Confessions of a
Spiritual Thrillseeker

Medicine Teachings
from the Grandmothers

CONFESSIONS OF A SPIRITUAL THRILLSEEKER

Medicine Teachings from the Grandmothers

ORIAH
MOUNTAIN DREAMER

Published by:
MOONFOX PRESS
Box 22516, 300 Coxwell Ave.
Toronto, Ontario
Canada M4L 2A0
(416) 466-5350

Publisher and General Editor: Michael Owen

Canadian Cataloguing in Publication Data
Mountain Dreamer, Oriah
    Confessions of a spiritual thrillseeker

ISBN 0-9695361-1-9

1. Mountain Dreamer, Oriah 2. Indians of North America -
Medicine. 3. Indians of North America - Religion and
mythology. 4. Indians of North America - Women.
5. Shamans - Canada - Biography. I. Title.

E98.M4M6 1991   299'.7'092   C91-095063-6

Cover: *Woman Shield* by Oriah Mountain Dreamer

Printed in Canada by Hignell Printing, Winnipeg.

For my grandmother, Merle Sylvesta Hildreth,
and my mother, Carolyn Jean House.
From you I inherited the fire in my heart,
the courage in my belly and the sadness in my eyes.
To you I offer my story, my gratitude, my love.

Acknowledgments

I would like to extend my thanks to the many people who have helped and supported me during the living and writing of this story: to my sisters of the heart, Linda Mulhall and Liza Parkinson, for their company on the road; to my sons Brendan and Nathan, for their patience with a mother who learns as she goes; to their father, Des McCarville, for his accommodation to my schedule and willingness to let me dream, even when the dream took me far away; to editor and friend Margaret Rose Carney, for her loving pushes to "keep at it" and generous work in shaping this text; to my friends Spalding Gray and Mickey Lemle, for their love of a good story—your encouragement helped me see this may be one such story; to my brothers and sisters of the Dream Star Lodge, who have, for more than three years, listened to these stories, witnessed my struggles and celebrated my joys—I thank you for the opportunity to teach and learn with you.

I offer my gratitude to Raven, the medicine man, sorcerer and shaman who helped me see my own love for "pushing the edge" and who shared with me knowledge of how to live this dream. May Beauty surround you. To all the other Native teachers and elders who have preserved and shared the medicine teachings I send my thanks. May I, and those with whom I share these gifts, use the teachings you offer to hold and feed the Dream of Grandmother Earth.

Thanks feel inadequate to express my gratitude to Michael Owen. Friend and medicine brother of my heart, you have supported and loved me as I lived this story. Editor and publisher, you have guided and enabled me to offer it to others. Wherever your path takes you, may it bring you joy.

I have not lived or written this story alone. There have been many brothers and sisters beside me. The Grandmothers and Grandfather of the dream have always been with me. My heart is full.

Preface

Two years ago I.dreamed of a woman in a long, rose-colored robe. She came to me and smiled. "You will write a book entitled *Confessions of a Spiritual Thrillseeker.* It will be about your journey on the medicine path."

The title is not intended to dishonor the ancient teachings or ceremonies that have taught me so much, or the Native peoples who have preserved and shared them. I am grateful for their gift of knowledge. It is a reminder not to take myself too seriously and reflects the fact that the experience of the ecstatic is something I want in my life for the "thrill" it offers. Part of me does not understand why everyone would not want this—the rush that defies explanation and takes your breath away. The book is my "confession" because I have tried to include all the moments when I was particularly dense, embarrassingly naive or just painfully human.

All the people and events in this story are real. I have changed the names and some dates and locations to respect others' requests for anonymity, and in my desire to take sole responsibility for my recollection and understanding of the events that occurred.

The first half of this book was written more than a year and a half ago. It tells the story of my first two years on the medicine path. I felt it was complete and went on to write a second, more didactic text on the teachings I had received from a group of Grandmothers in the dream. But each time I sat down to write, I heard their ancient voices speak to me. "Tell the story, Oriah," they urged. "The wheels are in the story. Tell the whole story." I was reluctant. The second half of my journey had been fraught with struggle, doubt and a growing a sense of humility, an experience I was less willing to share. But I sat down and began to write the story as I had experienced it. Perhaps you will hear pieces of your own story in the telling.

Many of the teaching wheels I received from the Grandmothers in the dream are in the story, hence the subtitle, *Medicine Teachings from the Grandmothers.* By being offered a factual account of how these wheels were received, the reader is not limited to my own analysis and understanding of their meaning. All of the words from the Grandmothers are offered verbatim. In doing so I feel certain that new ways of seeing and understanding this gift of wisdom will be discovered by others.

I do not know what "enlightenment" is. I still get tired, catch colds and argue with my children about cleaning their room and eating their dinner. But my life has changed and I wake up most mornings eager to see how the adventure will unfold, knowing I have the energy, strength and humor to meet it with enthusiasm.

Toronto
June 1991

Part 1

Confessions

1

I'm ready. I have seen a demonstration of the required response to the command "hit the dirt." I have two T-shirts and two sweatshirts on under my fatigues. The command requires hitting the dirt with complete abandon, coming down on full face and body. The small but sharp star cacti make the multilayer look very practical—except for the heat. It is noon and about a hundred and fifteen degrees in the shade. We are not in the shade. We are in the relentless sun, running full tilt up a forty-five-degree slope, alternately crashing to the earth and running in a crouching zig-zag.

As I crash down on command for the sixth time, I realize that those tiny brown lumps I'm crushing my face into are sheep shit, and I wonder *why?* Why am I here, doing this, paying for it, using up all my holidays? And can I keep this up? Only a year ago my idea of physically pushing the edge was staying up until ten o'clock two nights in a row. What does "hitting the dirt" have to do with my goals for physical health and spiritual ecstasy (vicarious or enlightening)? Have I finally lost it? Scenes of my "previous" life of four days ago—cooking, cleaning, diapering, shopping—flash before me, looking surprisingly inviting. But there is little time for nostalgia as I join my squad, "taking" the hill.

Robert stands at the bottom and decrees in his sergeant-major voice who is shot "dead" because of an inability to get one's ass or head down far enough, fast enough. He declares Yvonne, a woman in my platoon, dead on the slope below. Yvonne has asthma, and the climb has proved to be too much for her. She retires to the shade of a tree.

Suddenly another would-be enlightened warrior screams as if she really has been shot, and we rush to her aid. Confusion reigns as someone uses the walkie-talkie to summon the real-life doctor, and we carry the downed woman the rest of the way up the hill to the shade of the one tree in the vicinity. It is unclear what has happened. She keeps crying and saying she doesn't want to die. As we lay her down, I finally get a coherent answer from her. She has twisted her ankle, and the pain and physical exertion have brought to the fore all the emotional devastation

1

of her disintegrating marriage. Hence the sense of and resistance to "dying." Relieved that she is not having a heart attack, and trying not to be unsympathetic, we all sit down.

The call comes to descend. Stupidly, I had thought this would be easier, but now I find that if hitting the dirt at a forty-five-degree angle is difficult heading uphill, it is excruciating heading downhill. About forty feet from the bottom, I hit the dirt on command and keep right on going down the slope, skidding to a halt in a cloud of dust. I land at the feet of Raven, the medicine man in charge of all this madness. He is sitting, binoculars in hand, obviously having the time of his life watching us. I do not share his levity.

The group meets at the bottom to debrief and check in. Everyone seems fine until Yvonne strides over and hysterically announces in a loud and shaky voice that she does not want to be "dead." She has been sitting at the bottom of the hill since Robert left her there, hallucinating about funerals, grave sites and her unwritten will. Whether because of the heat, her asthma or just the humiliation of being unable to make it up the hill, she is angry and crying. The group is dismissed and a couple of the staff stay with her. I return to my tent for lunch and a short break somewhat bewildered. All thoughts of looking breathlessly seductive or spiritually enlightened during these activities are completely gone from my head. Useful survival techniques and thoughts about probable group insanity are all that occupy me.

The gray leaflet I'd received in the mail was emblazoned with an image of a naked man and woman outlined in red. They stood next to each other with feet astride, muscles rippling, long hair flowing, brandishing swords overhead and radiating sparks. It was very intimidating. The so-called retreat was scheduled to take place in the Arizona desert during August. The leaflet described a rigorous two weeks of self-defense and weapon training, martial arts, survival techniques and combat psychology as well as shamanic teachings on ceremonial medicine—a kind of enlightenment boot camp. This unique if somewhat bizarre combination of activities was described as ideal for developing the ability to live as a "warrior," one who is always at "cause" and never at "effect" in life. As someone who had lived for a long time at the "effect" of constant physical illness, I liked the sound of this. I assumed the arduous physical training was designed to help us step out of our "heads" and into our "bodies." Traditional shamanic training involves physical deprivation and hardship for cleansing and shifting perspective. I guessed that the unusual form planned for this retreat was a modern version of this intent and a reflection of Raven's personal training and history: Métis with a ⸺ Native American mother and a white father, he grew up on the reservation and was trained as a medicine person and shaman. He'd been a U.S. Marine who had fought in Vietnam and was also trained in martial arts.

Physical prowess has never been my strong suit, a fact I have successfully concealed by never doing anything physically challenging in front of others. I've been getting away with this for years because most people mistake thinness for fitness, and I don't gain weight no matter what I eat. Many years ago I even had a job as a part-time fitness instructor in a local community center. I would demonstrate the exercises, taken from library books, put on the music and enthusiastically talk everyone through the routine. Since I needed to keep an eye on people's progress and make helpful suggestions, no one questioned why I never did the routine from beginning to end. The participants, mainly tired middle-aged moms, were so pleased at having a night out, and so impressed with my thinness, that they never doubted my physical qualifications.

In fact, it was because of my body that I became involved in studying and using shamanic medicine, a year and a half before this desert retreat. While I had always been a healthy child growing up in a small town in Northern Ontario, my health had gone into a steady downward spiral when I left home and moved to the city. This had culminated in five years of increasingly severe chronic illness after the birth of my two sons. Those years, in my memory, are ones of living in a kind of underwater state. I was always tired.

One week after my second son, Nathan—a twelve-pound baby—was born, I awoke in the middle of the night, terrified. I felt the sensation in the center of my body of a long, thin core of light. I waited, and after a moment the light snapped in half. Where the core of light had been I could feel a grayness that sent waves of nausea through me. I began to hemorrhage. Panicked, I woke my husband. "Something is terribly wrong—I feel like something just broke inside of me."

It was the beginning of the end of any semblance of health or physical vitality in my life for several years. Every day I awoke with caution, awaiting the ambush: swollen glands, sore throat, throbbing headache, aching joints, infected sinuses, chronic diarrhea and the ever-present exhaustion. I would go through the day of caring for my two small children with measured persistence. One step at a time: cooking, cleaning, diapering, nursing, shopping, only to drop into bed as soon as their father came home from work. Most weekends and holidays were spent, if not in bed then pushing myself to go somewhere for the sake of my family, only to collapse during or after the excursion. Often I felt too ill to read or even watch TV while lying in bed. This left a lot of time for thinking.

It wasn't that I didn't seek medical assistance. My doctor, a quiet fellow with an open mind, left no stone unturned. Tube after tube of dark blood was taken from my arm to be tested, eventually eliminating my worst fantasies of leukemia and other fatal illnesses. Finally he came up with the term "adrenal gland exhaustion." I was momentarily encouraged. I could certainly verify the "exhaustion" aspect of this diagnosis. My optimism was short-lived. The prescribed treatment? Rest. At home with two small children, trying to do part-time work for financial survival, this seemed like a limited option. And I was increasingly tired of resting! It didn't seem to help.

In desperation I entered the unknown territory of alternative, holistic health practitioners: homeopaths, naturopaths, herbalists, iridologists. Some of it made sense to me, some of it seemed crazy, and all of it was expensive. I went on a strict diet, which at times consisted of little more than miso soup and rice crackers. I took remedies, supplements and herbs. With great skepticism I let a man take photos of my eyes, which he enlarged and used to report on the history of my health, its current diagnosis and his prescription for treatment. He was surprisingly accurate. With even more skepticism and a lot of giggling I lay on a table while a naturopath placed bottles of vitamin and mineral supplements on my stomach and had me raise my arm in the air and resist as she pushed it back down. The strength of my resistance informed her which supplements in what doses were appropriate for me. I was dubious but desperate. My sole criterion: if it works, I'll try it.

And it did work—symptomatically. The treatments often helped speed the process of shaking off a particular infection. But my illnesses continued. I was on a very short leash of careful diet, naps, ten to twelve hours of sleep a night and being careful, careful, careful. I still had no stamina. By now I was really scared. I knew that I could not live this way. I also knew that sooner or later, if I could not find a way to boost my immune system, I would pick up something more serious than colds and flus, something that all the carrot juice in the world wasn't going to cure.

With my energy a bit higher, I spent a lot of my time in bed reading, primarily books on holistic health and more spiritual approaches to healing. I guessed that my lack of health was linked in some way to something fundamentally wrong in my life. I just didn't know what. It was a testament to my desperation when one spring I took a substantial amount of our very limited savings, and a week away from my family, to journey to Northern Ontario to meet and learn from Raven.

Leaving my family with a week's worth of frozen home-cooked dinners, a clean house, completed laundry, etc., I set off with a suitcase full of the herbal remedies, vitamin supplements and special teas that I felt were critical to my daily functioning. Arriving at the workshop in the afternoon, I was informed by the organizer, Katharine, that Raven was coming later than planned, so would not begin teaching until the next day, "sometime between ten and eleven in the morning." I was pissed off. The trip had been complicated, expensive and difficult to arrange. I wanted to ensure I got every penny's worth of what I saw as my one week of freedom.

At 9:45 the next morning I went into the lodge to get a good seat in the ring of chairs in front of the fireplace. A "good" seat was one that would give me back support, a clear view of the three chairs placed at the front of the room, obviously intended for Raven and his companions, and the opportunity either to fade into the woodwork or surreptitiously exit if things got too weird. Gradually the nineteen other workshop participants drifted in. We waited. Forty-five minutes later an attractive woman in tight jeans, a white sweater and cowboy boots came in with Katharine. They perused the room, held a whispered conference and Katharine sent a couple of men outside. They returned moments later with wood to stoke the already blazing fire, a bucket of ice cubes and several bottles and cans of cola. After a few more whispered consultations the woman left and went to the cabin nearest the lodge, where Raven was reported to be staying. I say "reported," because up to this point none of us had actually seen him, although we'd observed a steady stream of smoke pouring from the chimney despite the relatively mild weather, and the scurrying of Katharine and other staff to and from the cabin with food and drinks. We'd been reassured by an obviously anxious Katharine that Raven had been up all night, smoking his pipe, dreaming with each of us and creating the thunderstorm that had passed through. I was skeptical.

By this time I had resigned myself to trying to "go with the flow." I was being philosophical in the hope of transforming myself into one of those laid-back, take-it-easy folks who never get upset about times and agendas. After all, the money was spent, I was here, and I obviously could not control the situation, so why not sit back and relax? This new carefree, if somewhat forced, lethargy was greatly fostered by the roaring fire, which had by now raised the temperature of the room to over eighty-five degrees.

My newfound state of relaxation was only slightly offset by my rising anxiety about the number of smokers lighting up all around me. I'd been worrying about this possibility since my journey to the workshop. Joan, a participant I'd traveled up with, had been on a medicine journey with Raven the year before. She had shared with me her previous experiences and impressions. As I was soon to learn, a substantial amount of conversation before, during and after these gatherings focuses on Raven himself, who seems to inspire some sort of strong reaction in almost everyone.

Two things she told me had increased my anxiety: Raven was a chain-smoker and a nighthawk. I panicked. Here I was, on my way to learn from a purportedly great healer because of my desperation about my physical health, only to learn that two of his habitual behaviors were ones I avoided, quite literally, like the plague. I had resolved that I would simply go to bed and miss the late-night teachings. I seriously doubted if anyone could either teach or learn past midnight anyway. I later discovered that Raven comes into his stride around midnight and can easily teach full tilt until dawn.

The smoking, however, was not so easily resolved. Not only did Raven smoke, Joan recalled, but given his practice of chain-smoking, other smokers normally inhibited about puffing at a workshop on healing also lit up. As my anxiety about getting ill began to rise, so too did my somewhat self-righteous anger. I asked Joan why no one had challenged Raven about this. She assured me they had, only to be told that basically he didn't give a shit. He smoked as and when he liked and had no intention of changing, so if people didn't like it, it was their problem. I decided on a wait-and-see position, sure I could, with vehement and straightforward argument about the health hazards, change the situation. Waiting for Raven in the close, too-warm room, which was now filling with smoke, I tried to remain calm.

Just as the idea of a nap began to seem appealing, everyone started to rustle papers and sit up a bit. Someone near the window whispered conspiratorially, "Here he comes." An instant later the door flashed open, admitting some much-needed oxygen and three figures—the woman who'd been in before, Raven and a younger man.

Raven strode in and nodded to but didn't really look at the group assembled. He was dressed from head to toe in red: red track pants, red T-shirt and red headband, with large turquoise rings on his fingers, a lit cigarette and open can of cola in one hand and a brown briefcase in the other. His hair, held back from his balding head in a long graying ponytail, and his fair complexion belied his Native heritage. Most revealing of his ancestry was his stance and walk; slightly round-shouldered, walking softly but solidly, he moved like both the dancer and martial artist he is, with the feel of a stalker.

The impact of his entrance on me was totally unexpected, and dissolved, at least momentarily, all hope of having any control over the situation. I stopped breathing. I could hear my heart beating and beneath that a low droning, buzzing sound like a swarm of hornets or bees. My heartbeat reverberated through and around my head and body, making all other sound seem distant. A moment later my viewing point was from high in the lodge's beamed ceiling. I could see myself sitting very upright and still in my chair, and I heard a voice saying, "I am here, Raven, and I have something to give you. Teach me and I will help you with the special task that confronts you." The voice was mine, but calmer, stronger and more self-possessed than I have ever felt. I watched from my lofty perch, aware both of Raven's actions as he settled into his chair and of my body, seemingly not breathing but vibrating with the thuds of my heartbeat. As Raven introduced himself, his eyes swept around the circle. As their surprising blueness lighted on me I felt myself snap back into my body.

I was shaken and surreptitiously glanced around me to see if anyone had taken note of my behavior, but all eyes were on Raven. Breathing now, I consciously relaxed the muscles of my rigid back and leaned into the chair. Slowly my heartbeat resumed its regular tempo. *What the hell was that?* Maybe I'd had a heart attack and didn't know it. Had I imagined the whole thing? Had the stress of leaving my two children for the first time unhinged my mind? Perhaps being this far away from the familiarity of my mother/housewife identity was more than I could handle. What about hearing my own voice? Had Raven heard it? I hoped not. I had nothing to give him and I had no idea what his "special task" was.

I spent the rest of the day taking pages of notes as Raven taught until well after midnight. Lying in bed that night, listening to the wind and rain outside the cabin, I went over in my mind what had occurred. Why had this man's presence had such an impact on me? What was going to happen here? I had read a great deal in the last year of my illness about esoteric subjects and mystical experiences, but this was different—this was happening to me. My one brief encounter with anything even half as strange as this had taken place a couple of months earlier, during a crystal workshop with a woman visiting Toronto from the States.

Judy was a gentle, soft-spoken woman who taught people how to work with gems, crystals and other stones. In my never-ending quest for something to improve my health, I had signed up for a daylong workshop, a new adventure for me. I didn't know what to expect. I wondered if the other workshop participants would all have a weird, otherworldly look to them. It had turned out to be a pretty tame group, three men and eight women—housewives, therapists, a geologist, a librarian and a secretary. In the afternoon Judy had each of us close our eyes, hold out our left hand and calm our breath and thoughts while she placed a small stone in our upturned palm. We had been told to send our attention into the stone and just wait and see what we saw, heard or felt. As she placed a small stone in my hand I felt, for an instant, quite weightless. Suddenly a brilliant light seemed to be shining directly at me, and opening my eyes, I raised my hand to shield them. Instead of sitting on a carpeted floor at the workshop I was on green grass next to a small stream. The sunlight reflecting on the water was shining in my eyes. As I turned away from it I saw an old Native man sitting next to me. He extended his hand to me with a warm smile. "Welcome, Granddaughter."

Despite my astonishment I took his hand. Immediately I felt as if I would burst into tears. Never have I felt more loved, more welcomed, more at home. The old man's voice was so familiar and yet I had no memory of ever having seen him before, awake or in a dream. Emotion choked my throat and I could not speak.

He leaned closer. "There is no need. Now that you have found us again you may come and talk anytime you like. We are your family." As he spoke, a group of people—men, women, children of every age, with short straight black hair and brown skin—came up behind him. They gathered around us, touching and patting my shoulder and back, all laughing and talking at once, welcoming me "back." I was overwhelmed.

Then, from very far away, I had heard another voice. "Oriah. Oriah, it's time to come back." It was Judy. I closed my eyes again and opened them reluctantly. Her worried face looked into mine. "Whew! You were a long way out there. You O.K. now?" I nodded.

After that, usually at night, I often tentatively tried to contact the image of the old man. Closing my eyes and breathing deeply, I would call out silently, "Grandfather, are you there?" It never occurred to me to call him anything but Grandfather, or even to ask his name. Each time I called I would immediately see his face and the place by the stream in my mind's eye.

Confused and shaken by my first meeting with Raven, I called on Grandfather and his face appeared. "Grandfather, what is my relationship to this man Raven?" I asked.

Grandfather was silent for a moment. "Daughter," he said.

"What does that mean? I am his daughter? I was his daughter? I am like his daughter? He is like a father to me? He will be? I will have his daughter? He has a daughter I know or will know?"

Grandfather would say no more, only the one word. Confused and exhausted, I fell asleep.

The next day Raven continued teaching at high speed. I picked up pen and paper to capture all I could. In the next seven days I filled page after page with notes—the easiest way for me to focus my attention and retain what I learn. I suspect it also calms my anxiety by giving me a sense of being in control of something, if only my notebook. Raven lived up to his reputation for the speed and density of his teaching. Sessions ran daily from about ten-thirty in the morning to five in the afternoon. After a break for dinner, Raven resumed at seven o'clock and continued until two or three in the morning, sometimes later. Since breakfast was at eight, sleep was short and often busy with dream exercises and assignments. I did not leave in the evening but stayed each night to the end, unwilling to miss anything.

I resigned myself to the smoke, occasionally dealing with my worry about my ever-fragile health by visualizing a protective dome over me to shield me from any negative effects. I did not have time to make any of the herbal teas and forgot to take most of my supplements and remedies. I was tired by the end of the week, but I was not sick, and my sense of energy and vitality were greater than they had ever been.

At that first meeting I felt like parched earth soaking up the water of Raven's teachings. Taking a short break during the first day, I went outside and down to the lake. The lodge where we were staying was on a rocky shore dotted with tall pines. The afternoon was gray and cool, and I squatted on a huge rock and looked out across the water. My chest began to ache and my throat felt very tight. I was aware of how I had been just hanging on for so long, trying to get through the exhaustion and illness. Sitting quietly, I felt tears well up inside me and heard soft voices that seemed to come from the rocks around me. "Sit, sister, we have waited long for your return. Rest." I began to shake and cry with an incredible sense of relief. All I could think of was "I need a rest. God, how I need a rest. Why can I never really find a place to rest?"

By the time I'd committed myself to the two-week retreat in the desert it had been over a year since I first met Raven, and a lot had changed. I had left my marriage and found a full-time job to support myself and my two sons. My health had been stable for six months. I was still cautious.

Knowing that I would be required to do something physical in front of others, I set about getting in shape. The fear of public humiliation, even (or perhaps especially) in a spiritually enlightened community, proved to be a great motivator. For five months I did thirty to forty-five minutes of aerobic exercise every morning. I used a videotape of a local TV exercise show so I could be in pain in the privacy of my own living room. At first I was somewhat distracted by the show itself: two or three young women in body-hugging, moisture-revealing, color-coordinated outfits doing a seemingly innocent set of exercises, provocatively seen from every possible angle by the roving camera. Periodically and seductively they encouraged the unseen audience by panting phrases such as "Come on, come on, you can do it, you can do it" in time to the music. This was a long way from my childhood memories of my mother being gently but cleanly encouraged by Ed Allen. The soft-porn appeal of the video kept me going past the discovery that the moisture on those suits was real sweat from working muscles. By the end of five months I could easily do the workout and I was even getting a bit bored. I began to fantasize about the possibilities of not only not embarrassing myself, but of managing to look a bit attractive, in an Amazonian kind of way, as I climbed a rope ladder or crawled through the undergrowth.

This growing, if limited, confidence in my physical ability did not completely allay my fears about the two-week retreat. I had received a list of things to bring. In addition to my camping equipment, personal items and food, I needed a set of army fatigues, a rubber knife, a bamboo baton and a martial arts gi. The gi, a white pajama-style outfit, I liked. When I put it on, took what I imagined was a martial arts stance and gazed seriously into the mirror, I looked as though I might actually be able to do something. Furthermore, wearing just the top, which was the length of a very short mini, looked incredibly sexy. I couldn't see how I might take advantage of this fact, since the top and bottom are generally worn together, but I stored it away as useful information.

The fatigues were another thing altogether. I did not own any, and as a good socialist, feminist, Canadian woman, I was not thrilled at the idea of spending money to acquire them. In fact I wasn't sure how I felt about wearing what I saw as a symbol of the imperialist U.S. military machine. Luckily I discovered that a co-worker owned a set of very hardy khaki pants and shirt. It seems that in her earlier days, coming out as a lesbian, they had been part of her demonstrative wardrobe. She no longer used them and was more than willing to lend them to me. The mysterious rubber knife and bamboo baton were found in martial arts stores. I was all set.

I arranged for the kids to be with their dad, for someone to look after my house and for time off work. All of this put me in the position of trying to explain to other people what I was doing and why. Many of my friends, like myself, were suspicious of anything with a military ring to it. They pressed me on the sanity of my going, something I could only tentatively vouch for. I could not explain it. I wanted to put myself into the unfamiliar and see what I could do. I wanted to test myself. I knew that in addition to the physical activity there would be an opportunity to do ceremony in groups and alone on the desert. My experience of ceremony during the previous year and a half of studying with Raven had given me the chance to touch the extraordinary and unexplainable.

I had done my first vision quest in Northern Ontario when I first met Raven. He had explained that our night out would be spent doing a ceremony to look at and confront all of our fears. This was enough to make me nervous. We were given instructions on how to build, seal and move around a medicine wheel we would make of stones. The ceremony began at dusk and we were each to spend the night alone in the bush. Raven did a pipe ceremony, linking with each of us for subsequent monitoring during the night. We were told we could call on him, if we felt the need, by using his sacred name. I recorded the details of the ceremony in my notebook, although some instructions were indelibly etched in my mind: to never invite anything into my circle once I'd sealed it, how to banish anything negative from my circle and how to leave the circle in a ceremonial manner.

These instructions were accompanied by stories from Raven that further provoked our already overstimulated imaginations. On the first day of teaching Raven explained that he needed to be careful because a coven practicing dark sorcery worked a short distance away and was aware of him. Covens . . . dark sorcery . . . my skepticism had a field day. But as he finished telling us of his concern, the large double doors facing the lake crashed open with a gust of cold wind, sending dust and leaves swirling around the room. The doors had been bolted from the inside since our arrival. Like children we all jumped in our seats and looked at each other wide-eyed, our skepticism gone. Raven laughed at our reaction and casually asked one apprentice to close the doors. Although seemingly nonchalant, he did direct another apprentice to cleanse the room, smudging everyone with smoke from burning sweetgrass, sage, cedar and lavender. Now, as we prepared to go out for the night, he told of a time he had spent alone in the desert in a sealed circle. While he sat in the darkness, a friend of his, also involved in the medicine work, had come by. Although he knew her, he had hesitated to ask her into his ceremonial space. At last, frustrated by his lack of trust, his "friend" had become enraged and revealed herself in her true form, that of a dark sorcerer trying to trick him by appearing as his friend.

With tension knotting my stomach, I went to gather my supplies. We were not allowed to bring shelter or food. The weather by this time was consistently miserable, raining off and on, the temperature just above freezing. I put on every piece of clothing I had, including long johns, rain gear, hat, gloves, scarf and ski jacket. As an afterthought I put a cushion into a plastic garbage bag to provide me with a soft and relatively dry sitting place. As I left the main lodge Raven glanced up and asked what it was. Hearing my plan for this small measure of comfort, he shook his head. "They don't do vision questing like they used to." This did not dissuade me from taking the cushion, and in my own defense I want to point out that most of the ceremonies, including this one, were developed and practiced in the desert of the American Southwest, where environmental conditions do not remotely resemble those of Northern Ontario in May.

I was raised in a small community in the north and my family had always been avid campers, so I felt that spending a night out in the bush would not really pose the problems for me that it might for some of my more urban colleagues, who were worried about animals. Being absolutely certain of this I watched as everyone set off in one general direction; then I headed the opposite way, not wanting my nocturnal solitude to be disrupted by the sounds of fellow questers singing, speaking or doing whatever one does in the middle of a long night. This turned out to be a decision I regretted more than once.

Somehow I temporarily forgot all of my camping knowledge when picking a spot, and chose a site right next to a swampy area. Despite the cool weather, the spring mosquito population was doing very well. Anxious to be settled before dark, I collected the rocks needed to build a medicine wheel, asking each one if it would hold the energy of a particular direction for me, leaving a bit of tobacco and a prayer of thanks if I felt the rock's permission. I was concerned about my ability to "hear" the rocks accurately and hoped they wouldn't harbor any ill feeling if I moved them against their will. I consulted my notes carefully and, worried about the growing darkness, began placing the rocks in the given order: east, west, south, north, southeast, southwest, northwest, northeast. As I placed each stone, I held it to my heart and, feeling very awkward, spoke out loud. "Spirits of the East, I call on you to be with me here . . . to, uh, help me in this ceremony . . . to, ummm . . . so I won't be too afraid and can learn what I need to be healthy again." My words, timidly spoken, seemed incredibly loud in the stillness of the forest. It was not a very strong prayer and I hoped the spirit world was not judgmental about my stumbling and stuttering.

My voice grew stronger with each stone I placed and I began to feel less self-conscious. After all, who was there to see me—squirrels and mosquitoes? Checking my notes again for fear of making mistakes, I began to sprinkle tobacco over and between the stones, moving clockwise around the circle. As I sprinkled tobacco I was supposed to say the prescribed sentence for sealing the circle and banishing all negative energies from it. The problem was I had not yet memorized the exact wording and was afraid that any deviation might lead to a breach in my circle and subsequent attack by the aforementioned "dark" forces. I realized this was unlikely and reasoned with my terrified self that any self-respecting dark sorcerer who could manage to breach someone's circle and do the undetermined "something" to them was not going to bother with a novice on her first night out. Of course, I did wonder about the budding apprentices of such sorcerers. Where did they get their invasion practice? Surely they had to start somewhere, probably with someone posing little challenge, like me.

My anxiety-ridden mind would be satisfied with nothing less than following the directions exactly. So, holding tobacco in my right hand, notes in my left and flashlight under my armpit, I began to walk and read out loud. "I seal this circle with tobacco and banish from within it, through the power of LawJup, LawJup, LawJup, LawJup, any energies, entities or beings, incarnate or disincarnate, who do not love me or would do me harm. Begone from this place now!"

The ink on the page started to run as the rain continued, but not before I made it around the circle. It all felt pretty shaky. I doubted if any Native person had been walking around a hundred years earlier trying to read the markings on a piece of leather by the flame of a torch. I decided to seal and banish again, just to be sure, and managed to feel I was putting some intent behind the now-memorized words by the time I'd walked the circle for a second time.

Feeling a bit more secure, I sat down for a moment's rest in the pouring rain. Then I panicked. My previous state of fear had stimulated a bodily need not mentioned in the day's instructions. Should I leave my circle and find an accommodating bush? Walking back to the lodge was out of the question—it would be pitch-dark before I got back. Staying in the circle did not seem to be the proper use of this newly created ceremonial and sacred space. Would my going out breach the sealed circle? How should I leave? How should I come back in? Would I have to reseal? If I didn't, how would I know I was safe? What would keep me safe when I was outside the circle? Had my creation of the wheel alerted anyone or anything to my presence?

It was all settled in a moment as my body provided the incentive for action and I unceremoniously darted out of the circle to the nearby bushes and relieved myself. Running back into the circle, I sheepishly sent out my prayer: "I apologize to any and all I have offended. Sorry, I'm probably screwing this all up and I'm not very sure of what I'm doing. I ask for your patience." So saying, I sealed my circle for a third and final time.

Sitting in the middle of the circle, I again consulted my notes. During this ceremony we were to move around the circle, sitting in the various places and asking to see our fears from that place on the wheel. When this was complete we were to go around the wheel again, sitting in each of the four cardinal directions and asking to see our "shield" in that direction. As near as I could figure, a shield was a kind of symbolic representation of some aspect of myself. According to Raven, these shields have an actual energetic presence as balls of light in what he called our luminous cocoon, a kind of giant egg-shaped energy body around our physical body. The shields move around inside the auric egg, and our perspective is dependent on which is up front at the moment: little girl, little boy, man, woman or elder. As I reread my notes I got an image of a kind of schizophrenic Humpty Dumpty.

I decided I'd better get started and moved into the first phase of the ceremony—looking at all my fears. I began walking around the wheel inside the stones, sitting in different directions and asking to know what fears I had. Sometimes nothing happened; at other times I would begin to see images in my mind's eye of earlier times in my life: as a child, afraid I would not be good enough, pretty enough, smart enough for my parents, terrified of my mother's anger; as a student, afraid of not getting straight A's; as an adult, afraid of being tired and ill, afraid of dying in my sleep, of not having enough money, enough energy, enough love for my children . . . . It went on and on. Sometimes I would be wary and vigilant, terrified of every little sound in the bushes, struggling to keep a tight rein on my imagination, which could see bears, wolves and far worse coming to get me. For hours I moved around the wheel, feeling alternately mystified, peaceful, scared, cold, wet, miserable, ecstatic, strong, weak, bored, fed up . . . . There were moments when the frogs— spring peepers, I think they're called—which chirped incessantly in a great chorus, seemed to fill my head with their deafening sound. I wondered if this sound could make a person go crazy.

Having gone around the circle once, I decided to take a break. I began to feel that I had done enough. After all, I'd gone out in miserable weather, followed complicated directions and looked as honestly as I could at the fears within me. I knew only several hours had passed, but I was wet, cold, tired and increasingly bored. What was the point? If I didn't stay, who would know? If I somehow got warm enough to sleep, who would know or care? This was the first time since my children were born that I was not looking after someone else. Shouldn't I be relaxing comfortably? Shouldn't I be looking after myself or having someone look after me for a change? I'd probably not get a chance to be away for another five years, and here I was sitting out in the cold rain, doing a ceremony I hardly understood, looking for what? What if nothing happened? What if something awful happened?

The nattering in my head continued incessantly, offering reasons to leave, go to sleep, do anything except the ceremony. Finally, bored with the endless inner argument, I stood up and spoke out loud to myself. "O.K. So this is it. Either do it and see what happens or shut up and go back!" I wanted to go crawl into my warm bed, but couldn't bear the imagined humiliation of having my cabin mates know I had not completed the ceremony. Nor did I have the nerve to lie and make up a story of an event-filled night. I was stuck. I pulled out my flashlight and started to read my notes.

Moving to the south of my circle, I sat down and tried to relax. Tentatively I sent out a silent prayer asking to touch and know my Little Girl Shield. Unsure of what I should be looking for, I sat quietly, trying to keep my mind clear, focusing on my breath. I began to drift in and out of a very light sleep, feeling a warmth like the mist of a vaporizer swirl around me. With it came images of my childhood, of myself as a little girl and the feelings still alive within me from that time in my life. I saw my mother's disappointment at not having a pretty child and felt the shame of the little girl trying to look her best, do her best to make up for not being pretty. I saw my family camping and laughing together and felt the little girl's sense of belonging and comfort in the out-of-doors. I heard the voices of my parents, hurt and angry with each other, and felt the terror of the little girl lying in bed straining to hear, sure she must somehow be the cause of the terrible fighting. One after the other, in a steady stream, the pictures and feelings moved through my body and mind. I laughed and wept with the child. Gradually the images slowed and stopped. I sat, exhausted and unmoving, for a long time.

Finally, I got up and moved to the north of my circle, stretching and jumping up and down in an effort stay awake. Sitting down, I again sent out a silent prayer to anything or anyone who was listening. "I ask to know my Woman Shield." I waited. Nothing happened, so I repeated the prayer, but still nothing occurred. I felt more awake now but increasingly impatient. Raven had said that this particular shield was the part of us that took care of the business of life: home, job, money, future plans. I had always felt reasonably competent in these areas so had expected some ease here. I began to think about my current situation, at home with small children, going to school and working part-time. I wondered where I'd be one or two years into the future. I realized I had no idea what lay ahead for me. It didn't seem to matter. I sat and sang from this place for a while and then got up to move to the west of the wheel.

I sat cross-legged and checked my notes. According to Raven, the west was the place of my Man Shield, my inner warrior. Feeling more confident, and wanting to get on with the next step, I spoke out loud, tilting my head back and looking at the dark sky ringed with the silhouettes of treetops. "Great Spirit, I ask to see my Man Shield, the warrior that lives within me." The instant the words left my mouth the figure of a man in a squatting position began to appear in front of me on the other side of the lit candle I had placed in the center of the circle. Something about him was familiar, but he was not anyone I knew. He was a handsome, tanned man with strong features, a very muscular body, blond hair and blue eyes, wearing only a loincloth and gazing openly at me. As non-threatening as his manner was, the fact that I could see him materialize across from me scared me half to death. I was paralyzed, unable even to look away or close my eyes. My breath was shallow and I could hear the rapid pounding of my heart. I knew I had not invited anything external into my circle, so reasoned with my terrified self that this figure had to be an image of my own Man Shield, which I had just asked to see. As my fear rose, the figure began to fade. When I could calm my breathing, he became clearer and more lifelike, until I could see him breathing and blinking in a normal fashion. Holding my fear at bay was draining and after only a few moments I gave up and my head dropped onto my knees. When I looked up seconds later the figure was gone.

I wanted to leave. I was scared and did not want any more surprises. The only thing that kept me from running back to my cabin was an even greater fear of leaving the circle by any means other than the prescribed ceremonial manner, which at the moment I could not recall. It was a long run back to the cabin in the dark, through the woods, with plenty of opportunities for something to get me.

I sat still for a very long time, thinking about the man I had seen. Was he really some aspect of myself? Is that why he seemed so familiar? It was hard to imagine he didn't exist somewhere outside of myself. Was there a man walking around in the world who looked like him? If so, what would that man be to me?

The next shield was the Child Spirit Shield, my little boy. Raven had warned us that this was the hardest to feel because it is the aspect of ourselves that truly knows no fear, which could, if we let it, teach us how to fly. After my experience of my Man Shield I was a long way from feeling fearless. It took hours of patiently sitting, praying and waiting to begin to get even a glimmer of what this aspect of myself felt like. As last, feeling quite calm and unafraid, I realized that I could see in the dark. Wherever I looked, the ground, both inside and outside my circle, was lit by a gray light. There was still no hint of dawn in the sky and yet the previously impenetrable and threatening darkness beneath the overcast sky seemed now to reveal everything down to the smallest detail. I could see branches, leaves, stones as if I had an infrared camera. I stood up and looked around, enjoying myself and feeling completely unafraid. We'd been told to ask for a sign if we thought we had touched the reality of our Child Spirit Shield, because it is a difficult one to find. I raised my voice to the sky and asked, if I was indeed seeing through the eyes of my little boy, that some sign be given to me. The moment I uttered the words the spring peepers, which had been relentlessly singing in chorus since darkness had fallen whether I was silent, singing or speaking, abruptly stopped croaking. The silence was more deafening, in its suddenness, than the constant song, and renewed my sense of both wonder and fear. They were silent for about three minutes, which felt like an eternity, and then began again and continued all night.

The rest of the time passed relatively uneventfully, and just before the dawn light returned I decided to leave. Throwing some tobacco across the stone in the west, I declared the circle open and as quickly as possible took each rock and placed it in the surrounding woods. Outside the protective security of my wheel I felt nervous and, glancing all around, I made my way back to my cabin. As I neared the lodge, I noticed the lights in Raven's cabin were on and headed that way with some vague notion of getting elucidation of the night's events. As I approached and knocked on the door, I suddenly had a very clear image of myself sitting out in the dark, as observed by bewildered squirrels and raccoons. There I was—great white bwana raised in the north, not afraid of being out in the night—scared of my own shadow and wanting to run home. Raven said, "Come on in," and I stepped inside, giggling at the image. When he asked what I wanted, I stood at the door, shaking my head and laughing, and said, "Never mind, I just can't believe what a silly fool I can be sometimes."

Looking at me as I stepped out, he smiled, and called out, "Now you're getting it."

Whether I got it or not, I was hooked. I wanted more.

2

T he desert retreat offers us combat and survival training on alternate days. I'll admit, it's an unusual schedule for people seeking spiritual enlightenment. Our platoon's uphill run takes place during the first session of combat training. Robert, one of Raven's apprentices, is the staff person in charge. Robert did two tours of duty in Vietnam. He is a mystery to me, a man in his early forties who often looks as if he is suffering a deep personal crisis. Dark circles under his eyes, which I imagine have to do with the collection of memories he holds, give him a kind of haunted look. I've met him before and he's always been warm and courteous, but I sense his discomfort with me and end our conversations quickly. I often wish I could find a way to help him relax when we are talking.

I feel a kind of uneasy fascination with the Vietnam War, and with those who participated in it. Wars are something that seem very distant, relegated to history books and movies. Here are men of a very similar culture and age to my own who have actually been to war, and I sense the horror and appeal the memory of that experience holds for them. There are several Vietnam vets present, including Raven. As we gather in the morning, the vets talk about their struggle with getting into fatigues again, the memories it brings back, the actual physical pain. Robert begins the session by talking about his combat experience: the horror of shooting a small child holding a hand grenade, the determination to come back alive, the closeness of men living and dying together. He invites everyone to speak about their own "combat experience." Although most are not veterans, very few have not directly experienced violence in their lives, in their homes or on the street. I listen to the stories of rape, beatings, sexual abuse, muggings. Suddenly war feels very close.

This is Penelope's first and last session of the two weeks. Penelope is a beautiful petite redhead of almost forty, who looks twenty-five. She dresses in wispy white gauze dresses and often carries a wand and wears those headbands with stars suspended on long springs like little antennae. She talks a lot about learning to do "Goddess play" and often adds to gatherings with lighthearted dramas and songs. When it is her turn to speak she tells us of her seventeen-year-old son, who was beaten by three young men on the street until almost dead. Her rage and her desire to find and kill the men who have done this spill from her involuntarily. Shortly afterward she leaves the retreat. The pain of her own anger and the reality of the violence in her life are things she can touch only briefly.

I keep my own story short and factual. I had been beaten in my first marriage. I had also been raped. It had not occurred to me as I'd signed up for this retreat that either of these two events from my past would be touched on here. As I share my story I begin to get a very uneasy feeling about what lies ahead.

My medicine name, received from Raven at our first meeting in Northern Ontario, is Mountain Dreamer. Raven had led us through a process of shamanic journeying, a kind of guided meditation using active imagination and drumming, in order to meet and bring back from the world of the dream our totem animals. Before we began the process, he was quizzed endlessly by participants, anxious to do it "right," about how we would know if our experiences were "real" or "just imagination." In our everyday world this is an important distinction, but for the shaman the dream is as much a part of reality as my sitting at this computer, and imagination is the road to new realities.

I was hesitant about the whole process, but I wanted to give it a try. Lying on the floor of the lodge where we were meeting, I relaxed my body as instructed and followed the sound of the drum. With my eyes closed I listened intently. The drumming filled my head and I felt my body sinking into the floor and going down a long, winding tunnel into the ground. After a few moments I came out the other end into a grassy clearing in the middle of a forest. It was not unlike my childhood image of Alice coming out of the rabbit's hole into Wonderland. I sat where I had landed, and then, still following the sound of the drum, tentatively rose and began to walk around looking for animals.

Based on our date of birth, we had each been given eight animals who were our allies. We were to find them and see if we could, with their permission, pull them into ourselves, to bring their energy and guidance into our everyday reality. Wandering through the densely wooded area, I was confronted by a huge brown bear, my birth totem. My heart beat faster, and it seemed to me that the drumbeat had quickened. With a shaky voice I greeted the bear as I'd been instructed and asked if I might have its energy and medicine to teach me in my life. I'm not sure what I expected—a kind of Walt Disney-cartoon bear I think, a cross between Smoky and Yogi—but the bear I confronted looked, smelled and sounded like a very real bear. As it moved closer, grunting, sniffing and drooling slightly, I froze. Slowly the bear came up to me and, beginning at my feet, sniffed me all over until it stood erect before me. Then, with deliberation, it moved forward and embraced me. From far away I heard Raven's voice reminding us to pull the animal into ourselves. I raised my arms and, putting them around the bear, pulled the warm fur toward me. As I did so the bear seemed to dissolve into my chest. For a moment I felt my own heartbeat and that of another, slower rhythm thudding through my chest.

The journeying continued and I similarly met and retrieved each of my animals: a cougar, turtle, beaver, snake, flicker, snow goose and coyote. Each experience was unique and yet similar. The journey through this world seemed physically very real to me. My breath became labored and my leg muscles ached as I climbed a low, rocky cliff. Coming to the top I saw a nest with three baby owls in it, mouths open, waiting for food. I left them alone. We had been told not to bring back any animals not on our birth wheel unless we saw them at least three times, in different forms. If we did, this would be our first power animal. Later I stopped to rest on the edge of a precipice. A huge horned owl glided to a graceful landing on the rock, three feet to my left. We observed one another for a few moments before he flew off. Having retrieved all of my animals, I started back to the place where I had originally come into the forest. As I walked into the clearing two large owls flew straight toward me at incredible speed. I jerked to a stop, and in a flurry of wings, talons and feathers they lighted gently, one on each shoulder. They sat for a moment. I sensed they were mates. As they flew away I called for an owl to bring back with me. One appeared from the surrounding trees, flying in a kind of blurred slow motion, its huge wings furling and unfurling. It flew steadily toward me. I opened my arms and felt the bird fly up to and dissolve into my chest. Not knowing why, I began to cry and, following the sound of the drum, journeyed back up the tunnel to my body lying stiffly in the lodge.

It was from sharing the story of my four encounters with the owls that Raven gave me my medicine name, Mountain Dreamer. The owl, in his tradition, is the bringer of the dream. It was my first power animal. A medicine name is one that tells you something about who you are and what your work will be in this life. Mountain Dreamer is one who always looks for and wants to live in a place of pushing her or his edge, one who

can help others to find and push theirs. I liked the sound of that. It held
out the hope of a life that did not entail endlessly slowing down, holding
back and being cautious. I wanted to find the places where I could start
to push that edge.

The desert retreat looks like a great place for edge-pushing. Although
only two weeks long, I arranged for three weeks off work to give me
time to both prepare and recuperate. My motives were mixed. I wanted
to arrive at least thirty-six hours in advance for two reasons: to get over
the three-hour jet lag before anything physically rigorous begins, and to
see Mitch, have unbridled sex and figure out where we stood in our
relationship. Mitch is from Toronto and we first met at the workshop in
Northern Ontario and began a relationship after a medicine journey to
Jamaica, six months later.

Mitch is now living in Arizona, studying with Raven. We are both involved with other people and have not had a very smooth time of being
together when other lovers are around. I arrive at the retreat hoping we
can come to some mutual understanding of sleeping arrangements, so I
will not be wasting a lot of time and energy wondering, watching and
worrying. I have brought my own tent to keep my options open and my
independence intact.

I want this trip to be perfect—a kind of compulsive desire I have not
yet surrendered despite my experiences learning with Raven, which always have a kind of chaotic rhythm of their own. Previous experiences
with him have done a lot to loosen the grip of, but not entirely banish,
this need to set things up "perfectly."

While I am prepared to try to go with whatever happens at the desert
retreat, I still want to set it up as flawlessly as I can. With this in mind I
rent a car at the Phoenix airport so I have my own transportation. Everything goes smoothly. The plane is on time, I get the car, a sleek red one
with air-conditioning and stereo, and hit the freeway with my map. I feel
like a free woman off on high adventure. By the time I've stopped to pick
up food and a cooler it's 5:00 P.M.—8:00 P.M. to my jet-lagged body. I am
just in time to hear the radio announce that there have been no new
shootings on the freeway. I pause. It seems I have arrived on the day
someone has taken to shooting at cars on the freeway. This does not feel
like a good sign. My spirits are somewhat subdued. I head for the
campsite in the mountains at the edge of the desert. The trip, while un-
eventful, is into unfamiliar terrain: long stretches of flat dry land with lit-

tle vegetation, moving up into rolling brown hillsides and low mountains.

By the time I get to higher ground the sun is setting. I am too concerned about arriving in the dark and getting lost to stop and enjoy the sunset. I keep thinking, *Look at that, what a beautiful sunset. Here you are, independent woman of adventure going up into the mountains as the sun sets and the stars come out. It's like a movie. Pause and savor it— this could be a life-changing moment.* Unfortunately, images of sleeping in the car and being stalked by ax murderers wandering the desert wasteland keep me moving. By the time I reach the campsite it is dark, and there is no one at the gate. There are a few signs pointing to the dusty tracks that pass as roads, so I know I am on the right trail.

As I gaze over a seemingly endless expanse of low hills I see a small point of light weaving down one hillside. I head for it. It is Mitch, camped at the top of the hill. He has seen the car and guessed that I am lost. The retreat is not scheduled to begin for two days, so there are only four or five people around, all apprentices working to get the area ready.

It is good to see Mitch, and after a brief visit with the others we pitch my tent, go to bed and indulge in the anticipated unbridled sex. As a delicious orgasm ripples through my body and his I feel a tug at the top of my head and find myself out over the valley, in the starry night sky. I can see the tent, the surrounding hills dotted with the lights of the small town nearby, the highway and the mountains in the pale moonlight. I can also feel someone near me, and very carefully and softly, while maintaining my view of the valley, I whisper to Mitch, "Can you see it?"

To my amazement he responds and slowly begins to describe the same view of the land. I look up into the midnight blue and the shower of stars and ask, "And the sky? Can you roll over and see the sky?" He cannot. I know out-of-body experiences are less-familiar territory for him, so I ask if I can touch him and turn him to view the sky.

He says yes, but as I reach out, I feel him leave. He has fallen asleep. I am alone in the sky.

I spend most of the next day resting and adjusting to the environment. The place we are camped is about one mile high, something that inspires in me, and in many others as they arrive, a migrainelike headache for the first twenty-four hours. It is blisteringly hot in the daytime and constantly windy, which means that the biggest problem is dust. It becomes more of a problem as time goes on. I am camped quite close to the road, which despite the multiple warning signs is treated like the Indianapolis Speedway by some of my fellow warriors-in-training. After a week of rigorous training I begin to visualize myself grabbing a bumper as some speed demon races by and ripping the car off the road.

I also find myself hoping for rain to settle the dust. Understanding that it will not rain is probably the biggest cognitive leap during my stay. For someone from Northern Ontario, rain and mosquitoes are synonymous with camping. Despite what I was told, I brought both insect repellent and rain gear on the trip. While I adjust rapidly to not slapping myself silly or basting myself in poisonous liquid, I keep looking for clouds and waiting for rain. None falls. The lack of water is a whole new experience. A very dry creek bed is the only evidence that moisture has ever been here. I feel a bit lost, camping where there is no lake. I experienced this as a teenager camping with my family on the prairies. Where do you go when there is no lake? For a walk? To meet strange men? To commune with your soul? Without a lake all of these worthwhile endeavors feel like aimless wanderings.

The other environmental factor I have to adjust to is the rapid temperature change at dusk. One minute I am wearing shorts and a T-shirt; fifteen minutes later I need my jeans and ski jacket as the temperature falls with the sun. Both the lack of water and the temperature change give me a feeling of uneasiness, as if I am on a different planet, or in a dream where the spirit of what happens cannot not be held by things outside myself for more than the moment in which it exists. It occurs to me that there is truth to this at all times.

I get up early the first morning despite the time difference, just as the sun is coming up over the mountains. There on a hill, silhouetted by the rising sun, is one of the gods. The most magnificently proportioned man I have ever seen is going through a series of slow-motion martial arts exercises. Even from a distance I can see he is tall, about six foot three or four, and incredibly muscular. The sun shines on his ebony skin. He is clothed in a loincloth and moves with the grace of a dancer. I am mesmerized. As Mitch emerges from the tent I whisper, afraid it is all a wonderful creation of my imagination, "Who is that man?" According to Mitch the man is Steve. He is very real and on staff for the retreat to teach survival techniques. I take this as a very auspicious beginning.

Everything at the retreat is organized on a military model—the Marines, to be precise, since Raven has been a Marine. In fact, the whole two weeks are very much a reflection of Raven's personality. As I watch other would-be warriors arrive I think back to what my expectations of a medicine person were before I met Raven: someone sensitive and powerful, gentle but strong. While he can be all of these things, the Raven I met in Northern Ontario was certainly not what I'd expected.

There I was: a Canadian woman who for many years had identified herself and worked with the feminist communities of the political left. I saw my spirituality and politics as inseparable and I liked it that way. It had a neatness about it, and I could back my beliefs with eloquent arguments and clear precedents, both personal and social. In varying degrees I was suspicious of, if not deliberately hostile to, people who did not share my prejudices: Americans, men, wealthy people, those on the political right, etc. You get the picture. I was wary about trying to learn spiritual knowledge from a man, but desperate enough to give it a try.

And then there was Raven: not just an American but a Texan. As I soon discovered, there is being American and then there's being Texan, a kind of heightened state of Americanism. He was an ex-Marine (I'm not sure you can ever say "ex" for someone who's been a Marine) who was not only unapologetic about U.S. imperialism, but was openly proud of his strong patriotism. He never included Ronald Reagan in his examples of tyrants in the world. I was appalled.

On a personal level I had expected to meet someone living and espousing a somewhat ascetic lifestyle: plain food, quiet removal of self from the daily concerns of the world, an elimination or careful containing of sexual energy and activity, etc. I had thought that the elimination of many "worldly" pleasures in my life might well be the price I was going to have to pay for renewed health, a price I was willing to pay out of sheer despair. No doubt some of this came from the "no pain, no gain" philosophy of my Scottish Presbyterian background, and the fact that, in my ill health, I didn't have the energy to indulge in many of these pleasures anyway.

But contrary to my expectations, Raven was a man who fully enjoyed all of the worldly pleasures and had little use for opinions that held them as less than spiritually correct. I was confused but relieved. Having lived in a community where things were always judged by their "political correctness," I didn't need any more rules. Raven smoked because he liked to and felt it grounded him. He ate lots of red meat, constantly drank cola and was very open about his enjoyment of sex—in many different forms. He spoke of this with a unique combination of the poetic eloquence of ancient Native teachings, which always honored the sacredness of the spirituality within the heart of sexuality, and a raunchy explicitness that celebrated the physical vitality of passion and lust.

This manner of speaking about sexuality never failed to offend many, which I suspect it was designed to do. I won't say I wasn't surprised. I had not expected to sit down in front of a spiritual teacher and hear him use words like "cock" and "pussy," with an undeniable twinkle in his eye. I even thought I should probably be offended and object in the name of feminism, or some other "ism." But the truth is I found his directness a relief. On the first day I heard Raven speak, someone asked him if he would share some of the teachings on spiritual-sexuality. Seeming reluctant, he agreed and began to talk about the four levels of orgasm. He had my attention.

In fact, one of the concerns in my life was my complete lack of sexual energy. Although this initially took a back seat to my concerns about not being able to get up in the morning or carry out a normal day's activities, as my health began to improve I worried more and more about it. Although I had not had a wide variety of sexual experiences, having been monogamous in my two marriages for a total of thirteen years and having had only one brief relationship between the two, I had always enjoyed lovemaking in my second marriage. My husband was a sensitive and caring lover. But while I enjoyed the times we made love, I basically had to be coaxed into it, not really caring one way or the other. This worried me. I had stopped using my health, the kids and life in general as an excuse and begun wondering what I was going to do about it. Raven talked about sexual energy as the catalyst energy in our lives and gave it an important place in overall health. I was surprised and intrigued.

This, of course, was an area that repeatedly gave rise to much speculation and gossip among those who had heard of Raven. Several months after first meeting him and hearing some of the teachings on spiritual-sexuality, I went to a workshop with the two friends I'd shared a room with on my first medicine journey in Northern Ontario—Bea and Joan. The all-women workshop was led by a woman who had taught with Raven and gave similar teachings combined with Eastern philosophy. One of the participants asked her what she thought of Raven. In response, she told the woman to check with a medicine teacher before working with him to see if sexual intimacy was a requirement of being a student or apprentice. Bea, Joan and I looked at one another in surprise. Had we missed something? Was it true that sexual intimacy was a requirement to learn with Raven? I was torn between feeling relieved that Raven had not, in any of our time alone or in the group, made this demand, and wondering if I should be insulted that no such prerequisite had applied to me. The women in the group, knowing we had worked with Raven, began eyeing the three of us with renewed curiosity.

Excited by all I had learned with Raven in Northern Ontario, I had journeyed to Jamaica to do another medicine journey with him six months later. When I returned from this land of sensuously warm moon-lit nights, my sexual energy and interest skyrocketed. Ending my marriage was both terrifying and exhilarating. It was like living my fantasy of "Ah, to be seventeen again and know what I know now." Four months after leaving my husband I flew to Phoenix to attend a spiritual-sexuality workshop with Mitch—a whole four days of teaching and practicing the techniques of spiritual-sexuality—I had rested up in preparation.

When Mitch and I arrived at the workshop the group of about thirty men and women were sitting in a circle. Each person introduced him- or herself by name, sexual preference and current relationship. The first woman I heard as we joined the circle introduced herself as Bo, and said she was "omnisexual" and "free-dancing." I was lost. I'd traveled three thousand miles to a workshop and I didn't understand a thing she'd said after her name. I was not ready for this. I tried to stay calm, reminding myself that I was tired, in a different country and a different culture and not that far from California. Eventually I figured out that a free dancer is someone who is not in a relationship but is interested in possible sexual partners. Omnisexuality is less easily defined, but refers to the ability to feel sexual energy in relationship to anything, not just people, but rocks and trees and birds. It's obviously a broader definition of sexual energy than we use in our genitally focused culture. I thought, *This woman must be from California,* but I did have some sense of what she meant. Even as a child, camping in the bush or canoeing across a lake, I had ex-perienced a feeling of physical aliveness and energy not unlike sexual passion.

Two months after the spiritual-sexuality workshop I experienced om-nisexuality more directly, while at a Sundance ceremony. We needed to cut down hundreds of small trees to build the arbor for the dance site. The man whose land we were using had a particular area he needed to have cleared. Women were asked to go ahead of the people with chain saws and axes, to say prayers to each individual tree that was to be cut, asking its permission to be taken for our purposes and honoring its giveaway of life with a prayer and offering of tobacco. I volunteered. It sounded like physically easier work than cutting and hauling.

Eight of us set off, tobacco in hand. Last-minute instructions made me wonder about the wisdom of choosing this task. We were reminded to watch our feet to avoid stepping on any rattlesnakes. I had figured out only the day before why so many people, including the children, wore boots with everything from jeans to bathing suits despite the heat—it was to protect themselves from snakebites! As someone who lives in an area with no poisonous snakes I was terrified of being bitten, despite reassurances that snakes are not aggressive and bites rarely fatal. As we set off, the man in charge of the tree cutting told us that if we were bitten we should sit down, make our breath and heartbeat as slow as possible, wait for the chain saws to turn off and then yell "Snake!" Calm my heartbeat after being bitten by a snake! And just what would the snake be doing as I'm sitting, breathing deeply? I decided to walk very slowly and watch very carefully.

We fanned out over the area. After about two hours of cutting I came out to a small clearing where all the other women were sitting together, each lost in her own thoughts. I sat down. More than half of the group, including myself, were crying. We began to talk about what we were feeling. As we had approached tree after tree, saying our prayers, asking them to come with us and sending our energy out to meet the tree's, we received again and again the answer, felt in our bodies or heard in our minds: "Yes, sister. I will gladly come and give my life and body for your ceremony." Once in a while there was a sense of a negative response, that the time was inappropriate, so we marked that tree to indicate it was not to be cut. But the overwhelming response, which had touched all of us, was a freely given "yes." Our tears and the ache in our chests were for both the incredible generosity and beauty of the trees' giveaway and for all the times we two-leggeds have taken life without regard for the life we affect. We all felt the same. Our hearts were full.

While not a sexual feeling in the narrowest sense of the word, we felt an awareness of the energy of other forms of life and of our ability to link with that aliveness. I'd lost a lot of that feeling, and my sexual energy and health with it, when I moved to the city. I wanted it back, and I was amazed to find teachings and a teacher that did not separate sexual and spiritual passion for life. I felt I really didn't have any choice. It was either learn how to live with passion in every aspect of my life, or die.

3

I begin to meet and get to know my fellow warriors-in-training, particularly those in my platoon. We are each assigned a rank, squad,
platoon and company. I am a sergeant, which makes me the leader of a
squad. This means nothing to my nonmilitary, Canadian mind.

My tent is gradually surrounded by those of newly arrived participants. On one side is Garth, a man I had met at a Sundance, who is
often Fire Keeper for ceremonial gatherings that require special fires.
Garth is a very large man who appears to be at least part Native
American, with long hair and a beautifully tanned and muscular body
much lusted after by many of the female warriors-in-training. He has a
kind of innocence about him, accented by his quiet soft-spoken manner,
that in no way detracts from his strong masculinity. We'd spent time at
the Sundance in pleasant conversation together and I feel somewhat reassured by his proximity and the easy laughter between us. Garth has just
come from another Sundance where his skin has been pierced, and the
wounds on his chest and back are still healing.

At the Sundance I went to, after ceremonial cleansing in the Purification Lodge, I danced for three days, together with more than a hundred
women and men, back and forth to the center tree. We danced in a large
circle, to constant drumming and singing, offering our time, energy and
sweat as a giveaway, a symbolic sacrifice, for the healing of Grandmother Earth and the People. In some traditional Sundances the dancers
have their skin pierced on the chest and/or back, a thin bone is inserted
and a thong attached to the bone. The thong is then tied to a buffalo skull
or to the center tree and pulled on by the dancer until the skin breaks, as
a further sacrifice of energy and blood.

Raven's group does not do piercing Sundances. For most of us the
rigor of dancing without food and water for three days, from 6:00 A.M. to
2:00 A.M. in the heat of the desert was challenging enough. While the
dance itself was physically taxing, the hardest part was the work of getting the site ready. The mailing I'd received had said that all dancers had
to be on-site four days before the dance. With my usual compulsiveness

I assumed this was an absolute rule, and arrived on time, with Bea. Unfortunately not everyone had taken the instructions as seriously as ourselves, which left a very small group, about eight of us, doing the work of preparing the site. For two days we piled thousands of small rocks from the dance ground onto tarps, hauled them away, spread sand, and raked and raked and raked in the hot sun.

Conversation was intermittent as Bea and I worked. On the second afternoon, as we raked side by side, she suddenly looked at me and said, "Oriah, what's your shoe size?"

"What's your hat size, Bea? I think you'd better get out of the sun." I figured her brain had just blown a fuse in the noonday heat. She insisted, so I finally humored her and shared the secret of my shoe size, after exacting a promise that she would take a break. The next morning I found a beautiful pair of beaded moccasins outside my tent, exactly the right size, a gift so I could dance in comfort on the burning sand.

Other dancers did begin to arrive by the third day and we started to build the huge circular arbor. While the dance area was open to the sky, the leaf-covered arbor provided each dancer with a shaded area about three feet by six feet in which to rest and sleep. Each dancer, wearing the traditional costume of fringed skirt, ribbon shirt and sash, hangs a painted shield at his or her place in the arbor.

In the midst of the color, the heat, the drumming and the dancing, my energy soared, and I decided to apprentice with Raven. Bea and I also decided to hold ceremonies and share the teachings with others when we returned to Toronto. The traditional offering to become an apprentice is a blanket and tobacco. I had brought a special blanket, a quilt made by my great-grandmother, in a pink-and-green eight-pointed-star pattern. After I began to study with Raven, my mother told me that, according to an old family story, her father's father, my great-grandfather, had been part Native. We did not know if it was true, although it made sense in terms of family history and events. If true, it was probably kept secret out of shame and racism. I brought this particular blanket as a way of acknowledging the mixed blood that may have been denied in my own family.

The effect of the Sundance stayed with me. For days after I got home I would jump up as the alarm rang, saying, "No, I can't dance yet. Go ahead without me." My body was exhausted, but strangely, I did not get sick. For weeks I felt I was living with one foot in the material world and one foot in the world of spirit I had touched in the dance.

Phyllis arrives at the desert retreat shortly after Garth. Her mother is with her to ensure she isn't getting involved in some weird cult group, and to keep a sharp lookout for signs of extreme behavior. Phyllis is about forty, a kind of Tugboat Annie—warm, exuberant, literally captain of her own fishing boat, married to another fisherman. She dresses in an unusual mix of flowing skirts and practical overalls, with a wide-brimmed straw hat colorfully decorated with long printed scarves that billow out behind her in the wind. I do my best to be welcoming and helpful and appear as normal as possible for her sixty-five-year-old mother. All seems to be going well when, just as we finish putting up her tent, Garth comes by. Now, I'll admit that Garth's size, hair and obvious strength are themselves noticeable. But Phyllis' mother turns a deathly gray at the sight of him. It takes me a minute to comprehend; then I realize that Garth has his shirt off, and she is staring in horror at the scars on his chest and back from the piercing Sundance. This is evidence of her worst fears: ritualized physical disfiguration of her daughter. She begins to take down Phyllis' tent, telling her to get in the car, they are leaving. I try to explain the scars, and how we will not be doing anything remotely resembling that here. Phyllis, who obviously knows her mother better than I do, motions for me to be quiet and somehow just bundles her into her car and sends her off, still protesting. I am impressed.

Michael and Toni, a couple from New York City, arrive late at night. In the dark, I help them set up their tent. Their marriage is not going very well, and with the help of Raven and the support of their platoon, they use the two-week retreat to break up. Michael is a gorgeous, flirtatious man of about twenty-five chronologically and fifteen emotionally. He has gone from Mom to air force to marriage with Toni, a single mother five years his senior. The first clue that all is not happy in their tent is when Toni begins, when Michael is around, to make loud, pointed comments about hearing Mitch and I making love next door, and how she would give anything to have a reason to make those noises herself. It's downhill from there.

Gradually the area begins to fill with tents, cars, people and dust as about seventy novice warriors gather for training. Mitch is camped a short distance away and after negotiating nighttime visits, I move my sleeping bag into his tent. This is fine until another lover of his, Darlene, arrives from Phoenix. I wait to see what will happen but decide I have no reason to discontinue my mealtime or bedtime visits unless requested to do so. I know that dealing with this kind of situation directly is not exactly one of Mitch's strengths, but I am not about to let him off the hook by quietly disappearing.

We are often in different parts of the camp, and on the first night after Darlene's arrival, I go back to his tent and crawl in before Mitch arrives. Some time later I hear he and Darlene approach the tent and sit down. I move around and moan a little to make sure he knows I'm there. To my amazement he starts to talk about his relationships with women in general, and she and I in particular, as he calmly explains his attraction to both of us. I suppose there are some who might feel sympathetic to a man in his situation. I am divided. Half of me wants to get up and lunge out of the tent, without undoing the zipper, to protest this insensitive display of cowardice as he tries to placate both of us without really speaking directly to either. The other half of me is being reasonable. After all, it is a difficult situation, I knew what I was getting into . . . let's not get attached to what he does . . . there is no competition between sisters . . . . The reasonable side wins out temporarily and I say nothing. In the morning I get up, go outside and raise my arm to brush my hair—a simple, low-risk activity particularly for a warrior-in-training—and throw out three vertebrae in my back. Repressed rage is having its revenge. I can't move.

Luckily, at these kind of things there are always a plethora of bodyworkers and new age healers, some of them quite skilled and legitimate. After the careful manipulations of a chiropractor and a masseuse I am able to walk, although I can't move my head. Warrior training is out for the day. I wander, feeling emotionally and physically miserable, wishing Bea had not decided to stay at home for this trip.

I had first met Bea on the trip to Northern Ontario. Katharine, the workshop organizer, had told us she'd meditated on the names of the participants to decide who to put in the same cabin. When I arrived she told me she had put me in a room with Bea, a very dear friend of hers. Room was a misnomer for the space we shared. Large closet would have been more accurate. Bea, arriving after I did, was very gracious about how the anxiety-inspired contents of my overpacked suitcase all but filled the room. I liked her immediately. We had gone on several medicine journeys together since that time, giving each other support and humor in our worst moments with the men in our lives, men who sometimes were involved with first one of us and then the other. Mitch is one such man and I want her here now to commiserate with me.

Eventually, as I wander around, I meet Joseph. Joseph is a pipe maker and teacher of Tai Chi. He also does some kind of body work. He has taken to calling me "Witchy Woman," finding me what he calls "mysterious." I am not sure what he means, but I like the way it sounds. Noticing my physical discomfort, he offers to do some work on me. I have nowhere to go but up, so I agree. He talks to me as he gently massages my back, and I begin to relax. I tell him the story of the previous night, and much to my surprise he is angry, not at my unwarriorlike attachment and reaction, but at Mitch's insensitivity. Raven's code of enlightened, if somewhat glorified, promiscuity is frequently and eagerly embraced by group members. Within this subculture my reactions are seen as possessive, attached and spiritually incorrect, as Mitch, the masseuse and the chiropractor have all been happy to point out. Gently Joseph asks if we can be friends. I hesitate . . . and then he wonders if I've ever had a man as a friend without some expectation sexually. I can't recall one who wasn't gay, and for some reason this makes me cry and think of my grandfather. Still working on my back, Joseph asks me to tell him about my grandfather. I can hardly speak, but slowly, still crying, I do. The memory that keeps coming to mind is of my grandfather, whom I called Baba, teaching me how to ballroom dance in his living room. My grandparents had the first stereo hi-fi I had ever seen and a wonderful collection of classical and big band records. He would put some music on, stand up and dance around the room to the strains of "Rhapsody in Blue," with me hanging on and giggling. I loved that record, not because of the music, but because of the dust jacket. It was a picture of a beautiful, dark-haired woman in a blue dress dancing so that the yards of gauzy material in her full skirt expanded endlessly as she twirled. I must have been about nine years old.

A nameless well of sadness and grief seems to rise up inside me as I tell the story. I cannot explain it. The feeling isn't new, but it's one I touch only briefly, my self-control always keeping it at bay. Occasionally something will happen that seems to put a finger on this hidden and unexplainable sadness.

Gradually, as the tears and the talk flows, my back unseizes. When I leave, Joseph speaks quietly. "Next time get out of the tent, even if you have to fucking crawl out. But don't lie there and take it!" I move my sleeping bag back to my own tent and decide to concentrate on the training sessions and forget about men, a vow I've taken often enough to think of it as a sort of intermittent mantra.

4

T he days are full. Wake-up is at six, a fact I am painfully aware of for the first few days because Mitch, a musician, is responsible for playing reveille. The day begins with an hour of Tai Chi, led by Joseph, followed by four to six hours of martial arts training, two hours of combat or survival training, and two to four hours of teachings by Raven or other staff. In the evening we do ceremony, often Purification Lodges or individual all-night ceremonies. We begin again the next day at six if we are able. Occasionally I am not able.

The ceremony in the Purification Lodge at the end of a very long day is a welcome way to cleanse and relax before sleeping. Often more casually referred to as the sweat lodge, it is constructed in a very precise way, bending saplings to form a small round structure resembling a geodesic dome. This is then covered with blankets, rugs or hides. Inside, a small pit is dug to hold red-hot rocks, heated on a ceremonial fire. When everyone files in and sits down, the rocks are placed inside and the blanket over the door closed. The person leading the ceremony, the Dance Chief, pours water on the rocks as special prayers are said. Ideally the sweat is completely dark, and it can get very hot. Representing the womb of Grandmother Earth, the ṣweat is a powerful ceremony for cleansing and healing.

I had my first sweat during my first workshop with Raven, after spending time alone with him for a healing. At the end of our first day at the workshop Jamie, the female apprentice accompanying Raven, asked anyone who wanted a healing to submit completed healing sheets by the next morning. I had no idea what this would entail, but didn't want to miss any opportunity to improve my health. I filled out the sheets and handed them in, stating my desire to improve my immune system and increase my overall energy so I could have a third child.

The next morning, in the middle of teaching at his usual breakneck speed, Raven stopped abruptly, looked up at me and said pointedly, "Why do you want to have a third child?"

With all eyes in the room on me, I displayed my cunning verbal skills in this, my first exchange with Raven, by uttering a series of "uhs" and "ahs." I finally muttered something about enjoying children and wanting to bring more of this enjoyment into my life.

Raven replied abruptly, "You already have two children—why add more?"

Seeing my inability to respond, several other women attempted to come to my rescue by offering reasons women might choose to have more than two children. I recall one saying it was like having different kinds of pie for dessert. While their reasons were not mine, I was grateful for their obvious attempt to support me. Finally, just as I gathered my wits, Raven returned to the teachings as abruptly as he had left them and barreled on.

I was told to be at Raven's cabin at eleven the next morning for my healing, and to bring a medicine gift and some tobacco as an energy exchange. I panicked. I had never heard of such a thing, had brought nothing with me and did not have the time or transportation to go out to buy a gift. I returned to my cabin to rummage through my things. In my insecurity about the trip I had packed almost everything I owned, and from these chose a small container of carved stone inlaid with abalone shell. I didn't know if it was appropriate, but it had been given to me by a friend and felt like it met the "heart gift" definition I'd been told about. Bea gave me a package of the cigarettes Raven smoked and I was all set.

The next morning I showered and changed after breakfast, somehow having the idea I needed to go to the healing as clean as possible. I arrived at Raven's door precisely at eleven, with butterflies in my stomach, medicine gift in hand, determined to go through with whatever happened. Jamie answered, clad only in a T-shirt and underwear, her head wrapped in a towel, and asked me to come back in half an hour. My anxiety rose. I joined the others in the lodge, where Gunner, Raven's senior male apprentice, was beginning the teachings of the sweat lodge, which had been built the previous day. I assumed I would not miss much during the healing and could get someone else's notes before we did the sweat.

I reappeared at Raven's cabin at eleven-thirty. Jamie let me in and directed me to the threadbare couch in the living room/kitchen area. Raven sat drinking cola and smoking, in a large armchair opposite the couch. As I settled down he asked me again, in a gentler tone, "Why do you want to have another child?"

This time I was ready for him. I'd sifted through all my possible answers and came up with the one that seemed the most legitimate and closest to the truth: I'd felt an incredible sense of power when giving birth to my two sons. They had both been born at home with the assistance of midwives and a doctor. It was during their births that I had had a real sense of my own power and spiritual heart, a feeling of being able to do anything. I wanted that feeling again.

Raven was silent for a moment and then responded, "So long as the patriarchy can convince you that this is the only place you will be able to feel that power, it has nothing to worry about. Now," he went on, as if reading my thoughts, "this may sound strange coming from a man, but I speak to you from my Woman Shield." Even as he said it I could see some difference in his face. His features were rounder, softer. I blinked, thinking it was a trick of my vision. He continued. "From my Woman Shield I can speak to you and say that the Sisterhood must take back its power. If it does not, the earth will not survive. And as a man there is nothing beyond sharing my teachings that I can do to make it happen."

His eyes had filled with tears. Lighting another cigarette, he told me there were, on the medicine wheel, eight different ways of giving birth, only one of which, in the west, was the physical birthing of a child. He asked me to look at the other aspects of myself and my life that were seeking birth and not to confine myself and my sense of power to only one of the eight. He paused and asked again, "What else? Why else do you want to have another child?"

This time I spoke without hesitation. "I have two sons and I want a daughter." I braced myself for anticipated criticism.

"Ah," he said, "I understand that. I wanted a daughter more than anything in the world. And I have six sons. How many children are you willing to have to get a daughter?"

We played with this for a while, discussing the genetic probabilities given my family and my husband's. Somehow his acceptance of my reason as legitimate made it easier for me to consider how far I would go, and what my chances of having a girl were.

We talked of something Raven called my Sacred Dream, my own particular path with heart, my reason for being born. He spoke of learning to dance my own dream awake to live to my fullest potential. I was elated and I knew this was why I was ill. I was not living my Sacred Dream. I leaned forward eagerly as he spoke.

"And now," he said, "You'd like me to tell you what your Sacred Dream is, wouldn't you?" I nodded and held my breath. "Well, I can't,"

he replied, laughing softly. "That's what you have to find for yourself. ∨
That's why you're here." I knew there'd be a catch.

Our conversation continued and broadened. Finally he called Jamie in
from the other room and asked me to lie down on the couch and relax.
While Jamie placed pulsars—plastic discs filled with spirals of tiny crystals—on different parts of my body, Raven asked what I could hear, see
or feel. At one point I could clearly hear my mother's voice, although not
the words.

Raven asked, "What did your mother tell you?"

I responded without thinking. "That she would always love me no
matter what I did."

"And what did that tell you?" he asked.

"That sooner or later I would do something very terrible," I answered,
surprised.

"Does this scare you?" Raven asked.

"Yes," I replied. "I am afraid I will misuse my power."

"You will not," he stated with a sureness that seemed to root the statement in my body. Then he asked me to focus on the top of my head as
Jamie placed a pulsar there. I did, and saw a brilliant, beautiful blue light
that seemed to flood my whole being.

"This is your Hokkshideh, your higher self," Raven said. "Ask what it
has to tell you at this time." I did so, and heard a clear androgynous voice
speak softly. "There are new things to be birthed here. You must first
learn to take your power and live at peace with this earth lodge, your
body." I began to cry.

Jamie removed the pulsars, and after a few moments, I sat up on the
couch. Every movement felt weightless, as if I needed to move very
slowly or I would throw myself right off the couch. I could hear the
others leaving the main lodge and was surprised. How much time had
passed? I felt as though I had been there for about thirty minutes. I later
discovered it had been two hours. I handed Raven the gift and tobacco,
wrapped in a silk scarf. He opened it and whispered with real delight,
"Ooh, my little girl likes that!" Again I could see the features of his face
changed so that the eyes and smile of a small girl were apparent. I
thanked him and walked out.

Everyone else had returned to their cabins, presumably to prepare for
the sweat. I headed for mine. Raven's was on top of a steep hill. For a
minute I paused at the top of the path leading downward, feeling as
weightless as air, and considered just stepping off and floating effortless-

ly down the hill. I decided my judgment might be impaired, so began to walk down slowly.

Back at the cabin, Bea and the three other women we shared the cabin with were racing around getting ready for the sweat. They were probably just moving at the usual pace, but in my time-warped perception it seemed they were running around frantically. Suddenly it occurred to me that I was about to go into a sweat with no idea of what I needed to do or what was going to happen. I began to plague my cabin mates to recap in five minutes the two hours of teaching they'd just received. They didn't mind pausing to answer my questions, but it seemed that the weightlessness had gone to my brain and I couldn't retain any of the answers they gave me, so I kept asking the same questions repeatedly. Barbara was the only other person in the cabin who had children, so I assume she knew something about dealing with incessant questions. Finally, in sheer exasperation, she grabbed me by both shoulders. Looking squarely into my vacant eyes she said, in an imperative tone, "Oriah! Take off all your clothes. Pick up you blanket and towel. Come with us." She kept repeating these three simple instructions over and over as I moved about the room, and I finally managed to follow them.

Ready at last, we trooped out, naked except for blankets or raincoats. It had begun to rain. On the way to the sweat I again tried to get Bea to give me a condensed version of what they'd been taught that morning. Having learned from Barbara's example, Bea told me firmly to just follow her, do as she did and listen to instructions that would be given in the sweat. Not in any state to feel worried, I joined the others at the sweat.

My perspective at that point was a little askew, but the sight of all those men and women standing in the cold wind, nude except for rain jackets casually flung open, with goose-bumped legs stuck into rain boots, struck me as hysterically funny. While I managed not to laugh, I couldn't seem to wipe what I'm sure was a mindless grin off my face. It was such a different scene from any I had anticipated on the "path to enlightenment." Gunner, who was leading the sweat, reminded everyone that although they could get out of the sweat in the first three quarters, no one would be allowed leave in the fourth and final round of prayers. "If you think you're going to die in the last quarter, you might as well, because it's the only way you're going to get out," he said. I sobered right up.

I remember very little about my first sweat. I sank down into my tiny spot in the crowded lodge on the cool earth and drifted into the blackness, rising heat, songs and prayers. I assume I said my prayers in the proper sequence and did nothing to embarrass myself. As I was to learn in many subsequent sweats, feeling hot or uncomfortable is much more dependent upon my mental and emotional state than on the level of heat or room available.

At the Sundance all the dancers were required to do four sweats before dancing and one afterward. I was nervous about it. I've never been able to sit in saunas for very long without becoming dizzy and was not sure how different this would be. The first one was not very hot, although it was long because of the number of people saying prayers, and very crowded. I had to sit with my knees up under my chin. By the end my lower back was aching. I was too busy enduring to really allow the ceremony to touch me.

The second sweat was led by Jack, a huge man about six foot five, with a kind of dark brooding energy that made me nervous. Although I was not sitting very close to the hot rocks, I knew from the start I was in trouble. I felt simultaneously dizzy and nauseous as the heat started to rise. My legs ached, my back ached and I felt that I had to get out. At the end of the second set of prayers, Jack told us that anyone who needed to could get out for some cool air for a few minutes while they added more hot rocks to the pit.

Using every bit of self-control I could muster, I did not bolt for the door over the bodies of the others in the sweat, but left in the correct ceremonial manner. Once outside I lay down immediately with my stomach on the ground, oblivious to dirt or cacti, sucking in great gulps of cool air. I felt quite desperate. I had traveled a long way to dance, and there was no way I was going to live through three more sweats. If I didn't sweat, I couldn't dance. I would be left wandering around all week helping out where I could. Jack called us to come back into the sweat. I didn't move. He came over to see how I was doing and, very close to tears, I told him I didn't think I could do it. With incredible gentleness, he helped me sit up and talked to me about how to deal with the heat. He showed me a "hand tie," a specific way of holding your hands, which when focusing your breath can help move the heat through you. What I remembered most was his telling me over and over not to fight the heat. This was, of course, exactly what I'd been doing—trying to grit my teeth, think cool thoughts of snow and ice cream—to make it through. I was not completely convinced, but my desire to dance took me back into the sweat.

It worked. The rest of the sweat was much easier, and I did complete the others necessary to dance. The final one before the Sundance was led by Marsha, Robert's wife and a woman with a reputation for being very tough when she ran sweats. It was a hot one, and in the middle of the third round, staring into the inky blackness, I could suddenly see huge circles, like painted shields, spinning around the sweat. There were four of them and I tried to capture their images to remember later. After the sweat I went out and lay on the ground to cool off. All at once I felt as though I were lying on a huge animal. I could feel the earth beneath me very subtly expand and contract as if it were breathing. I could hear a very distant thudding, like a giant heart beating. It was the feeling I'd had when I was three years old and had touched the side of a cow at my grandparents' farm with my tiny hand, a sense of touching a huge mass of life. I started to cry as my belief that the earth is not a static mass of inanimate material, but rather a living, breathing entity, became knowledge I held in my body. It gave me real hope that she was not just going to lie there passively and allow whatever destruction the two-leggeds decided to wreak upon her to happen. She could and would fight back. Marsha came over to see if I was all right. I told her about the shields I had seen in the sweat, which I now realized with disappointment I could not remember in detail. "It's O.K.," she reassured me. "What you receive in the sweat is always with you, whether you can consciously remember it or not."

Each sweat is unique, but to this day I know that when I am having a difficult time in a sweat lodge I have to look for where I am resisting, trying to hang on too tightly. Now, when the first pour of water hits the rocks and the steam hisses up and fills the sweat, I relax and with my breath welcome the heat into my body as fast and as gently as I can, as if I'm greeting a lover and aligning our two fires.

I have plenty of opportunity to perfect this technique at the desert retreat, as we do more than a dozen sweats. Some are unusually long and hot, having been designed by Raven for special purposes. By the middle of the second week we are doing a sweat designed to help us step out of our normal consciousness into a place where we can see into what is called our Book of Life. The Book of Life is understood to be a record of all of our lives, past and future. Seeing into it gives us some understanding of the patterns we keep repeating and, hopefully, some insights about why we do what we do. This is not viewed fatalistically; we are the ones who write our own Book of Life. But as soon as we enter a particular life, we can't seem to remember why we're here or what we decided we wanted to learn. It's a kind of karmic amnesia. I don't know if the ceremony will work or if the Book of Life even exists, but having had two marriages end and an on-going illness in my life, I am more than willing to learn what I can about my own patterns of behavior.

This is an unusual sweat. There will be six rounds of prayers instead of four and the door will not be opened between any of the rounds. This means all the rocks, about eighty, are placed in at the beginning and the heat builds the entire time. We are told that to avoid disrupting the heat or the energy, no one will be allowed to leave, so everyone needs to consider carefully if he or she wants to go in. There is no pressure to participate, and in fact people who have had difficulties with the heat in previous sweats are urged to consider skipping this one.

Tania insists on being included. Tania is a small Israeli woman with the foulest mouth I have ever heard. It isn't that she swears, although she does frequently, it's that she does not care what anyone thinks or feels about what she says. I am overwhelmed with repulsion and admiration. I first saw Tania in action at one of the group sessions where everyone attending the retreat was invited to air their grievances. Needless to say, with our strenuous schedule, the heat and the dust, everyone's true nature came out. Politeness is at a premium when seventy people have lined up for the four available showers at the end of a long, sweltering, muscle-wrenching day and the hot water runs out. Peace, love and other spiritual aspirations are put to a hard test.

Tania is outspoken to the point of brutality. At the first grievance session she rails on mercilessly about some "gorilla" who had, without regard for her, lain down on her legs in the previous night's sweat. She demands to know who he is. A large, quiet man puts up his hand. I think he deserves a citation for courage. He explains in a soft voice that he thought he was either going to pass out or throw up, and that lying down had been unplanned and involuntary. Tania is not sympathetic and is just warming up for a tirade, when she is cut off by Raven, who comes to the man's defense. Tania is switched from her original company—I think she'd worn them out—into mine in the second week, and I get some firsthand knowledge of just how ruthless and vulnerable she can be.

The truth is that Tania is scared to death in the sweat. I suspect she is claustrophobic and that her iron-willed resistance to showing any vulnerability means she fights the heat tooth and nail, and usually "loses" in her own mind, and has to leave partway through. So when Tania says she wants to do the six-round, one-door sweat, we are all dubious. The Dance Chief, Marsha, talks to her for some time, suggesting she be the person who sits outside the door, or that she help in some other capacity.

Tania is adamant. She can do it, she wants to do it and she will do it. After being warned a dozen times that under no conditions will she be allowed to leave, she is in and sits on my left in the sweat.

The heat builds gradually and I pull it into my body, until it fills me completely and I feel like a shining, living flame. Almost all of us lie down, with our heads at the outside of the circle. It is cooler close to the ground and tiny drafts of fresh air sometimes come in under the blankets at the edge of the sweat. It is also much more comfortable for my back, particularly in a sweat where I'm trying to relax enough to leave my body. The prayers flow smoothly and the energy builds higher and higher. As we start the fifth round Marsha instructs us to pull our energy up and out, and to say our prayer for opening our Book of Life. As I do I find myself once again above the desert in the starry night sky. A ribbon of light like a road seems to shine among the stars, and as I say my prayers, far below me in the sweat I hear Tania's voice next to me saying, "I need to get out."

Everyone gasps. Those who have found their way out of their bodies struggle to keep their attention from being drawn back too soon, knowing that if the door is opened the energy will be lost. The Dance Chief speaks calmly and reassuringly to Tania, suggesting ways she can increase her comfort. Nothing helps. Tania becomes increasingly agitated and belligerent about leaving, suggesting that the Dance Chief is trying to kill her. I concentrate on waiting, on holding my place in the stars until what is happening in the lodge is over. Finally in exasperation, seeing that gentleness is only making matters worse, Marsha lays down the law. "Tania, hold your space. You will not leave!" This shuts Tania right up, although I can sense the rigidity in her body next to me. After a moment, keeping my view of the night sky, I slowly move my left hand and gently place it on her navel, whispering almost inaudibly, "Breathe here." My hand is cool on her burning skin and I feel her begin to relax and focus on her breath. Leaving my hand resting on her, I turn my attention back to the path of light in the sky, and journeying across it, seek images from time past and time future.

One scene is repeated. I have seen it before in different sleep dreams, although a new sequence now completes the action. In it I am older, I guess about thirty-seven years old. I wear a deerskin tunic over my white blouse and skirt, with the image of a red, stepped pyramid painted on the back. At the top of the pyramid is a crystal skull. Two blue snakes are crawling up the steps on either side of the pyramid. My hair is longer and there is a bit of gray at the temples, but I look youthful, energetic and healthy. I carry in my hands a human-sized skull made of clear quartz crystal, radiating a rainbow of tiny, flickering lights.

Raven, Mitch and several other men are with me. We approach the low, dark entrance of a cave and are greeted by an old woman. She is tiny and stooped with age, leaning on a polished wooden walking stick. She holds out a gnarled hand to me and moves to usher me through the cave entrance. Raven moves next to me, but the gray-haired woman looks at him sternly and raises her hand to indicate that neither he nor the others are allowed to enter. I hesitate. I can see Raven's face, scowling and red. He is furious that she will not let him come with us. A ripple of fear runs up my spine. Gently she takes my arm and moves into the cave. We walk through a short passageway, dimly lit by a light ahead of us. The smell of damp earth surrounds me. The passage opens into a round, high-ceilinged chamber lit with torches set in the stone walls. A circle of old women, each wrapped in a beautifully patterned blanket, sit before me. They motion for me to place the skull in the center of the circle on the hard-packed dirt floor. As I do the cave is suddenly lit with spinning lights of every color, and the sounds of drumming and singing fill the room. I begin to dance within the circle, twirling and laughing with in-credible energy and agility. As I dance the lights seem to follow me, out-lining the pattern of my movement in neon streaks of brilliant colors: a series of infinity loops or figure eights, overlapping in different positions within the circle. The women around me, obviously enjoying my ex-uberance, encourage me, clapping and nodding in time with the drum-ming, smiling their approval.

The scene repeats and the dancing continues. I don't know how long I have been there. Time in the sweat lodge is different from the time we wear on our wrists. I later discover we were in the sweat about three hours. As I hear Marsha's voice calling to us to return to our bodies for the final round of the ceremony, I am reluctant to leave the old women in the cave. I thank them silently, tears filling my eyes, and they nod their goodbyes. No words have been spoken. As I return to my body, lying on the earth in the steam-filled lodge, I am aware of Tania, still next to me. She is breathing normally now. We file out.

As we leave the sweat I feel calm and relaxed, although a little light-headed. The man who helps me step out takes my arm and looks at me, surprised. "What did you do, take a hair dryer in there?" It's true. While everyone else is soaked, my long hair is dry and looks neatly combed. I don't know why. I just smile and sit down. The night is very cool and the moon, almost full, floods the desert landscape with an eerie blue-white light. Not everyone feels quite so composed. Many lie down immediately to bring themselves fully into their bodies and to cool off. The people who have been outside insure everyone is O.K. and covered with a blanket.

I walk in slow motion back to my tent. What did the images mean? One of the teachings Raven gave the first time I met him was about the crystal skulls. Gathered in the lodge in Northern Ontario he had told us a legend of thirteen crystal skulls, of flawless quality, here on earth— twelve clear quartz skulls representing the total knowledge of each of the planets with human life and one amethyst skull. These skulls, brought here from different planets by the Star Nation People, were used to build huge underground cities such as Atlantis. According to the story, the skulls were kept in the Jaguar Temples of the Mayans, but two were stolen by Cortez and his men with the aid of a woman from the temple. One was recovered in Italy during the Second World War and the other was discovered by an archeologist's daughter in what is now Belize. According to Raven, the latter skull contains the knowledge of the planet Earth. He said it was still with the archeologist's daughter, now an old woman living in Canada. The legend says that when the crystal skull is returned to and completes the wheel of skulls, the knowledge of the universe will be accessible. For this to happen, though, there must be a level of peace and justice on this planet that does not yet exist.

I had reacted strongly to the story. Something about it was familiar, although I couldn't say what. I had never read or heard anything about crystal skulls that I could recall. When Raven spoke of the skull, I instantly felt drawn to it and wanted to see it. In contrast, I felt physically ill as Raven related the part of the story about the woman who had helped Cortez. He referred to her as the "Scarlet Woman" and said she had been Montezuma's daughter. His tone changed as he spoke with passion and anger about how she had betrayed her father, her people and the other priests and priestesses of the temple. Falling in love with Cortez, she'd given him the precious skulls and had aided him in murdering those in the temple. As he told the story I felt flushed and dizzy. The buzzing sound I had heard when Raven first entered the room returned, making it almost impossible for me to hear his words. Immediately I felt short of breath and sick to my stomach. Although the feeling passed in a few moments, I had wondered if the long hours and smoke-filled room were taking their toll after all.

Even as a child I loved rocks and minerals and had a rock collection. As a student I took geology courses and always felt pulled to areas where rock formations were the predominant feature. I'd been aware from the age of four or five that I could "hear" rocks and stones speak, or at least give off a feeling or image, although instinctively I knew never to mention it to anyone. When I had taken the daylong workshop on crystals I was relieved to hear that other seemingly sane folks had had similar experiences.

Hearing about the skull in that first meeting with Raven, I later spoke with other workshop participants and discovered that the woman who had the skull was living only forty minutes from my home. When I returned to Toronto I immediately tried to track down her telephone number or address, but without success. Finally, nine months later, I met a woman who mentioned that her astrologer had been to see the crystal skull. With renewed energy I called the astrologer, got the telephone number and address of the woman, Samantha, and arranged an appointment.

Leaving my youngest son, Nathan, with his father, I went with my eldest son, Brendan, then six, and a close friend. I didn't know what to expect. We arrived at the address given to us by Samantha's secretary, friend and housemate, Elizabeth. It was a bungalow in a very ordinary suburb of a small city. We were greeted warmly by the gray-haired elderly women, both wearing floral print dresses, and by their two Pekingese dogs. The whole thing felt like a Sunday visit to relatives you don't see very often, who you have very little in common with, but think of fondly. Their home was simple and pleasant. Two things were unusual—the huge, silver Louis XIV mirror in the corner of the room and the crystal skull on the coffee table in front of the couch. The mirror, they explained to us later, had been a gift from a visitor, and had been used by Marie Antoinette herself.

The skull rendered me speechless, somewhat of a minor miracle for those who know me. I immediately sat on the floor in front of it, remaining there motionless for about an hour. Sounds, colors, images, feelings and sensations flashed through me. At different points I could hear a clear, androgynous and not unfamiliar voice speak. It gave me three ways to always stay connected to the energy of the skull. First, it had me recall a dream I had while very ill, only two weeks earlier. In this dream I had fallen into a river, where a huge fish had begun to devour my flesh, leaving my skeleton to sink to the mud-covered bottom. Suddenly a large bird dove into the water and, gathering my bones in its talons, took them to a nest on a mountain. There the bird reassembled the bones and placed crystals where each of my chakras and eyes would be. Slowly the flesh reformed over the bones and crystals. Since that time I had been able, when I focused my attention, to feel the sensation of the crystals placed in my body. This, the voice from the skull said, was the first way to remain connected to its energy, by feeling the crystals and their link to the skull's energy.

Then the voice asked me to look up to my right in my mind's eye. As I did so I saw a brilliant star. "This," said the voice, "is where we are both from. If you wish to connect with the skull, look for the star and pull its light into yourself." Then the voice asked me to be aware of my own skull. I focused on the bones of my head, and could clearly feel them beneath my skin. Suddenly I was equally aware of the shape and size of the crystal skull and had a sensation of my skull and it being alternately superimposed. First my skull was within the crystal, and then the crystal was inside my skull. "Focus on this feeling," the voice said, "when you want to dream with the skull."

Sitting on the floor in front of the skull, I focused on feeling these three ways of experiencing the energy of this magnificent crystal. Then the voice spoke again but with a more imperative tone. "You will dream me back to the Council of Grandmothers," the voice said. I was confused. Who were the Grandmothers? What did it mean to dream something back? Was there something I was supposed to do? I recalled Raven's story about the skull needing to be returned to the circle of skulls, and tentatively asked if it was O.K. for it to be with Samantha and Elizabeth. The voice was reassuring: "All is as it should be at this time. These two are the guardians of the skull."

Samantha and Elizabeth graciously served us tea and told us stories about their experiences living with the skull, while Brendan, sitting on the floor, devoured cookies and cautiously got to know the dogs. All at once, sitting on the floor next to him pouring tea, I had the strongest déjà vu experience of my life. I "remembered" it all as it unfolded: pouring tea, the china cups and saucers with their pattern of tiny pink roses, chatting about the dogs, the people who had visited, feeling the pile of the carpet beneath me. It went on for several minutes. The whole afternoon was a bizarre combination of the extraordinary and the mundane. In thanks for their hospitality I gave the two women a small wooden carving of a Goddess.

Two years later, returning to see the skull with another friend, I was greeted warmly again by Samantha, who said she remembered my previous visit. I was doubtful. They have hundreds of people visit, many of them famous and noteworthy, so I could not see why or how she would have remembered me. As we left I again gave them a small gift, a round wooden box with a buffalo carved on the lid. As Samantha accepted it she said, "Oh, I'll put it up here next to the gift you brought last time. Isn't it wonderful—it's made of the same wood." So saying she went directly to the small Goddess statue I had brought two years earlier, sitting on a shelf. It was indeed made of the same polished red-brown wood.

Returning home from my first visit with Samantha, Elizabeth and the crystal skull, I found my nights were full of vivid dreams. One month after visiting the skull I woke up in the middle of the night from a dream of being in a cave. Even as I awoke, I could see and sense the cave around me and I could not orient myself to my bedroom. I couldn't see the usual crack of light under the door or through the blinds on the window. Everything was black. I couldn't feel what was up or down, right or left.

Frantically my mind tried to find some way of orienting myself, and I felt around for something familiar. I stood and felt for the wall, and instead of the smooth painted surface of my bedroom walls, I felt the roughness of cool rock. I was terrified. Desperately I continued to grope along the wall, feeling I might pass out with fear. Just as I couldn't bear it any longer I touched the light switch with my hand. I flipped it on, flooding the blackness with harsh light. I was in my room, standing by the door.

For several moments I stared at the objects in the room, indelibly imprinting them on my mind to try to keep my bearings when I turned the light off. Flipping the switch, I dove back into bed. Immediately the blackness and disorientation returned. This time I did not get up but drifted in and out of a fitful sleep. Much later I awoke and heard the voices of women chanting. Very clearly I heard a woman's voice say, "You must be naked to meet the Grandmothers." I dreamed I was pregnant, in labor and giving birth to a tiny baby girl. Again I heard the woman's voice, echoing within the cave. "You have been called by the Dreamers." In the morning the T-shirt I had worn to bed was lying in the corner, although I had no recollection of taking it off. The elusive memory of the drumming came to me all day.

Lying alone in my tent at the desert retreat, after the sweat lodge, I remember each of these experiences and wonder what connection my vision in the sweat has with my dreams and the words from the skull. At the desert retreat Raven has a collection of smaller crystal skulls, carved in Brazil, that he says have been ceremonially keyed into the circle of large skulls. They are about fist size. Rising the next morning, I go to look at them more closely. With a loan from a generous friend at the retreat I buy one to use for dreaming, a dark, smoky quartz skull with red and gold rutilations, hairlike threads of other minerals, running through it.

I keep wondering what the images from the sweat could mean but I do not share them with anyone. The next day I find myself daydreaming as Raven teaches in the late afternoon. We are gathered in the only grove of trees, where Raven's camper is parked. As I sit in the cool shade my mind wanders. Raven is giving us some teachings on dreaming and understanding destiny. He is particularly intolerant of what he calls the "new age twinkies'" version of destiny, where people give up their power and responsibility for what happens in their lives, calling it fate. He does say, however, that some individuals choose to give up a piece of their free will, before entering a life, in order to play a particular role in healing the collective dream. This he calls destiny, accenting that it is rare. People know if this life is one of those rare ones where destiny has a role, if they are given a specific kind of vision. The vision will occur at least four times, in an especially vivid awake or asleep dream, with additional sequences taking the dream progressively further each time. In each the dreamer will see him or herself as aging and will be aware of both the teacher and lodge he or she is working with in the material world. The vision will be connected to repeated feelings of déjà vu in his or her waking reality.

I snap out of my daydream. This describes precisely the nature of the dreams I have had regarding the skull, culminating in the images I saw in the Book of Life sweat. I feel the blood drain from my face and hear my heart pounding. Joseph, sitting next to me, leans over and asks if I am all right. I nod dumbly. What scares me about this is that I do not understand the dream, or vision, if that indeed is what it is. If I have agreed to do something specific in this life, something important for the collective dream, I can't remember it. What if I blow it, miss my cue, screw up some small but crucial part?

The question nags at me for the remainder of the retreat. Finally, before leaving, my anxiety overcomes my fear of appearing unbearably inflated, and I tell Raven about the vision and my concern. Feeling cautious, I exclude the portion of the vision where he is not allowed into the cave and responds with anger. He listens very attentively and tells me there is no way of knowing if the dream has a literal or a symbolic meaning. More importantly he assures me that if it does indicate some aspect of destiny in this life, it would not be possible for me to screw it up. If, in fact, I have agreed to play such a role, it will happen whether I pay attention to it or not as part of the unfolding of the destiny set in place. I find this very reassuring and, while curious about how it might come about, I try not to add it to my list of things to worry about.

5

O n days when we don't have combat training, we have survival training. I am looking forward to the latter much more than the former because it's taught by Steve, the man with the godlike body that greeted my eyes the first morning, and because it's supposed to be about things I've always wanted to learn such as tracking, edible plants or finding water in the desert.

There is a lot of talk these days about Native prophecies predicting the demise of Western civilization as we know it, a collapse of the social and economic structure resulting in general mayhem. When I think about how far out of balance with the natural environment humans have become, I don't think this is improbable, but I'm cautious about how much I want to shape my life around the possibility. So I have an ongoing debate with myself. There has never been a time in history when there have not been predictions of downfall and destruction. Of course, there has also never been a time when human beings possessed such easy access to the means of full-scale global devastation. On the one hand I do not want to live in fear, nor does the idea appeal to me of stashing away food and equipment that I may be called on to defend at gunpoint from hungry individuals. On the other hand if the predictions are correct, and tales of oil spills, economic debts and the depleted ozone layer certainly add to the probability, am I just sticking my head in the sand by not preparing? I have two sons whom I love, and I do not want their lives shortened because I cannot face possible realities.

The inner debate could go on forever. I resolve it in two ways. I do not spend a lot of time listening to or reading the prophecies, knowing they only add to my anxiety and do nothing to move me into anything but hand-wringing inactivity. At this point, if I had to do without the local grocery store, my kids and I would probably starve. So where and when I can I learn about how to live off the land. Knowledge, unlike supplies, would not have to be defended and could be shared without any loss to myself or my family. It could be used for fun, or to add resources to our lives even in times of plenty, so it doesn't seem to add a self-fulfilling element to the prophecies.

Thus my enthusiasm about the inclusion of survival training in this retreat. While it's true the desert surroundings are drastically different from my home environment, I am assuming that the basic principles of learning to use what is available will apply. However I'm disappointed. It's not that Steve does not have the knowledge. He has lived off the land in many different places. But his teaching style and my learning style do not meet on mutual ground. The first day is spent in a slow-moving discussion about what we would look for if we found ourselves alone on this site. Steve's style is laid-back, soft-spoken and meandering. I walk away with a half page of information where I wanted twenty.

We are told to gather for our next session, a hike through the area, two days later, wearing only one piece of clothing. The item cannot be a T-shirt, shoes or anything that covers half of our body. This pretty well leaves us all standing around in our underwear, looking and feeling silly. As Steve arrives in his loincloth, some of the men begin to mutter that the whole exercise has been cooked up by Steve so he can show off his incredible physique. They get no argument from the women.

I assume that the point is to go out on the land without the usual protection and insulation provided by our clothing. Or else the exercise is just in keeping with this group's predilection for finding any excuse to drop their clothes. In either case I'm not pleased as I gingerly place my bare feet on burning sand, avoiding cacti, feeling the sun beat down on my unprotected head. Some people have chosen a hat as their one piece of clothing, seemingly a wise choice, until we are led into a narrow gully and asked to sit down. This is the only place where moisture exists, and therefore it's a haven for bugs, scorpions, snakes, prickly plants and God knows what else. I'm grateful for at least the illusion of protection afforded by my underwear.

I did not start my learning with Raven with a casual and comfortable attitude toward nudity, although I did learn to "push the edge" here also. In Northern Ontario Raven had given us teachings of the luminous cocoon, seeing the human body as energy. He began with the Stationary Assemblage Point, a point on the upper right chest that acts as a kind of tuning station for what we perceive as our reality at any given moment. He explained that most of us have our Assemblage Point stuck in what is called the Point of Confusion. This was not news to me. We discussed various ways of shifting the Assemblage Point to gain a new perspective and greater sense of centeredness.

One of the ways to shift it is with a special, round-ended crystal. Raven asked for a volunteer so he could demonstrate the technique. I can categorically say that in any group situation where someone has asked for a volunteer, I have never offered my services. In this case I came very close. I thought, *Come on, Oriah, for once in your life take a chance. God knows you could use a shift in perspective.* However, I was saved by this short exchange with myself as another woman stepped forward. I was left feeling self-righteously that this time I would have volunteered if I'd had the chance.

Two minutes later I did indeed feel "saved," as Raven asked the woman to take her shirt off and she, without a second's hesitation, did so to sit topless in front of the group. My stomach turned and the little voice in my head said, *That could have been you, you idiot! Let this be a lesson to you the next time you get any courageous notions of volunteering.*

Now, while nudity generally made me nervous, where my breasts were concerned it reached the level of acute anxiety. After twelve months of nursing each of my sons, my breasts had shrunk and sagged to a shadow of their former selves. Now they resembled what a friend so poetically called "two eggs over easy"—and the eggs being fried on a pan with a definite slope at that—and I was self-conscious about displaying them to anyone, let alone a roomful of strangers. I watched with real admiration as Rita, the woman who had volunteered, sat unself-consciously as Raven shifted her Assemblage Point. After describing and demonstrating the technique, which resulted in a pink flush over Rita's chest and a momentary look of disorientation in her eyes, Raven instructed us to choose a partner, preferably of the opposite gender, get a crystal and shift each other's Assemblage Points.

I had already decided that, despite Raven's reassurances that no one needed to try the technique who did not feel comfortable, I was not going to embarrass myself by revealing my terror of taking off my shirt. However, I also knew from watching the group that there were some men I would feel less comfortable with than others. Not wanting to leave my choice of partner up to chance or the Great Spirit, I moved the instant Raven said, "O.K., get started," to ask one man, Bruce, to work with me. We went to the side of the room, where, not wanting to delay the inevitable, I whipped off my shirt. My survival technique at this point was one I'd employed in physically uncomfortable situations, such as a medical examination or having sex with my first husband. I had a way of splitting my consciousness off from my body so I did not feel my own discomfort. Of course this occasionally useful skill was inextricably linked to the cause of my illness—a real alienation from my physical self.

My unsuspecting partner, perhaps equally ill at ease, began touching my chest in an effort to find where my Assemblage Point was, as we'd been instructed. While shifting the point is a relatively easy to learn technique, what takes practice for most people is "seeing" its location, whether visually or by touch. Doing so requires using the psychic senses and beginning to trust them. Raven, Jamie and Gunner were wandering around the room helping folks out. Gunner approached us and spoke with Bruce, encouraging him to be less tentative in his gentle poking, pointing out that this was probably his only opportunity to look so closely at "these beautiful little breasts." Outwardly I remained calm and smiling, inwardly I seethed over the offensive, if accurate, use of the term "little," conjuring similar phrases to vengefully describe a part of his male anatomy should the opportunity arise.

As Bruce finally determined the location of my Assemblage Point and prepared to use the crystal I noticed Raven watching us. Taking the three breaths as we had been told, I held the final breath as Bruce placed the crystal on my chest and his hand on my back. Suddenly I heard Raven's voice right next to me, speaking to Bruce. "Not so slow, shift her!" He grabbed the crystal and with a quick motion drew it across my chest and down the center of my body, turning it firmly about three inches above my navel and smacking me on the head with the palm of his other hand.

The whole thing couldn't have taken more than five seconds, but my experience of it was in slow motion. As Raven initially grabbed the crystal and moved it, a wave of nausea swept through me. My mind recoiled at the thought that my second direct encounter with Raven was going to include throwing up all over him. The nausea passed instantly, and a wave of heat flashed through my body from the base of my spine to the top of my head. Part of my consciousness seemed to follow the heat as it moved up and out the top of my head, to kind of free-float above my body. Another part of my awareness remained at the point of light and warmth emanating from my belly where he was twisting the crystal. With the smack on my head and the removal of Raven's hands, I thought for a moment I might pass out. The floor appeared to swim up to meet me. This, too, passed as quickly as it had come, and I blinked and looked into Bruce's concerned face. I assured him with a nod that I was all right and then gazed in wonder around the room. Everything looked brighter, cleaner, crisper, as if my vision had improved or some dullness had been lifted. I had no difficulty, after putting on my almost-forgotten shirt, with shifting Bruce's own Assemblage Point. While I've had my mine shifted countless times since then, I have never had such dramatic sensations, although the sense of both heightened awareness and clearer vision is often present.

Since then my discomfort with partial or complete nudity has dissipated. The strange thing about nudity is that it always feels like more of a problem in anticipation than when it actually happens. Thinking about taking my clothes off to do a sweat, going swimming or being part of a healing circle continued to raise my anxiety for some time. But once everyone had their clothes off and I was surrounded by a group of imperfect but beautiful bodies, I could never quite remember why I'd been so worried. The change in my own comfort was so gradual I hardly noticed it. Then one day, taking a break from preparing the Sundance site, I sat drying off in the sun after a swim. It suddenly occurred to me the three men I was talking with were as naked as I was—and I hadn't even noticed. All I could think was, *If my mother could only see me now,* and I laughed out loud at how much energy I had used worrying about even taking off my shirt.

Walking, crawling and sitting almost nude on the hard, hot ground during the survival classes is a different matter. I'm not embarrassed—I'm physically uncomfortable and bored. While it may be useful to know how to make strong rope from grass, after making an inch or two I feel I have the technique and do not want to spend hours creating several feet of it. I eventually begin to see the two-hour survival sessions on alternate days as times to catch a nap, which no doubt does add to the "survival adaptability" Raven is so fond of saying we need to develop. When we take a break for dinner Raven admonishes us to "eat and then go down." This is good advice. I discover that if I lie down for a nap before preparing one of the many freeze-dried culinary delights I have with me, odds are that I will keep right on sleeping and not eat. The descriptions on the food packages, promising gourmet lasagna, beef bourgignon or strawberry cheesecake if I just add boiling water and stir make a nap look good at any time.

Sandwiched in between Tai Chi at six every morning and combat or survival training at eleven is martial arts. Men and women train separately in these morning sessions. The women train with Delia. Delia is a beautiful woman about five feet tall, with a body that leans toward voluptuousness, though she struggles to keep it to a culturally defined thinness. She has long, thick, curly blond hair and large blue-green eyes. It's hard to believe she has worked in Hollywood as a bodyguard—until you see her in action. Delia is a black belt in karate and a martial arts teacher. She is there, as she puts it, to teach us how to effectively defend ourselves. No beauty, no style, just effective techniques to break, maim or kill, depending on the situation.

On the first day she predicts what will happen in our two weeks together. As we get into the training we will have mixed feelings about what we are doing, and will as a result become lazy, careless, tired and undisciplined, coming to class late, talking while she's giving instruction, injuring ourselves. She warns us that her response will be to tighten up discipline to keep our energy and attention high in order to avoid injuries and to help us learn as much as we can, as fast as we can. At the end of the two weeks we will be tested by actually being attacked by men she will bring in.

Each day we learn and practice techniques—with each other and by hitting, punching, and kicking huge mats. For the first two days the energy is high and everyone is excited. Then, right on schedule, people begin to unravel. Delia, true to her word, tightens up discipline. If you talk in line while waiting your turn at the mats, she demands ten push-ups or twenty sit-ups or you're out of the class. I never talk in line.

I have done women's self-defense courses before, although never quite so rigorously, so it comes as a surprise to me that I begin to feel ambivalent about attending the sessions. As I hit a mat, held by another woman, with my fists and feet, images of violence from my first marriage and memories of being raped flash through me. I am surprised, taken off guard. Ten years have passed and I'd thought I had already worked through my feelings. That was in my head. My body still holds all the memories: reeling across the room and feeling the footboard of the bed catch me across the lower back and kidneys; hiding under the card table in the corner of the bedroom, shrinking back farther and farther, making myself smaller and smaller, hoping I can somehow disappear so he won't find me; sailing through the air and crashing down on my back on the black-and-white tiles of the kitchen floor; looking up from the floor at the six-foot-five mass above me, trying to judge my distance to the phone and his proximity to the butcher knives; feeling my shoulders pinned to the bed, the air knocked from my lungs by his weight, a handful of hair ripped from my scalp as I try to move my head. The images come unbidden, and with each, my blows on the mat become weaker and weaker. Delia comes over and asks me what's happening. I can hardly speak. "The rape, the being hit, it's all coming back" is all I can manage to say. She has everyone sit down to talk. Many of the women are going through similar feelings. Out of forty, at least fifteen have experienced rape and assault. Delia sets up a special time for us to meet and deal with our histories of violence.

I leave the session feeling numb, uncertain of how I am going to go on. This is an unusual place for me, and I am more frightened than I have ever been. Always before, no matter how bad things were, I've always felt I could see a light at the end of the tunnel. Now I cannot. All I can see and feel is an endless abyss of pain, with no way out. These things have happened. I cannot erase them, and if I allow myself to sink into the despair, numbness, exhaustion and silent, screaming pain, I do not see how I can get myself out. Will I have to be ever-vigilant for the rest of my life to keep the blackness of the past at bay? For the first time I feel I cannot do it. I am too tired.

Desperately I seek out Raven. I know from what he has told the group that when he was in prison he was raped by a group of men. This is somehow important. I want to talk to someone who knows what I have experienced. I find him sitting in the shade outside his camper having a cigarette. Feeling very shaky, I tell him what is happening to me. He listens carefully and then speaks.

"Listen, hon, you've got to get this thing from the past out of your heart. That's where women have the difficulty. Men, they have a struggle getting things like this out of their heads. I kept going over the scene of my rape in my head a thousand times. But with women it's the heart. They may be able to stop thinking about it, put it out of their head, but it keeps right on living in their hearts." I sit numbly, listening.

"How?" My voice is almost a whisper.

"O.K." He sounds very matter-of-fact. "This is what I want you to do. I'm going to talk to Marsha about arranging a healing sweat for you with the women and then, when that's done, I want you to come and we'll talk. All right?"

I nod. "I don't feel like there's a way out of this. I can't see any way and this is the first time in my life I've ever felt like this." I begin to cry.

Raven's tone softens. "I know, hon, but there is. Let's do the healing and see what happens."

Thanking him, I get up and walk slowly, weary to my bones, back to my tent. I still feel weighted down by darkness, but I trust myself to the skills and knowledge of both Delia and Raven. I have no choice.

The next day the women who have identified themselves as survivors of violence meet with Delia. One by one each woman tells her story and Delia has her reenact it, with others playing the role of the man or men involved. Some are stories of incest and beatings in the home; others are of total strangers breaking into apartments or attacking women on the street. All are heartrending. A lot of tears are shed, but as we relive the events, one thing becomes apparent. Except where the woman was a child when the violence occurred, there were in every case things she could have done to get out of the situation or stop the man if she had had the knowledge and confidence. We each see how this was true in our own situation.

This does not make us to blame, but it does help begin to dispel the feeling of helplessness and the fear that the situation may reoccur. Delia can give us the techniques, but we know that is not enough. We have to feel we have the right and the ability to really defend ourselves. The fact that very few women feel this vehemently is a testament not to our failure, but to the success of the training we received as little girls and young women. We are indeed the daughters of patriarchy. Delia finishes the session with a meditation that helps us keep the memory of the violence from the past intact, but removes from it all the emotional energy that continues to drain us of our power. I leave feeling a little lighter.

The first healing I ever saw was on the last night with Raven in Northern Ontario. Three healings were done in a circle in the lodge. Having had my healing alone with Raven and Jamie in their cabin, I did not know what to expect. As I was to learn, healings take many forms. The three people asking for a healing were told to undress and lie down in the center of the circle formed by those who had gathered. Raven sat on the circle and told each of us the particular energy we held for the healing by virtue of the direction in which we sat. I was sitting in the west with another woman, the place of the earth and the body, of death and change, of introspection and intuition. Since the west is also the place of the feminine, we were told to call into the circle all aspects of the feminine we could think of, naming the Goddesses and Grandmothers in our minds. I felt good about this. Our other task, as a group, was to learn and sing a particular healing song that would continue uninterrupted for the duration of the healing—about four hours. It sounded pretty simple, but singing the same rhythmic chant from 1:00 to 5:00 A.M., without spacing out so you are still holding your particular place and energy in the circle is not easy. Gunner and Jamie were doing the actual energy work on the three in the center, with crystals, fans, gourds and some talking.

Of the three having the healing done, two were women from my cabin, Bea and Charlotte. Bea had had recurring kidney weakness and vaginal infections. Charlotte was seeking healing for herpes. The third person was Mitch, who had a prostate problem. Each had a very different healing, but Raven told us the premise is always the same. In the healing paradigm he works with, a condition is healed when the individual gives it away. The actual healing ceremony creates change in the fifth dimension, called the nagual—the place of spirit and dreams. This change then manifests in the tonal—the third or material dimension. The role of the healer is to facilitate this process by setting up optimum conditions alchemically and by helping the individual understand why he or she might have chosen this illness at this time. It's a tricky business to avoid self-blame for the illness while at the same time taking responsibility for what can be done, and to feel you have the power to do so.

I remember very little about what happened with Mitch. Gunner did some crystal work with him and had him verbally give away his anger at some of the women in his life. It seemed pretty straightforward. While Jamie was doing some general crystal work on Bea, Gunner began to work with Charlotte. Charlotte was a unique woman and more than a little eccentric. Tall and thin, with huge, red-rimmed eyes and long blond hair that always looked windblown, she made a living channeling spirit entities and teaching about crystals, and was a very talented artist. I'd only seen Charlotte in two moods: hysterically laughing and partying or dreamily trancing out and seeing all kinds of weird and wonderful things. The term "space cadet" was invented for her.

As Gunner worked, Charlotte's body began to shiver and twitch and she started to shake from head to toe. Gunner was obviously working hard, moving quickly around her and speaking to her while using the eagle fan on her chest. Then she convulsed, stiffened for an instant and went completely limp. From where I sat, three feet away, it appeared that she had stopped breathing, and I had a sickening feeling that her heart had stopped. Suddenly a headline flashed through my mind: Woman Dies in Cult Ritual—Twenty Arrested. *What am I doing here?* I wondered. *What do I really know about these people and what they're doing?*

The moment Charlotte went limp, Raven was on his feet and into the circle. I don't think I've ever seen him move so fast before or since. The rest of us were scared and our singing wavered. "Don't let the song drop," Raven commanded, "All you have to do is keep it going." We raised our voices with renewed vigor, as much to calm ourselves as to contribute. Raven leaned over Charlotte and placed two fingers of one hand on the side of her neck. Her whole body convulsed the way bodies do in TV medical dramas when they're given electric shock to restart the heart. Her muscles stiffened once, twice and then relaxed. She started breathing evenly and her color returned. Immediately she regained consciousness and began coughing, indicating she thought she might throw up. Gunner had her sit up and then continued to work with her, while Raven, smiling mischievously at all our wide-eyed stares, returned to his place in the circle.

Meanwhile, Jamie had completed her work on Bea and was talking quietly to her. Raven explained to everybody that Bea was going to insert a small crystal egg into her vagina, and that she was to give birth to it while taking back her feminine power and giving away her illness. Bea, with a dubious look on her face, squatted and inserted the egg. Giving birth to it wasn't so easy. She sweated and strained, trying and trying again, and still no egg. The women on the circle who had children were easy to pick out. We were the ones leaning forward, holding our breath and trying to help her "push." Finally Raven looked up and called on myself and two other women, all mothers, to go into the circle and help Bea. We couldn't move fast enough, we were so relieved at being given something to do. The three of us immediately moved into place around Bea without even having to consult one another. With Bea squatting, I supported her with my body from behind, while the other two women held her on either side. Then we talked to her, using everything we knew from the births of our own children, six among the three of us, to help her relax, focus and push. A few minutes later the egg was born to jubilant shouts and the announced "time of birth."

Three things impressed me about this and subsequent healings. One was the almost immediate transformation of those having being healed. Afterward they radiated an energy of change that was unbelievable. Another was the incredible ability of those in charge of the healing, Raven in particular, to pour everything they had into it with obvious caring and then walk away without any attachment to the outcome or the people involved. The third was an awareness of how everyone who participates in a healing also receives from it. As Bea and I returned to the cabin at five-thirty in the morning, I went into the bathroom. As I glanced in the mirror I stopped, rooted to the spot. I didn't recognize the woman who looked back at me. I was different. The eyes that gazed back at mine were not the eyes of a desperately ill housewife and mother, but rather the calm and smiling eyes of a stranger. I called Bea in and asked her to look. She stared in disbelief into the mirror at the two unfamiliar faces. We stood there for a long time.

Sometimes what I've received from a healing has been less welcome, although no less valuable. In Jamaica we held a healing for a woman called Carly, a stunningly beautiful woman married to a man named Ken. Ken was the epitome of everything I loathed. He was loud, bossy and overbearing, a rich, white American male who treated everyone as if they were his servants, particularly women and especially Carly. I was later to discover that he was equally generous, caring and genuinely unaware of how his manner made many women want to hit him. The healing, requested by Carly, included the cutting of the karmic tie between she and Ken.

When we are in an intimate relationship with someone there is often a karmic connection between us, patterns we are reenacting from this life or past lives, often patterns of pain. When someone decides to cut this tie they may or may not stay in the relationship. In either case they are indicating that they choose not to give away their power in relationship to someone by acting out of old patterns. Cutting the tie, seen by the medicine person as an actual luminous fiber of energy coming from the navel, helps to act from free-will choice in the relationship. I have seen karmic cord cuttings done for people about to be married and for others dealing with relationships long over, perhaps even with someone no longer alive. Although the actual cutting is done by the person doing the doctoring, the intent of the person seeking the healing is the most important factor, since the cord will reconnect immediately if the person is ambivalent about severing the connection. Often the ceremonial pipe is used to look into the Book of Life of the patient and this enables the person holding the Karma Pipe to see the karmic patterns of the relationship. This knowledge adds to the patient's understanding and strengthens his or her intent in the cord cutting.

Raven knew Ken and the kind of feelings he evoked in many, particularly women. At the beginning of the healing he looked around the circle and asked, "How many of you really want Carly to get this healing?" Many enthusiastic female hands went up. Raven cautioned us that if we were attached to the outcome of the healing, if we wanted Carly to get it whether she wanted it or not, we would feel it later. We all went through a prayer for giving away our attachment to the outcome. I sent out my voice with the others. "I cut my karmic connection with this little one, Carly, releasing her into her circle and I into mine. I give away all attachment to the outcome of this healing."

When it came time in the healing for Carly to cut the tie with Ken, Raven asked her if she was ready. She hesitated. "Do you want to do it, hon?" Raven asked. "I don't give a shit—it's up to you."

"I'm worried about Ken," Carly replied. The groan that rose from the women in the room was silent but shared. We knew that the cord cutting would be partial at best because of her obvious ambivalence.

"Don't worry about the brother—we'll take care of him. Do you want to do it or not?" Raven asked.

"I do," she replied, and Jamie cut the cord.

After the healing Raven looked around the circle slowly and said, with a little smile, "So how many of you have a bellyache?" Most of the women and some of the men put up their hands, including myself. I had an ache around my navel that seemed to go through to my backbone. "That," said Raven, "is because you were too attached to the outcome of the ceremony. You wanted her to do it, regardless of whether she wanted to at this time or not. You stepped into her circle. Now go out and find a tree, ask its permission and then give away the ache in your belly to the tree. And consider why you got so attached to this particular healing. What does it tell you about where you have a hard time taking power in your own life? That's why you got so attached to this healing." Feeling chastised, I went out and found a palm tree on the shore and did as he suggested. The ache in my body disappeared. It was no mystery to me. For every relationship where I have given my power away to some man, I wanted Carly to completely and cleanly cut her cord with Ken. Just another version of wanting someone else to do something that I was having trouble doing for myself.

Any anxiety I am feeling about having a healing for myself at the desert retreat is outweighed by my desperation to find a way out of the immobilizing blackness I feel as I reexperience the rape and beatings. Thirty women gather for the sweat arranged by Raven for my healing. Marsha is the Dance Chief and another woman is doing the crystal doctoring. As everyone files into the sweat I am deeply moved by the fact that all of these women are doing this for me, for my healing. They sit close together in a single circle on the outer edge of the sweat, leaving room for me to lie down in the center, and the crystal doctor sits next to me.

As the door closes darkness envelopes us and from somewhere very far away I hear a moan. Is it the wind sweeping across the desert? The water hisses on the rocks and steam fills the tiny lodge. The sounds of the women's voices rise in the darkness, singing and praying. They pray for their own ability to hold the circle for the healing and to call into the lodge the spirits of my totem animals and ancestors to help and guide me. They say prayers for me, for healing the wounds left by the violence done to my body and spirit. They raise their voices in steady chants that call to the Goddess for strength. As they sing, the doctor moves over my body in the darkness, using her breath and the crystal to increase and balance my energy.

Marsha tells me when it is time to send out my prayers. I am not sure to whom I pray, but I send out my voice, letting it rise with the heat. "Help me face the blackness. Help me to understand the pain of the past and give away any connection I have with the men who have abused me, a connection that still drains me." I feel as if my body is floating. The doctor asks if I am ready to cut my cord with these men, and I answer, "Yes." As I focus on each man separately I can feel a cord coming from the center of my body, out my navel. It has a dull ache.

The crystal doctor says, "Now," and I feel her hand lightly brush the skin at my navel, although the ceremonial knife used to cut the cord never touches me.

I call out as I have been told to. "I give away any attachment or connection I have with this one, releasing him into his circle and I into mine. I cut my karmic tie with him. I give it away!" I yell it into the blackness of the lodge with all the intent and focus I can muster from my heart, mind and body. The doctor rubs corn paho on my navel to seal the place where the energy has been cut. I feel as if I've been suddenly dropped onto the earth. My whole body is watery, relaxed and completely supported by the ground. More water is poured on the rocks and the steam rises as prayers of thanks are said.

As the ceremony ends, Marsha calls for the door to be opened. The moon is full, and through the open door it floods the tiny enclosure with blue light. Marsha tells me I can lie there for a few moments while the others get out, and then join them outside. I wait. I hear the rustling of moving bodies and then all is quiet, but I can still feel the circle of women sitting around me. I wonder if I have misunderstood. Why are they not leaving? Wondering if they are waiting for me to do something, I sit up. All of the women who were in the sweat have left. In their places are twelve old women, wrapped in colored blankets, watching me. I can see them clearly, their long braided hair streaked with gray, their brown wrinkled skin, their dark eyes holding me with their gaze. All I can do is sit and stare. I know they are there for me and my heart aches with a sense of fullness. Quietly the fullness spills from my eyes and tears stream down my face. Finally the old woman closest to the door nods toward it, indicating that I should go out. I don't want to leave their circle, but feel I cannot disobey. In the darkness I whisper to them, "Thank you, Grandmothers," the term of respect and love coming easily to my lips. Slowly I move toward the door and crawl out into the night. As I stand I see all the women who were in the sweat. They have formed a circle around the doorway and stand silently, steam rising from their bodies like blue mist into the cool air, silhouetted by the full moon, huge and white in the starry sky. I stand at the door for a moment, at the center of the infinity loop created by the two circles—Grandmothers within the lodge and Sisters outside. I wait for a moment on the edge between the two worlds and then move forward into the circle of women before me. They break their silence with laughter and greetings, welcoming me with hugs, the circle closing around me, holding me. I know the Grandmothers can see us and are pleased.

The next day I wake up full of energy. To my surprise, there are tiny cuts and scratches in a circle around my navel, although I know the crystal doctor did not touch me with the knife. They do not hurt and are healed over by the end of the day, so quickly that I wonder if I imagined them. In Delia's class I am able to concentrate on the instructions and moves. The tiredness is gone. Halfway through the class I am punching a bag held by another woman, when I realize it is very quiet. Everyone else has stopped practicing. Looking up, I see them gathered around watching me, eyes wide, mouths open. I pause and look at Delia. "What happened to you?" she asks with a grin. "You're hitting right through that bag." It's true; I am able to focus all my energy on my blows and the poor woman holding the bag can hardly stay on her feet. It isn't that I feel angry—in fact I am more relaxed than ever before. It's that I feel free of something that was holding me back.

As I leave the training area and head back to my tent Jamie, on staff for the retreat, calls to me. "Raven is at his camper now and would like to talk with you right after lunch." This gives me time to shower off the morning's sweat and dust, change into a cool cotton dress and grab something to eat. I pick up the painting I have brought from home for Raven and take it with me. I want to offer it as a medicine gift for arranging my healing.

When I reach the camper, a small unit on the back of a pickup truck, there does not seem to be anyone around. I wonder if I am too late. Tentatively I knock on the door and Raven calls out to come in. I step inside. He is sitting cross-legged on the double bed and motions for me to sit on the bed across from him. I kick off my sandals and sit facing him.

"So, how did the healing sweat go? Tell me about it," he says. I tell him about the karmic cord cutting and how much better I am feeling. I do not tell him about seeing the Grandmothers in the lodge, somehow feeling cautious about putting words to the experience so soon.

"Good. Now let's talk about what happened when you were raped." His tone is matter-of-fact, businesslike. "Tell me what happened." Somewhat reluctantly, but without the fear I had felt before, I tell the story of being raped. I am able to emulate his tone: calm, factual, relaying details without feeling emotional.

"And what did you learn from this?" he asks as I complete the story.

"I'm not sure."

"Well, what did you find out? What did you experience?"

I hesitate, unsure of what is being asked of me. "I found out what it was like to feel completely powerless and degraded," I say at last.

"And what did that teach you?" Raven presses.

"That I will never allow it to happen again!" I say vehemently.

"Good! What else? In the abuse that occurred with your first husband, where do you see you were responsible?"

I begin to feel confused and frightened. I was not responsible for what my husband did. Panic rises within me. I was immobilized at the time of the abuse, and for years afterward, by my feelings of shame and responsibility for what had occurred. I do not want to step into this again. But I want to trust Raven. I am grateful to him for all he has done for me. Meeting and learning from Raven has changed my life. I feel indebted to him. I want to understand what he is trying to teach me. I want to get it right, to be the adept apprentice, worthy of his time and energy. Anxious, I lean forward and sit silently while Raven continues.

"What could you have done before the situation became violent?" I think. It's true there were plenty of signs that the relationship was not a good place for me to be, that my husband was not very stable. I had wanted something else to be true. I stayed even after the first time he hit me.

He spoke again. "Were there times when he let you know how he was feeling and you did not respond? Did you tell him how you were feeling or did you try to avoid it?"

"Well, I remember trying to get to bed and pretend I was already asleep when he came in because I didn't want to make love with him. I would roll over and hope he wouldn't try to wake me. I was frightened."

"So, you did not let him know what was going on."

"No. I guess there were lots of things I could have done. I could have told him more about how I felt. I could have left as soon as the violence began. Instead I stayed and hoped it would stop, hoped things would change, pretended it wasn't as bad as it was."

Raven looks into my eyes. "And that's the place where you were responsible. Do you see that?" *YES,*

I nod, wanting to please, feeling confused. I desperately want to know anything I can about how I contributed to the violence so it will never happen again. Suddenly Raven's tone and posture change. He leans back against the wall and relaxes. There is a sense of completion. He smiles and speaks more softly and casually. "So, how are you finding your time out here? How is it going now with men in your life?"

I can feel myself blush self-consciously. I am flattered and confused by his interest. "Well, I've only been out of my marriage for six months and it's been a long time since I was part of the dating scene. I don't feel too sure of myself. Mitch and I are still seeing each other, although it's not always easy." I tell him about one of the other men, Tom, who is at the retreat. Tom and I were lovers briefly at the Sundance gathering two months earlier. We wrote a few letters back and forth after this, and he arrived at the desert retreat expecting us to spend time together and continue to be lovers. To be fair, I had also considered it, but something happened. As he arrived I became aware that while I was more than willing to spend time together socially, I did not want to sleep with him. There was no specific reason. It just didn't feel like the appropriate time or place. The lovemaking we shared in the spring was pleasant but it passed. This was a breakthrough for me: to gently but firmly say no to someone with whom I'd been lovers, without animosity or complicated explanations. Tom has not responded well. He is very angry, and I wonder out loud to Raven if I have not handled this well. It has been so long since I was in anything but a monogamous marriage that I don't know what "rules" apply. I am also surprised to find that being with me is so important to Tom and wonder if it is a fluke. Somewhat embarrassed, I tell Raven, "I really expected when I left my marriage to be sitting home alone." *No problem*

Raven's smile broadens. "Hon, basically men are very simple beings. If you put it out, they'll line up at your door. Just don't dangle that body of yours like the cosmic carrot." Raven leans toward me across the bed. "Personally I like the long lithe look . . . ." I can hear his voice continue, but I feel very strange. Surely he's not coming on to me? I'm confused about exactly what he's saying. I can hear only occasional words and phrases—"spirit husband," "spirit marriage." There seems to be something wrong with my eyes. My vision feels black around the edges, and once again, I begin to hear the strange droning sound. It grows louder and louder, filling my head.

A split second later I find myself standing by the door, my back against the wall. I feel frightened, my breathing is shallow. I feel as though I've had a close call of some kind, but I cannot understand why. I don't remember getting up from the bed. Raven is sitting relaxed and smiling, leaning back against the wall, his tone light and jovial. He has not moved. "So it sounds like you're getting it." He does not seem to think anything out of the usual has happened. I try to clear my head and sit down tentatively at the edge of the bed. Picking up my bag, I offer him the painting as a gift. He takes it and thanks me and seems genuinely pleased. It is a painting from the Kwakiutl, a tribe in northern British Columbia, and we talk for a short time about their art. Thanking him again, I put on my sandals and leave the camper.

Outside I feel my head beginning to clear and I mutter, "What was that?" When I return to my tent, Mitch is waiting, wanting to hear about my conversation with Raven. As I relay parts of it to him I wonder but don't talk about my strange "blackout." I assume Raven must have been talking about my relationship to Mitch when he used the terms "spirit marriage" and "spirit husband." What happened to me? Too much sun and physical exercise? I shake off the feeling of fear that creeps over me when I try to focus on the sequence of events. Why can't I remember getting up from the bed? Why did I stand up? Why was I backed against the wall? What frightened me? What happened to my vision and hearing? I shove the nagging questions aside, determined to learn all that I can during the remaining time at the retreat.

6

We take time out from our regular routine at the desert retreat to prepare for overnight ceremonies. Since the first one in Northern Ontario, designed to face and conquer my fears, I have done another all-night ceremony in Jamaica. I am nervously anticipating a third, not because of what happens while I'm out on ceremony, but because of what happens when I return. After my first ceremony I decided not to have a third child. After the ceremony in Jamaica I returned home and left my marriage. As I approach another ceremony I wonder, "What next?" There is no way to predict what will happen and I've learned that whatever I expect, something different will result.

I didn't have many expectations when I went to Jamaica, I was just thrilled to be going. Even without my thirst for the teachings and ceremony, leaving Toronto in November to go to the Caribbean was incentive enough. Of course, I justified the trip in my own mind with the fact that I was going to work, not just to have a vacation. As we arrived I became aware of how much the place shapes the experience. Northern Ontario in the rain and cold is a long way from balmy, laid-back Jamaica. A kind of party atmosphere was immediately fostered, one I had trouble adjusting to. It was a definite challenge. Could I maintain my dedication to work, work, work in the middle of paradise?

I had been clear in my own mind that part of my purpose in being there was to again find my own sexual energy, so dismally missing for several years. Most of the medicine journey groups are predominantly female, a fact I generally enjoy. However, this one turned out to be weighted on the male side. While couples stayed at one location, those of us there alone—four women and eight men—were at another group of villas about a mile down the road. This fact, combined with the party atmosphere, my stated intent and warm moonlit nights, almost sent my much married self into full flight.

Raven and his wife, Susan, arrived a day later than planned, leaving us to our own devices for the first twenty-four hours. Some members of the group went off in pursuit of the ganja weed for which Jamaica is so famous. Six of us went into the village in the evening to check out the local bar and dance spot. Our means of transportation was Johnny and his van. Johnny, a Jamaican, was something of a local celebrity, since he had somehow managed to get enough money together to buy a shiny new van. Eager entrepreneur that he was, his price for taking you somewhere often tripled on the ride home. We were in a sparsely populated area and the small, private resort we were staying at was a good distance from any town, so he generally got his price. Johnny's van was recognizable by the booming music than emanated from it wherever he went. He had rigged up two speakers in the back that constantly poured out rock and reggae at ear-splitting decibels. It took us four days to convince him that we really wanted the music turned down, which he did reluctantly, cranking it up again as we approached small villages so the locals would know he was arriving. Ever the opportunist, Johnny polled all of the women in the group to see who was unmarried. He was very clear about his intentions: he wanted to marry a Canadian woman so he could come to Canada. Suddenly all the women were very married.

The bar he took us to was a giant patio carved into the rock next to the ocean. The dance area was under the stars and the reggae bands sent their steady beat out over the waves. The place was filled with local folks and American tourists. As the band started, the six of us got up to dance. We were joined by two or three local men. I couldn't figure it out. Why wasn't anyone else dancing? The music was great, the spot was beautiful and the place was full of people. I felt as though there were two movies playing simultaneously, one of us on the dance floor, and the other, going at a much slower speed, of everyone else. I asked the others what they thought. Looking at me as if I were ten years old, someone replied, "Because they're all stoned." Feeling incredibly stupid, I realized it was true. Most people there were smoking dope. Looking around, I had the feeling that many of them, especially the tourists, had been stoned for days. Part of me didn't really understand. Why come all that way for a holiday, where the night and the music were so wonderful, and then not really be there?

I have never really tried drugs. I've taken three or four puffs from a marijuana cigarette twice at parties, and felt as much light-headedness as I did when I tried tobacco at fourteen. It's not a moral question for me. Most of the time I do not have the urge, and on the rare occasions when I've considered it, I was too scared. Maybe I'm just afraid of what I might do or say, but I've never come up with a good enough reason to give it an all-out try. Drinking more than two beers makes me very sleepy, and I hate having less energy the next day. I had enough of that from years of poor health.

On the second night in Jamaica some of the group arranged a party at the place we were staying, hooking up music and bringing in refreshments. In particular, they went to the local "special" bakery for some Jenny-cakes, brownies laced with hash. I hadn't heard about this, and when one of the men came up with a big bag of brownies and offered me one, I wondered if this was the dessert we'd all said we were missing at supper. I took a bite, and as I swallowed I heard another woman in the group ask if they had hash or heroin in them. I choked. *Oh, my God, heroin! That's it, I'll be a junkie for life. This is the kind of thing my mother warned me about.*

Getting a grip on my inner thirteen-year-old from Northern Ontario, I calmed down and, feeling no effect from my one bite of brownie, went and joined the party, sticking to ginger beer from then on. I was not, as it turned out, the only naive one. Another woman, from Michigan, had similarly limited experience with drugs. Small and pale, the fifty-year-old woman honestly thought the brownies were dessert, and ate two. I don't think anyone was trying to trick her; it just never occurred to them to tell her. Drink in hand, she joined a group of us out on the porch. About an hour later, not having said more than two sentences in the flow of conversation, she suddenly sat up very straight, eyes wide, and said, "Oh, my God, I know why I feel like this after one drink. Those brownies had drugs in them! I'm stoned! How will I ever get home to Michigan?" Reassuring her that she needn't worry about Michigan right then, I found someone to see her back to her cabin. She was very sick the next day, and surprisingly good-natured about the whole thing, once she could sit up without passing out or throwing up.

The problem with being the only one in a group not stoned is that you are painfully aware of how people are not nearly as brilliant or funny as they think they are, and you are the only one who knows it. As I was about to go back to my room, I noticed Richard, looking quite normal and conversing with the others. A financial investor, Richard is a tall thin man with a tiny mustache and a precise manner about him that reminds me of an English gentleman. He kept saying, "I don't know what the big deal is. I ate three of those things and I don't feel anything. I feel perfectly normal." Suddenly he paused, mid-sentence, got a funny look in his eyes and just fell over, passed out cold. Richard was unable to join us for the next two days.

After all of this I didn't know what to expect from the week. But Raven soon got down to daily teachings, and we began preparations for a night-long ceremony called Life Doll, Death Doll. I was nervous about the night out. Since I was used to the bush of Northern Ontario and yet had been frightened during my first vision quest there, I figured I'd be terrified in the jungle, where God-knows-what was lurking.

Preparation for the night out felt disjointed. The laid-back, don't-worry atmosphere of Jamaica ran counter to my feeling that I should be frantically preparing for a life-changing ceremony. I flipped in and out of taking it all very seriously. Even Raven's teaching was at a slower pace. It focused on an understanding of energy patterns and the ways in which different people's energies come together. As we are aware of our own energy, we step into what Raven called a web of energy. As we merge in part with others we are aware of a maze, an energy configuration that appears to have no methodical pattern. As our energy and awareness rise we are able to see or sense how all things are connected in the same pattern, a matrix. It is from within this overall pattern or matrix that we are able to do healings, manifest what we need and experience a sense of effortless ease with the flow of our life. It sounded beautiful, but I wasn't at all sure I understood the "how" of getting there.

For our night out we had to make a Life Doll and a Death Doll. Part of me felt it would be fun, and another part was reluctant to get into the work, especially since there were very detailed directions for making both. All materials for the Death Doll had to be collected and put together after dark, and all for the Life Doll in the daylight. Both dolls were made ceremonially, one representing the deaths we needed to bring into our life at that time, the other our celebration of life and beauty. There were specific items needed for both. In particular the Death Doll had to include something dead from the animal world.

In retrospect it sounds like a pretty easy task. We could have just gone to the kitchen and retrieved a chicken bone, or found a dead animal hit by a car at the side of the road. For whatever reason, my mind, perhaps underused in my search to rekindle my sexual energy, was not operating clearly. I consulted my friend Bea, who for her own reasons was similarly incapacitated, and somehow we convinced ourselves we had to go out and kill an animal to obtain this critical component for the doll. And, of course, we had to do it at night.

Without consulting anyone else, the two of us set off. Bea had the foresight to bring a flashlight, and we walked down a path that crossed a large field between the jungle and the road. We didn't really have a plan.

I think we were both hoping the other would find a way out of the task. Moving across the field, we became aware of the sounds of small animals around us in the grass. Bea scanned the ground with the light and we saw dozens of huge toads, each about the size of a large fist, hopping about. They seemed the most likely candidates for our purpose.

We now tried to devise a plan. How would we kill it? We decided we would have to hit it on the head with a rock. Throwing rocks at moving targets in the dark seemed futile, so we set out to catch a toad first. We crept about, trying to get close, but the toads kept hopping away into the grass. I kept hoping we wouldn't be able to catch one. Then Bea said a prayer, asking a toad if it would do a giveaway for us—offer its spirit that we might learn what we needed about death and change in our own lives. I added my prayers to hers, and lo and behold, one very fat toad sat without moving as we approached. He really did seem to be offering himself.

I was closer, so Bea whispered to me, "Grab him!" I did, but I was not prepared for the feel of the dry, coarse skin and the body wriggling in my too-tight grasp. With a very unwarriorlike shriek I dropped the toad, which hopped several steps away and then sat immobile again. Bea could see this was not going to be one of my more reliable moments, so she suggested that she grab him and I hit him quickly on the head with a rock. I agreed. Praying once again, we approached the toad. He did not move. Bea easily and gently grabbed him and held his head on the ground. I picked up a large flat rock and brought it down, inwardly praying for his forgiveness. I hit him twice, then sighed with relief, and Bea released the toad.

To our horror, the poor animal began to hop off into the grass. I had not hit him hard enough! Seriously wounded, he was now going off to die a slow and painful death! I felt frantic. We had to find him. Simultaneously we broke out of our paralysis and pursued him through the dark, off the path. By some miracle Bea found him, and having learned not to trust my halfhearted efforts, quickly hit his head several times with a rock. He died immediately. We sat, worn out, looking at each other in the dark, the dead toad between us. I felt terrible. We said some prayers to honor the spirit of the toad, and cutting off his legs to take with us, we left some tobacco with his body and returned to the room.

As I worked on my dolls, I got quite attached to them and their strangeness. Carved from wood and embellished with seashells, plants, bones, feathers and bits of material, they had a kind of strange charm. The Death Doll had a fierceness about her, with a hard line of a mouth smeared with a tiny bit of my own blood, a tiny toad-bone necklace and huge gaping eyes. The Life Doll made me think of mermaids. I planted a piece of turquoise in her navel, wrapped a strip of blue silk scarf around her neck and attached some branching coral to her forehead with a dab of bright pink nail polish. She was beautiful.

The afternoon before we went out to do the ceremony Raven asked us each to write a will. This did nothing to calm my fears about wild jungle beasts. I had not brought a flashlight with me and was concerned about getting lost. One of the Jamaican men working at the place we were staying filled some empty pop bottles with kerosene and a wad of cloth to make torches for those of us who wanted them. I don't know what he or the other staff thought of these crazy white people going off alone into the jungle for the night, but he good-humoredly gave me a bottle and waved goodbye, wishing me luck. Bottle and dolls in hand, I set off just before the sun set.

I walked down the dirt road for about half an hour, then decided to head into the jungle toward a tall white cliff far off in the distance. I reasoned that if I walked straight for the cliff, I could find my way out on my return by keeping it at my back until I hit the road. I walked for another forty minutes. The walking was easy, much of the area being open grassland with small bushes. I stopped where the trees and growth of the jungle began to thicken, staying in a bit of a clearing. Setting up my medicine wheel, I settled into my spot and waited as darkness descended.

It was a clear starry night, cool but comfortable. Small animals made sounds and scurried through the tall grass around me, and I waited for the anticipated fear to arise, be confronted and conquered. Nothing. Not even a glimmer. For reasons I still do not understand, I was not at all afraid. Not of the night, the animals, the ceremony, nothing. I was disappointed. How was I going to learn anything about myself—my fears, my courage, my strengths—if I couldn't find even a glimmer of terror to defeat? I waited. I walked around the circle. I said my prayers.

"Great Spirit, I ask to know the deaths I must welcome into my life at this time, the changes I must make to more fully live." I sat. Nothing happened. I was bored.

Finally I began to get angry. What was the point of this, anyway? Here I was in paradise, my first and possibly last trip to a Caribbean island, and was I having fun, was I out dancing, partying, playing like any normal person? No, I was sitting alone in the jungle waiting for something to happen that would tell me the direction my life needed to take—and nothing was happening.

As I got more angry, I began to pace around inside my circle. My anger turned to rage. Not knowing what else to do, I picked up my gourd and continued to walk, shaking it and feeling a burning sensation rise up from my stomach to my throat. I picked up my Death Doll and kept walking, and began to speak out loud.

"What the hell are you doing here? This is all fake. As fake as you are. This isn't going to work because you're not being honest. You've never been honest. Too much control. Always in control. Perfect life. Perfect husband. Perfect children. Perfect little life. Except you're sick all the time. How come you're always so sick if everything is so fucking perfect?" It went on and on as I moved with the Death Doll and my rattle. I felt possessed by some part of me I had never touched. It was out of my control, spewing forth my anger at my husband, my children, my body, my life. Part of me stood back in shocked surprise. Where had all this come from and where had it been hiding? I raged and yelled and screamed at the sky until, my voice hoarse and my body exhausted, I fell to the ground. I felt numb. I sat in the dirt breathing irregularly and clutching the Death Doll in my hand.

I closed my eyes and tried to regain some sense of control. Immediately a clear image appeared. I could see myself lying in a hospital bed. I was thin and weak-looking and I knew I was dying. The thought of cancer crossed my mind. My husband and my two sons were standing beside the bed. The kids were older, about nine and twelve, and we were clearly saying goodbye. I was being very brave, very strong, telling them how much I loved them and urging them to take care of each other. I knew I was not going to live much longer.

Abruptly the image vanished, as if someone had turned the TV set off, and I was once again in the dirt in the jungle. The message seemed clear. If I continued the way I was going I would not live a long life. I was going to die of some illness and it would be before I hit forty. I knew without any shred of doubt that I had seen the future I was headed for.

Something snapped inside me. In the blink of an eye I made a decision and, looking into the black jungle, I roared "No!" Instantly I felt very calm. Rising, I ceremonially buried the Death Doll, digging a hole in the ground with a stick and then resumed my seat in the center of the wheel, holding my Life Doll. I waited, but this time with a sense of calm, watching the stars. Shooting stars streaked across the sky; they seemed close enough to touch. I waited some more. Focusing on one star, which seemed to glow brighter and brighter, I could hear a song in my head. I began to sing it. It was a healing song, a song of touching myself and others with beauty instead of anger. I was amazed. I had heard of people receiving power songs during vision quests but had never even dared hope I would receive one, given my lack of musical ability. I sang it over and over again. I was afraid I would not be able to remember it. Only later did I realize that it would be impossible for me ever to forget this song. I sang it for hours for everyone and everything in my life, dancing in the circle with my Life Doll and singing to the stars.

Almost imperceptibly the sky began to lighten as dawn approached. I decided to gather my things and leave. Feeling calm and fully awake, I put the cliff of white rock, visible even in the semidarkness, at my back and began confidently to walk out of the jungle. But every time I took a few steps in any direction I was confronted with a dense tangle of bushes. Trying to push my way through them, I found they were full of long thorns that ripped into my clothes and scratched my skin. I backed up, veered to one side then the other, only to encounter similar bushes after a few more steps. I couldn't get out! Lighting the torch only made things worse, it lit the space around me but cast the area ahead into blackness. In exasperation I stopped and sat down.

I was frustrated and angry. I'd wanted to return to the group the picture of tranquility, glowing with the radiance of ceremonial ecstasy. Instead I was beginning to feel hot, weary and disheveled. Why was this so difficult? I had walked straight to this spot, of that I was certain, over relatively open ground. Now it was like trying to get out of a maze . . . . Something clicked—a maze! I had just spent five days hearing Raven teach about the maze and the matrix of energy. He had told us to ask for a sign during the ceremony if we thought we had been able to step into one or the other. I had forgotten.

I started to laugh. "O.K.," I said out loud, "I get it. I made it into the maze. That's how I was able to hear the song." The ceremony had enabled me to step into the energy pattern moving around me and had allowed me to be in alignment with the earth and stars. I had not been conscious of this shift in reality. I/seemed that the dense bushes had collaborated with the universe to ensure I got one of the lessons I had been sent out to learn. Acknowledging my own denseness, I stood up, noted the location of the cliff and walked straight out to the road without encountering a single obstacle.

Returning home from this ceremony, I knew I had to leave my husband and live on my own, sharing responsibility for our two sons. We had been together for nine years. It was a painful time for both myself and my family. My second husband had never been abusive and had clearly made the children and I the center of his life. Desperate to keep our marriage together, he pleaded with me to consider ways we could rearrange our schedules, our house, our relationship that would allow me to do what I needed to do. He was willing to be flexible in any area I needed to change. The problem was that the change I needed was not external, it was internal, and I knew I did not have whatever it took to make that change and maintain it while I was still married. Late one night shortly after my return from Jamaica, we sat on the bed, both of us crying, and I tried to explain.

"I have been sick for so long. I know something at the core of how I am living is wrong. It is not who I am. It's not because of you. It's not because of the kids. But I am afraid that if I do not move now, if I don't take this opportunity to change now, it will not come again. I feel like I am trying to save my life and I don't know any other way to do it but to be on my own."

My husband took both my hands in his. "What do you want me to do?"

My whole body shook with sobs. "If you love me, let me go. Don't make it any harder. Don't try and stop it."

"Are you sure?" he asked, his voice barely a whisper.

"Yes."

And he did. From that moment on he did not try and talk me into staying or making a new arrangement. I know it cost him a lot. And I know he did it because he loved me.

I was scared—no job and no child care. I'd been told the waiting list for government-subsidized day care places had more than four thousand people on it. My husband was willing to leave the house we were renting if I found him another place to live. The vacancy rate in Toronto was less that one percent, with dozens of people vying for every available apartment. I felt desperate. Without any planning or consideration for alchemy or ceremonial form, I found myself sitting on the floor of my bedroom praying. I spoke the names of every Goddess I could think of and begged them for their help. I had no ambivalence, no question about what I needed. I had to have a job, child care I could afford and a place for Des to live, and I had to have them fast. I asked for help with every cell in my body.

Exhausted, I lay down on the floor and stared at the cracked plaster in the ceiling. All at once I heard a strange sound, like the droning of a thousand bees or the beating wings of hundreds of hummingbirds. At the time I only had a dim recollection of having heard it before. It grew louder and louder and I felt petrified. I clasped my hands over my ears but couldn't block out the noise. At the same time I felt the floor begin to move and sway beneath me. Panic-stricken I raised my head slightly and saw the floor in the middle of the room buckle upward and tear open, a long crack running down the length of the room. I opened my mouth to scream, but the only sound I heard was the droning that filled my head with its now-deafening clamor. It seemed to come out of the cracked floor. Then, above the droning, I heard a woman's voice. "Now is the time when all things are rent!" Blackness engulfed me.

Sometime later I awoke, still on the floor, drenched in perspiration from head to foot. The floor was intact and everything in the room seemed normal but my body was quivering and I could still hear the echo of the woman's voice.

Twenty-four hours later all that I had asked for had occurred: I had a good job, a place in a local day care center covered by government subsidy and an apartment for my husband.

At the desert retreat I prepare to do my next all-night ceremony, one spent in a gravelike hole in the ground. It occurs to me that whoever designed these ceremonies was not into marketing. I am told this is a dreaming ceremony of going inward and learning to "meet death as an ally." I'm unsure of what this actually means. Intellectually I understand that having Death as an Adviser means asking myself: "If this moment is my last, is this how I want to be living it?" The question has crossed my mind more than once during the retreat.

Traditionally the ceremony is done by first digging a grave for yourself in a remote spot, one long enough to lie down in and deep enough to sit up in without having your head above the ground. After being sent out with a pipe ceremony by a Dance Chief, the apprentice lies in the hole, which is covered with a blanket, from dusk to dawn, trying to stay awake and moving in and out of a dream state. The hole is both a grave for all the deaths and changes desirable at the time, and a womb for the birthing of new life.

Some improvisation is necessary in the desert environment. Two other people doing the ceremony have already gone out and tried unsuccessfully to dig graves. The ground is so hard, dry and rocky that they made little headway and broke one spade handle. Raven decides that the ceremony will be done in one of the sweat lodges, as the sweat is alchemically and symbolically the womb of Grandmother Earth. I am pleased. The idea of toiling out in the hot sun digging a hole had not appealed to me.

Since childhood, I have had clear dreams almost every night of my life. I am looking forward to a ceremony that focuses on stepping into the dream. When I first met Raven I was surprised and pleased to hear that the medicine teachings he works with are those of a path of dreaming. I didn't know exactly what it meant, but thought it might be a place for me to learn to use my ability at dreaming for something other than entertainment. On the second night in Northern Ontario Jamie showed us a particular way of intertwining our hands as we went to sleep to enhance our ability to have and remember clear lucid dreams. A dream is lucid when you know you are dreaming. It becomes a controlled dream if you can direct your action, using the time and space of the dream to learn lessons that will affect your waking reality. After Jamie gave us the hand tie, Raven told us he would come to one of us in the dream that night and give us something.

Returning to the cabin very late, I climbed into bed, put my hands together in the prescribed manner and placed them under my pillow to keep them that way. I wondered if the hand tie enhanced dreaming by making you sleep in an uncomfortable position and not drop off too deeply. I fell asleep quickly and did dream. In my dream I was walking outside by the lake. I was aware that I was dreaming. Raven came up beside me and extended his hand. As I held mine out he placed into it a smooth gray object, oval-shaped and flat on top, like a button. As soon as I took it I was aware of how much energy it was taking for me to be "awake" in the dream. I thanked him and said I needed some deeper rest now and, without waking up, took my hands apart and slept until dawn.

The next day as we gathered Raven asked how the dreaming had gone and if anyone had got the object from him. I was hesitant to speak. What if it had just been my own dream and nothing to do with him? But I wanted to know. Briefly I told him my dream. He listened, nodded and said, "Good, you got it," and pressed on with more teaching. I never had the chance to ask what the object was or what it meant.

The trouble with trying to accomplish specific tasks in your dreams is that doing so is not easily controlled by the conscious mind. After my first workshop with Raven I would go to bed, night after night, using all I had been taught about going into and preparing for controlled dreaming. My dreams remained vivid, sometimes lucid, but I was never able to take conscious action in them. I gave up. Then one afternoon, about seven months after I'd first received the teachings on dream techniques, I was alone in the house. Feeling exhausted, I lay down for a nap. I had only an hour before I had to go out, but I could not fall asleep. Finally, feeling very frustrated, I decided I might as well get some work done if I wasn't going to get any sleep. I got up and walked into the hall, noticing as I did so that my eyes were not functioning properly. Everything had a kind of glow to it, an edge of luminosity. I looked around at the white walls and saw writing suddenly appear on one, in bright blue handwriting. I couldn't read it or even look at it directly. Something very strange was going on. I walked back down the hall and, passing the bedroom, noticed a pair of legs under the covers of my bed. I stopped and backed up. My body was lying in bed, apparently asleep. Then it dawned on me—I was asleep, and dreaming in a lucid, controlled dream! This is what I'd been waiting for! I'd made it! I immediately remembered hearing that most folks when they begin to dream lucidly either get very frightened or very excited and wake themselves up. I calmed down, determined to continue.

Unfortunately, in my excitement I forgot everything else I had been taught about being in and using this state of dreaming for learning. Instead of going to a mirror to see my reflection and to stabilize myself, I went downstairs to my living room, which was used for ceremony. I couldn't decide what to do next. I felt exactly as I had the first time I'd been left alone in the house after giving birth to my first son. His father had taken him out and I was overwhelmed by the silence and the opportunity to do anything I wanted. I decided to lie down and nap, since I was always tired and could rarely nap when Brendan was home. But as soon as I lay down I thought, *No, this is crazy. I can't waste the time napping—it'll be over too soon. I should get something done that I find hard doing with the baby around so I'll feel like I really used the time.* I began to race around and do some household chore, then thought, *No, now this is really crazy. I never get a chance to just relax. I should be reading. I never get to read anymore.* But when I lay down to read, I started to doze off. I went around and around like that for the entire time, neither resting, relaxing nor getting anything done.

This same sense of indecision overwhelmed me as I stood watching the strange luminosity of the living room. Suddenly I remembered that I was supposed to call for a teacher, and forgetting all I'd been taught about how to do so in a way that would ensure my own safety, I said indiscriminately, "I call on a teacher to come to me."

Instantly I heard someone behind me and turned to see a small woman race down the hall toward me. She was stooped as if with arthritis and had on a bright-pink polyester suit and a gray wig sitting crookedly on her head. She had a wild, demented look in her eye. I wondered if it really was a woman, or rather a strange old man dressed to disguise himself as one. She grabbed my arm, and too late, I realized I had not asked for a "teacher from the light." The woman terrified me and I could not think of the words used to banish negative forces. I muttered something completely ineffectual like "Go away." She started pulling me down the hall.

From out of my amnesic haze I remembered Raven's sacred name, used to call him in the dream, and called it out loud. He immediately appeared in the hall. The woman did not wait for him to speak but instantly disappeared. Raven looked at me and shook his head. "If you're going to learn to play on this plane," he said, "you're going to have to remember what the fuck you're doing. Don't do that again! Just wander around and get a feel for what it's like to function on this level." He was gone as fast as he had appeared and I was left feeling rightfully chastised and cautious.

I decided to follow his advice and just move through the house. I kept pinching and lightly hitting my arms to get a sense of what my body felt like in the dream. Everything was very similar and yet different. When I hit my arm I did feel it, but there was a delay, as if the action was filtered through a substance that makes all movement slower and more observable. I walked to the bottom of the stairs and wondered if I had to walk up or if I could just think myself to the top. I thought of seeing myself at the top and was instantly there. For a long time I moved around the house, enjoying the sense of fluidity. Finally I knew it was time to wake up, and finding myself back in my body, woke up in bed.

One of the things about stepping so completely and consciously into the dream was the frustration that followed when I woke up and thought of all the things I could have tried. Why didn't I go outside, move an object of furniture to see if it was moved when I woke up, go and touch my own body in bed, call for a teacher from the light and get great wisdom on the mysteries of life in general and directions for my life in particular? How could I not have thought of these things? How could I have used the time to practice going up the stairs? My sense of failure was only enhanced by talking to other apprentices, similarly awaiting the opportunity to step into this experience, who were sure they would do better and incredulous that I could have been so stupid and frightened.

I went to bed for weeks afterward eagerly anticipating another lucid dream where I could do all of these things. None came. Leafing through one of Carlos Castenada's books shortly after my first controlled dream, I came upon a description one of the characters, Don Genaro, gives of what he calls his first doubling dream. How he felt very much paralleled my experience. I was elated, then, reading on eagerly, was equally horrified to learn that after his first experience he did not have another dream of this nature for fifteen years. I gave away my expectation of nightly forays into controlled dreams.

I did not have to wait fifteen years, however, and at intermittent if unpredictable intervals continued to have similar controlled dreams, where I did remember all I wanted to try and how to do it without endangering myself or needing to call for Raven's help. As in my first vision quest image of my Man Shield, I repeatedly realized that it was my fear that would limit how far I could go and what I could learn.

The all-night dreaming ceremony in the desert seems like the perfect opportunity to do some lucid dreaming. Philomene, a woman from California, dance chiefs the ceremony. I don't know her well but like her immediately. She is a tall thin woman with frizzy hair that seems to change color regularly. After giving me instructions on how to set up and enter the ceremonial space she leaves me alone.

I feel a flutter of nervous anticipation but no real fear. After building and sealing my medicine wheel around the sweat lodge, I enter and lay my pad down so my head will be in the west. The light fades. Inside the sweat it is soon pitch-black. I cannot see my hand in front of my face. I have carefully placed a flashlight by my right hand just in case I need some instant light. I wait and I think. Periodically I break the silence by singing ceremonial chants.

Soon the sweat begins to feel like a tiny pressurized capsule, any sense of what lies outside dropping away. I begin to imagine myself in a small black womb floating in space. How do I know the desert is still out there? How do I even know there are people still out there? There could have been a nuclear holocaust and everything and everyone I knew is gone. How long have I been here? Maybe I've always been here and all the rest—my life, my children, my home, this retreat—is just a dream I have had while sleeping here. Or perhaps I am at home right now in my bed, dreaming I am here doing ceremony in the desert. I lose all sense of time and space. I am not afraid, but I am aware of how I construct my sense of reality in a particular way, tied to reference points that have now been removed.

I drift in and out of sleep and dream, not quite knowing when I'm asleep and when I'm awake. I hear a woman's voice telling me it is time to go to the sacred marriage. I have no idea what this means. Suddenly I hear something moving on my right, a kind of gentle scraping and slithering, the sound of a snake moving over the hard, bare ground, and it's very close. Terrified, I sit up and listen, staring blindly into the solid blackness. The sound of my own heart pounding makes it hard to hear exactly where the movement is coming from, but I am sure it is inside the sweat. I reach out for the flashlight—and can't find it. Desperately I paw around and realize I might touch, antagonize and be bitten by whatever has joined me. I pause and take several gulps of air, trying to clear my mind. Whatever has entered the sweat, and by now I am convinced by the sound that it is a snake, is not coming closer but continuing to move along the wall to my right. I note that there is no rattling sound. Relieved, I decide to lie back down.

Lying with every muscle tense, I listen. Somehow I gradually begin to relax, and fall into a light sleep. I dream of a snake made of blue lightning and awaken to see the after-image glowing in the blackness above me. I drift again into sleep and am awakened by drumming. Philomene is drumming to let me know dawn is here and it is time to leave. A dim light filters into the sweat and I am amazed to find I am now lying with my head in the east. I have no memory of turning around, but by the look of the ground I have been moving a lot during the night. The blankets on the sweat are pulled up a little on the side where I heard the snake, allowing enough space for one to pass in or out. My flashlight has rolled out next to the opening.

Leaving the sweat, I feel a little shaky and am grateful for the solid images that meet me in the dawn. Philomene provides tea and we talk about the night's events. I ask her if she has ever heard of blue lightning. I have heard of specific meanings for red and black lightning, but neither of us has heard of blue lightning and I wonder if my own unconscious just made it up.

Later I ask Raven about it. He answers without hesitation. "Blue Lightning is one of the awakeners, and the snake is the symbol of the energy of spiritual-sexuality. This is probably an indication of your sacred same that you can verify in the Ancestor Speaking ceremony." I begin to put it all together. A sacred name is one you use in ceremony and dreaming with others. It tells of your Sacred Dream—the potential that you can live. Blue Lightning Snake, by Raven's definition, would translate to the "awakener of spiritual-sexual energy." It sounds like a potential I'd love to work at realizing. Later in the day, Raven goes over the different colors of lightning used in the symbolism of the medicine path and he names blue lightning as "Chaos that brings Death." Now, even given an understanding of death as that which brings rebirth, this sounds a little scary. So Blue Lightning Snake is one who creates chaos to bring death through spiritual-sexual energy? Not exactly something you'd include in your computer-dating application. An ex-lover who knows my sacred name listens to the explanation of blue lightning and looks at me with a knowing nod of confirmation.

Two nights later I walk out alone on the desert to do another all-night ceremony. The purpose of this ceremony is to find and speak with your spiritual ancestors, asking for their guidance and for a sacred name. The night is beautiful, full of stars and very still. I feel drawn to a hill and stop halfway up to build my medicine wheel and begin the ceremony. This ceremony requires that a small fetish of each of my medicine animals be placed in the appropriate direction. No one told me about this until an hour before the ceremony. I'm pissed off. The apprentices who live near Raven have received advanced warning and have arrived with small carvings and fur, feathers and bones from the appropriate animals. Some generously share with me a few of the animals I need, but I do not have time to hunt for all of them. I improvise, using earrings and bracelets that have representations of the animals on them, and in exasperation draw a few on small pieces of paper. I wonder if the ancestors will see this as shoddy planning and disrespect for the ceremony. I hope not, but feel I wouldn't blame them if they did. Are the ancestors as judgmental about lack of organization as I am?

Feeling very sleepy, I sit in my circle, send out my prayers and wait, my head nodding, eyelids drooping. As my unfocused vision rests on the dry grass in front of me, I notice eight tiny blue lights shimmering about three feet away, four inches off the ground. Immediately I am wide awake. I keep feeling that the tiny lights are "looking at me," and realize that these must be the Tolilaquai, the first beings of the ancestor world—the little people, the fairies, elves, gnomes, as they are known in other traditions. For the rest of the night there are always at least a half dozen in this same spot in front of me, dancing around. They make me feel very lighthearted and unalone.

I continue, with renewed energy now, to say my prayers to the ancestors. Images of a variety of men and women appear in different directions, and I ask for their guidance and help in my life. Finally I ask for my sacred name, but do not hear anything within or without. I wait. The night is cool and I wrap my blanket closer. I wait for hours but feel no impatience, enjoying this unusual state. My eyes scan the surrounding hillside. One tree grows near the top, about forty feet from where I am sitting. As I glance up toward it I am aware of a strange glow among the branches that was not there before. As I watch, the glow begins to take on shape and color, until the image of a rippling snake of clear blue luminosity appears. I wonder if it is a trick of my eyes, so I blink and rub them. The image remains, clear and shimmering. I look away and focus on the opposite horizon. When I look back the blue snake remains in the branches of the tree. For hours I sit quietly and gaze at the shimmering form. It does not move. As dawn approaches and the sky lightens, it begins to fade. I offer my thanks to the ancestors, disassemble my wheel and slowly return to my tent. I have my sacred name.

7

Paint-ball games are scheduled for the end of the first and the second weeks of the retreat, and provoke a lot of argument and discussion. These games are a new form of entertainment throughout North America. It seems some enterprising individual figured out that there is a small fortune to be made from providing adults with an opportunity to play "war." The games are held on large tracts of land. Participants are dressed in khaki fatigues and face masks, and given guns that fire paint pellets. The "teams" wear distinguishing armbands and try to capture the other side's territory and flag, shooting each other with the pellets, which splatter red paint upon impact.

This is not my idea of a nice way to spend a Sunday afternoon. As a mother who won't allow her sons to play with violent war toys, I have my share of skepticism about the value of the exercise. As the first week of training comes to a close, discussions around the camp focus on the game and people's feelings about it. Some folks, particularly some of the men, are entering the experience with youthful enthusiasm, remembering the boyhood games they loved. Others feel they are here for serious self-discovery and spiritual enlightenment and resent those who see it as only a game. Still others feel their years of commitment to antiwar movements prohibit participation. The Vietnam vets are quiet, no doubt having their own feelings about crawling through the underbrush and taking aim at humans down the barrel of a gun, however harmless.

There are also mutterings among the women. Many wonder about the safety of the game and are worried about one participant in particular, Nicholas. There is no doubt that Nicholas is an unusual character. About forty, slim and attractive with graying curly hair, he seems at first glance perfectly normal. However, during various sessions it becomes clear that Nicholas's mind is not always functioning clearly and coherently. Often during a training session he interrupts, apparently to ask a question, only to go into a long, disjointed soliloquy. As he does so, he becomes increasingly agitated, the rising color in his face and the bulging of his large blue eyes giving him more than a slightly deranged appearance.

My direct experience with Nicholas comes during a session on anchoring, a technique for dealing with negative emotions that includes "anchoring" a positive emotion to a place on the body that is easily touched. When asked to get partners, Nicholas zips up beside me and asks me to work with him. The technique involves having him focus on a particularly positive emotion while I touch him, in this case lightly with my finger on the back of his right hand. When the exercise is complete, Nicholas, grinning broadly, explains in a loud voice that he is thrilled I chose to touch his right hand because it's the hand he masturbates with. People around us stop talking. I calmly nod and say, "Oh, I see," declining to share my thought that I had a fifty-fifty chance of being right and since a majority of the population is right-handed its unlikely to be an indication of a cosmic soul-mate link between the two of us, a revelation he seems certain of. Notwithstanding this, Nicholas tries to persuade me to leave the retreat with him and go to his home in San Diego. I decline. While he is clearly not operating from within the same framework of social norms as most of us, I have not seen anything to make me believe he is dangerous. I am not, however, disappointed to hear that Raven has decided Nicholas will sit out of the game with him, observing.

The arguments about the merits of the game continue. Raven asks that we give it a try and see what we can learn. I figure that since I've come such a long way and spent a lot of time, money and energy on this, I'm not backing out now.

We load into cars and trucks to go out to a more remote part of the desert—rolling hills covered with low bushes and dotted with a few trees. It's hot and dusty. Dressed in fatigues, we line up for our face masks, guns and ammunition. The men who own and rent out the equipment show us how to use the guns and we take a few practice shots.

This is one of the places where I experience the difference between the Canadian and American cultures. Guns do not have the same meaning in these two countries. In every culture there is at least one issue that is a rallying point for common identity, something almost everyone agrees upon regardless of their political viewpoint or affiliation. In Canada it is the environment. You could ask almost any Canadian how they feel about acid rain and get the same heartfelt expression of concern regardless of their place on the political spectrum. In the States, this consistency of feeling cutting across political lines rallies around the inalienable American right to own a gun. There are those who don't feel this way, and there's much controversy about gun control but I've met in-

numerable Americans, from Marxist-Leninists to those on the far right of
Attila the Hun, who own and cherish handguns, automatic and semi-
automatic weapons. As people line up, load and practice shooting their
weapons, I feel this difference acutely. I know how to shoot a .22 for
hunting, but am completely unfamiliar with the look, feel and use of
handguns. The only Canadian I ever met who owned one was a cop.

Much to the disappointment of the game enthusiasts, the guns have little accuracy and often jam, making the possibility of any impressive one-
man Rambo manoeuvres remote at best. There is a growing nervous tension in the air, and despite myself I feel some urgency to get started.

Tony, the local owner/organizer of the game, is a large man with long
hair, dressed in a loud Hawaiian shirt. For some reason he makes me
think of Berkeley, California, and the sixties—ironic given the game he's
selling. He tells us the rules. There will be referees on the site to settle
any disputes about who has been shot. When someone is shot he or she
must put on an orange vest and leave the playing area. Masks must be
left on, and shots to the head are illegal. Each team will have a few moments to position their flag in a safe, guarded spot and set up a strategy
for going after the other side's flag. We will be playing three thirty-
minute games, marked by whistles.

Raven has decided that members of the team winning two out of three
rounds will receive a massage from any member of the losing team at
their convenience. This announcement causes a chuckle of anticipation
and somewhat lightens the mood. When the instructions are complete,
Tony asks the group if everyone understands, and in one voice the ap-
proximately sixty participants respond with a strong "Ho!" In many Native traditions "Ho" or "Aho" indicates agreement, understanding and an
adding of one's heart energy to another's words. Tony knows nothing of
this and assumes the mysteriously unanimous syllable must have been
"No!" Bewildered, he shakes his head and says, "O.K., I'll go over it
again." Laughing, we assure him we did understand. He raises his eyebrows and asks, "How long all you folks been out here?"

The two teams gather at opposite ends of the large playing area and
position their flags. Quickly we divide into squads and decide on an aggressive strategy for fanning out and going after the other team's flag. As
the whistle blows, my squad heads out and, using the hand signals
learned in combat training during the week, begins to zigzag into enemy
territory. I'm concentrating on keeping up with the others, when suddenly we hear the popping sounds of guns being fired. Not three minutes
into the game I feel the sudden sting of a paint-ball exploding on my left

temple, the only spot on my head not covered by my hat or mask. I can't believe it! I am the first person to be shot! And in the head! It's illegal! As I stand there, shocked, red paint oozes behind my mask and through my hair, and a sizable welt begins to rise on my temple. A second shot from my concealed attacker hits me on the leg and I am out of the game. I haven't even fired a shot. I put on my orange vest and begin to walk off the playing area, more than a little humiliated, to wait out the game.

Neither team captures the other's flag, but our team loses miserably, having lost the most players. We regroup and reconnoitre. We decide it will be meaningless to capture the other side's flag if we lose all of our team, so we change strategy. We decide to play a completely defensive game, with a goal of keeping all our people alive and protecting our own flag. We fan out in a circle, concealing ourselves in the bushes around the small hill and clearing where we have positioned our flag. The group elects Michael, one half of the soon-to-be ex-couple camped next to me, to be lookout for our side. He remains on the hill, where he can see the enemy approaching from all sides but is out of the range of their guns.

This game feels very different. I position myself in a small gully halfway down the hill and wait. I have decided that the message of the bruise on my temple is to stay low. The difficulty is I can't see anything but bushes. Other team members are concealed around me, but I cannot see them. We have worked out a password and response to avoid shooting one another if we hear movement close to us. I wait, gun cocked, and listen. The heat is unbearable and sweat trickles down my face under the mask. The tension builds. My life is not in danger. This is a game. Yet still I can feel my senses strain and sharpen, listening, watching. I'm reminded of a story Raven told of sitting for more than twenty-four hours in a jungle swamp in Vietnam. Surrounded by Vietcong, he remained motionless, alert, waiting, silent. That was not a game.

The sound of gunfire fills the air and I hear Michael's voice from up on the hill "There's some coming up on the south side, and a sister who needs help there. Stay low! Keep in touch with your squad!" My squad is on the north side of the hill, so we don't go to the woman's aid, others are closer. We quietly give password and response to check in with our squad members. The game continues in this way. Michael shouts out encouragement and warning when the other side is coming up the hill, and who needs help. He does so always in terms of the family—aiding a brother or sister, protecting the family. Michael has been a firefighter with the U.S. Air Force for many years. He slips immediately and realistically into role: working the team together, depending on one another, defending yourself and your teammates. The whistle blows, announcing the game's end, and we emerge from our hiding places. Only then do I realize how much tension I have been holding in my body. A count is taken. Not surprisingly, neither side has captured a flag. We weren't trying to, and with Michael's warnings, our defenses were virtually impenetrable. Our team has lost three members, two shot by our own side in confusion. The other side has lost fifteen. We've won game two.

We regroup for the final game. Feelings have changed. We like the way the second game felt and are surprised but pleased at how easily the nonoffensive strategy succeeded. We figure the other team will adopt the same strategy for the final game. Then what will happen? Will we both just surround our own flag and not battle at all? This is it! We've figured out how to end world war. Surely everyone's priority is to protect that which they love, and seeing that being nonaggressive is the best way to do that, they simply won't fight. This must be the point of the game. And we got it! Not only that, but our side got it first. Now we can share, by example, our enlightenment. We fan out and position ourselves for the last round.

Again I am lying in the bushes, although this time with less tension as I wait. All is quiet, as we expected, and my mind begins to wander. After a while I hear another squad member nearby say he's going to move out a little and explore. He's obviously bored. A couple of others follow suit, and I doze in the sun, gun under my arm. Suddenly a volley of shots is fired close by on my left and I hear Michael shouting from the hill "Six of them coming up the northeast side—watch out!" Another volley of shots rings out. "Others coming up the south and the northwest! Wake up! They've hit three brothers and more are coming in!"

I'm amazed. What the hell are they doing? They're using the same strategy as before, just more aggressively. I send out my squad's password and wait for response. Nothing. I try again in a louder whisper. No response. The squad has fanned out too far. I am alone. I hear a branch crack behind me and, wheeling around, say the password clearly. Giving one second for the response, which does not come, I come up on my knees and fire. The paint from my pellet explodes red on the chest of a man from the other team and he yells, "Shit, I'm hit!" Two more steps and he would have been in view of my hiding place.

A teammate crawling through the bush behind him calls out, "Rob, is that you?"

"Yeah, I'm out of it. There's a bitch in the bushes here and she just got me. Get her!"

The vehemence in his voice makes my stomach turn. Four men coming up behind him call out to one another and begin to move faster in an effort to find me. Now it's no longer a game. I have to move; he's seen me and is verbally guiding his companions to where I am—supposedly illegal for someone who's been shot dead, but there are no referees around. I start to crawl under the bushes as fast as I can, face in the dirt. They are much closer. It is impossible to move absolutely silently, and they are close enough now that if I move they will find me. I lie completely still, hearing their footsteps come closer.

"Where is she?"

"Don't worry. She couldn't have gotten far. We'll get her!"

Right away I see one man not more than ten feet in front of me, scanning the bushes. I cannot believe that he can't hear the pounding of my heart, and I struggle to keep my breath even and silent. I know if I move one muscle he will have me. His gun is cocked and ready. Although I have reloaded since I shot his companion, I know that if I shoot him, one of the other three stalking me will get me before I can reload. The tension is unbearable. I lie and wait. I can hear Michael still calling out directions, including telling team members of the four men ascending on my side of the hill. Apparently he cannot see me trapped here, or perhaps he is wisely not calling for assistance so as not to let my attackers know I am still here. They wait.

"She must have moved away."

"No way, she couldn't have got that far."

Suddenly a shot rings out. "Somebody coming down from above us— let's get out of here." They move away, out of range of the person who has fired from above me, and the whistle is sounded, indicating the end of the game.

We all begin to walk back to the meeting place—some talking, laughing; more, like myself, very quiet and reluctant to take off their masks despite the heat. I do not want my mixed emotions to show. My body aches and part of me wants to sit down and weep. Another part of me is enraged. Why were they so stupid? Why did they come back so aggressively? We gather for the score to be tallied. Again, no one has captured a flag. Our side has lost six players, theirs twenty-three. We have won the best two out of three, and we pile into the vehicles to return to camp, to gather and debrief.

Raven asks us to talk about what we have learned. It's hard to articulate what has happened. Some felt it was fun. More were frightened by what they saw in others or in themselves—the capacity for violence, revenge, aggression. Talking helps relieve the tension, although we all know it will take time to sort out what the game meant to each of us.

I've heard about this game being played in a similar way at a peace conference in Canada. Participants, all of whom were members of politically active disarmament groups, were playing the game to look at the nature of war and violence. Many were committed pacifists. The game had to be cut short. Participants were yelling, in tears, arguing. Many left, angry and upset by what they had experienced, before the conference was half over. It is not easy to face our own shadow, even in a game.

Not everyone stays for the second week of training. Some cannot afford the time off work and others have decided that one week of this intensity is all they want for now. By the end of the second week, discussion again focuses around the upcoming paint-ball game. Feelings of ambivalence are even higher. Many, including myself, learned a lot from the first game but see little need and are reluctant to repeat the experience.

Raven tells us that the second game will be structured differently: no breaks, but one ongoing, three-hour game, with two opposing countries and a small group of terrorists. The scenario: one group wants to take over the land and ancestral home of the other because they need it for their expanding population. War ensues. The rules: people shot in the legs or arms must put on their vests and sit out ten minutes. Those shot on the body or head are "dead" and must go to a central area for twenty minutes, after which they may reincarnate back into the game on the side of their choice. There are no other rules.

A rumor circulates that this is a test, of our ability individually and as a group to do what we want, to not give power away to the teacher. In the Cherokee tradition the women were the ones who declared the start or end of a war. The women wonder if this second game is a test of our ability to declare and keep the peace by stopping the game. Raven has told us that he himself will head up a terrorist group at the beginning of the game. Other terrorists are not named, but it is assumed that they will come from the retreat staff. Rumors abound that many of the staff will play double agents in both camps. Since Raven has declared that no other rules apply, and that all is considered fair, one group decides to kidnap Raven and cancel the game an hour before it is to start. They seal off the back door to his camper while he is inside. Too late they realize they have not sealed off the truck doors, and in an instant Raven climbs through a cubbyhole in the camper into the cab of the truck and out.

Others begin to discuss capturing the terrorists before the game, and as Clark, a young man of sixteen, passes the group heatedly debating this strategy, he is tackled and brought roughly to ground by an enthusiastic woman yelling, "I've got one!" Whether Clark is a terrorist or not, his mother, one of the women on staff standing nearby, is enraged and screams at the woman to get off her son. Chaos reigns.

The problem is that no one knows how seriously to take the game. Should we stop it? Go ahead and participate? I am amazed at the level of feeling and commitment to one strategy or another among participants. I have a lot of feelings, but none of them strongly indicate what I should do, so I say nothing. It's unlike me to be so quiet or so undecided. Raven does not appear to participate in this week's discussion, no doubt enjoying from a distance the chaos he has generated.

We are told by one of the staff which side we will be on for the game. By this time much of the discussion has degenerated into declarations of personal distrust and anger which continue for the next hour. Our team, or "country," meets in circle a short distance away. We sit silently. We are to be the side that is being attacked for our ancestral lands. What will we do? Will we fight? Two women on staff bring out their ceremonial pipes and begin to fill them. They say prayers not just about the game but for guidance, centering and calmness in a group whose bodies and emotions are raw after two intense weeks together. We pass the pipe, and each person speaks from the heart: about their discouragement with the arguing and fighting, their confusion about the game, the feelings of fear it raised for them the week before and their willingness to participate as best they can. We sit quietly for a few moments and then prepare to leave. I am not looking forward to this, but I want to see it through.

At the site we quickly and quietly get our equipment. Tony is looking nervous about the new "game" he has agreed to let us play. We walk together into the bushes and gather to plan strategy. Getting organized is difficult. Some feel we should take a defensive stance; others feel we cannot do so for three hours but must find some way of immobilizing the other side long enough to get them to talk about peace. After much argument and some shouting, with time running very short, one man, a senior apprentice, takes charge and begins to bark orders. People hesitate. He is a staff member and a prime suspect for being a terrorist or spy. There's no time left to argue. I'm assigned to a small squad, three men and three women, who are to take a long route around the other side's territory, come down from a hill behind their headquarters and capture their leaders.

Our squad separates from the larger group. Will, a gentle man I've come to know and like in the past two weeks has been appointed squad leader. The other two men I do not know well. Gayle and Ginny are the other women. Gayle, a staff member, is clearly eager to do well in the game. Ginny, a beautiful woman from Atlanta, has been in my squad for the full two weeks. We have camped near each other and become friends over tea at the end of the long days. We strike out, staying very low and making a wide circle around the central area where shots are being fired. The territory is large and it takes us more than thirty minutes in a back-breaking, crouched run to cover only half the distance we have to go. Several times we stop and sit motionless while squads from the other side pass by. The men are impatient with this strategy. As we go deeper into the other country's territory and encounter more members of their army, they stand and fire. One by one they are shot and must remove themselves. Gayle, Ginny and I continue, finally reaching the rise of land on the far side. We begin our descent, seeing their headquarters below us. Here we pause. There is a ring of guards in the bushes around their head-quarters. How will we get through? And if we do, then what? Are we to shoot all their leaders? Hold them hostage in order to negotiate? We decide to get closer to hear and see what's happening.

We spread out a little and proceed to crawl on our bellies down the hill. As I do I hear a man's voice behind us. "Got one," he shouts to another man close by as he fires and hits Ginny. From under the bushes I can see her. She has been hit in the leg, so will be out for ten minutes. I can see the man, Jack, who has shot her, but he has not seen me or Gayle. He reloads and steps up in front of Ginny "O.K., bitch, declare yourself dead or I'll shoot you again!"

What? This is illegal! According to the rules you cannot shoot some-one already shot, nor can you shoot someone at point-blank range. At close range the pellets could do some damage. He has only wounded her and now is insisting she take herself out of the game.

"Come on, bitch, do it or I'll shoot you again! Get the fucking vest on. Now!" Given his size Jack is intimidating even in his best moments. This is not one of his best moments. He has clearly lost it. I can see Ginny and she has taken her mask off, looking frightened as she frantically searches for her vest. I feel enraged, a red haze swims before my eyes as I watch him scream and wave the gun over her. Every molecule in my body wants to shoot him, and I'm only partially aware that the gun I hold con-tains only paint-balls. I want him dead! Now! I shift my weight to fire, and feel an arm on mine. It's Gayle. She shakes her head and points to the man behind Jack. If I stand and shoot him, I will no doubt be shot by his partner. Part of me doesn't care, but the interruption makes me pause. What if Jack really has lost it? Will my shooting only escalate things?

His partner walks up. "Hey, man, take it easy." They move off after they have seen Ginny remove herself. I lay shaking with mixed emotions: surprise at the depth of my rage and my capacity to want to do someone real harm; amazement that even with this feeling I did not act blindly but paused; bitter disappointment that I didn't shoot him regardless of the consequences. Gayle moves on down the hill and I rest for a moment and then follow. Suddenly I hear a loud voice over a bullhorn.

"Blue Nation, we call on you to come and join us. Let us declare peace between us and negotiate a solution to our land dispute so that we can handle the terrorists together."

Gayle and I sit and listen. We are part of the Blue Nation. What if it's a trick? We inch forward and watch the clearing below. There are more people there, many of whom began on the blue team. But what if they've reincarnated on the other side or were double agents to begin with? Most have removed their armbands all together. We watch as several others with blue bands emerge from the bush and walk into the clearly. They are not shot but are greeted with cheers as they gather to receive some water and fruit being shared there. It looks like the offer is sincere. We come out with our weapons held up and join the others near a central tree. Slowly others come in and gradually the two nations stop their war.

Elsewhere, the terrorists, still led by Raven, are wreaking havoc, shooting members of both teams and spreading rumors that both sides are continuing the war. We organize ourselves into small squads and go off to hunt down and either kill or capture them. I am with a group of seven that finally catch sight of and surround Raven. Raven has apparently already been surrounded and almost captured several times, but by feigning surrender has managed to escape. Several who have already witnessed this do not give him a chance again and fire mercilessly until he is declared dead. Raven, obviously having the time of his life, removes himself from the game. The squad continues up a hill where a whole group of terrorists are under siege.

Then, right in the middle of the shooting, running and shouting, comes Jamie, dressed not in fatigues but a long skirt. She is beating a hand drum and singing a chant to end the fighting. I watch, mesmerized. Although the fighting does not end, she walks unmarked among the flying paint pellets. The terrorists have obeyed no rules up to this point. I cannot see why they don't shoot her, but even though I see several aim in her direction, she is not hit. It's as if she is protected by something unseen.

Finally the whistle sounds, indicating the end. It is not so easy to step out of the game this time. As people pile into vehicles to return to camp, I lean against a small yellow car. Jack strides up and opens the driver's door. It is his car. "Hop in," he calls to me with a smile, as his partner, Sherry, climbs into the passenger seat. I hesitate. Do I want to ride with this man after what I have witnessed? The other vehicles are pulling out. Jack sticks his head out the window. "Hey, Oriah. Wake up! Are you coming or what?"

"Yeah, I guess so." I get in the back seat. The ride back takes no more than five minutes. Sherry and Jack laugh and talk about the game, good-naturedly commiserating over losses. I can see Jack's eyes in the rearview mirror, smiling and open. They are not the eyes of rage and violence I saw an hour before. I go over the scene in my mind and know I did not imagine his uncontrolled anger. This is the same man, who now lovingly puts his arm across the car seat to massage the tired neck muscles of his lover next to him. They drop me off by my tent.

I sit by the tent, too worn out to move, feeling numb, watching the dust roll across the valley before me. A sense of knowing something ripples over me like a wave. The man in the car, smiling, loving, laughing, is the same man with murderous rage in his voice towering over Ginny. Just as the hands in my lap, which have lovingly bathed my sons, could have shot him or any man I saw threaten someone I cared for. I have known all of this in my head before now I know it in my body. I'm not sure I want to know.

8

The final day of the retreat dawns: testing day. I wake before the bugle sounds and lie waiting. My stomach is in knots, refusing breakfast. All the women who have trained with Delia for two weeks will, if they choose, be tested by being attacked by men. We have known about this from the beginning. Delia has recruited six men, five retreat participants and one colleague from California. All are martial artists most are black belts. They will be well padded, we will wear no protection. Their instructions will be to attack all out, with intent to rape, until they hear Delia yell, "Cut." Delia will do so after the woman has delivered two or three "take-out blows," hits that, without padding, would break, maim or kill. We will each be attacked three times.

I am concerned, knowing that Tom is one of the men chosen for this task. He is obviously still angry at me for not spending time with him during the retreat and I wonder if the testing will be a place for him to vent some of his rage.

We gather at the spot we have used for training. Gym mats are spread over a thirty-by-sixty-foot area of ground under an awning, which provides some respite from the relentless sun. Delia introduces us to her colleague, Hubert, and he goes with the men to give them some last-minute instructions. I cannot take my eyes off Hubert, a very attractive, very massive black man. He's a karate black belt, stunt man and martial arts instructor who is well over six feet tall, weighs at least two hundred and fifty pounds and is solid muscle. His bicep is about the size of my thigh. I begin to pray.

I notice that despite all my wonderful recent experiences with spirit, I send out my silent prayer to the Scottish Presbyterian God of my childhood Sunday school. I try to make a deal. I'll do this thing, I'll put myself in there to be tested, if He will just see to it that Hubert is not the one to test me.

Delia stands with the women for a moment. No one is giggling or chatting this morning. Faces are tight with tension. She reminds us that it is our choice whether to be tested or not. Some women are absent.

Several women say they do not want any men from the retreat around watching. There is a murmur of impassioned agreement. We do not want to provide entertainment for those not directly involved. Delia does not seem surprised by the sentiment and asks men who are in the vicinity to leave. Only Raven and the six men participating will be in the area.

I am scared, but I want to be tested. In previous self-defense classes I "graduated" when I was able to chop a board in half, but this does not reassure me when I am on the street alone at night. Some of this training I had done before I was raped and beaten, and I had never even thought to use it in those situations. I want to know how I will physically respond if threatened or attacked again. Of course, I know this is not a real life-and-death situation, but it is as close to the real thing as one can get. I need to know if I can do it.

Delia divides us into small groups and a man joins each group to do some sparring exercises to warm up. The physical activity helps loosen the tension. The men move slower than they will for the testing and we know when it is our turn. Suddenly there is a yell. A woman lies on the ground and the man who has been sparring with her is bending over her in concern. They have been struggling, he has flipped her and somehow her leg got twisted behind her. In obvious pain and unable to walk, she is carried to the side and stays to watch the testing. X-rays later show her leg is broken.

The incident shakes everyone. We all know there are risks and have signed numerous waiver forms reminding us of this fact. But theoretical risk and a sister in pain are two different realities. Delia tells us it is time to begin. All women who want to be tested are to stand on the mat at its perimeter. We stand there, tense and silent.

"What the hell is he doing here?" A woman points a man standing just outside the awning.

"I thought we said no spectators," another says to murmurs of agreement. We are all scared. We would rather be angry.

"I asked him to be here as medic." Rhonda, the medical doctor on staff, speaks. She is to be tested herself and feels the need to have someone else present to help with possible medical emergencies. The man looks stricken by the response to his presence and eagerly offers to leave. Delia asks the group to let him stay so Rhonda can have the same opportunity as the rest of us to focus on her own testing. There is reluctant agreement.

The testing begins. One at a time the men wander inside the circle of women, sometimes talking about what they are looking for, what they want to do to a woman.

"My old lady pissed me off last night. Now somebody's going to pay. Some bitch is going to squirm under me, yessir. I know what women really like and I'm going to give it to one of them."

"I like 'em young—ten, eleven, twelve. I like seein' how scared they look, how they beg you not to hurt them. The look in their eyes—it's a real turn-on."

Sometimes the man just silently strolls around the circle, staring. Sometimes, quick as lightning, he grabs a woman who looks off guard and flings her down onto the mat. Other times he tries to start a conversation, as if in a social situation, and slowly reaches out to take her arm.

"Hey, honey, how's it goin'? You are really looking good tonight. How about you and I just take a little walk together, get to know each other?"

The women are alert, tense, silent, on guard. It is hard to wait, not knowing when my turn will come. It is hard to watch as women I know, women whose stories of rape and violence I have heard through tears, are grabbed and start to struggle. Tom approaches the youngest woman in the group, a beautiful sixteen-year-old. He has barely touched her, when she flies into action, taking him out before he even gets a full grip on her and throwing a kick at him as he retreats. We laugh and applaud. Other women are not as ready. They struggle and flail, wasting energy on frantic, useless motions. Again and again Delia calls to them. "Think! What are your weapons? What are your targets? Don't wear yourself out! Make every move count!"

Two of the men involved in the testing are brothers—Will, my squad leader in the last paint ball game, and Rick. Both are karate black belts, quiet gentle men in their twenties from Texas. I've come to know them over the two weeks and have a kind of sisterly affection for them both. Will wanders the circle, gazing at all of us. I see him coming as he moves quickly toward me and pulls me to him, hooks my leg out from under me, and in an instant I'm flat on my back with him astride me. But I feel okay. We have practiced repeatedly a technique for getting out of this position, one I feel confident about doing since it primarily uses the muscles of the lower body. I have very little upper-body strength, but having given birth to a twelve-pound son, I know without any doubt where the strongest muscles in my body are. As he talks to me, telling me how he's going to fuck me and hurt me, I slowly bend my knees and bring my heels up under my buttocks. He has my arms pinned over my head. Without warning, and with a "kyi" that scares even myself, I push up with my legs, arch my back and throw him over my head. As he is catapulted over me I reach up for the second part of the technique, to grab, twist and pull his balls. The protective cup he's wearing prevents this.

Raven has taught this technique to hundreds of women and swears that it will render a man fully unconscious within a second. He claims to have tested it himself by having his partner use the technique on him while he held an unloaded pistol to her head. According to the story, he was unable to pull the trigger before she had him out. Raven has had women practice this technique by grabbing two ripe plums in a sock until they can immediately burst the plums. After hearing this story neither men nor women look at plums quite the same way again.

Will is not unconscious but on his feet immediately and coming back at me. I use my legs again and land blows to his knees and groin that would, without padding, have taken him out again. Delia yells "Cut," and we stop. As I leave the mat I hear Raven call to me to keep moving, keep walking, to not sit down. I feel as if all my joints are being pulled apart, apparently a reaction to the flood of adrenalin brought on by the attack and best worked out by continuing to move for a few minutes. Someone takes my arm and keeps me slowly walking for a few moments. The testing continues until everyone has fought once and then we take a ten-minute break.

I'm beginning to feel a little better, like maybe this won't be so bad after all. All of the women attacked managed to defend themselves— some quickly and neatly, others with more of a struggle, but all effectively. As we gather again at the edge of the mat there is tension but less fear. It begins again. Occasionally, as women are attacked, Raven calls to them to use their Wind Sword, their mind, encouraging them to talk to their attacker and see a way out of the situation. Most are too focused on using their physical defenses to even try. Len, a man I don't know, attacks Cheryl. A tiny thirty-year-old woman who looks twenty, she has a youthful innocence about her that gave even greater poignancy to her story of being raped by a man who broke into her apartment late at night. Len immediately has her on her back, and is sitting on her chest. "What's your name?" he demands.

"Golden Dawn," she replies in a childlike voice.

"What the fuck kind of name is that? Bet you're one of these new age space cadets, aren't you? Well, Golden Dawn, do you know what I'm going to do? I'm going to fuck you!"

"Wow, that's great! I've been looking for a real man. None of these new age guys really has what it takes to really fuck me."

No one, including Len, can believe it. Her words are just too incongruous with the image she presents. In genuine bewilderment he looks around and falters. "What? Fuck this!" He hurriedly gets off her. We laugh and cheer, amazed. It's not a technique that would work with many, but it did with him. She used her Wind Sword and we are delighted. Laughing, I glance over at Rick, who's standing just inside the circle. He is laughing and shaking his head, smiling at me. I feel more relaxed.

In a flash he is on me, grabs me and throws me through the air. I am taken totally off guard. Worse, the attack has come in a moment of shared levity. I feel my body arch through the air and come down hard on my back, all of the wind knocked from my lungs. My body remembers the motion. It is identical to the way I was thrown and landed when I was raped. I hear the sharp intake of breath by the women on the circle. Many were there for the reenactment of my rape and know how this situation physically parallels it. Suddenly everything slows down and I feel a flood of overwhelming tiredness and warmth flow through my body. Rick continues to attack and I kick at him, but my motions are slow and half-hearted. I just do not care. I want to go to sleep. I don't care if he kills me; I am just too tired to fight. I hope he kills me quickly. Scenes from the past flash through me. One moment I can see the blue mat beneath me; the next moment I see the black-and-white tile of the kitchen floor I hit so many years before. One moment I can see Rick's goggled face and blond hair, and the next I see the dark hair and beard of the attacker in my past. I don't want to fight.

Delia's voice penetrates the haze. "Oriah! Don't do that! You've been here before—don't check out on me!" Slowly, using every bit of will I can gather, I begin to fight back, aiming blows, watching for his next move. It seems to take forever. but I finally pick up speed, and after several hits Delia yells "Cut!" I move off the mat, stunned. Everyone is shaken and Delia calls a break.

Body aching, I move off alone to the top of the nearby gully. I sit and weep. I am overwhelmed with the realization that I would rather have died than fight. The lethargy that overtook me was so complete that I feel I could have gone to sleep in the middle of the whole thing. What if Delia had not yelled at me? What if it had been a real attack? Would I have chosen death? I am frightened at how beyond my control it felt. Where was the inner warrior Delia has talked so much about?

Will comes and sits next to me. He tells me that Rick has taken himself out of the testing; he is too shaken by what he saw me go through and feels he cannot do it anymore. I walk to the washrooms to buy some time before deciding if I will put myself back at the mat for the third round. Ginny joins me as I walk and puts her arm around me.

"I wanted to jump in there and help you so much," she says, beginning to cry.

"I know."

"Will you go back?"

"I don't know. I don't know if I can."

The call comes to begin. We have already been there for four hours and the strain shows on everyone's faces. I move to the edge of the mat, numbly feeling I have not really decided, but my body is deciding for me. One of the men circles, talking about how he likes to attack older women, little gray-haired ladies who are too helpless to do anything. He begins to leer at one woman under five feet tall, in her late forties, with gray hair. Still talking, he lunges for her, but he has made a mistake. The condescending talk has made her furious and she is ready for him, flying into action almost before he has touched her. One by one women are tested and pass for the third and final time, receiving a certificate from Raven and hugs of congratulations from others who are finished. There are only a half dozen of us still on the mat. I'm not sure I'm really committed to being there and stand with only my toes on the mat. Maybe they won't know if I'm in or out and will pass me by.

Hubert begins to circle the mat. *Please, God, anyone but Hubert.* But I know even as I send out the thought that this is it. He wanders by, seemingly unaware of me, then turns and grabs me.

Something inside me snaps. I have a very clear image of a woman standing at the edge of the mat, with a little girl next to her holding her hand. The woman is me. She looks worn-out. The little girl is me at age six. Her eyes are wide with terror. Suddenly a third figure steps in front of them, an androgynous figure, possibly male, who moves into action against the attacker without a moment's hesitation or wasted movement. It is also me, and effortlessly I choose my weapons—fist, knee, foot— and my targets—eyes, groin, knees—and deliver repeated take-out blows with an earsplitting "kyi" that comes from my belly. From far away I hear a voice. "Cut, cut, cut! For God's sake, Oriah, I said cut!" It is Delia.

Hubert stands with his hands raised defensively. "Whoa, girl." I stand dazed, then look at Delia, who begins to laugh. Everyone applauds and cheers. He didn't even get me down on the mat.

The testing is completed. We have been at it for six hours. We sit in circle beneath the awning, men in the center. We are all bruised and spent. Despite the padding, the men have been injured, although none seriously. One at a time they speak of their experience of the fights, their fear for the women, their fear for themselves, their fear of seeing the potential rapist and attacker in themselves. One man explains why he volunteered for the testing. A year earlier his mother, sixty-five, had been raped and murdered in her home. His feelings of helplessness and grief compel him to do whatever he can to help women learn to defend themselves. We cry with him as he talks of his mother. All the women have brought medicine gifts for the men, gifts from their hearts in exchange for the profound giveaway these men have offered us on this day. The men take turns choosing from among the beautiful gifts of blankets, feathers, beaded pouches and crystals.

Delia speaks for a short while. She warns us that for the next few days we will all probably feel a bit on edge, ready and waiting for anything, dreaming of fighting, perhaps distrustful of men. We discover this is no exaggeration and that it lasts much longer than any of us expected. Two days later, getting ready to leave camp and return to Phoenix with Mitch, I am approached by Tom, who asks me go to town with him and have breakfast. Feeling guilty about not having spent any time together, and aware of his disappointment, I agree but have some misgivings. I return to my tent to pack up and wait for him to come by. Finally he does— much later than planned—he has been delayed by work. Somehow my relationship with Mitch has survived the retreat and I am returning to Phoenix with him. I still have some packing to do and want to be ready to leave when he is. I tell Tom it will have to be a short trip into town for what will now be brunch. He tells me not to worry, that if we're not back in time he'll take me into Phoenix. It dawns on me that he has no intention of getting me back to camp in time to catch my ride. His anger with me is only thinly veiled with forced jokes and coaxing. I tell him I'm not going and start to walk away from the car. He reaches out and grabs the waistband on my shorts. Without hesitation I spin around, the words clicking through my mind: weapons—claw hand; target—eyes. He is still holding on to me. I pause for only an instant and, looking him in the eyes, say, "Drop it!" Obviously shaken and furious, he does. I walk away.

It is like this for many women. Men in the camp joke nervously about making sure they announce themselves when approaching the tent sites of any of the women who have been tested. We're not feeling particularly aggressive, just capable, for the first time in our lives, of defending ourselves and somewhat on automatic if threatened.

Delia says the acuteness of this explosive energy will pass, but the confidence in our ability to protect ourselves and those we love will not. Finally she leads us in a guided mediation of visualizing the inner warrior—the part of myself that stepped forward when Hubert attacked me—that can do whatever needs to be done, without fear or anger, to protect my inner woman and child.

As we walk back to the tent I am elated. "I chose to fight—I choose to live" runs through my mind like a chant.

The retreat is over. Most of the participants stay for ceremonies planned for the next day, and new people begin to arrive. The ceremonies are open to public participation and are aimed at collectively healing the planet and bringing together the human family in the great Gathering Together Circle. Several hundred people are expected.

Retreat participants are more inclined to celebrate their own survival of the previous two weeks than they are the dawning of a new age. Ginny, Will, Rick and I with several others pile in a van and go into the nearby town to eat at a restaurant and party. Not much is going on in the small town, so we head back out to the camp, park the van on the desert under the star-studded sky, crank up the music on the tape deck and begin to dance across the sand to Paul Simon's "Graceland." It is a beautiful night and we dance for hours. While we were in town about a hundred people have arrived for tomorrow's ceremonies. They are now all in bed, their tents filling the previously spacious camp, small domed structures that have popped up like little pods on the desert floor. Despite the purpose of the ceremonies and our desire to welcome these newcomers, we're all feeling slightly invaded. What we have shared in the past two weeks has formed a very close community, and it is hard not to feel it's "us" and "them."

Finally everyone wanders off to bed. I am still wide awake and sit with Rick, watching the stars and sharing a blanket against the cold. We talk of the testing that occurred earlier that day and I explain to Rick what happened to me when he threw me. I am aware that, despite all of the others present and Delia's coaching, what happened is something only the two of us shared as surely as if we'd been alone in a back alley, in a real fight. We sit silently, just watching and letting the events of the day sink in. Rick puts his arm around me and kisses me gently on the cheek. He asks if we can spend the night together. It feels like the healing we both need. We walk together back to my tent.

There are a lot of different ways to make love: as passionate lovers, as friends, as brother and sister on the same road together. It doesn't really matter. As long as there is an open heart-to-heart touching, some healing will always take place. I lay down shyly next to the man who had, in his willingness to play a part in the testing that day, given me a chance to find my warrior within and be freed from the fear of the past. He undresses me slowly and smiles. "I feel very honored to be here with you tonight," he says, and I know he speaks from his heart.

My heart feels full as I see mirrored in his words and his eyes an honoring of the feminine, of woman, of myself. It's something I have not seen or allowed before. His body is bruised, scratched and battered from the combat testing, but our lovemaking is quiet, soft, gentle, a soothing for the wounds of the day for both of us.

The next day newcomers and retreat veterans gather to prepare for the evening ceremonies. There are some complaints from the recent arrivals. They feel they have come for a serious and meaningful ceremony and want to prepare with some quiet meditation. They complain that our exuberant spirits, loud music and boisterous rehashing of the weeks' conflict-ridden activities are not conducive to the mood required for inspirational ceremony. One woman comments with horror that she overheard retreat survivors jokingly make up bumper-sticker logos that poke fun at spiritual aspirations to which she is committed. It's true. There have been some laughter-filled discussions of "ungrounded" new age groups and possibilities for bumper stickers. "Your body—don't leave home without it!" or "I kicked ass during the Harmonic Convergence," referring to the August 17, 1987, date seen as a potential turning point in human spiritual development. These are not sentiments she wants in any way to support. Raven laughs and asks for her indulgence, attempting the almost impossible task of explaining the past weeks' events and their unusual, if temporary, effect on us all. He also appeals to those who have been here for two weeks to welcome the others. He reminds us that we will all be returning home soon and could use this opportunity to begin the process of reentering the broader community within which we live.

The ceremonies planned are to begin at 8:00 P.M. and run all night, with a sweat lodge ceremony at midnight, one at 4:00 A.M. and one as Grandfather Sun comes over the mountains around 8:00 A.M. Preceding all this will be the Warrior Returns ceremony for all Vietnam veterans present. This ceremony is traditionally done after a war for all those who fought, to cleanse them and heal the wounds they endured for the sake of their people. As darkness begins to fall, the one hundred and seventy people gathered come together in circle to say prayers for the veterans who sit in the center. One at a time we will go to each of these men and offer our heart energy for his healing and cleansing. Although many gathered opposed the Vietnam War, all welcome the chance to participate in some small way in healing the wounds it left on so many.

As the ceremonial pipe is lit a car races across the desert and comes to a halt in a cloud of dust behind where I am standing. It is a convertible, and the man driving stands up in the car and begins to shout. "Heather? Heather, where the hell are you? Get over here, we're getting out of this place." He is loud, belligerent and perhaps drunk. His tone is threatening. Heather, a quiet woman who has arrived only today, looks apologetically at all of us and begins to walk to the car. Several women, including myself, move instinctively to stop her. We are still on the edge that the combat training has given us and nothing would make our day more than going over and physically dealing with this bully. Garth, the Fire Keeper, motions us back to the circle and strides out to the car, speaking to the man in a low, steady tone, asking him to leave the area. I'm disappointed. But I realize I'm probably not capable of being able to settle this without escalating it. It's too soon. The man drives off as fast as he arrived and we resume the ceremony.

The night of ceremony is, for me, a going down into the dream. As we gather I start my moon cycle, beginning my menstrual bleeding. This often happens when a lot of ceremony takes place. In some Native traditions women on their moon do not participate in ceremony or touch ceremonial objects. Women on their moon are understood to be most in their power and aligned with spirit. This energy does effect a ceremony, but here it is the responsibility of the ceremonial Dance Chief to know how to use and incorporate this energy for the benefit it can bring the whole community. However, when I am at a ceremony from another tradition, I respect their ways and remove myself if I am bleeding.

As we enter the first sweat I tell the Dance Chief I am bleeding and she asks me to sit in the west of the lodge, place of the feminine, of intuition and introspection, of death and change, the body and the Grandmothers. I sit in the west with Rick on one side, Will on the other and a third man in front of me. I have with me the smoky quartz crystal skull I chose from the collection Raven brought to the retreat. As the heat begins to build I feel myself sink into the coolness of the earth beneath me. It is as if my body is a vortex of spiraling energy going down deeper and deeper into the darkness of the earth, past rocks and roots, through sand and time. It is a place of incredible peace and comfort, where neither time nor space matter. I rest there.

As we leave the sweat I take the sense of this place with me and have some trouble walking. Will and Rick support me, and once we are dressed we go to sit under some trees apart from the larger group. Both men are concerned about me, but I assure them I am fine, just reluctant to leave this space. They tell me they were aware of feeling my energy going into the earth in the sweat. I lie down and Rick puts my head and shoulders in his lap, supporting me. Will sits at my feet and two other men, friends of theirs, join us, sitting on either side of me. They decide to work with their pipes, and as I drift down into sleep again I hear voices saying prayers as tobacco is added. Someone covers me with a blanket and I struggle to wake up. "Sleep if you can," says Rick, "and we will draw on this wonderful energy of the dream that comes to a sister on her moon. I will wake you for the next sweat."

I relax, held and cared for by this small circle of the Brotherhood. I am surprised and delighted at the trust I feel. I do not need to fight here. I drift in and out of the dream, visited by images of Bear and Wolf, who come to speak to me. The men around me smoke the pipe and sit in silence. I dream of a circle of Grandmothers. I can hear their drumming and singing.

And then I see the whole two weeks like a film: practicing hitting the bag over and over; lying alone in the night ceremony; sitting in the circle of Grandmothers in the healing sweat; emerging into the arms of the sisters under the moon; watching Jack scream at Ginny; flying through the air and hitting the ground; confronting Hubert; making love with Rick; lying in the circle of men.

I smile and drift into deeper sleep. Perhaps I can rest here.

Part 2

Out of the
Land of the Father

1

S omething is terribly wrong. I look around my living room trying to orient myself. Nothing is where it should be. The furniture is gone, the room completely bare. The door to the hallway is on the south side of the room, the fireplace on the north. Everything is a complete mirror image of what it should be. Immediately I realize what this means: I must be asleep and dreaming. I wonder if I should go upstairs and check to see if my body is still in bed, but I am afraid to leave the room. There is something here, something that shouldn't be. I can feel my heart pounding, my breath coming in shallow gasps. A man I do not recognize enters the room. I know he and I have been married. He is concerned for my safety. Before we can speak to each other a dark yellow streak with a dull luminosity enters the room and zooms around our feet. It looks like a tennis ball with a tail—like a miniature, three-foot-long, dark comet.

"Look out," the man yells, "he will try to enter your body!"

Paralyzed, I know that whatever this is, I must stay away from it, and I begin to banish, using the words I have been taught by Raven. I am surprised that despite my fear I am able to remember the words exactly. "I banish, into all eight directions, by the power of LawJup, LawJup, LawJup, LawJup, all energies or entities, incarnate or disincarnate, who do not love me or would do me harm. Begone from this place now!" The yellow streak leaves the room, but moments later flies back in, about six inches off the floor.

"Keep banishing, keep banishing! If it enters you it will be impossible to get rid of!" the man screams at me.

I continue to banish, strengthening my tone and taking care to say the words correctly. Each time I do, the yellow streak circling menacingly around me leaves the room for a minute or two, but returns immediately. My banishing only seems to keep it at bay.

The man leaves the room as I continue to banish and returns with the vacuum cleaner. He plugs it in, turns it on and, holding the hose close to the yellow streak, sucks it into the vacuum, immediately detaching the hose and unplugging the machine. I am surprised his strategy worked but wonder how long the vacuum can hold this thing. The man looks at me. "It is the energy of a dark sorcerer. He is trying to possess you." I nod, watching the vacuum cleaner. It has begun to glow and shake and I know somehow that whatever this is, it will find a way out. I continue to banish.

Suddenly a glowing, twelve-inch wooden ruler, like the ones I used in elementary school, but with writing on the back of it I cannot read, slides noiselessly out of the front of the vacuum and flies straight at me. It hits me in the center of my body, dissolving into my solar plexus and knocking me to the floor. Stunned, I sit on the floor, feeling a warm tingling moving around my navel. The man is frantic now. "Oh, my God. He's done it. Banish! Banish now and don't stop!"

My mind is clear and calm. I know that I have only a few moments to rid myself of this thing within my body. Once it is there for more than two minutes, I know it will be almost impossible to get out without a great deal of help, and may do me permanent damage. I also know it will be useless to continue to banish as I have been doing. I know I must increase my intent and focus, remain calm and gather my will, taking all the time I can to do so. If I rush I will not have the focused energy to be rid of this thing. If I take too long it will be too late. I must take all the time available and not one second more. I must not panic.

I sit and follow my breath into my body, relaxing all my muscles and feeling my weight drop to the floor. I pour all my energy and attention into my words, like focusing the light of the sun beneath a magnifying glass to start a fire. I speak quietly but with force, my tone low. "All that is evil, get out! Begone!" A murky yellow light streaks from my body and out the door. It is gone. With a jolt I find myself back in my body, awake, lying in my bed. I can feel heat in my chest and belly. Was any damage done? Sending my attention down into my body, I check it out. Everything seems fine except for a blossoming headache. I touch my belly, my solar plexus and, moving my hand up between my breasts, realize my necklace is gone. I had gone to bed the night before with a silver chain around my neck—a Goddess figure hangs from the chain, arms upraised, holding a round piece of polished, deep-blue lapis lazuli—now it is gone. I search the bedding, the bed, the room, but it is not there. I feel disturbed by her disappearance. Where could she have gone?

Feeling shaky, I get out of bed and go downstairs to make myself some tea. Everything in the living room looks normal. Taking my tea back upstairs, I quickly bathe and dress. Going into my workroom, I sit at my desk and begin to write about the dream in my journal, a pink loose-leaf binder. As I finish, I sit quietly for a few moments, focusing on my breath, relaxing my body. From deep within I hear the voice of an old woman. "Read the dreams. Read the dreams." What does she mean? I begin to leaf through the pages of my journal, rereading dreams of the past few months.

The echo of the voice continues, persistent, urging. I have kept notes on both dreams and out-of-the-ordinary experiences for years, filling loose-leaf binders and stacking them away on my bookshelf. I have never gone back to reread them. I go to the bookshelf now. Which dreams should I read and why? At random, I pull out a binder and begin to look through it. There are five large binders and numerous smaller notebooks dating back six years. I pull out others, hoping my random actions will lead me intuitively to what I need to see right now. It's like looking for a needle in a haystack.

It's been almost three and a half years since I rested in the arms of my newfound brothers at the end of the desert retreat. Memories come back vividly as I read my journals from this time.

I came home from the desert retreat with a feeling of purpose I had never known before. I knew I had found what Raven called my path with heart, a tradition of teachings and ceremonies that touched my mind, heart, body and spirit.

I also came home with more physical and sexual energy than ever before. As Delia had predicted, the sense of physical power stayed with me after the martial arts testing. A week after I got home from the retreat I overheard a friend, a guest in my home, on the telephone. A small gentle man, he had been regaled with stories of the retreat since my return. "Oriah?" he said on the phone as I eavesdropped. "Oh, yes, she's home again. She hasn't any need for a key since she came back. She just walks up and rips the door right off the hinges!"

Bea and I began holding ceremonial gatherings in my home on the new and full moons and I started teaching classes, sharing what I had learned from Raven. The second time I had met Raven, on the trip to Jamaica, he had urged me to begin teaching the medicine wheels. Surprising numbers of people interested in doing ceremony began to appear, and the classes were filled with twenty-five to thirty people each week. Bea and I invited others who had studied with Raven to participate in the building of a community. With advice from Raven and the ever-present inner guidance of the figure I knew as Grandfather, I cautiously proceeded to learn and teach. The community and my love for shamanic work grew. I could not imagine ever wanting to do anything else and used all of my holidays and any money I could muster, to travel and study with Raven. I knew I had learned only a fraction of what he could teach me. I wanted more.

Three months after I returned from the desert retreat, Raven came to Canada to do a workshop on spiritual-sexuality not far from my home. After the desert retreat Mitch and I had resumed our long-distance relationship and we decided to do the workshop together. The night before the workshop I was excited and a little nervous. I went to bed early and lay awake, unable to get to sleep.

As I drifted into sleep my body felt peculiar—light and airy as if it were floating up toward the ceiling. With one part of me aware of this unusual physical sensation I moved into a dream, one I had had about six weeks earlier. I was in an open-air amphitheater built of stone. At the center was a circular stone floor surrounded by three tiers of stone steps. On the top tier there were seven stone pillars that rose behind a large chair or throne sitting on the second tier. Raven sat in the chair crying, his head in his hands. The light was fading and streaks of orange and red lit the sky as the sun set.

In the center of the amphitheater stood a woman. I couldn't see her face as her back was to me. She was tall, with long blond hair, and wore a plain white dress. The dress had long sleeves and a tight-fitting bodice that revealed her slender figure. The skirt hung full from her hips to the floor. The dress seemed to shimmer with a blue-white light as she moved across the floor below the spot where Raven sat. She began to dance in front of him, spiraling around the circular floor in smooth, beautiful movements. Just then I saw two children, a boy and a girl, sitting on the step below the throne, one either side of Raven. He and the children watched, mesmerized, as the woman danced. She motioned for them to join her and the two children bounded down the stairs, each taking one of her hands and spinning around with her. The three laughed and danced, motioning for Raven to join, them but he sat watching, immobile.

Finally the woman stopped before him and, releasing their hands, waved the children away. Slowly she mounted the steps to where Raven sat and extended her hand to him and spoke for the first time. "It is time. Come." Her tone was not harsh, but it had a compelling quality that made refusal impossible. Slowly, with resignation, Raven took her hand and they walked together up to the final tier of stone surrounding the amphitheater. Walking on top of the broad curved wall, she led him to a place past the seven pillars, and removing her hand from his, she nodded toward the darkness that lay beyond. She turned and walked away, leaving him at the stone precipice. He stood for a moment and then suddenly jumped over the edge into the darkness. I gasped. As he fell his body began to glow with red-and-black patterns until he was completely covered with them. On his head was a giant red-and-black bird mask with a huge beak and his arms were covered with feathers of the same colors. He looked like a giant Hopi Kachina falling into the abyss. Plummeting into the blackness, he burst into flames, flared briefly and disappeared. I awoke with a start, panting and covered in sweat, feeling as though I had been dropped onto the bed.

What was this dream? I had dreamed it several times before. I resolved to share it with Raven during the workshop if I had the opportunity. I was always reluctant to actually speak to Raven about my own dreams. At all the teaching workshops and journeys there were always dozens of people lined up to tell him of their experiences and seek his advice. I was quite sure my dreams and experiences were not unique and I did not want to appear as yet another groupie of a new age guru. Something that happened in Jamaica, however, had made me a little less reticent to share dreams that had an unusual quality to them.

While preparing to go on the journey to Jamaica, I had a repeated dream of Raven, accompanied by the same unusual body sensation of floating up to the ceiling while sinking into the dream. In it I had seen Raven, looking tired and upset, walking through deserted sand dunes. Different people approached him. A little girl in a white dress ran to him and wrapped her arms around his neck, kissing him tenderly. A young Native man strode up to him aggressively, blocking his way and challenging him to a fight. Raven shook his head sadly and the young man moved away, bewildered. Finally a bird flew down and landed on his shoulder. Raven seemed to shake off his mood of lethargy and quickened his pace.

I'd been unable to put the dream out of my mind. On the last day in Jamaica Raven had offered to give each of us a Tarot card reading. We were to present him with a small medicine gift as an energy exchange. I could not decide what to offer as a gift. I had told Bea about the sand dunes dream and she had suggested I offer it as my gift. I was uncertain. Who was I to offer a dream to this medicine man? What audacity! What self-importance! But the idea, and Bea's persistent encouragement, wouldn't go away. So after my reading I had told him of the dream, reading nervously from my handwritten notes. As I finished I looked up. To my surprise Raven was crying. "This dream," he said, his voice choked with emotion, "is about what I need to know to face a ceremony I must do soon. You were right to tell me and I thank you. It is important to me. May I keep it?" He extended his hand for my notes and I gave them to him, moved and awed that the dream really had meaning for him.

Several months later, when I made my first trip to Arizona, Mitch and I spent a day exploring the local area. As we came over a rise in the sand dunes I realized that we were walking in the very same deserted landscape as the one in the dream I had shared with Raven in Jamaica. Excitedly I pulled Mitch along, describing to him the old oil drum we would find over the next hill, the view beyond this stone, the tree we would see farther on. Each description proved completely accurate down to the smallest detail. I had never been to Arizona before in my life. Somehow the dream had taken me there. I could hardly believe it. Mitch, on the other hand, seemed fairly blasé, and cautioned me that I was never going to be a great sorcerer if I got so excited over every little unusual thing that happened. My enthusiasm was not dampened.

My reticence was lessened by this experience, which seemed to confirm that my dreams were not just for me. I did not know if the dream, of the woman in white and Raven jumping into the abyss, meant anything to Raven. As my teacher, he often appeared in my dreams, and I assumed they had symbolic meaning for me—after all, they were *my* dreams. It was not hard to see that he, or what he symbolized, was becoming important to me, both internally and externally. Still, there was something about this dream, its recurrence, the body sensation, the clarity, that reminded me of the dream I had shared with him in Jamaica. Would this dream similarly have meaning for Raven?

At the spiritual-sexuality workshop I put any possible embarrassment aside and sought Raven out at the conclusion of the second day. We sat alone in the room he was using for the weekend, sitting cross-legged opposite each other on his bed. It was late and it had been a long day of teaching for him. I had been touched by the caring he had shown for many people there, particularly for some of the women who were afraid and wounded from past sexual experiences.

Looking into his eyes, I spoke softly, not trusting my voice to contain the emotion I felt. "I want to thank you for today. For the way in which you honored the Sisterhood here. I have been touched and moved by the way you approached each woman with respect. It was good to see." As I spoke Raven's eyes filled with tears and he nodded, unable to speak. "And now . . . ." I straightened up and cleared my throat, passing over the emotions we were both feeling. "I want to tell you about a dream. I don't know if it has any meaning to you, but I offer it." Quickly, without embellishment, I related the dream of the woman in white and his jump into the abyss. He listened intently, nodding occasionally. When I was finished he spoke.

"The place you saw was the kiva where I did my ceremony. What you witnessed is what happened to me there." He seemed in a quandary as to how much he wanted to say. "You will have to discover for yourself why you dreamed it at this time." I wanted to know more, but as he finished, Mitch and Katharine, the workshop organizer, burst into the room talking and laughing. They were anxious to know what was being discussed, but we shifted the conversation to more mundane matters and did not speak of the dream again. I wondered if Raven knew why I had dreamed it at this time.

2

I sit at my desk, sipping tea and reading over the dreams in my journals, moving through the memories, amazed at the pieces I have forgotten. Along with my dreams, the journals contain my notes from various medicine journeys.

For several years in a row, Raven had met with apprentices in different parts of Mexico for special teaching sessions and ceremonies. The trip scheduled for the winter after the desert retreat was to the ruins in Tula. I was determined to go. The trip was supposedly by invitation only, which really meant if you wanted to go, be there. Bea had also decided to go. We received a note telling us to meet the group in a Mexico City hotel. I made my flight, child care and work schedule arrangements early in December. Nothing was going to stop me.

And nothing did, but a few things made me pause. On December 31, running downstairs to open the front door for a friend with whom I was about to celebrate New Year's Eve, I suddenly sensed what felt like a hand on the middle of my back. I catapulted straight out into the air, completely missing the last four steps, and landed on the side of my ankle. Later, X-rays showed I had broken a bone where the tendon had torn. I had to have a full leg cast, which wouldn't come off until three days before my flight to Mexico. But I was undaunted. I was going!

Two days after breaking my leg, an older woman who had joined us for ceremonial gatherings, called me. She sounded strained and cautious. "Oriah, are you and Bea still planning on going to Tula?"

"Yes, we are. Why?"

"Well, I had a strange dream last night. I don't want to be alarmist, but I do feel it's important. I . . . well . . . I wonder if it's really a good idea to go."

"Well, tell me the dream. What happened?"

She was reluctant to go into details. "It just felt like it might be dangerous . . . like it could mean . . . well, someone could die."

"What do you mean 'someone'? Do you mean me? Bea?" I asked, growing more and more impatient.

"Well, yes. I mean, you never can tell with these things, but it seemed in the dream that the place could be dangerous for you both and might result in one of you at least getting badly hurt."

We talked for a while longer, but she would not be more specific. I was unnerved. This woman had a long history of working with dreams and did not easily panic or exaggerate. On the other hand, I was determined not to miss out on this chance to learn more with Raven.

The next day, another woman who had participated in the medicine classes I taught, called me. She seemed embarrassed, uncertain if she should talk to me. She told me a friend of hers whom I had never met had had a lucid dream about Bea and I the night before. Her friend taught courses in lucid dreaming and took this kind of thing very seriously. The dream warned that Bea and I would die if we went to Tula.

I hung up the phone and sat still for a moment. What was going on? One of Carlos Castenada's books sat next to my desk. I'd been reading it the night before. Distractedly I picked it up; the page fell open and I began to read. In the story Don Juan was warning Carlos against going to Tula because it was a place where the ancient sorcerers were mesmerized by their own sorcery—a dangerous place to go! I couldn't believe it. What was happening? Was there really some risk in going to Tula? Bea and I talked it over, but our resolve was unshaken. With an updated version of my will in safe hands and a cane in my own, I limped onto the plane with Bea and headed for Mexico.

Often on these trips Bea and I roomed together. On this trip we had made different arrangements. I was going to stay with Mitch and she with Bill, a friend and lover from Virginia. It was a choice we later regretted more than once. We arrived in Mexico City early in the evening and were told there was a meeting in Raven's hotel room at nine o'clock. When we arrived at his room it was packed. It seems the rumor mill on this particular trip had been working overtime and seventy people had showed up to see what would happen. People filled the room, sitting on beds, chairs, bureaus and even in the bathroom. I managed to get on one of the beds so I could elevate my now-aching leg. Mitch sat next to me.

No sooner had we sat down than Gunner slid over to me and, sitting very close, began to talk. Originally from Europe, Gunner was an attractive man in his early forties with a reputation for having a different lover on each medicine journey. I had first met him in Northern Ontario and while I had been impressed with his ability during the healing ceremony and Purification Lodge, I had been mystified by his general attitude and demeanor. A quiet man, Gunner appeared only minimally interested in the complex teachings Raven enjoyed so much. He did, however, spend all of his time traveling with Raven or teaching the medicine on his own. Raven had named him as his successor in the group and he held a position of considerable prestige and power, but except for the regular seeking out of sexual partners, he generally removed himself from the group and socialized with very few people.

He spoke in a low tone. "And how are you doing, pretty lady? It's good to see you. I'm going to a much warmer spot in Mexico once this week is over and everyone else has gone home. I know a place that's very beautiful, near the jungle, with incredible waterfalls and nice hotels. I would like very much to have you come along and have some fun with me. What do you say?"

I couldn't say much. I was speechless. Not only was his proposition unexpected, it had been heard by the ten or more people sitting around us, all of whom, except Mitch, looked amused. Discretion was not Gunner's greatest gift. I finally found my voice and told him that it sounded very nice, but I had to get home to my job and my kids, which was the truth. Looking disappointed, Gunner asked me if I could find any way to stay just as Raven called for quiet.

He told us he had arranged a special training session for us—stalking the apprentices of another sorcerer who were going to be in and around Tula. These apprentices had trained longer than any of us and could, according to Raven, shapeshift. This meant they could take on forms of different people at will. We were given their names and descriptions of their various personalities. It was unclear why we were going to stalk these people. I assumed that it was to develop and test our dreaming and stalking abilities—a kind of junior Olympics for neophyte sorcerers.

The next morning we all piled on a bus and headed for Tula. It's a small town, not used to a lot of gringo tourists, but the ruins do get a few visitors, primarily Mexicans. Overnight our group filled virtually all the hotel rooms.

It was cold, windy and dusty. For a week we all wandered the streets and ruins, alone and in groups, gazing into the eyes of unsuspecting Mexicans. Although other things may change with shapeshifters, the quality and color of their eyes are supposed to remain the same, and therefore provide identification. Raven's information on the apprentices we were seeking had included detailed eye descriptions. If you are a blond, blue-eyed female sitting alone in a Mexican town square, gazing into the eyes of Mexican men, you can attract a lot of unwanted attention. I was not having a good time.

I was not at all sure if there were any sorcerer's apprentices to find, and if there were, I felt pretty certain they would find it easy to avoid large noisy groups of Americans running all over town. All subtlety was lost in the competitive bid to be the first to "make a hit," as Raven called it. Sitting at lunch one day with five other members of the group, in a small restaurant off the town square, two of the men seated across from me vaulted over the table and sprinted out the door. Turning around in my chair, I watched them run toward a woman with red hair walking through the square. One of the apprentices we were looking for was supposedly a tall woman with red hair—a rarity in Mexico. My lunch companions returned a few minutes later looking disappointed. The poor unsuspecting woman was not one of the people we sought. If I were the redheaded shapeshifting apprentice, I would certainly consider paying a few Mexican women to rinse their hair with red dye just to watch the commotion.

Sharing a room with Mitch turned out to be less fun than roaming the dust-filled streets. We had agreed to share a room all week, an arrangement that immediately sent him into claustrophobic withdrawal, fearing it would be seen as making a "commitment." More than once I was tempted to see what space was available with the ever-friendly Gunner.

Periodically I would go out to the ruins and sit. I always feel my imagination inspired when I visit ancient ruins. As I sat on top of the highest pyramid, leaning against the tall, rectangular figures carved in stone, said to be Atlanteans, I couldn't help but wonder about what it had been like when it was built. Not the grand ceremonial activities, but the mundane details. What kinds of shoes did the feet that climbed this pyramid wear? Who cleaned the chambers below the temple? Probably a woman. Did she bring her children? Did the children behave? Were they allowed to run and play among the pyramids? Was she tired as she swept? Happy? In love? Plagued by troubles at home? What did she feel? What were her dreams? Who were her lovers? What was her relationship with the priests and priestesses of the temple? Did they treat her as an invisible underling? Did she watch them, admire them, fear them?

It was early one morning during one of these mental meanderings that a man approached me as I sat at the top of the pyramid. Ever on my guard, and fed up with trying to get rid of Mexican men, I watched him approach out of the corner of my eye. I relaxed a little as I recognized him. He was employed by the Mexican government and was at the ruins each day to answer tourists' questions. He was a friendly, quiet man whose English was much better than my Spanish. Some of the other apprentices had gotten to know him, and he'd joined us for dinner and gatherings in the evenings. He squatted in front of me and looked intently into my eyes for a few moments.

"I have seen you sitting here often by yourself," he said. I nodded. "You are a beautiful woman who seems to have a lot of fun with your friends here."

"Here we go again," I thought jadedly, "another come-on."

"But you have a great sadness like no other behind your eyes. Is your life unhappy?" he continued softly.

I felt as if I had been hit in the stomach. I could not breathe. There was something in his manner that made my abrupt denials irrelevant. Whatever he had seen and touched with his words rose inside me and threatened to spill over in tears. Standing up, I ran down the steep stairs of the pyramid as fast as I could with my cane and bandaged ankle. I was overwhelmed with a sense of deep sadness, of grieving for things lost, of having longed for something all my life. It was the same feeling I'd had at the desert retreat when Joseph worked on my injured back and listened to the stories about my grandfather. I fled the place, the Mexican man's observant gaze and the feelings it evoked.

I walked around the ruins fighting back tears and finally sat down in a deserted corner, letting the noonday sun warm me. I felt exhausted. I did not want to go back to the hotel, wander the streets of the town nor encounter the Mexican man on the pyramids again. I sat for a long time soaking up the sun, leaning against the ancient crumbling wall.

Feeling stronger and wanting to fully enjoy this first day of sunny weather, I decided to return to the pyramid. The Mexican guide was no longer around and I climbed to the top. I was greeted by the voices of several people I knew from Raven's group. They sat together talking and laughing, apparently at the expense of one member of the group, Gerry. A soft-spoken Italian man now living in California, Gerry had arrived at the ruins late that morning. Wandering around the entrance, ever on the alert for sorcerer's apprentices, he happened to look in the guest book that visitors to the ruins were asked to sign. There, dated that same day was the signature "Manuel D'Or," the name of one of the apprentices we were seeking. Gerry was ecstatic. He went racing into the ruins, examining every innocent tourist and announcing to everyone from Raven's group, "He's here! He's here! Manuel D'Or came to the ruins this morning!" Somehow he never wondered about the likelihood of a sorcerer's advanced apprentice declaring his presence by putting his name in the guest book. In fact, one of Raven's apprentices, bored and looking for a little amusement, had left the signature. Finally, unable to watch Gerry continue his excited search through the ruins any longer, one of the women in the group told him the truth. The whole group, including an embarrassed Gerry, was sitting on the pyramids enjoying the joke and the sun.

I waved hello and, wanting to be alone, sat slightly apart, at one of the corners of the flat surface at the top of the pyramid. There were a few tourists coming and going; climbing the steep stairs to have their pictures taken with one of the Atlanteans. The breeze was light and the sun continued to shine in an almost cloudless sky. The stone beneath me began to feel warm and I relaxed, enjoying just watching the people. At times there were a dozen people wandering about the top of the pyramid. At other times I was alone.

The shadows of the Atlanteans grew longer. There were very few people still around. As I sat alone, an old Mexican woman came up the steps with a young man about twenty years old. They did not look around at the view or gaze at the Atlanteans the way the other tourists did, but went straight to the corner opposite where I sat and, kneeling down on the stones, began to empty a leather bag the young man carried. The woman spoke in low tones. My Spanish was not good enough to understand what she was saying, but she was clearly giving him some kind of instructions. The young man listened intently and did not speak, nodding occasionally to indicate he understood.

Standing up, he took off his T-shirt, revealing a muscular brown torso. He had straight, short black hair and wore faded blue jeans. He removed his boots and stood barefoot on the stones. The woman, who I assumed was his mother, tied a leather strap around his forehead and a band around each upper arm. Beautiful green-and-blue macaw feathers hung from the arm bands. He picked up a large conch shell and several other items I could not identify, all of which had been taken from the bag, and began to walk around the top of the pyramid. He circled the perimeter once, passing close by me, and continued walking. On the second turn he paused and stood in each of the four directions. Saying something in Spanish, he put a small horn to his lips and blew. The thin high note rang out four times in each direction. Sitting in the sun watching him, I felt a sense of timelessness and wondered how many young men had come to this place over aeons of time to perform and learn ceremony. I felt honored to be witness to this clear reminder that the ancient ways were still alive among the Mexican people.

As the young man finished his tribute to the four directions, several of Raven's apprentices bounded up the pyramid stairs. Marsha, her husband Robert, and Hank, a friend of theirs from Texas, had obviously seen the ceremony and come to investigate. They watched from a distance as the young man returned to where his mother sat and began to speak with her in hushed tones as he removed his head and arm bands. Marsha, Tim and Hank were beside themselves with excitement, and after waiting a moment, they approached the woman and her son.

Raven had given us clear instructions. If we thought we had found one of the shapeshifting apprentices, we were to have a "medicine talk" with him or her. A medicine talk, as far as I could figure, was a conversation filled with double entendres. To the untrained ear it would appear to be an exchange of small talk about the weather, where you're from, where you're headed, etc. But there would also have another level of meaning full of symbolism apparent only to the two people involved. It sounded complicated and not unlike many of my interactions, particularly with the opposite gender. If we felt we were engaged in a medicine talk with someone we suspected was one of the apprentices we were seeking, we were to try to get information from them without giving any. When we felt sure this was our quarry, we were to confront them by asking if their name was that of the person we sought. If asked directly, they would have to respond honestly. Finding and identifying them would be an act of "counting coup" and would entitle us to receive a one-on-one medicine teaching from the apprentice "across the pipe." In this and other Native teachings speaking "across the pipe" means one must speak from the heart, taking great care to say what is one's truth. If no actual pipe is present, the intent is represented by a specific hand signal. We were to make this signal to the apprentice we found and wait until he or she repeated the sign.

I had carefully written down all of Raven's instructions. When the young man and his mother had initially appeared on the pyramid, I had wondered if either could be one of the people we were looking for, but as they proceeded to do what was obviously a ceremony, I'd dismissed the thought. Surely those we were seeking would not come marching up in front of me to do a ceremony. Neither the young man nor the old woman fit any of our descriptions. Now, watching Marsha, Robert and Hank approach them, I wondered if I had dismissed the possibility too readily.

Had I missed my big chance to be the one who found an apprentice? I watched.

Hank spoke a little Spanish. Combining this with hand gestures, the three began to speak to the woman and her son. I felt uncomfortable and very embarrassed watching these three gringos pursuing the two Mexicans. There was nothing subtle in this approach, nothing resembling a "medicine talk." The woman and her son were friendly, but they clearly knew nothing about the mission these people were on. I moved to the other side of the pyramid, watching from a distance. I couldn't hear what was being said, but Hank and Robert repeatedly made the hand gesture indicating "across the pipe" to the young man. He looked bewildered and finally raised his hand to his heart. Marsha had continued to try to communicate with the woman and the two of them were nodding and smiling together.

Suddenly I felt very tired. What was I doing here? What were we all doing here? Were there really any apprentices to find? Without saying anything to the others, I descended the pyramid stairs and headed back to the hotel, feeling discouraged. I showered and changed and wandered out into the hotel courtyard to see who was around. Passing Raven's room, I noticed the door was open. He was seated at a small desk writing, and several of the women in the group were sitting on the bed examining some purchases they'd made that morning. They called to me to come in. I went in, sat on the bed and looked at what they had bought— some pottery and jewelry. The women chatted about the Mexicans they had bought the items from, a young man and his family who had a private collection of artifacts. As I listened I moved over and sat in the chair about three feet in front of Raven's desk. Raven continued to write, occasionally glancing up and adding his comments to the discussion.

Gunner came in and joined us. He smiled warmly at me and, leaning over, gave my shoulders a squeeze. Bending close to my ear, he spoke in a loud stage whisper, one eye on Raven. "You are looking especially lovely." Raven looked up at him.

I smiled nervously and said, "Thank you," my face flushing. Something did not feel right. The comment was intended as much for Raven as myself. I wanted to get up and walk out. I wanted to say, "Don't do that! Whatever is going on between the two of you, don't use me, leave me out of it." But I said nothing, distrusting my own perceptions and certain that both men would tell me I was crazy, imagining things, if I said anything. It was not the first time or the last that I did not trust my own knowing.

Suddenly Marsha and Robert burst into the room, looking as if they had run all the way from the ruins. Breathlessly they began to tell Raven about the man and woman at the pyramid. They described the young man's clothing, his ceremony and his response to their words and gestures. According to Marsha, the woman was indeed the young man's mother; she was teaching him ceremony, and he was apparently apprenticed to someone who lived not far away. She had given Marsha her name and the name of a small restaurant she owned in Mexico City, inviting the whole group for a special dinner and ceremonial dance upon our return. "So, is this it?" Marsha asked Raven. "Have we found one? Is it a hit?"

Everyone in the room waited as Raven sat, head down, gazing at his hands on the desk. After a moment he nodded and spoke. "Yup, yup, it's a hit all right. If it's not actually one of them—it's one of their apprentices. That's it. You've made our first hit."

Marsha and Robert were ecstatic. I was dazed. All this seemed very nice and, while it was an honor, as visitors to their land, to meet and be welcomed by people involved in similar spiritual practices, the fact that we had met them didn't make them the apprentices we sought. No medicine talk had taken place. They did not respond to the questions or gestures by identifying themselves and they did not match any of the descriptions. That was it? That was a "hit"? I doubted if they were in any way connected to the apprentices we were looking for, but if they were they certainly didn't know anything about the game we were playing. They had wandered unsuspectingly into our midst and found themselves to be the prize we were searching for. This was counting coup?

Confused, I left the room and stood on the balcony overlooking the motel courtyard. Gunner followed me out and asked if I was going to dinner.

"Yes, I guess so. Maybe we could go together and talk."

He agreed and we headed off to a local restaurant. I waited until we had ordered.

"Gunner, you were in the room just now. What did you think?" I asked, trying to be tactful. I did not want to put him in the awkward position of contradicting his own teacher.

"Not much," he responded.

"Well, I mean . . . do you think it was, as Raven calls it, a hit? Do you think those people were part of the group we're looking for?"

He looked at me ruefully. "I think," he said with an edge of thinly veiled disgust, "that a couple of people's self-importance has finally gotten away with them."

I wanted to ask him why he thought Raven had pronounced it a hit, but his manner did not invite more discussion of the matter. We ate our dinner and talked about our experiences dreaming. Raven had called a meeting for that evening in a room above one of the other local restaurants, so we set out shortly after we finished the meal.

The meeting room was crowded and smoky, with everyone gathered around a long table. Mitch had already arrived and I joined him at the end of the table. We had not spent much time together, as Mitch made it painfully obvious he preferred the company of the people from the Arizona community of which he was now a part. He did not want our relationship to diminish his status as "unattached" and available. I did not know many of the people there, and with Bea spending most of her time with Bill, I spent most of mine alone. I felt disappointed with Mitch's coolness and distance but was unwilling to pursue him.

Raven arrived late and I realized this was the first time since our arrival in Mexico that I had seen him outside his hotel room. Although we had done a group ceremony at the ruins earlier in the week, Raven had not been present. Susan had led the ceremony. The never-ending rumors held that Raven was devastated because Jamie, his senior female apprentice, had gone to work with someone else—Lorne Fire Dog, a man who had declared himself a shaman and Raven's enemy. The group had said special prayers for her during the ceremony, expressing concern for her safety, certain that the man she was with worked on the "dark side." I was unclear what this meant and reluctant to ask questions. An air of secrecy and fear surrounded the subject. Although I had never gotten to know Jamie at the apprentice gatherings we'd been at together, I hoped she was alright.

Whatever the reason, Raven looked worn and discouraged as he entered the meeting room. As everyone quieted down he stood to make an announcement. "Well, everyone, we did it. Today we had a hit!" Most of the people in the room had not heard about the young man on the pyramid. They clapped and cheered. After four days of roaming the streets and ruins, they were surprised and encouraged to hear that someone in the group had been successful. Raven turned the meeting over to Marsha and asked her to tell the story.

As she began to speak, I again heard the droning sound I had experienced in the dream when the woman told me, "Now is the time when all things are rent." I could hardly hear Marsha or the comments Raven added. I felt flushed and nausea swept over me. The room was warm and full of smoke. I needed some air.

I couldn't understand it. I was willing to take Raven's word that the apprentices we were looking for were in Tula. I was even willing to concede that we might not be good enough in either our dreaming or our stalking to find them. If we weren't good enough, we weren't good enough. We'd just have to learn more, work harder. I was willing to say we'd failed. I was not willing to say we'd succeeded when we hadn't.

Raven spoke again after Marsha finished, encouraging everyone to work together, get organized, pay attention and get out there and find the other apprentices. I barely heard him. My chest and throat ached. Raven then launched into giving a teaching on personality types based on Carlos Castenada's account of Don Juan's teachings. According to these teachings everyone has a basic personality type, or mask they wear: Space Cadet, Do-gooder or Fart. In addition everyone has a mood they present to the world—a projecting mood—and one that comes out if they are pushed—an anchoring mood. These are any two of Cunning, Ruthlessness, Sweetness or Patience. Raven asked everyone to say what they thought they were and then he told them what they were by shamanically "seeing" a spot on their energy body.

I couldn't think straight. Slowly my breathing and hearing had returned to normal, but my head felt full of cotton batting. I had no idea what "type" I was. When my turn came I stood up and faced Raven.

"Well," he said, "what do you think you are?"

"I have no idea." I felt so off balance I was unwilling to even guess. Raven gazed at me intently.

"You're a Cunning Do-gooder who projects through Sweetness."

"Sweetness!" Mitch snorted from his seat beside me. "You must be kidding. I've never seen any of it." I felt my face flush with embarrassment. I sat down.

"Yes, sweetness," Raven repeated, looking directly at Mitch with disdain. "Next." The process continued.

I was surprised. The do-gooder mask I would have guessed if I had thought about it long enough. I was often trying to please, to help. Cunning as an anchoring mood also made sense. I did rely on my mental facility to work my way out of or around situations, especially if I felt pushed. But I never would have guessed sweetness. I initially came across as sweet?

Raven completed the discussion of personality types and returned to developing a plan for finding and counting coup on the other sorcerer's apprentices. He had decided to organize us into small groups of five and began to assign people to their groups. As he designated people, those of us remaining put up our hands to indicate we still needed a group. He repeatedly put individuals who were rooming together and in relationship in the same small group. When he came to Mitch and I he placed us in different groups. Part of me was relieved, given Mitch's ongoing ambivalence and hostility. Another part of me was confused. Why would Raven deliberately split us up? It was not the first time this had happened. He knew we had been in a relationship for the past year. He and I had discussed my relationship with Mitch and yet he seemed unwilling to acknowledge its existence in a collective situation. Was he trying to tell me something? I felt like a little girl. I wanted him to acknowledge me as an adult woman in a relationship with a man.

As Raven concluded I looked around the room. People were congratulating Robert and Marsha on finding an apprentice. I felt sick as I watched. I needed to get out. I wanted to beat the crowd and headed for the door, arriving at the top of the stairs just as Raven did. We stood opposite each other for a few moments, silent, looking at each other. Suddenly I felt all the sadness touched by the Mexican tour guide well up inside me. Raven's blue eyes held mine and everything else—the laughing, talking men and women moving around the smoke-filled room, the scraping of chairs on the linoleum, the guitar music filtering up the stairs from the restaurant below—faded into the background. It was as if we had momentarily stepped out of time and space. As we stood there I knew all of my emotions—the sadness, the confusion, the longing, the disappointment, the questions—were there, naked in my own eyes, and I knew he saw them. And as I looked into his eyes I saw what I had not expected to see: a mirror of the same overwhelming sadness and longing. I turned and escaped into the darkness of the cool night air.

3

The time in Tula had not allowed for individual ceremony. Raven worked within a system of "gateways"—a series of individual and group ceremonies that marked a progression of learning and apprenticeship. There were fifteen gateways in all and twenty-two levels within these gateways. Each gateway ceremony was progressively longer and more complex. I had completed all the ceremonies in the first gateway and most of those in the second.

I wanted to do more, to learn faster, but the demands of life as a single working mother did not mesh well with constant trips and time alone. Of the hundreds of apprentices I had met only a handful had children. Even fewer had small children who lived with them. More than once, as I tried to figure out how to get time off and the money to cover the cost of traveling to do another gateway ceremony, I wondered if I should even be attempting to walk this path with my particular resources and responsibilities. I enjoyed my job, but the small social service agency I worked for depended on private donations and government grants, and paid its workers well below the general rate for social workers. I financed my trips with the evening classes I taught on the medicine work.

Late at night, after a full day at work, picking the kids up from day care, putting them to bed, making dinner and lunches for the next day, throwing in a load of laundry and cleaning up the house, I reached down within myself to find the energy to study, call students who were seeking assistance, or plan and lead one of the classes or ceremonies that were held in my home two or three times a week. The trips were exhilarating and full, but I returned tired, with my money and time off depleted and my children needing extra attention and energy. I wondered if people with children were supposed to be doing this work at all.

Before leaving Tula, Raven and I had met briefly in his hotel room. He'd urged me to get through my gateway ceremonies at a quicker pace. I wanted to do as he asked, but was already feeling stretched to the limit. I also wondered at the wisdom of doing these life-changing ceremonies in rapid succession. Would this give me sufficient time to understand and integrate their meaning into my life?

I returned from Tula weary, confused and somewhat discouraged. The group had not found any apprentices except for the young man on the pyramid. I realized I needed to end my relationship with Mitch and told him so shortly after returning to Toronto. I had grown weary of his ambivalence about being in a relationship and his subsequent come-here-go-away behavior. It had not been fun. I plunged back into working, studying, teaching and building a community of people interested in medicine work.

About a month later I received a notice from Raven about a gathering in Arizona for all apprentices, planned for early September. The group was going to meet and do individual and group ceremony on the Navaho reservation. I hesitated. I wanted to continue to learn but felt I needed to be more deliberate and conscious about my use of resources. I prayed for a sign to show me if this was a trip I should make for my own learning.

Early June arrived and I still hadn't decided if I would go. I sat down to figure out the costs, and the decision seemed clear. I simply did not have the money to pay for the airplane ticket. Sitting on my couch, budget in hand, I spoke out loud. "Well, Great Mystery, here it is. If I'm supposed to go on this trip, someone is going to have to materialize an airplane ticket, because I don't have the cash to buy one." No sooner were the words out of my mouth than I heard the mail being pushed through my door slot by the postman. I went and picked it up and there among the bills was a letter from American Airlines informing me that I had accumulated sufficient mileage to receive one free round-trip ticket anywhere in the United States or Canada. I could hardly believe it!

Raven had told us many times that if we asked for a sign and got one, we should take it and not quibble. But I was in a particularly skeptical mood. Sure, the means to go had been provided and that was pretty impressive, but it did not indicate that I should necessarily use the ticket to go on this trip to the American Southwest. I continued to pray for a sign. That weekend I went alone to my trailer, a small, ancient, no-longer-mobile unit with a wood stove and propane lights, set on a remote lakefront campsite that I leased. It was several hours north of the city and provided an inexpensive retreat for myself and my children. All weekend I asked and watched for any indication from spirit that I should go on this trip. I was sure the undisturbed natural setting would provide the perfect opportunity for receiving a medicine sign.

Nothing happened that I could interpret as a sign. On Sunday I loaded my car and, standing at the door to my trailer, sent out one final prayer. "Well, this is it. I ask for a clear, easily understood medicine sign if I am to go to Arizona on this medicine journey." I got in my car and started down the narrow dirt road. About halfway out to the main highway I saw a bird on the ground at the left-hand side of the road. At first I thought it was a partridge, which are plentiful in the area and often walk across the road like chickens in their own barnyard. But as I drove forward slowly I could see it was much larger that a partridge. It was a red hawk. I had seen hawks before, flying overhead or sitting in trees. But I had never seen one on the ground. I expected her to fly off long before I got close to her. The red hawk is considered the messenger from our higher self and its presence is often seen as heralding change. I drove closer and the bird did not move. She sat watching the approaching vehicle, and seemed to be waiting for me. Keeping my speed steady, I drove up beside her. Only then did she spread her wings and rise effortlessly into the air not more than a foot from my window. Keeping pace with the car, the magnificent bird flew beside me at eye level, barely moving her wings to maintain her position. I was close enough to touch her and I could see every detail: the powerful wings, beautiful red-brown feathers, curved beak and gleaming eyes. I kept my speed constant, and to my amazement, she continued to fly next to me for several minutes. Then, with an effortless surge of energy, she moved slightly ahead of me, turned sharply and flew diagonally across the hood of the car, up into the sky through the trees. I stopped the car and watched her go, sending a prayer of thanks to the spirit of the hawk for her presence as she flew toward the southwest. The Southwest! I was going!

This time I went alone. My flight took me in three phases to a small airport in Arizona. The last leg of the journey was in a small twenty-seat plane. There was a lot of turbulence and I arrived feeling a bit airsick and fatigued from twelve hours of travel. Loading my camping supplies into my rented car, I found a grocery store and bought food and bottled water for the week. By the time I headed out of town on the highway it was getting dark. I hoped I could find the motel where we were supposed to meet. It was a three-hour drive across the desert and I stopped repeatedly to check my map. I knew Raven and the group would be leaving in the morning to go to the ceremonial site and I did not want to lose my way, miss the group and spend the week roaming around Arizona trying to find them.

The road was a ribbon of asphalt running straight across the flat open desert, a landscape of sand, stone and scrub brush. There were few cars but many signs warning motorists to watch out for cattle, which apparently ranged freely in the area. Normally I'm relaxed when driving, but the ever-present signs, and the knowledge that I was very tired, made me hunch forward in my seat, peering intently though the darkness for cattle and driving slower than I wanted. I did not think hitting a cow would endear me to the local farmers or the car rental company, much less be a good way to begin my week. I wondered about the medicine of the cow and what significance hitting one might have.

The clock in the car said ten minutes to ten as I finally rolled up beside the motel that Raven's letter had designated as the meeting place. There were a lot of cars parked in front of the rooms, but the office lights were out. I knocked. The sign said they closed at ten o'clock. Finally a light went on and a very sleepy, disgruntled-looking man came to the door. I told him I wanted a room. He informed me that they closed at ten. When I told him it was not yet ten o'clock, he just looked at me with disgust and motioned me inside. I registered and paid for the night, angry at his attitude but too fatigued to fight. As I left with my room key, he spoke. "On the reservation it is eleven o'clock. We do not change our clocks to suit the business world here. We follow the natural rhythm of Mother Earth." He closed the door before I could respond.

Feeling I had once again revealed my ignorance of the lives of the people whose traditions and knowledge I was attempting to learn, I walked to my room. I recognized Raven's camper outside one room and, knocking, was told we would meet the following day at a local campground. "Get some sleep and be there on time," Raven called out as the door closed. I went back to my room and crawled into bed.

The alarm woke me too soon. I struggled out of bed to have my last shower for days and headed out, with just enough time to fill the car with gas, eat some breakfast and drive to the meeting place. There were only five apprentices there as I arrived, five minutes early. Over the next two hours more and more apprentices wandered into the area, pulling out folding chairs and catching up on news. The majority, including Mitch, who was still living in Arizona, were from Raven's home lodge. There were about thirty of us altogether.

Finally Raven drove up in his camper and sat down in a chair. "Well, this is what we're going to do. We're going to drive out on the reservation to some land where I know some folks. They are the friends and family of Many Shields, the Navaho man who was my teacher. They know we're coming and we'll spend some time with them. My teacher, Grandfather, had eight daughters. They're now all grandmothers. Seven of them, and many members of their families, will be there. We're going to honor them by taking a feast out for them. For the rest of the week I will do some teaching, and I want each of you to do as much personal ceremony as you are able, to get through the gateways. This is a very powerful place and the spot where I did a lot of ceremony. Questions?"

Chris, an outspoken, earnest woman I had met before, put up her hand. "Raven, I'm wondering what guidance we should have about interfacing with these people." I stifled a groan. People using words like "interface" are one of what Raven would have called my "closed symbols"—something I have a knee-jerk negative response to. Raven began to answer her, stating the obvious guidelines for guests anywhere: be polite and courteous; don't make a nuisance of yourself, etc. I wanted to add my guess that not using words like "interface" would probably help.

We got in our cars and formed a long caravan behind Raven, who led the way out to the highway and then down a dirt road into the hills. We drove for about an hour until we came to a small cluster of buildings— two houses and a hogan, the Navaho ceremonial meeting place. Raven got out of his truck and motioned for us to drive around, forming a large circle with our cars, marking the perimeter of our camp. As I drove around I remembered all those old childhood movies where the settlers circled the wagons to seek protect themselves from the "hostile Indians."

The Navaho family was anything but hostile. They came out as a group—elders, children, men and women—to greet us. Many had come from other places on the reservation to welcome us and, no doubt, to satisfy their curiosity about these strange white men and women who wanted to learn their medicine ways. There were very few men in the group of thirty to forty Navaho. Many of the men had been forced to leave the reservation and seek work in the cities, trying to send money home and coming back for visits when they were able.

The "feast" we brought was from the local fried chicken franchise; in my mind a contradiction in terms. We created a camp complete with portable toilets under makeshift blanket tipis for privacy, conspicuously set out on the endless flat desert. A particularly large and poisonous black spider had been seen in the one available outhouse on the property. We decided to respect the sacred spider medicine and create our own facilities.

Navaho and apprentices gathered in the hogan to share chicken, chanting and drumming well into the night. Several of the grandmothers spoke, welcoming us to their home and thanking us for honoring them with the visit. Raven in turn expressed our gratitude for their hospitality.

We met the next morning in the hogan. Raven began teaching in preparation for a group ceremony to be held the following night. The teachings focused on lucid dreaming and something he called the Night Warrior army. He had talked of it before: a group of dreamers, of which Raven is the leader, who work in the fifth or dream dimension to battle the dark side, which has its own army. Since everything that happens in the third or material dimension has already been dreamed of in the fifth dimension, the hope is that defeating the dark in the fifth will forestall its manifestation—wars, poverty, murder—in the third. The purpose in bringing us together in the third dimension was to build our skills and relationships so we could be more effective and lucid in the fifth dimension.

I wasn't sure how I felt about all of this. On one level it appealed to me. When I began studying the medicine I'd wondered what use I could make of my skill in lucid dreaming, beyond personal entertainment and self-understanding. The stated purpose of the Night Warrior army appealed to my desire for, and history of, working for social justice. I had no problem sensing the "darkness" of war, poverty, ignorance and violence in the world, and I was fascinated with the idea that we could do something about this before it took place. My participation in political movements, trying to bring about change once things had happened, had always felt like too little, too late. But my struggle came with the model of an army, with its attendant images of violence. Raven and Susan had described their Night Warrior mantles, the costumes they wore in these nocturnal battles. Both included fierce masks and weaponry.

I had had limited but frightening experience with the night battles Raven described. About two months before I'd found myself in the middle of a lucid dream. I was standing on a desert with a group of Raven's apprentices. I knew I was dreaming and was surprised—this was the first time I had "woken up" outside my own home in a dream. The group of about twenty was discussing an upcoming battle against another group, apparently nearby. Two male apprentices I knew were in charge of the group and they told us to follow them.

As we came over a small rise we saw the other group. About ten tall, brown-skinned men, all with long spears, gazed at us openly. I was confused—I was sure these men posed no threat to us and felt someone had made a mistake. We were in the wrong time or the wrong place. Before

I could say anything the apprentices in charge ordered us to attack. I held back and watched in horror as the apprentices were struck down one at a time, in spite of their superior numbers. I wanted to leave, but watched mesmerized and confused as the battle continued. Suddenly I caught a movement out of the corner of my eye and, turning, saw a woman, an apprentice I knew coming up behind me. I felt frightened. Why? True, we were not friends, but we were on the same side, weren't we? Even as the thought took shape I saw her raise her hand. Something flew from her fingers and struck me in the middle of the back. Pain seared through me, up to the back of my head and down to the base of my spine.

I woke up in a cold sweat. It was 3:15 A.M. The pain wouldn't go away and I cried out in agony. My whole body felt aflame. Moving slowly and painfully, I found the thermometer in the bathroom. My temperature was 104.5 degrees. I lay immobile in my bed for the rest of the night, trying not to cry, trying to subdue the pain by relaxing my body. If I was in the Night Warrior army I wanted out! Why hadn't I trusted my gut feeling and left the minute I knew something was wrong? At dawn I called a friend and fellow apprentice, Morgan, who lived close by. He came over, gave my sons breakfast and sent them off to school. While he bathed my aching head with cool cloths we discussed what we should do. I could hardly move. Morgan went home and returned with his medicine items. My sons were to stay at their father's house that night so we were alone. In the hours that followed my condition did not improve and finally, later in the day, Morgan used sucking medicine, a shamanic technique for removing medicine arrows or other foreign objects of the spirit realm from the body. After he finished I fell into a deep and dreamless sleep. Later I awoke, it was still dark. My fever had broken, my face felt cool and the pain in my back had been reduced to the dull ache of a bruise. I looked at the clock. It was exactly 3:15 A.M.

The whole incident had unnerved me. Yes, I wanted to work with other dreamers to create a better world, but I did not want to get hurt. Next time would I have the courage to follow my own intuition so I wouldn't get injured?

A month before the trip to Arizona I'd had another lucid dream. I stood in my home before the full-length mirror in the upstairs hallway. I was wearing a beautiful dress made of luminous blue-white fabric. It fitted my upper body perfectly and hung full from my hips to the floor. On both arms were gold bracelets in the shape of cobras, winding from wrist to elbow. I wore a white headpiece that fitted over my head and down around my neck and upper chest. It had a gold cobra at the forehead, over my third eye. My boots were of soft white leather. But most impressive was the gold belt that encircled my waist. I studied the intricate, embossed pattern intently. As I stood gazing into the mirror, I heard the voice of Grandfather say, "This is your Night Warrior mantle." I turned, and as I moved the skirt glowed with a shimmering light. I was surprised at the costume, it seemed far less battle-ready or fierce than either Raven's or Susan's. As soon as I awoke I drew it in detail.

As we sat in the Navaho hogan listening to Raven, I felt my desire to participate rekindled by his stories of the Night Warriors. He told us to ask repeatedly during the ceremonies of the week for a sign about which direction on the medicine wheel we were to hold as part of this Night Warrior army. As we took a break for the evening meal, Raven asked to speak to those of us who were going to do a gateway ceremony while we were there. Anxious to take advantage of this chance to advance in my gateway work, I went to see him. Although there were two shorter ceremonies I still needed to complete, he urged me to do a three-day solo ceremony. I could do the shorter ones at home with less monitoring. I agreed and Raven assigned Gwen, an apprentice who had done the ceremony, to teach and monitor two other women and myself.

I liked Gwen, although I had never seen her at any other gatherings. She was about fifty years old and seemed very at home with herself. She sat with us as the night fell and went over the ceremony. The two other women were both in their sixties and relatively new to the medicine path. I felt good in the company of these older women.

We were to go out at dawn the following morning and spend three days and two nights on the desert. By the time we returned at dusk of the third day, people would be preparing to leave the reservation the following morning. Although I would miss what happened at the main camp, I wanted to do the ceremony. I felt a longing to seek some confirmation and guidance as to the direction my life was taking. The ceremony had a specific purpose. We were to call upon the four enemies of the warrior— Fear, Death and Old Age, Clarity and Power—and then capture them in calcite crystals to make them our allies. We were allowed to take one quart of water, a bed roll and a blanket, but no food.

In the morning we sat with Gwen as she did a pipe ceremony to monitor us in our time alone. She gave each of us a small personal medicine item that belonged to her, to enhance her ability to stay connected with each of us. Then, picking up our packs, we set out together, walking along a dry riverbed gully. We were warned not to stay in the gully for fear of flash floods. While it might not rain where we were, it could rain up in the hills, high above the mesa. If that happened a wall of water would rush down the gullies, sweeping everything in its path. The evidence was all around: debris of every description, including an old refrigerator embedded in the silt left behind by the torrent of water.

One by one the other women moved off in different directions to seek their ceremonial places and Gwen finally turned back toward camp, leaving me alone. I continued to follow the riverbed for another half hour. I was not feeling well, that morning I had woken up with a headache and the beginning of my moon cycle, even though it was not due for more than a week. I grumbled to myself as I walked along. We had been warned about the number of rattlesnakes in the area and told to look out for a "snake stick," a stick whose shape and energy holds the power of, and offers protection from, snakes. We had also been warned about the roaming coyotes and cougars descending from nearby cliffs. Armed with tampons and ziplock bags, I was anxious not to draw any animals to me with the smell of my blood.

I finally climbed the river embankment and surveyed the area. In every direction, as far as the eye could see, the terrain stretched flat and sandy, covered with cacti and scrub brush. It was a wonder to me that anything could grow out here. Far to the east, where the mesa I was standing on dropped away to a lower plateau, the sky and ground met in a clean straight line. Far to the south there were tall, red-brown sand cliffs. The most overwhelming thing was the blue, cloudless sky. There was so much of it. To someone used to living in the Canadian Shield, where every horizon is closed in by trees, rocks and hills, it seemed immense and endless. I pulled my hat down farther to shade my face and began to walk south.

Suddenly, out of the corner of my eye, I saw something poised above the ground. I froze, not wanting to provoke what I was sure was a rattlesnake about to strike. Nothing moved. I waited. Cautiously, sweat beading on my forehead, I turned. There, about three feet to my left, was a piece of sun-bleached driftwood, arched in the perfect shape of a snake poised to strike. I let out the breath I hadn't known I was holding and sat down weak-kneed, laughing at myself. It was a snake stick! Carefully I picked it up and said a prayer of thanks for the gift. Leaving a bit of tobacco, I set out once again to find a place to build my medicine wheel.

It was hard to choose. One spot was just like another: flat, hard, dry, sand, with lots of little cacti and bushes. Carrying my snake stick, I wandered around, trying to find the place that "felt right." I began to feel irritated. I needed to sit down and rest. How could I find my "spot" in a place like this? I remembered reading about Carlos Castenada trying to find his "power spot." It took him all night to find it on a porch. How long would it take me with a whole desert to choose from? No one had given me any guidance on how to do it and I didn't want to be stuck out there for three days in the wrong spot. I began to feel angry and sorry for myself. This was always the way it was: sent out to do something without sufficient preparation and guidance. My head and lower back ached.

I stopped and sat down. Silently I sent my prayer to Grandfather. "Please, Grandfather, help me. I don't want to blow this ceremony, but I really do not know how to find the right place. Maybe it doesn't matter, I don't know. Can you help me?" I sat and waited, focusing on my breath. At last I sensed his face before me and his voice within.

"Granddaughter, breathe through your womb, pull the breath and energy in and out below your navel. Relax your body. Let its weight drop down to be supported by Grandmother Earth." I did as he instructed. "Now, keeping your body relaxed and your breath even, stand up." I stood. "Focus on your navel. Pull your breath in through your womb and send it out through your navel. See it like a long, luminous fiber in your mind's eye, shooting out of your navel ahead of you, scanning the ground all around until it finds and fastens on the place you must go. Turn as you do this." I followed his instructions, turning around where I stood. Suddenly something tugged at my navel. It was as if a line had been attached to my body inside, at the center. Grandfather spoke again. "So? What are you waiting for? Follow it." I jumped, startled. Follow it? Oh, yes, of course, I needed to find my spot. I moved straight ahead, following the feeling of tension in the center of my body. All at once it was gone. I was released. I sat down. This was my spot. I thanked Grandfather and got to work.

I spent the rest of the morning speaking to and gathering Rock People to hold the energy of my circle. I found some other pieces of sun-bleached wood, stuck them into the hard ground and stretched my blanket over them to create a tiny bit of shade in the center of my circle. But even in the shade and with a water-soaked handkerchief around my forehead the heat was unbearable.

I sealed and cleansed my circle and sat down under the blanket. I raised my medicine pipe to the immense presence of Father Sky and said my prayers for guidance. "Great Mystery, see this little one, Blue Lightning Snake. I come to cry for guidance for myself and my people. I offer thanks for all the gifts I have been given and ask you to teach me. Teach me how I can best live my medicine to touch myself, life and others with Beauty."

For the first two days of the ceremony I followed the instructions Gwen had given me for calling and capturing the enemies. One by one I called on Fear, Clarity, Death and Power and, using my pipe, directed them into the crystals, asking them to speak as my allies. On the first night I crawled into my sleeping bag as the temperature fell and the sun set, sending streaks of purple and pink across the endless sky. With no trees or hills to blur the horizon, it was easy to feel I was lying in the midst of the galaxy itself as the sky darkened to a deep blue-black and a million stars came out. I drifted into a light sleep listening to the coyotes howl in the distance.

Suddenly I awoke and sat bolt upright. Something was wrong. I grabbed for my flashlight and then realized what it was. The energy of my moon time had increased unexpectedly, leaving me lying in a pool of my own blood. I was frantic. This had never happened to me before. What about the cougars and coyotes? I had been so careful with my tampons and ziplock bags and now there was blood everywhere. Quickly I got out of my sleeping bag. Using my flashlight, handkerchief and the precious bottle of water I cleaned up as well as I could. As I did I had an image of what I would look like to a passing UFO or other night visitors. What was that woman doing down there, alone in the middle of nowhere with her flashlight and wet cloth? I would hardly look like a dignified warrior engaged in a sacred ceremony.

Having done what I could, I lay back down, keeping a wary eye out for four-leggeds. As I laid my head on my rolled-up jacket, I felt a buzzing in my ears and a rushing sensation in my head. My nose started bleeding. Incredulous, I sat up and grabbed my handkerchief. What was going on? It seemed I was destined to do this ceremony covered in my own blood. Before I had left the camp, Daphne, a medicine teacher and friend, had said to me, "Remember, this is not the time for sacrifice." I began to wonder.

I finally fell asleep and dreamed of the circle of Grandmothers I had seen during my healing sweat at the desert retreat. One of them spoke clearly. "You will hold a position in the northeast." She said it several times. I awoke wondering if this referred to my position in the Night Warrior army.

The days passed slowly. The trouble with such a large unencumbered view of the sky is that you get to watch the sun move across every inch.

In the heat of the day, watching and waiting, I felt that I had been and would be there forever.

The last day of the quest was my thirty-fourth birthday. I awoke at dawn just as the pink-gold streaks of sunlight streamed over the eastern horizon. Sitting up, I greeted Grandfather Sun, grateful this was my final day out alone. Some people sleep in on their birthday and have breakfast brought to them in bed. Some people party. I was sitting alone on the desert without food or water. At that moment I couldn't remember why.

Suddenly I saw a movement in the distance. There, directly in front of the slowly rising sun, were three wild horses, one black, one bay and one red-brown. They galloped in a line, nose to tail, moving southward along the horizon, tails and manes flowing. I was mesmerized by their beauty. As I watched I thought I heard a sound on the ground behind me, and ever wary of snakes, I turned quickly. Nothing was there. I turned back to watch the horses—and they were gone! I stood up quickly and scanned the horizon but they had disappeared. I thought they must have gone over the edge of the mesa on which I sat but their sudden appearance and disappearance gave me a strange feeling.

I sat back down and watched the rising sun, singing a welcoming chant to the new day, the new year of my life. All at once, I felt overwhelmed by exhaustion, as if I had not slept all night. I lay down on my sleeping bag and right away moved into a strange dream. There were no images, only a blue-gray mist surrounding me. I heard the pounding of horses' hooves and heard a voice, neither male nor female. "It is time. You must leave the distractions of other work and make your medicine your work. You must leave your job, and begin to teach the medicine full-time."

Instantly I was awake. Leave my job? How could I do that? How could I support myself and my sons on money from teaching? All my life I had worried about money, and many times had lived very close to the edge financially. The job I had did not pay much, but it did provide a steady and secure income. Could I face the insecurity of being self-employed? My anxiety went into orbit just thinking about it. I sent out a prayer. If this was what I needed to do, I needed to know how.

Closing my eyes, I immediately saw an image of figures written on a sheet of paper . . . a balance sheet? A budget! I looked at it carefully. There, laid out, was a precise plan for income and expenditures for the next year and a half of my life. I opened my eyes and, rummaging through my knapsack, found a pencil and piece of paper and began to write it all down. When I finished I sat back and looked at what I had written. Not only was it a budget, based on leaving my job at the end of December, but it was one that would work, assuming people came to the planned classes and workshops. I could hardly believe it. I had never heard of anyone on a vision quest receiving a "vision" of a budget! I shook my head and laughed. My incredibly organized, ever-budgeted mother might not approve of what I was doing or where I was going, but she would be proud to know I never made a move, not even one in the nagual, without a budget.

After the excitement of the early-morning events, the rest of the day passed slowly and uneventfully. I daydreamed about leaving my job and being able to work more with the medicine. I felt some sense of completion and wanted to go back to the camp for a hot meal and cold shower, but we had been told to return at dusk on the third day. The sun moved so slowly I thought at times it had stopped altogether. By late afternoon I had completed the ceremony for capturing the enemies and sat smoking my pipe. I was feeling increasingly excited about my future plans. I wondered if returning at dusk meant literally as the sun hit the horizon or just late in the day. As I debated this, I was surprised to see movement, on the horizon to the south.

A small cloud of dust seemed to be coming toward me. As it came over the low rise a short distance away, I sat up. A small herd of sheep and two sheepdogs came over the hill with the dogs instantly on the alert as soon as they saw me. We had been warned about the dogs by the Navaho. They were not pets but working dogs, trained to independently protect and herd the sheep across large areas of open land to new grazing areas. They would take the presence of anyone or anything, two-legged or four-legged, as a threat to their charges.

One dog ran around the sheep, trying to herd them away from me, while the other moved a bit closer and barked incessantly, its hackles raised. I tried to sit very still and look as nonthreatening as possible. The dog continued to growl and bark. I tried speaking to him. It made things worse. I smoked my pipe and said my prayers, but that only seemed to incite him to greater heights of frantic barking and growling. I decided to lie down, hoping I would appear less threatening. It did not seem to reassure him. Even lying down, with my head propped up to watch the dog, any movement, no matter how small, increased his agitation and brought him closer. I was pinned down. We had been warned that the dogs, if feeling threatened, would attack a human and could seriously harm or kill someone. Watching the dog, I had no doubt about this.

The sheep moved very slowly and the other dog was having trouble getting them rounded up by itself. The sun was nearing the horizon and I couldn't move. Here I had come into the desert to bravely confront Fear and Death, and I was pinned to the ground by a sheepdog! I knew horses were considered the Carriers of the philosophies and belief systems of human teachings. Dogs were the Keepers of the same. I wasn't sure how both fitted into the day's events or the ceremony I had done, but here I was, immobilized by the Keeper of philosophies and belief systems. Was somebody trying to tell me something?

At last the sheep moved off to the east with the one dog. I waited for the other dog to go with them. But Fido, as I was now unaffectionately calling him, was a cautious fellow. He kept me immobilized for another half hour to allow his companion and their charges ample time to get away. Exasperated, I gave up and lay down flat, watching the never-ending blue sky, listening to the incessant barking, which had now been going on for more than two hours. Several minutes later Fido stopped barking and ran after his companions. Warily I raised my head, only to see him turn periodically and watch me, barking a clear warning not to pursue them.

Relieved, I began to pack up and dismantle my circle. The sun was just above the horizon and I wanted to get back to camp, about an hour's hike along the riverbed, before dark. Completing the ceremony, I put on my pack and headed out. I was immediately aware of how weak three days in the hot sun without food or water had left me. Trying to stay clear-headed enough to watch for snakes, I made my way unsteadily toward the riverbed. It was only a short distance away and I knew by following it I would not get lost. I stumbled awkwardly down the riverbank and began to walk.

The longer I walked the dizzier I became. Although it was beginning to cool off, the exertion of walking, even with my small pack, sent sweat running down my face. I did not remember the hike out being so long and began to worry that I might be going the wrong way along the riverbed. Finally I sighted some rocks laid out in circles on the ground. I guessed that they had been placed there by fellow-apprentices doing personal ceremony. I was encouraged. I was getting closer to the camp. I wondered why they had not dismantled their wheels at the conclusion of the ceremony. As I proceeded I came across more and more circles of stones. From the tire tracks I could see someone had obviously driven a truck through and around many of the circles, scattering stones and leaving deep ruts in the sand. Why would someone want to destroy the wheels?

At last I came to the path leaving the riverbed. Mounting the embankment, I saw the camp. The air was cool now, the sun below the horizon. Feeling stronger I walked into camp and went directly to Gwen's tent. She greeted me with a hug.

"Welcome back. We were wondering if we would have to send a search party out. The others have been back for hours." I moaned inwardly. Why must I always be such a rule keeper? Gwen brought out some canned chicken and lemonade and I ate and drank while telling her about my time out. We needed to do a closing ceremony together, but I wanted to clean up before the light died completely. I went to my tent and put my solar shower full of water up on the roof of my rented car. The water had long since cooled off, but it felt wonderful to rinse the sweat and sand from my body and hair. Putting on a clean white shirt, light-brown full skirt and my soft suede boots, I felt like a new woman. I returned to Gwen's tent.

The person who sends someone out on this ceremony is required to "read" the apprentice's calcite crystals when they return to determine to what degree they were successful in capturing the enemies and making them allies. The reading is given as a percentage and I had been told beforehand that most people's figures the first time they do this ceremony were between 10 and 20 percent for each of the four enemies. The ceremony can be repeated to give the apprentice an opportunity to gain more knowledge of and access to the enemies, making them allies.

Gwen sat in her tent holding her pipe and one of my calcite crystals. I sat cross-legged in front of her. One at a time she read the crystals: Power—78 percent; Death—86 percent; Fear—82 percent. Gwen was amazed. She had never seen such high readings after this ceremony. I was feeling pretty self-satisfied by this time. Every childhood memory of pride in being at the top of my class came to the fore. Gwen spent a longer time on the last crystal and then spoke. "Clarity—17 percent."

Seventeen percent! How could that be? Clarity was the enemy of the north, place of the mind, my strongest place on the wheel. I gazed in shocked disbelief at Gwen, who looked somewhat apologetic. My sense of accomplishment in capturing the other three enemies was forgotten. I had failed! Miserably! I opened my mouth to protest, to question her ability to read the crystals accurately. Suddenly I could see myself sitting there: puffed up like a little toad, indignant, protesting, sure I was being evaluated unjustly and ready to do something about it.

Instead I started to laugh. "What a set-up," I said. "I sit here and get wrapped up in my competitive bid to do better than anyone else, then discover I blew it in the area I'm most confident. Of course it would be Clarity—that's my biggest enemy. I always think I can figure it out, think it through. I'm always sure I can 'get it' with my mind." I couldn't stop laughing. "It's O.K.—I get it."

Gwen closed her pipe and we wandered outside. There was going to be a gathering in the hogan for our final evening on the reservation. As I walked through the camp, people welcomed me back and asked how I was. I felt wonderful, full of energy and excitement. To my astonishment, one by one, the men of the camp came up to give me a hug and chat for a moment. Several asked about my nighttime plans. One man approached me with a broad grin on his face. "Well," he said, "I can see all the brothers are lining up."

I looked at him surprised. "What do you mean?"

"Well, you've come back just sparkling with energy. We all just want to see if we can get a little. Some of us would like a lot, but my guess is that a little is all we're going to get. Right?"

Clarity might be my enemy, but I got his meaning. "'Fraid so. I plan on sleeping alone tonight."

I was anxious to hear what everyone had been doing while I was out alone. Raven had given everyone a personal nighttime ceremony to do, one to enable them to see their Night Warrior mantle and know their position on the circle of those working in the dream. Several other apprentices had also just returned from time alone on the desert and were preparing to go out and do this ceremony. I did not want to go out again so soon and went to find Raven. I found him sitting in the hogan, waiting for people to gather.

"Raven, I've heard about this ceremony. A month ago I had a dream where I saw my Night Warrior mantle, and while I was out on the desert I had a dream about the direction I was to sit in. I just came back in from the three-day ceremony, and I really don't want to go back out—today's my birthday . . . ."

Raven laughed. "O.K., write down a description of your mantle and hand it in." I rose to leave. "And happy birthday."

I sat outside the hogan with my flashlight and wrote a description of the costume I had seen in the dream. One of the men came up beside me and looked at the picture I was drawing of the belt and its intricate design. "Where did you get that?" he asked abruptly.

I looked up. "I saw it in a dream. I was wearing it. Why?"

"You didn't see or hear Raven's description of the Night Warrior mantle?"

"No, I was out on the desert. Why? What's going on?"

He pulled a piece of paper from the notebook he was carrying and held it under the flashlight. There on the page was a picture of the belt I had just drawn, identical in every detail. I looked at the page, amazed. "Where did this come from?"

"It's the belt Raven described to us. We were supposed to dream it in to know if we were part of the Night Warrior army or not. Are you sure no one told you about this?"

"No. I just got back in. I saw this in a dream more than a month ago." My stomach turned. This was pretty hard to explain away as the power of suggestion or some kind of trick.

One of the women called everyone into the hogan. We had been told at the beginning of the week to always enter the hogan with respect, walking around within the eight-sided room in a sunwise direction, never cutting across the center. I went in and took my place on a blanket on the floor. The hogan filled with apprentices and Navaho. It was a Saturday night, so more men were able to join us. Seven grandmothers sat along one wall in aluminum lawn chairs. The evening was one of sharing. They sang their songs and we sang ours. The women demonstrated and tried to teach us a simple ceremonial dance. After an hour Raven announced a break and everyone left for a breath of fresh air.

Outside I asked several people about the medicine wheels I had seen in the riverbed. Why had they been dismantled? What had happened to some of them? I found out they had indeed been built by apprentices and Raven had instructed them to leave the wheels together for further ceremony. But someone had gone out with a truck and raced through them, deliberately breaking the circles. Not everyone on the reservation felt good about our being there.

As we talked I became aware of a Navaho man speaking with one of Raven's female apprentices. His voice was getting louder and he leaned toward her aggressively. "It's not right. You people don't show respect for our ways."

"In what ways have we shown a lack of respect?" she asked.

"When you walk in the hogan. I have seen people walk in with a lit cigarette. That is not the way it should be. You don't care. These are our ways, not yours." His voice got louder and louder.

Abruptly one of the Navaho grandmothers walked up to him. She was a small round woman, not more than five feet tall. She spoke with a thick accent and looked up at the Navaho man. Her words were forceful, spoken for all around to hear. "If you cannot tell who is truly family, beyond the color of a person's skin, you are not my son!" She turned on her heel and walked toward the house.

We were all stunned and embarrassed for the Navaho man. It was true he had been aggressive and angry, but disowning him seemed harsh. We stood silently in the dark, shuffling our feet and staring at the ground. Someone called for everyone to reassemble in the hogan.

The mood in the hogan had changed. None of the grandmothers had returned. The Navaho man stood at the door. It was clear the grandmothers would not return until this was resolved. Hesitantly he moved into the hogan and spoke. "I am an Indian," he said, sounding angry and nervous.

"So am I," Raven responded in a neutral tone.

"I am upset with what I see. Not everyone here respects our ways. I have seen people enter the hogan improperly." The man went on to explain his frustration with living on the reserve: the poverty, the violence, the spiritual ways that had been lost because of the deliberately destructive policies of the white government. His rage and his pain were clear. There had been and continued to be many injustices. His people's way of life had been destroyed. "I have to work for a living. I cannot come out here and do these ceremonies. I have to journey to the city away from my family to make money for them. And still there is not enough."

I thought ruefully about my life of working, studying, mothering, scrimping pennies and time in order to be here. It was ironic, but I could see why he would view us as rich white people coming to "play Indian."

Raven watched him intently but did not interrupt. Everyone listened with their full attention, absolutely quiet. His tone began to soften and his words slowed. "Many times I have put up the tipi to call the people together to do the ceremonies I am learning. Sometimes no one comes. Sometimes a few. And now you arrive and everyone gathers, everyone comes." He stared at the floor, discouraged. "I am sorry if I was too harsh with the woman outside. I was upset because I thought you were not respecting our ways. I heard there was a sweat the other night." He looked up, a flash of anger rising again for a moment. "I hope the men and women were not in there together. That is not our way!" He paused again. "I just wanted to say these things . . . and to say I am sorry if I offended. I meant no harm . . . . Sometimes it is hard."

We all sat in silence, waiting. Finally Raven spoke. His tone was firm but not without compassion. "I understand what you are saying, brother.

If any of these people stepped across your way of doing things it was out of ignorance, not out of disrespect. People need to be taught, to be told the proper way to do things. When we do our sweats men and women are together. I know this is not the Navaho way. We respect the ways of others and while we are here on your land we have not stepped across it. The men and women did not sweat together. These people have worked very hard to learn the medicine. We are here because I made a pledge to my teacher, Grandfather, to help support his family after he was gone. The money we bring is a gift from the heart. He was a powerful man and I know the family misses him." Raven lowered his eyes. "I miss him too."

Raven adjusted his chair and shifted his weight. Everyone began to move slightly, clearing throats, whispering, passing drinks of water around. The air felt lighter. The Navaho man who had spoken sat down. One of the young Navaho women left. After a few moments several of the grandmothers returned, offering to teach those who were interested a traditional Navaho dance.

I was exhausted, the day's events finally taking their toll. I wandered outside and headed for my tent. Mitch walked with me. We watched the stars and talked about what had happened in the hogan. I was touched by how Raven—unapologetic and direct—had dealt with the man, listening to everything he had to say. Mitch put his arm around me. I looked at him suspiciously. "I am not going to sleep with you," I said with a smile.

Embarrassed, he dropped his arm. "I didn't ask you to, did I?" he said defensively.

I laughed. "Good night, Mitch." I crawled into my tent and fell instantly asleep.

In the morning we packed up our cars and got ready for the final ceremony, gathering in the hogan with our medicine pipes and crystal skulls. This ceremony was to create a cohesive circle among those who worked together in the dream for the light. As we went in I realized I had not told Raven where the Grandmothers had said I was to sit, in the northeast. As each apprentice entered, one of the men, with Raven's list in hand, read off the position on the wheel. As I walked through the door into the dimly lit hogan he looked at me and consulted the sheet of paper. "Oriah . . . here you are. You sit in the northeast."

4

R eading about my journeys and dreams suddenly triggers a connection: the woman in the white dress, dancing in the dream where Raven jumped, flaming, into the abyss, was me! It was the same dress shown to me later as my Night Warrior mantle.

A month after returning home from Arizona I'd received a list of everyone who had participated in the ceremonies on the reservation. Each person had been listed according to his or her place on the circle, medicine name and Night Warrior name. Apparently, when people went out alone to seek a vision of their mantle, they'd been told to also find a name. No one had mentioned the task of finding a name to me, and I had not asked for or been given one in my dream of the mantle. I had already heard of several people's names. Most matched the strength and ferocity of their costumes: Raging Panther, Crimson Eagle, Screaming Spear.

As I'd flipped through the list, I had wondered what kind of name would match my luminous white dress. I had been surprised to find that Raven had recorded a name for me on the list. Even more surprising was the name itself: Strikes Fear. My Night Warrior name was Strikes Fear? While most of the names were nouns and adjectives that created a picture, mine was a verb and described an effect on someone else. Not only was the name inconsistent with the person I thought I was, incapable of really scaring anyone, it didn't seem to match the nonthreatening nature of my costume. Where had the name originated? While it disturbed me, I also liked it. It was, after all, the name for that part of me that fought against the dark in the dream dimension. And what strikes fear in the heart of darkness? Light.

It is only now, reading through my journals, responding to the Grandmothers' continued urging to "read the dreams," that I see for the first time the connection between the woman in the dream that I offered to Raven and my Night Warrior mantle. I wonder again about my name. Is it a description of his response to me in the dream? In whom do I strike fear? In Raven? It seems unlikely.

Certainly I had felt some fear, as well as excitement, upon returning from Arizona. One week later I gave notice at my job. I told my supervisor I would stay until Christmas to complete some work, give them time to find a replacement and get ready for self-employment. I was excited and scared.

My experience on the desert had renewed my desire to continue learning with Raven. The next gathering for apprentices was scheduled for Palenque, Mexico, in mid-February. According to Raven, Palenque had been the ceremonial site, hundreds of years ago, for a group of people working for the light in the dream dimension. We were going there to ceremonially reawaken both the power of the place and our memories of any past life participation we may have had in this or any other circle of dreamers. With my memories of last year's visit to Tula only slightly dimmed, I once again got on a plane and headed south. Bea had decided not to go, but Morgan and Joan did. We flew to the small airport closest to Palenque, and with some other apprentices from the U.S., hired a cab and drove to the hotel. I was elated to see how this area differed from Tula. Where Tula had been cold, cloudy and dusty, with little vegetation, Palenque was set in a lush tropical jungle. It was warm, humid, sunny and green. The hotel had pleasant rooms, with a wonderful view of the valley and a beautiful central pool lined with rocks and surrounded by greenery. Arriving in the late afternoon, we were told to be at the pool at ten the next morning. Joan had decided to stay at another hotel, and went to get settled while Morgan and I had dinner in the large open-air dining room, visiting with other newly arrived apprentices.

Some of the women on the trip to Arizona had talked about meeting during the medicine journeys to do ceremony specifically related to the Sisterhood. With people living so far away from one another, opportunities to do this were rare. While I appreciated Raven's incredible knowledge, I knew that he worked from the viewpoint of a man. I wanted the chance to sit with other women who were on this path and talk about the teachings from a more feminine perspective. As I talked with Chris, the eager apprentice who'd been concerned about "interfacing," I told her of my desire to have this happen.

"What do you think, Chris? I don't know how busy our schedules are going to be, but I would really like to have a gathering with the women. Maybe we could do some kind of simple ceremony together."

"Oriah, I think it's a great idea," she replied. "I would really like some time alone with the other women." We decided to talk with other women we knew and, after the week's schedule was apparent, set up a time for a gathering.

The next morning Morgan and I went down to the pool around ten. People started gathering, enjoying the sun and the water. More than an hour later Raven appeared and sat in the shade at one end of the pool. He looked terrible. Ill with the flu, he was pale and run-down. Some of the apprentices had wandered back to their rooms or to the restaurant while waiting for Raven to appear. One of them reappeared now and Raven yelled at him, "Where have you been? Let's go, we're ready to start!"

Another apprentice called back from the far end of the pool. "Where was he? Where were *you*?" The apprentice looked at his watch; it was now eleven-thirty. "So much for 'be there on time.'" His tone was bantering, but there was an underlying hostility and tension.

"Well, I'm here now. So let's move it." Raven replied, sounding angry and looking around as everyone congregated.

There was something unnerving about the whole exchange—a strange beginning for a week of ceremony. Morgan leaned over and whispered to me, "As we begin so shall we continue." I hoped not.

Raven jumped straight into a description of the ceremony we were going to do. The purpose of the ceremony was to cast a dome over the Mayan ruins nearby, and "fire" this dome to create an ideal dreaming space to be used now in the tonal, and later at home, in the dream. After the collective ceremony to create this protected vortex of power, Raven would give us individual ceremonies to do inside the dome at the ruins. The dome was to be created by ceremonially planting crystals in the earth around the ruins. It would be "fired," or energized, by a ceremony inside the ruins using a large crystal skull. Apparently dreamers in past times had used the crystal skulls in this location.

People were divided into teams and each team was to go to a different direction around the ruins, and plant their crystals. Local authorities were not open to having groups do ceremonies at, or close to, the ruins, so we would have to work well away from the ruins, back in the jungle. Everyone was also divided into different groups for getting the elaborate instructions on planting the crystals, calling in all the powers, blessing and awakening the place and doing complex sets of conjuring to increase the energy. I was in an all-women's group. I wrote everything down and gathered my belongings to go out into the jungle.

As we waited for the teams to get ready, our women's group sat at the side of the pool. Chris asked Jo, the senior apprentice in charge of the group, if she could take the opportunity to put forward an idea to her sisters. Jo nodded and Chris rose to speak to the thirty women gathered.

"I want to tell you about a vision I have had. In a meditation on this site I felt the Goddess speak to me about a coming together of the sisters."

I listened, incredulous. Either I had just attained divinity or she wasn't talking about our brief conversation the night before. She continued, "It feels clear to me that we need to spend some time here coming together as women. I have read that there is a site within the ruins where the priestesses gathered. Perhaps it would be appropriate to do a ceremony there. Or maybe we could gather here. It doesn't matter, exactly, but I did feel called to put the idea out to the group. I feel the Goddess has spoken to me and has given me this task."

The women responded positively, expressing their willingness to meet together. While confused about Chris's approach, I didn't really care. Perhaps the Goddess had spoken to her. It didn't matter, so long as we had a chance to get together.

Jo raised her hand for quiet. "Well, this seems like a nice idea, if it's possible. I feel responsible for checking this out with Raven. If we're going to plan something like this it mustn't interfere with any of the things he has planned. I'll check to see if it will be O.K. I don't want to take time away from the tasks he's set and I want to make sure that any ceremony we do would not disrupt the energy of what Raven is trying to accomplish on this site."

The other women agreed to leave it in her hands. Some part of me felt uneasy.

We all set out to do the ceremony. I liked the idea of creating a dome of energy over a ceremonial site, but the preparation had felt rushed and confusing. The instructions were complex and the teaching had been chaotic, filled with interruptions, people leaving to find notebooks, pipes and crystals, and many questions had been left unanswered. The teams for doing the ceremony were different than the groups for receiving the instructions. There had been no ceremony to pull everyone together for our common task. There was no time for cleansing, or for finding a quiet moment to focus our intent and internalize the instructions.

I was to go into the jungle with another woman, Ursula, from Switzerland. Raven had taught in Europe several times and had attracted a number of people from Sweden, Austria, Switzerland and England. Ursula spoke very little English and I spoke no German—we would have to communicate by signs. When Jo told her to go with me I felt some uneasiness. From her work with Raven Ursula was familiar with ceremony, and although she could not help me with instructions I might forget, she would be there to witness any mistakes I made. I was sure I would make plenty. Feeling very insecure, I set off into the jungle with Ursula a step behind.

It was hard to know just where we were supposed to stop; the jungle was so dense and we couldn't see the ruins to judge how far we had come. We walked for a while through the thick foliage then, throwing my fibers out from my navel as Grandfather had taught me in Arizona, I found a place. Ursula and I sat down. Even though it was late in the afternoon the air was warm and close. Feeling very hot and sweaty I unpacked by knapsack and laid out my pipe. I tried to calm my breath and my thoughts to bring all of my attention to my part of the collective task Raven had set. As I sent out my prayers, calling on the spirits of the place and its ancestors to be with us, I slowly filled my pipe with tobacco. Ursula sat silently. The air was heavy with humidity and filled with the sounds of the teeming life around us: birds fluttering from tree to tree, tiny lizards racing through the leaves, insects buzzing around our heads. As I sent the thin spiral of smoke from my pipe up through the jungle, a shaft of sunlight caught it. The smoke seemed to hang immobile, suspended above our heads. Ursula smiled and suddenly I was glad she had come to share this with me. I offered her my pipe and she smoked. Together we planted the crystal, saying our prayers together in English and German. By the time we finished, the light was beginning to fade, and we made our way back to the hotel.

The following day the group met at the ruins for what Raven called the "firing" of the energy dome we had anchored by planting the crystals. It was a beautiful, warm and sunny. We gathered under a huge tree in the center of the ruins. Groups of American and European tourists, mostly elderly men and women, streamed off buses and followed guides through the ancient site. I sat watching in amazement as they climbed up and down the endless stairs of small pyramids and tombs, growing red in the face, chests heaving, wiping sweat from glistening foreheads. The tour guides moved and spoke rapidly, rattling off factual information about the site, looking and sounding bored. It was a kind of "fast food" tour, one I fully expected to leave bodies in its wake.

Raven sat with us under the tree and gave detailed descriptions of the ceremonies he wanted each of us to do in different parts of the ruins. The ceremonies were to help us balance our shields and discover more about our Night Warrior. A small group of apprentices was given the task of firing the dome with a large crystal skull and a beautiful Quetzal fan. The rest of us were asked to gather around them to hide them from the view of the security guards. I joined the group. As several apprentices crouched on the ground in the center of the circle, working with the crystal skull, the others began to mill around them, talking loudly, laughing and joking. The whole thing felt embarrassingly inept. There were many groups walking around the ruins and all we really needed to do was stand there. We were attracting far more attention with our noise and commotion.

I moved away from the group. Raven was sitting in the center of the square watching. I sat down a short distance away. The small but noisy group of apprentices moved from place to place. Security guards and tourists glanced at them, but no one seemed interested in the loud, partying gringos. Their strategy seemed to be working. I waited to see if I would sense the dome being fired. A slight tingling ran up my spine. I wondered if it was the dome or simply my desire for something to happen.

I spent the rest of the day at the ruins doing the personal ceremonies and exploring the various temples and tombs. My enthusiasm for the task was low. Finally, in late afternoon, I caught a bus back to the hotel and tried to revitalize myself with a shower. Feeling a little better, I decided to dress up for dinner and put on a short, bright-red dress. The dress, a soft clinging T-shirt, never failed to boost my energy and attract the appreciative glances of the opposite gender. I decided to go all out, painting my finger- and toenails a matching shade of scarlet and putting on some makeup. I needed to shake off the feelings of lethargy and disappointment from the day, and hoped a change in appearance would help. Joining the others in the restaurant, I sat down in the front row of the apprentices gathered.

Raven arrived shortly and settling in, looked around the group. "Well, I think we just did some of the finest ceremony ever in the past two days. How many felt that? How many felt it was one of the most powerful ceremonies we'd ever done?" I looked around the group. Only a few hands went up in agreement. Raven seemed surprised but plunged on. "I don't know how many of you noticed what happened when the dome went up, but I was sitting and just observing. As the ceremony to fire the dome was finished, you could feel it go up. So did everyone there. As the dome was fired the sky changed and all the people in the area looked up. Everybody, just for a moment, looked up into the sky as if they'd heard or felt something."

They had? I had also been watching and hadn't noticed this. Had I just missed it?

Raven began to do some teachings on dreaming—in particular, on fighting Night Warrior battles in the dream. He told of how Susan had just had her first "kill" in the dream, "taking out" one of the members of the opposing army of the dark. Susan recounted the dream while Raven interjected explanations. She had clearly been shaken by her experience. Raven surveyed the group. "A few of you have also made your first kill in the dream. Gwen has . . . Jo . . . oh, Keith has . . . and of course Oriah has." I was surprised. I remembered most of my dreams, but none of killing anyone. Raven continued, "If you want to know if you have or haven't made a kill, put your hand up and I'll tell you." Most of the group raised their hands and one at a time he looked at them and said, "Yes, you have," or "No, not yet."

People began talking. Raven waited for the chatter to die down. Suddenly he looked at me for a moment and then announced, "I want to talk about this area and its history. I want to talk about what happened here." He began to talk about his past-life memories of being head priest in Palenque when the Jaguar temples were attacked and destroyed by the Spanish. He said that Many Shields, the Navaho who had been his teacher in this life, had been Montezuma. Raven's brother in that past life, he told us, had been a warrior. When the Spanish had landed Raven, as the head priest had stayed, but his brother had led the people out of the area and up into what was now the southeastern United States. They had, he said, become the Tsalagi Cherokee people.

As Raven told this part of the story, Gunner shook his head and looked at him, frowning. "But Raven, the Cherokee were not in that area for another five hundred years or more."

An awkward silence ensued. Raven seemed confused by the interruption. "Yes," he said, raising his voice defensively, "but this is where they came from." Gunner did not question him further. Raven continued with the story of the Spanish arrival and the destruction of the priesthood.

I felt my heartbeat quicken and raised my hand. "Raven, is this the same story you told at the gathering in Northern Ontario, the story about the Scarlet Woman?" He nodded and once again told the story of the woman who had betrayed her people by helping Cortez destroy the temple of the Jaguars and steal the crystal skulls. Raven said many of the apprentices gathered had been there when the circle of dreamers had been destroyed. He talked about the incredible sexual and magical power of the Scarlet Woman. I listened carefully, my stomach churning. I felt a heat rise through my body and the low droning sound seemed to come from within my head. The story still affected me in the same way as when I had first heard it, but this time my mind was clearer. What was wrong here? The story held the all-too-familiar ring of Eve in the garden being responsible for the downfall of humanity. Why were the powerful Jaguar priests so easily defeated by the actions of one woman?

Raven ended the story. He urged us to go to the ruins the next day and complete our ceremonies. We were to do our Night Warrior ceremonies in what Raven called the labyrinth, beneath one of the temples. Apparently all the buildings had been connected with an underground system of passages. While only some were excavated, he urged us to face our fears of the dark, bats, lizards, spiders and getting lost, by doing our ceremony deep within the labyrinth. It seemed to hold the promise of high drama and I was looking forward to it.

"It is critical that you do these ceremonies at this time," he said. "The dark side is gaining power and momentum in the world, even in the United States." Apparently it came as more of a surprise to Raven than it did to me that the dark force was alive and well in the U.S.A. He continued, "You can see it all around. They're talking about more gun control laws, which will infringe on your rights under the Second Amendment."

Not my rights. As usual, Raven spoke as if everyone gathered was American. I had heard this tirade before and knew where we were headed. "I urge each of you, when you get home, to take out a membership in the National Rifle Association. They're the people who are defending our right to bear arms and they're in the middle of a big membership drive. The Second Amendment is the number two, and you all know that two represents the power of Grandmother Earth. So supporting the NRA is defending Grandmother Earth and the feminine." This was a leap I was not willing to make. "Send your memberships through our office so we can get credit for your joining. The organization that sells the most memberships receives a cash prize of several thousand dollars. It's a great way to raise money for our expenses and battle the dark side at the same time."

Morgan rose and left, a look of disgust on his face. I decided to wait it out and see if he would go on to do other teachings. Another apprentice from Canada raised her hand. I waited expectantly. Was she going to challenge his right-wing beliefs?

"Raven, I'm wondering if Canadians can join. We don't have anything like the NRA in Canada." I struggled to keep the groan of dismay from escaping my lips.

"I know you don't, but unfortunately you have to be an American citizen to join. Sorry." The woman shook her head, disappointed. "I know, and y'all have a real problem up there. The violence in Canada is getting worse and worse, and the socialist government is creating it." Raven got up to leave. The meeting was over.

Not in my wildest imaginings had I ever considered Brian Mulroney a socialist! I was used to Raven's political tirades, but, while I did not agree with Raven's viewpoint, I had long ago resolved to ignore his politics. I left the gathering still feeling unsettled. What disturbed me, once again, was the story of the Scarlet Woman. I decided to go see Paula. A woman in her late sixties, Grandmother Paula, as she was respectfully called, had studied with Raven and others on the medicine path. She and her husband had come to the gathering with some apprentices from Texas. With long gray hair flowing down her back and an agility that belied her age, she was outspoken and direct. I had liked her immediately.

Timidly I knocked on the door to her room and heard her call to come in. She and her husband were talking with another couple from Texas. Motioning me to a chair near her, she looked at me keenly. "Well? What is it?" she asked, never hesitating to get right to the point.

I paused. "Well, I'm just wondering . . . I'd like to hear what you think about the story of the Scarlet Woman."

Grandmother Paula smiled slightly. "Why? What do you think?"

I could see I was going to have to give if I wanted to get. "Well, I'm not sure. Something about it doesn't seem quite right. I mean, this one woman is responsible for the downfall of the Jaguar temples, Montezuma and the dreamers' wheel?"

Paula leaned forward in her chair, a bright glint in her eye. "Must've been one hell of a woman, eh? All those poor men so mesmerized they didn't know what was happening. Ha!" She leaned back and shook her head. She pointed a wrinkled finger to the gray hair at her temple and narrowed her eyes. "I've got this little thing in here and I call it my bullshit detector. I'll tell you what I hear when I hear Raven tell that story—bullshit!"

I stood and smiled uncertainly. "That's what I thought. Thanks." Feeling even more unsettled, I went back to my room and went to bed.

Putting the Scarlet Woman story out of my mind, I returned to the ruins the next day to seek out the labyrinth and complete my ceremony. Before leaving the hotel I checked in with Jo to see how plans for a women's gathering were progressing. She told me Raven wanted everyone to finish the assigned ceremonies before doing anything else that might interfere with this priority. My sense of uneasiness grew. Was it my imagination or did Raven not want this women's meeting to happen? There was plenty of time. Most people were spending a good part of each day eating, drinking and socializing in the local bars and restaurants. I told her I'd check back later that evening.

Map to the ruins in hand, I headed for the labyrinth and entered a small stone doorway under one of the temples. It took a few moments for my eyes to adjust to the dim light. The low-ceilinged passage was damp and musty. There were no signs of bats, but the smell of human urine burned my nostrils. I moved deeper into the passageway, stepping over puddles. I was anxious to move farther into the tunnel, away from the light of the doorway and the tourists moving in and out. Small alcoves branched off the main tunnel, and I could see fellow apprentices sitting quietly, doing their ceremony. I wondered why they were staying so close to the entrance. Were they afraid of getting lost? Anxious for adventure, for the opportunity to once again "push my edge," I moved on, determined to go into the depths of the labyrinth. The "depths" proved to extend no more than a hundred feet. Very little of the tunnel was excavated and the short portion that was received a constant stream of tourists, exploring and using the small alcoves as lavatories. While the passageway was dim, it was certainly not dark. There was no chance of getting lost, and all bats or other creatures had long since abandoned the much-trafficked tunnel. I was disappointed.

I stepped into a small alcove and sat on a damp stone ledge, hoping the dampness was just humidity. Trying to be philosophical, I prepared to do my ceremony. The challenge was not darkness, bats or the fear of getting lost; it was to step into the dream despite the noise of running children, light from the door, men stopping to whisper obscenities and poke at me, and the strong smell of urine.

I spent the afternoon in the tunnel, alternately going into a deep dreaming trance and keeping in touch with who or what was around me. The dream state was induced by singing a special chant Raven had taught the night before. The purpose of this ceremony was to find and see each of the five different aspects of my Night Warrior, the part of myself that battled the internal and external dark in the dream dimension.

One by one I saw images of the different aspects of my self in the dream. I saw a Japanese woman with long black hair dressed in a kimono of blue-green brocade. The kimono was trimmed in black satin and gold braid. The woman was calm and watchful. I knew she was not as demure and defenseless as she appeared. Her strength lay in her empathetic reading of others, which told her of their strengths and weaknesses. I knew she was the Night Warrior aspect of my Woman Shield.

Quietly I sang the chant again. The image of a young woman appeared. She was in her mid-twenties and dressed in a bright white-blue-and-pink T-shirt and tights. Her blond hair was pulled back into a ponytail and tied with a pink ribbon. I knew her innocent appearance was part of her defense. She would continuously be underestimated by others, particularly by the men she met. She wore sneakers and could jump and somersault with incredible agility, using the luminous fibers extending from her navel and hands to move through incredible distances at high speeds. She was the Night Warrior aspect of my Little Girl Shield.

I paused to write the descriptions in my journal. Again I relaxed my body and softly sang the ceremonial chant eight times. This time an old woman in a long dark turquoise robe stood in front of me. Her hair hung loose, falling past her shoulders, thick and gray. As she stood she raised her arms over her head. A light seemed to glow in the middle of her chest and I knew this was her only weapon: a pure heart. With this I knew she could face any darkness without fear of death. I heard her speak. "The depth of the heart space terrifies the dark," she said. The sleeves of her uplifted robe began to change into feathered wings and I knew she was a shapeshifter. This was the Night Warrior face of my inner Elder Shield.

Once again I sent out my chant and waited. The dim figure of a woman appeared before me. She wore a headpiece of pearls that completely covered her hair and draped over her neck and upper chest. Beneath this she wore a long dress of black velvet and soft, black leather boots. She held a burning candle in one hand and a sword swung from the gold belt encircling her waist. The sword seemed translucent, made of a shimmering light. But her most striking feature was her eyes: large and unwavering, they shone with the deep blue-green of glacial lakes. I knew her weapons were the sword, which cast light, and her eyes, which could pull another into the dream. She was the face of the Adult Spirit Shield of my Night Warrior.

For a final time I closed my eyes and murmured the ceremonial chant, seeking the face of my Night Warrior's Child Spirit Shield. Instantly a very small, muscular woman appeared. Her skin was bronze, her hair and eyes black. She appeared to be Mayan or Egyptian. She wore few clothes, her breasts and waist adorned with strips of leather embossed with the figures of snakes in gold, silver and copper. Blue-green peacock and macaw feathers hung from her upper arms. She looked fearless, and I knew her weapon was primarily the fear others would feel when confronted with her sense of power and the magic of the snakes she wore.

These were the faces of my five aspects of self, my shields, as they appeared in the fifth or dream dimension. The ceremony was complete. Leaving some tobacco and a prayer of thanks to the spirits of the place, I gathered my notes and I headed out into the sunlight and back to the hotel.

It was late afternoon. A number of apprentices were gathered in the hotel restaurant. I stopped by and asked if a time had been set for a women's meeting. No one seemed to know. There were no group plans for that evening. We had two days left and we were going on a trip the following day to a different ceremonial site. The ruins were closed at sunset, so anything we did in the evening would not interfere with people's individual ceremonial assignments. Why was this so difficult? There had been plenty of time for eating, drinking, swimming, sunning and socializing. Frustrated, I made a suggestion as Jo appeared. "Why don't we just pass the word around that any women who would like to gather can meet by the pool at ten o'clock tonight? Anyone who wants to can come, and we'll decide what to do when we meet." Several other women agreed and Jo added her reluctant assent. I went back to my room for a shower, telling women I met on the way about the meeting.

After dinner I headed down to the pool. There were about forty women on this journey and by quarter after ten, nine women, including Joan and I, had gathered. Apparently, after we had spread the news of a 10:00 P.M. women's gathering, Raven had asked Susan to do a teaching on the Sacred Pipe at the same time. Many of the remaining women were there.

The nine women sat awkwardly in silence next to the pool. Chris, having called the gathering, began. "Well, I thought it would be nice for us to have a chance to talk about what it is like for us as women, walking on the medicine path. Maybe we could just go around and have folks talk about what it means for them to try and learn about and act from the feminine."

There were a few uncertain nods. Grandmother Paula began. She spoke of the need for the women in Raven's group to learn how to hold the place of the feminine. She looked around the group in the darkness. "This is not easy. Raven is a strong man. But without the presence of an equally strong feminine, Sacred Law cannot be kept."

Her words touched a chord in me and I spoke. "I know that I am more adept at acting from my masculine. I have been well trained by my culture. But more and more I am feeling my way into the feminine, the place of soft power. It's hard to find, let alone hold, this place when I am at these apprentice gatherings. This worries me. Why is it hardest for me to sit in my feminine power when I am doing the thing that has brought me closer to my connection with spirit—these teachings and ceremonies? When I leave these gatherings it takes me several days at home to feel balanced again, to find my more feminine, feeling side. I want to be able to keep it with me when I am here, doing the ceremonies and hearing the teachings."

Everyone sat silently. Chris asked someone else to speak to their experience of the feminine on this path. She looked to the woman sitting next to me, a senior apprentice. She had studied with Raven for five years. She looked around the circle before speaking. "Well . . . this is the first all-women's gathering I have ever voluntarily attended, and I'm not sure why I'm here. When I was younger I was forced to go to wedding showers and I hated it. My experience with other women has been . . ." She hesitated, her voice growing hoarse with emotion. "Well . . . I have often felt hurt by other women. I guess I really don't trust that other women aren't going to try to do something to me." Several of the other women nodded in agreement.

Another woman spoke about Jamie. She cried as she talked about her struggle to maintain her connection with her friend and at the same time demonstrate her loyalty to Raven. "She has made a choice to work with another teacher, but we are still sisters. I don't want to abandon her, but it seems impossible. Raven is afraid she's trying to get information from me to pass on to this man, so he can use it against him. I have to be so careful about everything I say, so I can't really tell her what's happening with me."

There was a pause. "Anyone else?" Chris asked.

Patty, a young, energetic woman spoke up. "Well, I just feel very fortunate to have learned so much about the feminine from Cliff." Cliff was Patty's lover and partner. "He has shown me how wonderfully sensitive and aware a man can be. He supports me in everything I want to do and is very caring."

Lynn spoke next. Lynn was from Toronto and had been a student in some of my classes after meeting Raven. Several months before the journey to Palenque she had moved to Arizona to study full-time with him and was about to become manager of Raven's office. She spoke quietly. "Other women have always been very important to me. As I move into a position of working closer with Raven, I am concerned about my capacity to hold the place of the feminine. I have some sense of how hard that will be." She laughed nervously.

I leaned forward. "Lynn, I want to offer something to you, and to this circle. It is a dream that I had several weeks ago. It may give us some guidance in holding the feminine on this path. I know it has helped me in my understanding of what that might mean." I paused before continuing. Did I really want to do this? The dream felt personal. Would someone tell Raven about it later? Probably. Would he be angry? I didn't know.

"In this dream I was riding in a car. Raven was driving and I was sitting in the back seat with my two sons, Nathan and Brendan. He was driving wildly, recklessly, going too fast and careening around the road. I was terrified we would crash. I was worried the kids would be hurt or killed.

"Frightened, I crawled into the front passenger seat. Raven looked at me, enjoying my fear. I told him to stop driving so fast and he just laughed. I told him to stop or I would stop him. He laughed again and said, 'Go ahead and try.' I reviewed in my mind all the martial arts I knew, wondering how I could stop him. I glanced at the ignition key and thought of grabbing it to stop the car. Raven saw me and knew what I was thinking. 'Try it,' he said again. I knew that if we struggled for the key we would crash and the kids could be hurt or killed.

"I didn't know what to do. I looked out the window beside me and saw my reflection in the glass. Suddenly I felt my heart beating in my chest, and tears welling up inside me. With all the intent I could muster, giving voice to the ache in my heart, tears streaming down my face, I turned toward Raven and said quietly, 'Please don't do this!'

"Instantly, Raven slowed the car and pulled over to the side of the road. He looked dazed and said, 'I'm sorry. I don't know what came over me. I don't know why I did that.' I woke up crying and thought immediately, 'Damn, what a wimp. I used my tears to stop him!' But as soon as the thought crossed my mind, I knew it was not true. My words, spoken from my heart, were what stopped him."

Everyone was silent. Finally Lynn spoke. "Thank you, Oriah, I will try and remember this over the next few months."

I looked at her. "Lynn, if you ever need any help or support, just call."
She nodded.

We sat in the darkness beside the pool and continued to talk quietly
into the night. It was a fragile start, a whisper, an embryonic beginning of
something. Finally we ended our discussion and wandered off to bed,
each wrapped in her own thoughts. I was glad we had gathered, and
wished we could do more. I doubted opportunities would be plentiful.
Disturbed by all the questions that lacked answers, I drifted into a deep
sleep.

As the faint light of dawn filtered into the room, I was woken by the
people next door. The night before I had heard them discussing plans to
do a pipe ceremony at dawn. Rolling over, I looked at the glowing
figures on the clock dial and groaned—5:15. I lay awake, trying in vain
to get back to sleep. Eventually I gave up. As long as I was awake I
might as well get up and see the sunrise. I got out of bed and went to the
window. A wooden lamp and a strange wooden highchair were sitting
next to the window. I couldn't remember seeing them in the room before.
Slowly I turned to face the bed and saw my body, still asleep beneath the
covers. I was in a lucid dream.

My heart beat with excitement and I tried to calm my breathing. I
opened the curtain and looked outside. The clock next to the bed said it
was five-thirty and I could see the pale pink of dawn in the sky. Everything outside looked normal.

I decided to go out. Pulling on my clothes from the day before, I
opened the door and stepped outside, breathing in the fresh morning air
and listening to the birds. My mind reeled with the possibilities. What
should I do? Where should I go? I decided to head toward the small town
nearby and started to walk down the road. Then, remembering my experiences at home of "thinking" myself to different places, I started to
think of flying and immediately found myself skimming effortlessly
above the ground. In moments I was in the center of the small Mexican
town. Cautiously I wandered the streets, empty except for the occasional
stray dog. Some food vendors were beginning to open their stalls. I could
smell the smoke of charcoal burners being lit. I could feel the air, warming with the sun, on my bare arms.

I passed the door of a restaurant we had eaten at earlier in the week
and heard voices. Cautiously I moved inside, and saw Raven sitting in
front of a small group of apprentices. He glanced up as I entered the
room. I sat in a chair near the door. "The trick," he was saying, "is not
just to be able to hear the teachings in the dream but to know you are

dreaming. One of you here knows that right now. Who is it?" I raised my hand and he nodded to me. The others seemed not to have noticed. He continued. "The thing about dream walking is that you can do things your physical body would normally find taxing. For instance, although you may be too ill or tired on the tonal to make love, in the dream you can have all kinds of energy for great sex." Immediately I felt wary. Getting up, I went back out the door onto the street.

As soon as I entered the street I felt a tingling like an electric shock move up my spine. My hair felt as if it stood on end; my hearing and sight sharpened. Something was going to happen. In alarm I turned and saw a long black limousine drive up the street. The windows were mirrored so I couldn't see inside. As I watched it a tall, thin man stepped out from between the buildings and grabbed my right elbow. He looked like Morgan, but I knew it was not him. He spoke in a low menacing tone. "Just come with me and no one will be hurt." I could smell his breath, foul and hot on my neck as he propelled me forward toward the car. The back door swung open and I gathered my energy to fight being put inside. But as the door opened I saw two women sitting in the back seat, clearly terrified. Without hesitation I stepped into the car and sat between them. The door closed and locked behind me. The man slid into the passenger seat in front and nodded to the driver, a small man in a dark suit, to drive on.

As the car drove out of the town and into the surrounding hills, I observed my fellow passengers. Both women were young, probably in their early twenties. One looked to be about six months pregnant and very close to tears. I tried to make conversation and pretend nothing unusual was happening, asking them their names and when the baby was due. The other woman said she was three months pregnant. I sat quietly for moment. I was three days late for my own moon cycle, and although I was certain I was not pregnant, it was possible. I gazed at the profile of the man who had put me in the car. Softening my vision I tried to "see" him and measure his intent and power. Suddenly he turned and caught me watching him. Terror gripped me. Quickly I focused my vision, and wiped from my mind any effort to assess him. I knew his intent was evil and his power strong, too strong for me in a head-to-head confrontation. Suddenly I heard Grandfather's voice, low and urgent. "Don't let him know that you can 'see' him, that you have any idea about what is going on. Your only protection is in appearing unaware. You must look nonthreatening, stupid." He paused and I heard a chuckle. "Do you think you can do that?"

I wanted to make a retort but only thought, *Very funny!* Uncertain and suspicious, the man watched me for a few moments, then turned back to the view ahead.

The car pulled off the highway and moved down a long narrow lane surrounded by dense jungle. Finally it stopped in front of a huge gray stone building several stories high. The door opened and two men carrying machine guns pulled us from the car and led us into the building. We were escorted down a long corridor and into a huge room filled with about forty women. Most appeared to be in different stages of pregnancy. The room was pleasant and bright, the floor covered in orange carpeting and the walls painted a sunny yellow. The women sat or stood in small groups, speaking in hushed tones or silent. All of them looked haggard and frightened. The door was closed and bolted behind us.

I wondered what to do next. Again I heard Grandfather. "You're in your dream body. Explore!" Right! It had all felt so real I had almost forgotten that my physical body was back in bed at the hotel. In my dream body I could go somewhere just by thinking myself there. I reached out with my mind and felt around inside the huge stone house. Something was definitely going on here. Pushing my energy out, I moved to a similarly decorated room across the hall. Lying and crawling on the floor were dozens of babies. It was a nursery. Several middle-aged women moved among them, changing diapers or giving bottles. A feeling of dread started to overwhelm me and I heard Grandfather again. "Go down to the cellar."

Reluctantly I pushed my thoughts ahead of my body and went down into the space beneath the house. The room was dark and dank with the putrid smell of rotting meat and excrement. I gagged and felt like vomiting. I wondered if a dream body could vomit. Something brushed my cheek as it flew past and I repressed a scream as I jumped away. Bats! The place was filled with bats, hanging from the ceiling and flying through the air. My eyes began to adjust to the dim light and I looked with horror at the scene in the room. In a flash I knew what this house was about. The man I had seen was using the babies as food for the bats. I didn't know what he did with the women. I felt sick and dizzy. Again I heard Grandfather. "Oriah, be alert. There is great evil here. Understand what is happening. This man uses these bats, fueled by the intense life-force energy of newborn children, to go into the world and work for the dark. They are the sorcerer's messengers, and the messages they carry are of darkness, fear and cruelty."

Suddenly I was back in the room with the women—I knew Grandfather had helped me move out of the cellar. The door opened and the man who had brought us to the house entered and surveyed the room. I wanted to leap at him, to somehow stop this, and yet I knew I did not yet have the power to defeat him. I also knew I could not stay here without being detected. Quickly I moved toward the door, then I stopped. How would I get out! The man turned toward me. Grandfather whispered, "The dream. Use the dream!" Rapidly I turned my body and imagined it paper thin, slipping between the door and its frame. At once I found myself standing outside. I pictured my body back in the hotel room. I woke up in my own bed and sat up shaking.

I got out of bed and went into the bathroom. My face looked back at me from the mirror, frightened, pale. I backed up and leaned against the wall, sliding down to the floor. Sitting on the cold tiles, my face in my hands, I wept silently for what I had seen. Was it real or symbolic? Did such a man exist? Was there such a place? I got dressed and went down to the restaurant, anxious for human company and for someone to talk with about my experience. I sat with Morgan and Joan and began to tell them about my dream. My speech was disjointed, as if I was not entirely back in the tonal. I felt scattered. As I told the story, other apprentices arriving for breakfast stopped by to listen. As I finished, one of the women rose to leave. She looked at me with a half smile. "God, I hate you. I can't get a dream like that no matter what I do."

Another woman and a senior apprentice joined her. "Yeah, makes you sick doesn't it." They both laughed as they moved away. I was stunned. The comments, supposedly made in jest, held an underlying bitterness. I knew many of Raven's apprentices were frustrated with their own lack of dreaming, but my experience of the previous night had been frightening and painful, something I was struggling hard to see as a gift to be used for beauty. It had not been fun.

I decided to go and speak to Susan. I sensed she would understand my feelings of fear and anguish over the dream. I found her by the pool and told her the dream. She asked me how I was feeling now.

"I'm not sure. I still feel discombobulated, as if I'm not all here. Part of me wants to know how to go back and stop what was going on. I want to know how to beat this guy, how to find him. Another part of me wants to get as far away from here as possible."

She nodded, understanding my contradictory feelings. "I really think you need to tell Raven about the dream. I think he can be of more help than I can. I'll set up a time later today after the trip to Agua Azul."

"Thanks, Susan." I rose to leave. I felt better speaking to someone I knew had had a similar experience. I headed off to get ready for the trip.

The whole group was going to Aqua Azul, a waterfall about an hour from where we were staying. We were told the site was incredibly beautiful and the ideal place for the fifth gateway, Hanged Man ceremony. Although most of the group was in the third gateway, many were eager for the opportunity to do a more advanced ceremony.

I caught a ride with an apprentice from Jamaica who had rented a car and we arrived at the falls mid-morning, early enough to see only a few tourists. The site was truly beautiful, a wide river of deep turquoise water cascading over cliffs and rocks to create magnificent waterfalls and rapids. We gathered below the rapids where a single tree grew arched over the water. In the Hanged Man ceremony the apprentice is suspended head down over the water from a rope tied to one leg and then released, falling into the water. Gunner, who had led the ceremony before, gathered everyone around and briefly described the ceremonial logistics. He passed out sheets depicting body paintings and told us the ceremony would help us greet the deaths we needed in our lives. Everyone put on bathing suits and started painting one another.

I was hesitant, still preoccupied with the dream. My moon had begun and I was overwhelmingly tired. The intent of this ceremony was not clear to me and the preparation nonexistent. Where did the body paintings come from? What did they mean? What were we to focus on while we were hanging upside down waiting to be released? When I mentioned my doubts to fellow apprentices, several told me the intent was to get it "ticked off" the gateway sheet, the record of ceremonies completed. I was not immune to this motivation. My inner, always-get-straight-A's overachiever did not want to miss an opportunity. But another part of me balked. What was the point? If I was really going to utilize a powerful ceremony for personal transformation, shouldn't I take more than a moment to focus my intent? Was getting it ticked off the list a good enough reason to do it? With no preparation, no fasting, no pipe ceremony, were we honoring the tradition of this ceremony? More importantly could I not do it? Could I be there and pass up this chance, see others get ahead of me on the gateways and not do it because it didn't feel right? Or was this just an excuse? Water is not my favorite element. I am not a strong swimmer and I do not like heights. Was I just plain scared and looking for an excuse not to do the ceremony?

I watched the other apprentices, their bodies painted, line up, climb the tree and drop into the water in rapid succession—a kind of ceremonial assembly line. The Mexican tourists gathered to watch and comment on the crazy gringos. I felt sick. Maybe it was just fear— although I had done many things in ceremony that had frightened me—but I could not do it. I sat and watched.

We returned to the hotel by late afternoon and I went to look for Susan. She said Raven wanted to see me, so I went to his room. Three other apprentices were there and Raven was telling them about their Night Warrior statistics: data on the number of battles they'd been in, how they fought and how many losses they'd had. Each wrote the information down. I listened and watched. One at a time they left until we sat alone. "So," Raven began, "tell me the dream." When I had finished recounting it he continued. "Yup, it's definitely a Night Warrior dream. I know the guy you met. He's a bad one. Lives in Texas and practices satanic ritual involving children."

"Are you saying this man actually exists on the tonal?" I asked, my stomach turning over.

"Absolutely. You were lucky. He does have more power than you. Last night's battle was a draw. Even though you didn't engage in an actual fight, you did get away without him detecting you. Since you have less power, that counts as a tie."

"Wait a minute," I said. "I want to be clear. Are the women and children I saw real on the tonal? Are there really women and children being used in this way, by this man, at this time?"

"Yes."

"And how can we stop this, if it's true? Can I go back at will? Can I do anything about it?"

"Maybe, if you keep learning." Maybe? This seemed pretty vague to me. If there was a man out there doing these things, I wanted to know what to do about it. I also felt frightened. What was the risk? I had already been hurt in the dream once. If this guy or others like him were affecting real children on the tonal, what was to stop them from going after my sons?

"Raven, I want to know, would someone like this, someone working on the dark side, go after my children to get at me?"

"Absolutely, that's what happened to my sons. The dark side went after them."

"Well then, that's it." I rose and walked to the window. "I'm out. I'm willing to take risks, but I will not put my sons in that kind of danger." My tone was final.

Raven looked startled. "Whoa, wait a minute. It's not like that. My kids got tempted with drugs, alcohol, crime—that kind of thing."

I started to feel angry. This was important to me. "That's not what I'm asking. I want to know if any of these guys could step into the tonal and directly hurt my kids physically, mentally, emotionally or spiritually. The temptations you're talking about are there for all kids. I'll have to take my chances with them like every other parent, and I'll do the best I can. I want to know if my working in the dream could invite something into their circle that would do them direct harm, because if it does I'm out until they're old enough to look after themselves."

"No. No, it couldn't endanger them like that." His tone was definite. I felt confused. Why had he initially said they could? Why couldn't they? If anyone wanted to make me do or stop doing anything, the easiest way would be to threaten those I loved. Were they somehow protected? I wasn't sure what to believe but something in me sensed the truth: they were not at risk. I wasn't sure why.

Raven continued. "Do you want to hear your Night Warrior stats?"

"O.K." I was startled by the abrupt change of topic, but curious. I had heard that Raven had programmed his home computer with information about everyone in the Night Warrior army and then played out the games to see what happened in the dream. I was unfamiliar with the computer game and dubious about the whole process. I wrote down the information as he gave it to me. He told me I had had twenty-nine fights, twenty-five knockouts, two draws and two losses. I had good strength and endurance. My flaw was my hesitation to get into a fight, although once I did I would give it everything I had. I could absorb pain without reacting and would almost always take any opening my opponent offered. I wrote it all down. I wasn't sure about the Night Warrior battles, but it sounded like an accurate description of my patterns in personal relationships.

"Raven, I have to tell you something. It's interesting information, but I don't know if it's true. I remember a few of what feel like lucid Night Warrior dreams, like the one last night. You tell me I have had twenty-nine, but that doesn't really mean anything to me. I only know about the few I can remember. The rest are theory. How many people just take your word for it and how many really know for themselves?"

"More and more." Raven answered vaguely. "More and more all the time." A knock on the door interrupted us and Susan entered to ask about evening plans for dinner. I sat and waited. I did not know if my questioning had angered Raven, but I was not sorry I had asked. As Susan left he lit another cigarette and turned toward me. "What I want to know," he began," is what holds you back? Why aren't you giving me a complete commitment? I don't understand why anyone wouldn't completely commit to the light. I'm not getting enough from you. Why aren't you giving me one hundred percent?"

I felt confused, attacked, accused. My mind reeled. Did asking questions mean a lack of commitment? How did making a commitment to Raven equal a commitment to working on the light? It implied I might be working, at least in part, on the dark side. I forced my voice to remain calm. "What would a complete commitment look like, Raven? What would I be doing that I have not done? I've left my marriage and my job to study and teach the medicine full-time. I am at every apprentice gathering. I do the ceremonies and personal work. What would it look like if I was giving more?"

Walking around the room, he continued as if I had not spoken. "I just don't get it. Why won't you give me a one hundred percent commitment? Why? That's why I can't see all of your Night Warrior mantle in the dream. Some part of it is hidden to me. Why won't you give me a full commitment?"

"Raven, what would that look like on the tonal, here and now?" I repeated.

He did not answer but sat down on the bed across from me. My throat ached. I felt in some ways that I owed him my life. I had been so ill before I began to work with him. What did he want from me?

The door opened and two men came in, laughing and talking. Raven turned to them and they all began chatting about the day's adventures. I stayed and listened for a while, finally rising to leave. I turned with my hand on the doorknob. Raven nodded goodbye.

I returned from Palenque exhausted and discouraged. A nameless, nagging worry seemed to sit in the back of my mind. Feelings of conflict and ambivalence plagued me and I wanted them resolved. Rumors of people leaving Raven's group in Arizona, and growing financial concerns for the center he had started, filtered up to Toronto. On Easter Sunday I sat down and wrote a letter to Raven, reviewing my three years of learning with him and the incredible impact it had on my life. I had had several dreams since Palenque. In them I saw Raven ill and weary. Concerned for his well-being and disturbed by his vague demand for more commitment, I wrote:

. . . I do not know how you are doing but I want you to know how deep my concern for you and your health and wholeness is. It would not be a complete picture to talk about how much the teachings mean to me and have helped me in my sacred dream without speaking of the impact you, as the teacher of this knowledge, have made. There are a lot of different pieces to that: the personal struggles you have shared with those you teach, your ability to teach at great speed with mental agility, and humor. But none of these, as much as I have enjoyed them all, really point to that which has touched me most. From the first time I heard you teach, and each time since then that I have seen you in a group or alone, what has touched me is your heart. Beneath all the masks of fart, tough kid, wise teacher and unattached healer has clearly shone a good heart, one capable of, and often acting with great courage, tenderness and love for this tiny green planet and all of her children. It was there when you so consistently honored the Sisterhood and the child within in your words at the spiritual-sexuality workshop, when I came to you in pain about my history of rape and abuse, when I have watched you pour all your skill and ability into a healing, and when you speak of the teachings and your dreams for creating a world without ignorance. I do not know you Raven, in any personal sense, but all of my dreams and intuition tell me that any difficulties you are having now with your health or your work center around difficulties with your heart. I offer this to you, knowing it may be my own fantasy and illusion, or information you have, or cannot use. I give it with an offer: if there is anything you need, that you feel I could be of help with, if it is within my power you have only to ask. Finding you, and through you, the teachings, clearly brought me "home"—and home being where the heart is, is also where family is. You are family and I love you.

5

I read a copy of the letter and start to cry, remembering my desperate efforts to reassure myself and Raven that I would not leave him, that I remained loyal. Reading my notes, I relive the confusion, ambivalence and fear. I take a short break to get more tea and wander restlessly around the house. I am uncomfortable in the living room, the memory of last night's dream of the ruler flying out of the vacuum cleaner and into my body still vivid. I rub my belly where it entered, feeling the ache, and return to my workroom. Silently I send out a prayer: "Grandmothers, what is the point? Why do you wish me to reread, relive all of this? What am I to understand?"

I hear the voice within me: "There is a story here, Oriah. Hear the story. Continue to read."

Baffled, I open another binder of notes and continue.

Raven's teachings had most affected my life through the gateway ceremonies I had done. Feeling somewhat dissatisfied with the ones I had done in Palenque, I wanted to do a solo gateway ceremony as soon as possible. In early June I arranged for my sons to be with their father and set out to do my Two-Night-Hole-in-the-Ground ceremony. I was being monitored by Mitch, who had recently returned to Toronto to live. We had not resumed our relationship as lovers, but remained somewhat cautious friends. Mitch did a pipe ceremony with me in his home in the city before I got into my car and drove north to my wilderness campsite. Although Raven had approved the arrangement, I felt a little uneasy about being monitored by someone who was neither near the site nor adept at leaving his body.

I had enjoyed my One-Night-Hole-in-the-Ground in the sweat lodge in Arizona and was looking forward to this ceremony, which I assumed would be more of the same. The rock of the Canadian Shield had the same limitations as the Arizona desert when it came to digging a hole, so once again I was to do the ceremony, to greet death and change, in a Purification Lodge. This lodge was much smaller, about seven feet in diameter, large enough for both lying down and sitting up. It was a lodge I had built for myself and my family at our campsite. I was to go into the small structure of curved saplings covered with blankets and plastic at sunset one day, stay for two nights and a day and emerge on the second morning as the sun rose.

I spent the day relaxing and preparing: doing the tobacco ties, going for a canoe ride, bathing in the lake, tidying my small trailer. Throughout it all I moved slowly and methodically. More than once the deliberateness of my actions reminded me of those of the character played by Sissy Spacek in the movie *Night Mother*, a woman who was preparing for her own suicide, getting her mother's house and affairs in meticulous order before she shot herself. I shook my head at my own patterns and said out loud, "Just like the Virgo you are, Oriah. Leave everything neat if you're going to die."

I sat in the sun beneath the cedars singing and tying tobacco into small squares of blue, green and red cloth. As I placed tobacco into each small square of material and looped them in a row on a long string, I said a prayer asking the different energies of the universe—Grandfather Sun, Grandmother Earth, the Plant People, the Animals, the Humans, the Winds of the Four Directions—and many others to be with me during the ceremony. The process calmed my nervousness about the ceremony. It was a meditation.

When I was finished I had sixteen red ties and forty-four each of the blue and green ones. The red ties, holding the prayers of the South to help me step into the ceremony in trust and innocence, were hung from the forked sticks set in each of the four directions. The others, representing the colors of the spirit and material worlds, were strung between the forked sticks. I stood in the late-afternoon sun and surveyed the tiny lodge surrounded by the colorful ties and the special flags and feathers hung in each direction. The sun was still warm and the wind moved the tall pines and cedars above me. Suddenly, with a whirring sound, a hummingbird appeared and darted over the lodge, hovering within the area surrounded by the brightly colored ties and then darting between each of the sticks in the four directions. I knew the medicine of the hummingbird was that of the Great Choreographer, the one who teaches us to change direction, make different decisions, rechoreograph our lives. It felt like a good sign for stepping into ceremony.

I set up my medicine wheel around the lodge, speaking to the Rock People as I had been taught and sealing my circle with tobacco while banishing any negative energy from within. As the sun set I sent out my prayer in each direction, calling to all those ancestors who loved me to be with me and guide me in this time of aloneness.

Sitting within the lodge, I smudged myself and the small space with smoke from burning sage, cedar, sweetgrass and lavender and set up a small altar in the west. As evening came I filled my medicine pipe with prayers for myself, others and all the children of Grandmother Earth. With my head in the south I laid down, holding my pipe.

The time passed slowly and as the dusk deepened I was joined by many mosquitoes and blackflies. I tried to ignore them as I prayed for guidance on how to live my medicine, know my gifts and use them for healing myself and others. My prayers became more and more disjointed as I slapped at the buzzing insects. I tried to relax and say a prayer to the six-leggeds, asking for their help in this ceremony. I fell in and out of a light sleep, filled with lucid dreams of visitors to the lodge, who spoke to me of the people in my life I loved: my children, my friends, my family. I woke up hearing a woman's voice saying, "These are your people. Do they know you love them?"

I dreamed I was standing outside the lodge, and knew my body was inside asleep. Three Inuit people, one woman and two men, walked into the campsite from the road. As we stood outside the lodge it began to collapse and I worried about my sleeping body and how it would get out. The woman began to dance and chant. As I listened I began to feel dizzy. Suddenly she seemed to melt into the collapsing structure of the sweat lodge, and I knew her body had been transformed into the new structure arching over my sleeping form. I wondered out loud how I could get back inside, and one of the men turned to me and said, "Just think it and you will be back." I thought of being in my body and immediately woke up in the darkness. I felt I was inside a womb, the small dome over me the body of my expectant mother.

I continued to drift in and out of dreams. I woke up hearing a woman's voice. "Grandmother weeps for you." It was pouring rain and pitch-black.

The rain sent thousands of mosquitoes and blackflies looking for shelter, and my lodge was the perfect place. No matter how many times I adjusted the blankets touching the ground at the perimeter of the lodge they continued to find their way in. They buzzed in my ears until I felt dizzy, biting my legs, arms, face—anywhere they could find flesh. I could feel my face swelling. Frantically I smudged again, hoping the smoke would somehow discourage them. But the herbs in the abalone shell were damp from the constant rain and would not light. I struck match after match.

They flared in the blackness and sizzled out in the soggy leaves. I gave up, but not before I had struck twenty matches, creating a sulfur haze that hung in the tiny lodge, choking me. A dull ache began to gather behind my eyes. I recognized the beginning of a migraine.

I tried to sing, but my throat stung from the sulfur. Holding my pipe, I laid down and drifted in and out of a restless sleep, waking to slap at the insects buzzing in my ears and biting my face. Full of self-pity and more miserable than I had ever been, I began to cry. As the dim light of dawn filtered into my tiny shelter the rain continued, the bugs thickened and my head felt as if it would split in half. I had not prepared for this time of fasting in the proper way. I should have eaten only fruits and vegetables for a day or two beforehand to cleanse my system. Without food or water, my body was flooded with toxins and my headache became unbearable. Exhausted, I slipped again into a disquieted sleep.

I awoke hearing a little girl's voice. "I can't, I can't. Please don't make me do this." It took me several minutes to realize it was my own voice. I rolled on my side to vomit, the headache searing through me. I had no idea what time it was. The day stretched endlessly before me. I wanted to get out, but I couldn't move. I raised a hand to my face—it was swollen and bloody from bites. My tears felt cool on my feverish skin. Clutching my pipe, I called out to Grandfather. "Grandfather, help me. I cannot do this. Please . . . help me."

As my prayers left my lips I heard his voice. "Oriah, come with me." I felt myself being gently lifted by strong arms and carried from the lodge. The rain had stopped and everything looked green and fresh. Grandfather laid me down gently on soft grass beside the stream, putting a blanket beneath my head.

"Grandfather . . . I—"

"Sssh. Quiet now. It will be O.K. Just be quiet and close your eyes. Rest here." My crying slowed down and I allowed myself to relax. Grandfather leaned over me, talking and putting cloths soaked in the cool water of the stream on my aching head and bitten face. The coolness soothed the pain. "I will take care of you. Be still now. Sleep." His voice washed over my body like a sweet chant and I surrendered to sleep. Occasionally I roused from my dreaming. Grandfather was still there. I told him my dreams as he changed the cloths on my face and he murmured softly, "It is good. It is good to go with the Dreamers, little one."

I dreamed of being a midwife for a woman giving birth to a tiny baby girl. The baby was glowing, shaking her tiny fists in the air above her head. I dreamed of giving birth to the baby, and nursing her. The dreams were sensual and alive. Each time I awoke, Grandfather was there, bathing my head, speaking softly, feeding me flatbread and cool water. Each time he sent me back into the dream.

The faint light of the final morning filtered into my consciousness and I woke up in the lodge. The ceremony was over. My headache was dulled; I was unbearably thirsty and weak. Slowly, after saying my prayers of thanks to Grandfather and the spirits, I left the lodge and made my way to my trailer. I was shocked and trembling. The ceremony had been nothing like those I had done previously. The physical pain had been endurable only with Grandfather's help. Stumbling into my trailer, I drank some juice and put some water on to make tea. I was discouraged, my thoughts frantic. I was only in the third gateway. There were dozens of ceremonies in each gateway and fifteen gateways. How could I continue to learn in this way? It was too much. I could not do this. What was I going to do? This was the path I wanted to walk. I wanted to keep learning, but not like this.

Feeling faint, I ate a piece of fruit and collapsed into bed. Instantly I was in a dreamless sleep, waking hours later with the sun shining in my eyes. Feeling a little better, I got up and cooked myself some vegetables and rice. By the time I finished cleaning up, I was exhausted again. As the final light of the day began to fade I returned to the lodge and took down the ties, flags, feathers and medicine wheel. When I offered tobacco in thanks, my heart felt full of sadness. I could not imagine ever wanting to do another ceremony in solitude. I was unsure what I had learned from this one, but I felt quite certain I never wanted to repeat the experience. Discouraged, I went to bed.

I woke up late next morning, still feeling shaky but without a headache. Drinking some tea, I sat at the table in my trailer and began to write in my journal about my experience during the previous three days. The words flowed from me and filled page after page with dreams and descriptions of physical pain, emotional despair and the soothing comfort of Grandfather. I saw in the words the story of a woman who often ignored her physical body, who rarely asked for help and even less frequently could receive it. There was no one to talk to about my strange experience, so I wrote. I tried to put aside my anxiety about not wanting to do any more ceremonies and what this would mean for my apprenticeship.

As I finished I was surprised to see by the position of the sun that it was late afternoon. I had not had anything to eat, but strangely, I did not feel hungry. I felt restless, uncertain of what to do next. I did not have to drive back to the city to get my sons for another two days. Feeling unsettled, I wandered outside, finally coming in and picking up a book. I lay down on the bed to read, glancing periodically out the window, which overlooked the lake. It had been sunny for most of the day, but now huge gray clouds began to gather on the horizon. The wind seemed to be picking up and the air held the promise of a storm. As I opened the book I heard the distant rumble of thunder.

I tried to read but could not focus. I found myself reading and rereading whole paragraphs I could not remember. The sky became overcast and the sound of the thunder drew closer. I tried to ignore it. Normally I love thunderstorms and my sons and I always go outside or sit at the window, whether we are in the bush or the city, when the thunder, lightning, wind and rain begin. I love the sense of power beyond human control. Many Native stories are filled with the magic and power of words from the Thunder Beings. When I started teaching the medicine way, a thunderstorm gathered on each night of my first three classes as I put my prayers in the pipe. It had felt like a confirmation, a positive sign.

But this was different. I didn't want to acknowledge the Thunder Beings, I wanted to read my book in peace. I had done my ceremony, it had been difficult and I wanted to be left alone. The roll of thunder did not feel comforting. It felt like an elbow in the ribs, an unwanted voice calling for my attention. No matter how hard I tried, I could not concentrate on my book, and the thunder continued, although no lightning was visible and no rain fell. Finally, in exasperation, I threw down my book and said in a loud and somewhat belligerent voice, "O.K., O.K.! What is it?"

Instantly the thunder crashed directly overhead in an earsplitting crack, shaking me to the core. I was terrified. Feeling contrite, I continued in a trembling voice, "Sacred ones, I apologize. I give thanks for your presence, forgive me. I am tired and I do not know what I must do."

The thunder rolled in a deep, penetrating rumble. I pondered the meaning. Perhaps I needed to do a small ceremony to bring proper closure to what had occurred. Certainly I had not completed my ceremony in very good humor. I walked outside and offered some tobacco to the earth and sky, the four directions, the spirit of my ancestors, thanking them for my time alone and asking for guidance in understanding the meaning it held for my life. I walked back to the trailer, but as my hand reached for the door handle, the thunder rolled again, ominous and warning, above me. Clearly this was not enough. I sat down and looked upward toward the billowing, dark gray clouds piling up above me.

"O.K. Clearly I need to do something else, right?" The thunder rolled gently in confirmation. "What about a pipe ceremony? Do I need to do another pipe?" The responding rumble felt incomplete, as if that, too, would not be enough. I sat still and thought. A terrible suspicion began to form in the back of my mind. I raised my face skyward again. "I need to do another gateway ceremony?" The thunder bounced back and forth between the four directions, exuberant, confirming. I was immediately on my feet.

"No way. No, I can't! With all due respect, there is no way I can do another long ceremony alone right now. Even if I wanted to I don't have anyone to monitor me. I'm dog-tired and weak and I still don't understand what I was supposed to learn in the last ceremony!" I also didn't think it was a good idea for anyone to do ceremonies close together without time between for reflection. Angrily I called out, "I can't. I won't!"

As I uttered the words, the thunder cracked again directly overhead, once, twice, three times. The ground shook and I sat down feeling defeated. I took a few deep breaths, trying to slow my racing heart and clear my head. This was crazy. Was I really going to put myself through another ceremony because I thought the thunder was speaking to me? Was I finally, truly, losing it? This was ridiculous. I needed rest, recuperation, fun. Maybe the physical pain in the Purification Lodge had unhinged my mind a little. This was my imagination and nothing more. Determined, I stood up and headed for the trailer. Again the thunder cracked above me three times in succession. This was more than coincidence. Crazy or not, I could not ignore it.

I sat back down on the ground. "Isn't there another way?" I asked, my voice small. Resigned, I went into the trailer to get my notes. I knew I had been given a detailed description of the next ceremony, although I could not remember what it was. Pulling out my notes and reading them, I felt my heart sink even further. It was worse than I had thought. Next on the list to be done was a two-day, one-night ceremony. I was to call on the Tuolanani, my demons, and conjuring them through the pipe into a triangle of stones outside the unsealed medicine wheel. This was not a gentle, contemplative ceremony but one of seeing and confronting internal and external demons. It felt dangerous. The first half of the ceremony was to be done in daylight and it was already late afternoon. By the time I got set up it would be dusk and I would be doing this frightening ceremony as darkness fell. I knew that dusk was one of the times in the day when the "crack between the worlds," the veil between spirit and substance, is most open.

Discouraged, I went back outside, sat with my notes in my lap and sent out my prayer. "Sacred Thunder Beings, I thank you for speaking to me. I do not want to do this ceremony at this time, but I am willing to follow your guidance. If this is what needs to be done, I will do it." As soon as I finished my prayer, the thunder rolled, a long and sustained rumble that moved across the sky. I felt a tiny surge of energy, and stood up. "Thank you," I said softly as I went to gather my pipe and other medicine items needed for the ceremony. The clouds began to move off, the sky began to clear and the thunder rumbled gently into the distance, finally disappearing. There had been no rain, no storm, only an hour of conversation with the Thunder Beings.

With the decision made, I moved as quickly as possible, wanting to complete the first day's ceremony before darkness fell. Despite my tiredness I was anxious to follow the instructions for this ceremony exactly. I did not want any alchemical errors, particularly since no one was monitoring me or knew what I was doing. Having made all the preparations and set up my wheel, I stood with my medicine pipe and called on the Tuolanani, the demons, to show themselves to me. It was dusk, that time of day when all things are visible but have lost their color, the time of grays. The trees, rocks, bushes around me were monochromatic in the fading light, grainy like an old black-and-white TV picture. As my voice rang out the breeze fell. The birds were silent. Nothing made a sound. With my heart in my throat, I waited.

Before me in the triangle of stones outside my circle I saw a face. It was not human, not animal. It was the grotesque face a five year old might imagine when thinking of monsters, with a yawning black hole for a mouth. I stepped forward, without taking my eyes off the figure, into the blackness. As I did a memory washed over me with such suddenness and vividness that my legs almost buckled under me. I'd had the memory before as a mental picture, but now it was physical, felt in every cell of my body.

I was about four or five years old, lying in my bed listening to my parents arguing in the next room. I was straining to hear their words, sure I was the cause of their argument. Suddenly, from within my room, I could hear voices, soft and dark, wooing me. The feeling in my body was a kind of nausea, a sickly sweetness. There was a smell in the room and a taste in my mouth—harsh, metallic, like the smell of ozone during a thunderstorm or the taste if you put your tongue on a battery.

One voice was in charge, an androgynous voice, slightly more male than female. The voice asked me to go with them, though I didn't know what that meant. They promised me I would not feel lonely or afraid if I went with them. I would be taken care of, able to do or have anything I wanted. I was tempted to say yes but something in me resisted. I knew they were "bad voices." I knew that "God," the gray-haired old man from Sunday school classes, could not help me. I knew the choice was mine. With all the resolve a frightened five year old could muster, I told the voices to go away. Only then, after I had made the decision, could I call on this figure I knew as God to comfort me. I would picture myself lying curled up in his giant hand, knowing the voices would not return that night, that I could sleep safely. I do not know how many childhood nights were spent this way, only that the voices had persisted for some time and then stopped.

Coming back out of the memory, I found myself standing in the darkness, holding my pipe, surrounded by the trees. Keeping my pipe in my hands, I crawled into my sleeping bag in the center of my medicine wheel, mulling over what had happened.

I was amazed that although I had always kept this memory in my mind, I had spent very little time examining it. The feeling was clear. At a very early and vulnerable age something had tried to step into my circle and take advantage of a very lonely and frightened child. What most surprised me was the knowledge that even at such a young age I knew I had to choose whether to go with the voices or not. Although my connection with the God I knew had been very strong, I knew the decision was mine alone, that "He" could not help me until I had chosen.

My adult self was appalled at the unfairness of it all. How could a lonely, frightened child be responsible for such a choice? On the other hand I felt elated. As I learned the ways of magic and sorcery with Raven I had always had some concern about the possible temptation, in times of difficulty, to go with the "dark side," although what this would look like, I had no idea. But if I had already faced and refused these voices when I was a child, completely unaware of their meaning, could I not continue to do so as an adult striving to be more conscious? The choice had been made years before and I had chosen not to deal with my own pain by going with the voices that offered power and gratification.

Exhausted, I fell asleep. I dreamed again of Grandfather sitting beside the stream. We talked of my life, my hope, my fears. His lined face gazed at me kindly and his words lingered as I awoke in the early dawn: "Dare to dream it all, Oriah."

The day was one of journeying, of moving around the medicine wheel, smoking my pipe in each direction and finding an ally who would speak to me of my inner demons. In each place I sat for a long time, moving inward, listening to my breath and heartbeat, and heard the voices of old women, offering wisdom. The woman in the south spoke of my inner child's fear of abandonment. This was not new information. Impatiently I asked what I could do about this.

She replied instantly. "Face the reality of this, of your little girl's terror, and keep this knowledge with you at all times. It will take a long time for the child not to be afraid. You must care for her and watch that her panic is not in charge of what you do. You must not use her fear to cling to people when the woman in you does not have the courage to ask for what she needs. Do you remember the night your mother and father argued and your father walked out of the house? Your mother called out to him, saying, 'Don't you walk out on these kids!' meaning you and your brother. What she meant, but did not have the courage to say was 'Please don't leave me. It's scaring me.' Do not use the child's pain within yourself to provoke guilt or pity in others."

"But the pain I feel is real when I'm afraid someone is leaving."

"Of course it is. It awakens all of your inner child's fears and history of pain. It is very real. Acknowledge it, take care of it but do not add to it by using it."

I sat for a long time contemplating the Grandmother's words. As I moved to the west and sat I heard another's voice, deep and husky like the voice of an ancient being. She spoke to me of my years of physical illness and my ongoing fear of my own body, my fear that it would always let me down. Again I asked for guidance.

"In the face of real physical pain you cannot be better than you are. You can only be who you are. You fear others will see this vulnerability, which you see as weakness. You do not have to prove that you can endure pain. Accept your body as it is—neither less than nor more than others'. It is a fine earth lodge. Accept help when you need it. Soften to your own pain. Do not treat it or your body as the enemy. Think of your body as a part of Grandmother Earth, which it is! Would you exclude one part of Grandmother Earth, especially if it was in pain, from your heart?" Her words touched me and I felt incredible tenderness for this body I have so often neglected and cursed for its limitations of the moment. I was reminded of my physical pain in the previous ceremony and my inability to touch this pain with softness as Grandfather had done.

As I moved toward the north, I heard a voice before I had even asked for assistance. "This is the place you are least known to yourself because your mythology is so heavily dependent upon your 'superior' mental skill." I stopped in my tracks and opened my mouth to speak. "No, no, do not protest. But know that with mythologies come many fears. What if you are not as smart as you think you are? You have never really been tested. What if you are as smart as you think you are and it means nothing? You know that you have brains, but is this what really counts? Perhaps what really counts is something you do not have. Frantically you believe your brains will make you 'worthy,' but, of course, the tiny voice of fear niggles at you, the fear that you are No-Heart." Her voice continued, relentless, probing. "You believe you are known to yourself, but you fear those parts of yourself that are unknown, both light and dark, because they are uncontrollable. Your fear in the north is of losing control. You do not have the answers. You are only beginning to find some of the questions."

I was stunned by her words. "How can I stop this?"

She answered, her voice more gentle. "Give away your pride in your mental and verbal abilities. Dare to test yourself in writing a book, returning to school. Risk failing to do well. Learn to use this incredible gift of the mind to receive with caring all that is offered to you, giving those who offer you something all of your attention and treating their gifts as gold, for they are."

Fatigued, I returned to the center of the circle. I considered sitting down for a rest but felt the pull to continue the journey, to maintain the momentum in order to stay out of my head. I walked to the east and sat down. An image of the desert came to my mind and I sent out a prayer. "Sacred ones, I seek your guidance here. What is my demon in the east?" Silence answered and I waited.

Finally the voice of a woman came to me like a whisper. "Spiritual self-importance is your enemy here. On the one hand you fear being ordinary, not being able to 'see' the extraordinary, not being seen as someone who 'sees.' You doubt even those experiences that are real because you know your desire for 'spiritual thrillseeking.' You doubt everything because you fear your self-importance creates these experiences. On the other hand you are afraid to truly 'see.' What happens when something verifiable occurs? You are afraid! Afraid of your own shadow—literally, and of your power. Will it make you lose your mind, and your most prized assets, mental clarity and self-possession?"

Her words rang with truth. "How can I overcome this enemy?"

"Grandfather will help you. Listen to his voice. Let go of self-importance. Tell people of your errors and your visions with equal conviction."

I moved to the southwest, place of the dream, and sent out my prayer for guidance as I once again smoked my pipe. The Grandmother here spoke slowly. Her voice came from very far away. "The essence of all fears here is that of not being able to have what you really want, of being undeserving, of losing what you have, of asking for too much." She was silent.

"What must I do to conquer this fear?"

"Dare to explore everything you want, to envision all that your heart longs for. Give thanks each morning and evening to the Great Mystery for your life and go for it all!"

I felt complete, so I rose and moved to the northeast. The same voice continued. "The demons here are related to the southwest. But here the fear is of scarcity, that you will not have what you want and need because there is not enough. You fear that if you have others will go without, or will try to take from you." As she spoke a wave of nausea surged through me. I paused to regain my balance and asked how I could conquer this demon.

The Grandmother continued. "Remember the words of your friend and fellow teacher, Daphne. 'If you can't trust the universe, who can you trust?' and 'This is not the time for sacrifice.' Separate this frightened and sometimes stingy part of your lower self from your knowledge of who you really are. Make room for it in your heart as you do for the wounded child, but do not let it rule your actions."

I moved to the northwest and sat. A loon called out over the lake and I felt like crying. The long and lonely call of the loon always reminded me of growing up as a child in Northern Ontario, far from the dirt and activity of the city. I waited awhile and, smoking my pipe, sent out my prayers for guidance once again. The voice that responded was light, younger than the others. She spoke gently. "You fear never being able to go home. Here you fear that the deep longing in your heart that is touched by the song of the loon will never cease. It is the grief of loss of home and the fear that you will never find it because you are unworthy. You fear you are being punished for failing to be more than human."

As she spoke tears flowed silently. I finally asked, "How can I overcome this?"

"By a daily practice that acknowledges you are home, here in your heart, that you are never alone or separate. We, the circle of Grandmothers, are always with you."

It took a long time for my tears to subside. Wearily I moved to the final direction, the southeast, sat with my pipe and raised my face to the sky. I had started at dawn and now it was dusk, the sun just above the horizon. I had had nothing to eat or drink for two days and was emotionally exhausted. Holding my pipe, I raised my voice to the stillness around me. "Great Mystery, I sit in the place of the southeast, place of my ancestors, of my concepts of self. What is my demon here?" The wind began to pick up in the southeast, blowing the hair back from my face. I closed my eyes and focused, listening.

The voice of an ancient one came again. "Granddaughter, you fear you are not basically a good woman, that without rules and laws, watching and shaping you, you would be evil. This fear holds you back from taking any real power. You do not trust yourself as vessel. Love yourself, as you are. See how many of these fears were projections from your mother, who had them of herself. See yourself as you are, light and dark, and cultivate mercy and forgiveness for yourself and others. Be gentler with yourself. There is never a need for, or healing in, harshness."

I stood up and conjured the Tuolanani that was the amalgamation of all these inner fears. Abruptly an image of an old woman, an evil witch, appeared inside the triangle. Her clothes were rags, her limbs rotting, her teeth decayed. She laughed with a nasty crackle and nausea swept over me. She reached out her hand for me and shrieked, "You can't. You can't." I recognized the voice as one I have often heard in my head. Often skillful, melodic, reasonable, it has come many times, warning me not to be "unrealistic" about life and my abilities, not to hope or dream for "too much."

I banished the figure in the triangle, sending her away. I knew her only access to me was through the fears unacknowledged fears I held in my body and mind. I stilled her voice of doubt and criticism by focusing on my breath, remembering what I knew and would always know. Suddenly I felt a great tenderness for myself, a desire to take care of myself in a way I had never felt before.

I offered tobacco to all the directions and the spirits, in thanks for their guidance. Closing my pipe, my mind empty of thoughts, I dismantled the circle, gathered my belongings and walked back through the forest to my trailer. I was exhausted, but it was the fatigue at the end of a journey, the contented weariness of work well done. Putting my things away and drinking a cup of tea, I made a few notes in my journal and crawled into bed. I felt I had been gently but completely taken apart and put back together. I thanked the Grandmothers and fell asleep.

6

The darkness of the dream enveloped me. Even as I drifted into sleep I heard the voices of the Grandmothers calling me. I moved into the warm blackness and looked for the soft orange glow of the fire. The flickering light sent shadows to play on the stone walls of the kiva and across the faces of the old ones sitting in a circle. They sat quiet, still, gazing at me steadily, each wrapped in a blanket. A shiver ran up my back. There was one place empty on the circle. Nervous and uncertain, I approached the spot and sat down cross-legged. I felt I was sitting in the south of the circle.

The Grandmother in the north, sitting directly across from me, spoke first. My view of her was partially obscured by the fire in the center of the circle, though her face was visible above the crackling flames. It was lined and brown, her eyes keen and bright like those of a bird. Her hair fell in curling tangles of gray around her shoulders. The words came from her lips in a language I did not recognize—short clipped sounds— but I heard them in my head as English. "We have called you to begin the teaching. We will over time give you twelve wheels to guide the Sisterhood, for you to share with others."

She looked at me expectantly. I nodded to indicate I understood, my mind reeling. Twelve new wheels, given in the dream? How would I ever remember them? What were they? Why me? What would I do with them? Was I going to teach them? Write them? What if people thought I'd made them up?

"Oriah!" Her tone was commanding. She shook her head slowly and glanced at the other Grandmothers as if to say, "Keeping this one on track will be a challenge." More gently she spoke again. "Just relax and listen to the sound of my voice."

I took a deep breath, consciously trying to relax my shoulders and clear my mind, dropping my weight into the earth. "Close your eyes, little one." I closed them and from very far away began to hear the deep steady beating of a drum. It came from beneath the cave, from above us and all around us, growing stronger and stronger, as much felt as heard.

It was as if it came from the Earth herself and filled every part of my body. The beating became stronger and seeped into every pore, every cell. A pressure, a sense of fullness, began to spread through my chest and abdomen, and I felt my heart and womb expand and fill. Realization hit me like a flash of light and I spoke out loud. "My God, it's the heartbeat of the earth!"

"Yes, little one." The voice of the Grandmother softly reached me. "Listen. Feel." The heartbeat continued to fill me, and now I began to feel another rhythm, slower and softer than the beating, expanding and contracting. It was her breath. I felt myself expand with her inhale, relax and drop inward with the exhale. Tears began to stream down my face. "She is alive. She really is alive. Her breath is mine. Her heartbeat is in me."

"Yes." The Grandmother spoke again. "Now follow the sound of the beating heart, and feel within yourself how it is for you when you do not dream. Remember the days when your spirit was so tired that no dreams came in the night to offer guidance and comfort to you. Feel in your body the memory of that time." As she spoke I was gripped with anxiety and the feeling of weariness and desperation that comes to me when I do not dream. There have not been many such times in my life. I have had my dreams with me since I was a very small child. But brief periods without dreams have taken me into a place of cold darkness, a feeling of walking through the day asleep, unable to touch myself or others, off balance, wary, nerves taut, struggling to continue. I felt my body tense with the memory.

The Grandmother spoke again as I remembered this anxiety. "This is how it is for Grandmother Earth when the Sisterhood continues to give its power away. The Sisterhood carries the Dream of Grandmother Earth in its circles, its gifts, in the power of its heart and womb. Grandmother Earth is struggling to heal herself from the imbalances being created. She struggles not only for herself but for her children; the plant people, the swimmers, crawlers, four-leggeds, winged ones and human children. Her body is being torn apart by the two-leggeds, and she struggles, like all mothers, to continue to provide for these children. But the Sisterhood carries her dreams, and she needs this in the same way that you do, for strength, guidance and for the healing of the heart. Every time a sister betrays her own heart, the sacred circle is broken, a piece of that dream is lost and the Earth struggles with less than she might have. Feel it, see it, know what that is like for your mother, the Earth."

I could still hear her heartbeat in my body, her breath all around me. And now I felt her struggle. Images passed in front of me: men tearing holes in the earth to extract the minerals, her organs; huge rain forests slashed and burned; bare rocks where once there was soil and plant people, her skin raw and blistered; poisons flowing into waterways, her bloodstream dark and sluggish; otters and geese suffocating in the thick oil spills, her children dying. And I felt her struggle, felt her moving her huge mass in protest, in rage, not even for her own pain but for the children she could not nourish because of these wounds. I felt her reach down and pull on every ounce of strength she had to bring all things into balance. Her heart beat laboriously. I felt it in my own chest as it cleansed the polluted blood-flow of rivers, oceans and lakes. The breath burned my throat raw as she struggled to pull in the contaminates and breathe out clean air for her children. She moved her bones, her muscles and the earth heaved, cracked and shifted as she struggled to regain her balance. I felt her reach for more strength, more heart and beyond into spirit, into the dream.

New images appeared: circles of women singing, chanting, drumming, dancing, praying, passing the pipe, healing one another, honoring their bodies, laughing, crying, holding one another, holding their children, holding their brothers. And with each image, I felt her breathe a little easier, a bit fuller. But these images flickered. They were intermittent, an unsteady flow.

The Grandmother in the north called to me again. "The people need the Earth and Grandmother Earth needs her Dream. The Sisterhood must learn now. These wheels will help you in this learning."

Slowly the sound of the beating drum receded, but even when I could no longer hear it, I knew it was there. It was always there as was the expanding and contracting of her breath. I opened my eyes and looked at the circle of Grandmothers through my tears. My voice was hoarse and shaky. "I do not know if I can do this. I am afraid I'm not strong enough. To touch the world's pain and despair and my own within it . . . I am afraid that I do not have the strength for the task you put before me."

The Grandmother to my left, in the west, spoke. Even sitting she was a tall woman. Her face was strong and angular, her hair long, dark and straight. "What is the very worst pain you can think of? Pain you do not think you could bear?"

I answered without hesitation. "The death of one of my sons."

"Watch carefully," she replied, nodding toward the fire.

I gazed into the flames and scenes appeared in the glowing embers. I saw many women, white settlers in one-room cabins, Native women in tipis, women planting crops, cooking over open fires. All had children. I saw women strain in childbirth and reach down between their legs for the squalling, blood-covered infants; women walking through deep snow, babies wrapped in shawls held close to their bodies for warmth; toilworn women placing the greedy mouths of hungry babies to their breasts and drifting into restless sleep as the child nursed; women wiping tear-stained faces and offering comfort in their laps; women watching sleeping children, lightly kissing their heads and smiling. And then I saw scenes of the same women, rocking small lifeless bodies in their arms, keening to the sky, placing small coffins into the earth, putting tiny bundles on funeral platforms.

I heard the Grandmother's voice. "These are your ancestors. They bore their children knowing from the beginning, when they first came from their wombs, that they would bury at least one of them—taken by poverty, accident, disease, war, starvation, in a time when life was hard. Feel their pain and their strength as they give back to the Great Mystery and their Earth Mother." Suddenly I was in the body of a woman standing at the edge of a grave. A small rough coffin lay in the earth. I could see my boots and the bottom of my skirt. I could feel a pain in my chest as if my heart were being torn in half, and I longed to jump into the grave and howl. My arms reached out and I felt a spade in my hands. Slowly I began to shovel earth into the hole, covering the box and the body of my child. When the hole was filled I sat next to the raw earth and smoothed it with my hands. I felt quieter now and sat for a long time. The air became cooler, the light dimmer, and I rose to leave. I watched my feet move away from the grave, one step at a time.

"Feel her strength, and that of all the other women who came before you. This ability, to know life and death, they give to you. It flows in your blood. It is the strength that is part of your inheritance as woman. With it is there anything you could not do for your people?"

I felt the blood of my ancestors in my veins. I looked across at the Grandmother in the west. "Thank you, Grandmother." For the first time she smiled.

"And now we will begin with the first wheel."

With those words I woke up. I felt disoriented and, turning toward the clock, was surprised to see it was only one-fifteen in the morning. I felt as if I had been dreaming for hours. Groggily, half awake, I groped along the floor next to my mattress and found my notebook and pencil.

Without turning on the light I began to write down words, phrases that would keep the memory of the dream for me. Drained, I let the book and pencil fall, rolled over and pulled the blankets higher. I fell asleep immediately and, to my astonishment, woke up in the kiva.

Again I sat with the circle of Grandmothers, the fire burning in the center of the round chamber. The Grandmother in the east spoke first. She was a tiny woman, barely visible in the blanket wrapped around her. She spoke smoothly and quickly. "This is the first wheel, within which all twelve are contained." As she spoke I could see circles of light appear in the cave above our heads. It was as if her words materialized in the air, spinning in blues, greens, purples and pinks. "The Sisterhood holds the Dream. This wheel will tell you how. In each of the cardinal directions are teachings to enable women, individually and collectively, to hold the Dream. In the noncardinal directions are the different aspects of the Dream itself. I will speak first of the cardinal directions." She paused. "Do you understand?"

"I think so." How would I remember all this?

"Just relax and listen," the Grandmother in the north interjected, and smiled reassuringly.

The Grandmother in the east continued, "Great healing must take place for the Sisterhood to hold the Dream of Grandmother Earth with strength and consistency. In the south are teachings for balancing the inner child and healing the heart. The wheels of the south will guide you in touching your wounded spirit and brokenheartedness with real mercy. Without some tenderness for self, and others who are but a mirror of self, the Dream cannot be held. Each must know herself as worthy of having her own dream, as deserving of the love and guidance of her ancestors. These are the Wheels of Self-Love."

She paused again and then continued, "In the west are the teachings of the Birthing Wheels. Here is the knowledge and wisdom of the power of the feminine: Life-Giver and Death-Bringer. Through these teachings women touch the power of their physical ability to birth children and the model of wisdom this offers for birthing all that exists in the world. The knowing of the power women hold in their bodies, the wisdom they can touch in their moon cycles, conception, pregnancy, birthing, child-rearing and menopause are what enables them to hold the Dream. This does not mean all women need to birth physical children, but the Sisterhood must listen to the stories of this experience for the knowledge it offers. From these stories and this knowing in every woman's body, each individual learns to birth all that she is: dreams, ideas, work, health, home, creativity, relationships and much more. Collectively you give birth to the world of your children. Through her body each woman is connected to the planet itself, and to the power it holds." I felt her words stir the memory, in my body, of the births of my sons.

"The teachings of the north bring the sisters into alignment with all life on Grandmother Earth. Here is the knowledge that all are your relations. Coming into alignment with the other worlds of Grandmother Earth allows you to touch the common Mind that moves through all. You must feel at a cellular level the life-force that flows through you and all that is, how the blood that flows through your veins and the fluid moving up and down the body of one of the Standing Tree Nation pulses with the same energy. With this knowledge of the interconnectedness of all life comes the wisdom to ensure the life of the People. For the Dream to be held you must have this knowing.

"The teachings of the east are for balancing the masculine and feminine energies within and without. These teachings reweave the torn Marriage Basket, the container for re-membering those pieces of the Dream that have come before your time and will ensure the future. Here you must learn to still the war between the masculine and feminine, to truly create the Sacred Marriage that ensures the people will continue. In the east are the Heartflame Wheels, knowledge for holding the Dream with passion."

The Grandmother paused again. I looked around the circle, my vision blurred, and my head grew heavy and dropped to my chest—I felt worn out. I woke up in my bed. The clock read two-twenty-six. This time I turned on the light, anxious to make my notes complete. Quickly I wrote down what the Grandmother had said. It felt overwhelming, each piece the work of a lifetime and more. I turned off the light and lay back down, sure I would have trouble getting back to sleep. In moments I felt myself drift off and reenter the dream.

The Grandmothers sat waiting in the kiva. Again I sat in the south. The Grandmother to my immediate right, in the southeast, leaned forward and laid her hand on my arm. Her hand felt soft, wrinkled and warm. She spoke quietly, her voice husky. "You must not be discouraged. Remember all things are a wheel. This is not a linear process, an all-or-nothing proposition. Each woman develops all places on the wheel at her own pace. Each healing, each new real understanding, adds to her ability, and the ability of the Sisterhood circle as a whole to hold the Dream. Everyone begins in different places and moves in her own pattern and at her own pace."

I smiled my thanks to her.

The small Grandmother in the east resumed her teaching. "Remember, the wheel I am describing to you contains all the other teaching wheels. In each of the places I have briefly described to you there is a teaching wheel, with eight directions—a guide or key for developing the power I am describing. In turn each of the eight directions on these wheels will unfold to contain another wheel." As she spoke I could see a three-dimensional image appear above her head, a holographic picture of spheres appearing within spheres. I shook my head, feeling inundated. How would I ever remember it all? The Grandmother to my right again touched my arm.

"It will all unfold, little one. One petal at a time. One petal at a time."

The Grandmother of the east went on. "Now I will speak of the non-cardinal directions. In each sits two faces of one aspect of the Dream of Grandmother Earth, making this a twelve wheel, a nagual wheel. The two faces are two viewing points of that aspect of the Dream, one from the collective or macrocosm, the other from the individual or micro-cosm. I will start in the southwest. Here is the Dream of the Individual, each person's medicine, gifts, path with heart. In one face we see the individual's free-will choices during a particular life or dance. In the other face we see what appears to be fate or destiny, choices you have made before you entered this dance to participate in the Collective Dream. Together they show you the Dream for which you have taken birth."

I listened carefully. I have always felt a struggle between wanting to take full control of and responsibility for my life and needing to surrender to what seemed to be an unknowable larger plan.

She continued, "In the northwest we see the two faces of the Dream of the Planet. This is the Dream of places upon Grandmother Earth. In one face you see, or often feel, this Dream as a place of power on the planet—Machu Picchu, Dreamer's Rock, Mount Shasta. The brothers and sisters of the tribes in Australia have not lost the ability to hear the Dream of different places. In the other face we see the Dream of the places within, for each woman holds within her body a microcosm of the energy vortexes of the earth. When you are able to bring the two—the places within, and the places on the earth—into alignment, this aspect of the Dream is manifest, often in the ceremonial forms of dancing, singing, movement and prayer. Each person will find some places easier to align with than others. These are their places of power for this dance. Here they are able to hear and see the Dream of the Planet, the history of

Grandmother Earth's and their own changes and the movement between the two."

I thought about my trailer site in the bush. When I'm there I am aware of my body in different ways. I am aware of my womb, my hips and pelvis, their weight, shape, fullness and link to the darkness of the dense forest. I wondered if this was a little of what she meant.

"In the northeast we see the two faces of the Dream of the People. In one face we see 'that which feeds the people, that which ensures life for your children's children to seven generations. This is the Dream not only of survival, but of that which feeds the soul: Beauty. It is what you would call the Dream of bread and roses. In the other face we see how each individual's gifts and creativity can be used, fostered and honored to bring this food to the people.

"In the southeast we see the Dream of the Ancestors. In one face you will see us, your ancestors, and the love and vision we hold for you and your brothers and sisters. In the other face you will see yourself, the concept you hold of who you are as Granddaughter of the ancestors. In these two faces of the Dream you are guided to know what it is to be fully human." She paused and looked directly into my eyes. "In working with this wheel remember all that you have been taught. Each place mirrors its opposite. The powers of the cardinal directions stabilize the wheel— the Dreams of the noncardinal directions create movement and change. All happen simultaneously, interwoven and yet separate.

"The degree to which each aspect of the Dream is lived, corresponds to the degree to which the Sisterhood has developed their abilities to hold the two cardinal directions on either side of that aspect of the Dream. For instance, a woman's ability to hold the Dream of the Individual in the southwest, to know and live her own Sacred Dream, to surrender to and find joy in the tasks she has set for herself in this life dance, is dependent upon her ability to dance the south Wheel of Self-Love and the west Birthing Wheel. If she does not know, through the body of woman, the power of the feminine to give birth or bring death to all that is manifest on this planet, she will not be able to consciously dance her own dream awake. If she is unable to touch her own woundedness with mercy and love she will not feel worthy or capable of seeing and living her dream. Do you understand this?"

I nodded hesitatingly. "I . . . I think so. It feels like a lot."

Quiet laughter rippled around the circle. "It is," she replied. Again my vision became unclear and I had the urge to lie down and sleep. I woke up in my bedroom. Flipping on the light, I reached for my notebook and checked the time. It was four o'clock. Rapidly but carefully I wrote out all I could remember and switched the light off. I was exhausted again. Ruefully I realized what all those years of nursing my two sons through the night had been for: perfect training for waking up repeatedly in the middle of the night and going immediately back to sleep. It took me longer to drift into sleep this time, but again I found myself in the kiva with the Grandmothers. Once more the Grandmother of the east began to talk. "Now—"

"Grandmother, please, may I speak?" She looked at me and waited. "I cannot do more on this night. I thank you for your teachings, but I'm exhausted. I must rest. Can we do more another time?"

She looked around the circle. Several heads nodded, and the Grandmother beside me spoke to the others. "It is enough for now. We must remember her humanness. There will be time for more." She leaned toward me. "Rest now, little one." Feeling as if I could weep with tiredness, I nodded to her in gratitude and lay down on the ground. Darkness enveloped me. I slept.

The alarm woke me at seven. Half-asleep, I crawled out of bed and called to my sons to get up. I was ready to drop. I glanced at my notebook. Page after page was filled with words from the Grandmothers. I could hardly believe it. I was to be given twelve wheels for the Sisterhood?

I heard Brendan at my door. "Mum? Are you getting up or what? We're hungry."

"Yeah, I'm coming." Every move was a struggle. Shouldn't someone with a housekeeper or without children be doing this kind of thing all night? I stumbled downstairs to fix breakfast and lunches before the school bus arrived.

After my sons had left, I sat and read my notes. My memory of the night was vivid. My notes were detailed. I sat quietly for a long time, dumbfounded by what had happened. What should I do with all of this? Was it real? It certainly felt real, but how did I know? What if it was just my self-importance? I decided to talk to Raven about my experience. I was going to Arizona in less than eight weeks to attend a workshop he was teaching. In the meantime I would work with the wheels and see if I could use them in my own life.

In the next eight weeks the dreaming continued and the Grandmothers continued to teach me, although there were no more all-night marathons. I asked them about sharing the wheels with Raven. They were curiously quiet but did not object. I asked them repeatedly about my relationship to

Raven as my teacher, and the request he had made for more "commit-ment" in Palenque. Each time they gave only one reply: "You cannot save Raven." They would not elaborate. I couldn't see how this answered my question. Something about it filled me with dread.

Two months later I was in Arizona. I had arrived three days early for the weekend workshop in order to do a Walk-Talk ceremony and to have some time to talk with Raven. This was the last ceremony needed to complete the third gateway. It was a mandatory group healing ceremony to create death, change and rebirth in the apprentice's life by having him or her "taken apart" and "put back together" by the group. I had sat on such a circle for one woman during our journey to Tula. Sixteen people, guided by a Dance Chief, listened to the apprentice's life story and reflected back her eight different aspects of self, both light and dark. The dark mirroring provided the "taking-apart," and the light mirroring the "putting-together." Mitch and other apprentices had gone through it, and although I had not seen any apparent change in them as a result, all professed to feeling profoundly transformed. I was not looking forward to the ceremony, but Raven continued to urge completion of the gateways. At my request, Lynn, now in charge of Raven's office, had ar-ranged my ceremony for the second night after my arrival.

On my first night I dropped in for an evening class Raven was holding with advanced apprentices. When I arrived, very few people were around and Raven sat in the classroom, studying some notes. Three other people wandered around the room. I chose a seat in the corner opposite Raven. He did not look up as I entered, and I did not want to interrupt his read-ing, although I was sure he was aware of my presence. Slowly the room began to fill and Raven continued to read. As everyone settled in, Lynn held up a hand for quiet. "We still need a few people for Oriah's Walk-Talk tomorrow night. Is there anyone here who can come?"

Raven spoke without taking his eyes off the page in front of him. "This is a real important ceremony. We need a strong circle. Oriah is a strong woman and one of the strongest apprentices. It's important that we put together a good circle." He glanced up and, looking at me, feigned surprise. "Oh, Oriah! I didn't realize you were here." I squirmed in my chair as the other apprentices watched me. I was sure he had known I was there all along. I wondered what he was up to.

Several people volunteered for the ceremony, including Tom, with whom I had been lovers with two years earlier at the Sundance. At the desert retreat he had been furious when I had decided not to continue our relationship. He responded now to the request for volunteers with disturbing enthusiasm. "Put me down. That's one taking-apart circle I don't want to miss!"

By the end of the class they had put together a full circle of people for the ceremony, scheduled for the next evening. I had arranged with Raven to have a Mayan Book of Life reading the following afternoon, before the ceremony. The Mayan Book of Life is a Tarot deck designed by Peter Balin. Raven uses the major arcana to do a reading for the upcoming year, charting the tasks and energy needed in each aspect for maximum growth, pleasure and knowledge. I had not had a reading with him since the trip to Jamaica, two years earlier.

I arrived the next day with some trepidation. During the last reading Raven had told me I would become an apprentice and begin teaching, two things that did not feel like even remote possibilities at the time. Both had occurred within the year. He had also said that I would become a full medicine woman.

As I waited for Raven to prepare for the reading I sat down and visited with Susan. I was feeling anxious about the ceremony that night and the possibility of Tom seeking revenge for unrequited love within the context of the taking-apart circle. I had mentioned my concern to two other apprentices the night before, but they had chided me about my lack of courage and of trust in the Great Mystery to set up the circle I most needed for my healing. I hoped raising it with Susan now did not demonstrate a lack of trust in the Great Mystery but I couldn't help hearing my mother's Scottish Presbyterian adage, "God helps those that help themselves," contradicting this sentiment.

"Susan, I'm worried about tonight. Tom has volunteered to be on my Walk-Talk. I think he might have some ulterior motives." Susan raised her eyebrows in question. "A couple of years ago we spent some time together at a gathering. It was pleasant, but not something I wanted to continue. He was hurt and angry and I don't think he's gotten over it."

"How long ago was this?"

"Two years."

"And I assume that by 'time together' you mean you were lovers."

"Yes, but very briefly."

"And he's still upset about it?" She looked surprised.

"I know, it seems crazy, but he still seems very angry."

"Must have been quite a brief encounter." I felt myself blush as she sat and thought for a moment. "Well, you're right. It's not appropriate for anyone to be on a healing circle if they have unresolved personal feelings. I'll speak to him beforehand and ask Denise, the Dance Chief, to replace him."

I felt incredibly relieved and pleasantly surprised that she had taken my concern as legitimate. Lynn came into the room and told me Raven was ready to do the reading. I went to his office.

I had never been to Raven's office before. It was a small, windowless room, about eight-by-ten feet. A large desk, wall unit with television and VCR and numerous bookshelves filled the space. Martial arts trophies and plaques hung on the walls; medicine items lined the shelves. The air was stale and smoky, the light dim. The lack of windows gave a sense of timelessness: it could have been any hour of day or night outside. We sat in the tiny space on the floor in front of the desk, opposite each other. I had brought my recorder to tape the session.

Raven is a symbol dancer, someone who works wonderfully with symbols like those on the cards. As he flipped up the cards and put them in their pyramidal layout for the year, he spoke steadily and quickly, translating the symbols and their meaning for me in the upcoming year, pausing occasionally to ask me questions. As he spread the line of cards dealing with relationships he stopped and looked at me.

"So, what's going on with the men in your life?"

"Well, I am in a relationship with Morgan but . . . well, I'm not sure it has the same meaning for both of us. I'm realizing that I do not make relationship the center of my life. It's wonderful to have, but I know I would be O.K. without it. I think it is more central for him."

Raven nodded. "Good. Your medicine is the center of your life, not relationships. That's the way it should be." He paused again before laying out the next card. "This is your Destiny card, what your higher self knows you are destined to do and need to do at this time in your life." He flipped up the card, number two, the Priestess. "It is your Destiny to be a Phoenix Firewoman."

Instantly I heard the now-familiar distant droning sound in my head, as a slight dizziness washed through me. A Phoenix Firewoman is someone who is trained in the use of sexual energy and magic in healing. Many of the apprentices who attend spiritual-sexuality workshops aspire to, or at least train for, this position. As far as I knew the only way to learn how to use this knowledge for healing was in "hands-on" training with Raven himself. "Uh . . . Raven, I know a lot of apprentices who would like to be Firewomen, but this has never been something I've felt particularly drawn to. I've never asked to be a Firewoman."

"You don't choose it. You're chosen. That's the way it works," he replied.

"Uh-huh." I sounded as dubious as I felt. He pressed on with the reading. The final card, showing my path for the year was number twelve, the Hanged Man. Raven called it the path of the Heyoka Grandmothers, the old ones who teach by tricking. I wondered what that would look like.

As we finished the reading I spoke. "Raven, there's something else I'd like to ask you about." He nodded. "I have had a number of dreams where I see a circle of Grandmothers. They have told me they will teach me twelve new wheels for the Sisterhood and other dreams have given me some of these wheels."

Raven nodded again. "Sounds good. I'd like to hear about them sometime."

"I feel like I'm just learning them right now, but I would really like to share them with you down the road a little and get your reaction. I am thinking of sharing them with the women's Moon Lodge at home in an effort to see if I can articulate them and do them justice."

We had gone well over the time set up for the reading. I paid Raven and left. Feeling unsettled, I went to prepare for the ceremony. On my way to the car I ran into Tom in the parking lot. I paused to speak with him.

"How are things up in Canada?" His tone seemed friendly.

"O.K. I'm generally having a good time," I answered. "How are things with you?"

He hesitated. "O.K., I guess. How about the men? Break any new hearts lately?" The words were joking, his tone was not. I stood silently, looking at him for a moment, then spoke softly. "Tom, why are you still so angry with me? It's been a long time."

The anger drained from his face at my words. He spoke, his voice full of emotion. "It's not you I'm angry with—it's myself."

"Well, it sure feels directed at me."

He stared at me for a moment. "You just don't get it, do you?" He shook his head. "You walk in and I see what I want . . . and I know I can't have it. And it makes me mad!" I couldn't think of anything more to say. He climbed into his van and started it up. Leaning out the window, he smiled slightly. "You'll be happy to know I've taken myself off the circle for your ceremony tonight. Just didn't feel like the right thing to do." He pulled out of the parking lot. I felt relieved but sad.

The ceremony was to be held in the converted garage at Raven's home and I arrived half an hour before the scheduled start. To my delight and surprise, Will and Rick, the two brothers and martial artists from Texas I had spent time with at the desert retreat, were there. Will was to be on the circle. Rick and I caught up on old news as we waited for the ceremony to begin. Finally, an hour and a half later, Lynn called me inside.

I stepped into the garage which had been converted into a comfortable room for ceremony, and was greeted by the silent stares of a circle of sixteen men and women sitting in the nude. In most healings the patient, in this case me, must be nude. It enables those doing doctoring and dance chiefing to "see" the energy changes more clearly, and it certainly starts the process without the usual first line of defenses. For most healings the circle is similarly unclothed, primarily out of support for the person in the center. While it can be uncomfortable being the center of attention without your clothes on, it can be unbearable if all the other people in the room are dressed. I had been on enough healing circles to feel relatively comfortable with and appreciative of this practice. Many people who have never participated in a healing have questioned me on the need for nudity and the possibility of sexual misconduct as a result. But doing a strenuous and often difficult task together in the nude is not sexy, and I have never seen or felt any such misconduct in a healing.

I took off my clothes and jewelry and set them in the corner of the room. I was shaking slightly, probably more from nervousness than the coolness of the room. Denise was ready to do a pipe ceremony and motioned for me to sit opposite her. Denise had not been at the apprentice gatherings I had attended. It soon became clear that she had never dance chiefed this ceremony before. Crystal, a senior apprentice, was there to monitor and guide her—the ceremony was to be a training session for Denise. While I understood the need for training, I was disappointed. I had met Denise briefly the day before and had a short conversation with her about some of the teachings. While clearly sincere and eager to learn, she was very new to the medicine. Although full of doubt and trepidation about this ceremony, I really did want to utilize it to its fullest: to allow all my usually skillful mental, verbal and emotional defenses to be met and dismantled by the circle. I knew that Denise was no match for this. She was clearly intimidated by me and insecure about her ability to do the ceremony.

Putting aside my disappointment, I focused on the pipe ceremony. Denise filled her pipe, calling in all the spirits and powers to be with us, asking them to help me in my ceremonial healing. I had done a number of pipes for others, and many for myself, but this was the first time anyone had done a pipe for me. I was deeply touched by her prayers, by the time and energy she and everyone else in the room were giving to help me on my journey.

As the pipe was completed Denise directed me to sit in the center of the circle and face the man and woman sitting in the south. As I faced them I was asked to speak about my life in those aspects held by this direction: relationships, childhood, mother, father. When I felt complete I moved sunwise, to face the next position on the circle and tell more of my story. Slowly I made my way around the circle speaking of my dreams, work, health, sexual history, finances, past life memories, beliefs, lifestyle choices, religious upbringing, spirituality and self-concepts. As I spoke, the people on the circle listened carefully. They had clearly been told to remain impassive, to not show any emotion. I found it difficult not to entertain them. It is what I do—I teach through telling my personal stories, making the sometimes painful parts bearable with humor. As I slipped naturally into doing this, those on the circle struggled not to respond with laughter. When they laughed, Crystal reminded them again to "hold their place." It was clear only some had the experience needed to do so. I began to censor myself to make it easier for them, resenting the lack of opportunity to use, and have dismantled, one of my finest defenses, humor.

When I completed my story around the wheel, I sat silently, awaiting further instructions. Crystal spoke, "So how do you feel now?"

"Fine," I responded warily.

"Look around the circle," she instructed. "What is the worst thing you could say to the people sitting here?"

I looked at the faces around me. Most I did not recognize; some I did. What was the worst thing I could say? Several things ran through my head. *You don't know what you're doing. You do not have the skill to be taking anyone apart.* But antagonizing a group of people who, moments later, would be taking me apart, seemed overly self-destructive. I also dismissed the thought of leaving. Raven was urging me to get through the third gateway as quickly as possible and I wanted to continue to learn within the gateway system. This was a mandatory ceremony, the last to complete the third gateway. I knew if I left I would also have to deal with spoken and unspoken accusations of being too soft, unable to face my own "shit," unwilling to really step into difficult self-examination and change. I couldn't bear to appear to wimp out. I hesitated and then spoke, the words coming unbidden. "I don't trust any of you."

"Good," said Crystal. "Let's begin."

I faced the south again, this time hearing from one of the two people sitting there. They spoke in the first person, mirroring back to me the dark side of what they thought they had heard in my story. Some of it was difficult to hear, and I found my insides churning, my defenses crumbling around the edges, while my face remained impassive and my body still. But people had differing levels of skill and experience with the process. Some made comments that were clearly not applicable to me, giving me a chance to relax and listen with curiosity but no real response. Others, hearing the inaccuracy of their own words, would try to compensate by raising their voices, swearing and becoming very emotional. "I'm shit! I don't know what the fuck I'm doing! No one has ever been good to me . . . ." I could feel some strain in maintaining my composure, but it was not particularly difficult. One woman, frustrated by my lack of response, decided to add dramatic action to her words. She stood up in the southeast and looked at the rest of the group with scorn. "I don't even want to be here," she announced, a pretty good approximation of what I was feeling. Angrily she strode out the door, slamming it behind her. The impact shattered the glass in the door window. Everyone gasped and then laughed as she looked aghast at the result of her drama. Any meaningful impact was lost as she stepped out of role and tiptoed back to the circle.

Their goal was to make me lose my composure, take me apart. I felt a little guilty, and tried to respond more emotionally, allowing tears to come when a comment felt closer to the truth. "Daddy, why didn't you protect me from her anger?"

"I am the Ice Queen. Nothing touches me."

"Why can't the rest of you keep up? I'm brighter and faster than any of you."

"Why didn't you love me, Mum? Tell me what you want me to be. I'll do anything you want."

"I'd do anything just to be pretty."

It went on and on, full of self-pity, held anger, old resentments and insecurities. I did want to learn about those aspects of myself that kept me from being all that I could be. I was willing to look at the dark aspects of myself. But I wanted to feel the tension of my own defenses, to feel the circle was strong enough to have me push back fully. I knew it wasn't.

Periodically Crystal, who was clearly doing the actual dance chiefing, would have a man and a woman, who were not sitting on the circle, pull me to a standing position and walk with me, one on each side, rapidly around the outside of the circle. As we walked around, they leaned close to me and each repeated different phrases from the circle's story into my ears "I'm no good, I'm no good, I'm no good . . . ." The hurried movement, constant sound and the simultaneous phrases in both ears were designed to lower my defenses, spin my shields and take me apart. As we walked I felt myself relax. The feeling was not unlike the warmth I had experienced during the martial arts testing at the desert retreat—a kind of giving up, not caring what anyone did to me. In some ways the whole thing felt all too familiar. I had been here before—beaten, abused. I knew I could take it. I knew I could hide away an essential piece of myself where they could never get at it, as I had when I was raped. I stopped caring. It didn't matter what they did to me. It just didn't matter.

Outwardly I became a bit spacy but remained composed. I could feel the group's frustration with my lack of a more dramatic response. As I moved around to the northeast I faced Nicholas, the apprentice I had met at the desert retreat who had frightened more than a few women with his bizarre behavior. I was surprised that Raven allowed him to sit on these healing circles. Aside from the anchoring exercise we'd done, when Nicholas had voiced his enthusiasm for my choosing the hand he masturbated with, we had had no contact. He watched me now, silent, waiting. Suddenly he leaned forward as if to grab me. Instantly I was clearheaded and alert. I knew this was where I would draw a line. I would take whatever he or the others did verbally, but if anyone tried to push me by being physical I would use every bit of knowledge and training I had to fight. I could hear Delia's voice run through my mind. "What are your weapons? What are your targets?"

I spoke in a low menacing tone, looking him straight in the eyes. "Don't touch me!"

He immediately pulled back, resting his arm on his knee. He stared at his hand for a few moments before speaking. "This is my hand. See the spot on my hand. Strange spot. Funny spot." I had no idea what he was talking about or what it could possibly have to do with the ceremony. I wondered if it had anything to do with his memory of the anchoring exercise. He continued in a singsong voice, "All I see is this spot. Strange spot. Funny spot. This is all I see . . . ."

Others on the circle shifted uneasily, clearly uncomfortable with what was happening. No one intervened. I relaxed a little and again enjoyed the respite from the taking-apart process. When Nicholas stopped speaking, Denise asked me to turn and face the next direction.

After I had faced all the remaining directions, she directed the others to go out of the room, leaving me alone with herself and Crystal. Warily

I laid on the floor, feeling lethargic. Crystal asked me what I thought would help me in the putting-together process. What did I need? What did I want?

I did not want anything from these people. I wanted to go home. I also wanted to trust the ceremony and do my best to receive whatever lessons it held for me. Fearful, but determined to be as honest as possible, I said, "Touching, in a friendly nonsexual way, has always been difficult for me to receive. If people were to touch me gently on the shoulder or arm during the putting-together it might help me receive the light mirrors." Speaking felt risky. It exposed my vulnerability and was difficult, especially after the trying taking-apart.

Crystal responded brusquely. "Well, it's your circle! You will have to ask for what you need!" So much for exposing my vulnerability. Instantly I felt myself recoil, pull away to a distant place within myself. Crystal rose and called the others to come back in. The circle reformed and the process began again. This time I heard people reflect what they felt was the light side of my story. I don't remember what they said. Again, the man and woman periodically walked me rapidly around the circle, speaking phrases in both ears. I cooperated. I did what they asked. I heard the words. But I knew I was not taking it in; I was waiting for it to be over. I felt light, airy and knew I could easily leave my body. I heard Crystal urge the man and woman on either side of me to keep me alert, keep me with them. The woman on my left began to tell jokes and make sexual suggestions about the men sitting on the circle. "How about that one? Wouldn't you just love to sit on his face? Or that one?" I felt giddy, and giggled involuntarily. The laughter brought me fully back into my body. I wondered how long this would go on.

Silently I called to Grandfather. "Grandfather, why am I here? What should I do? Help me."

Instantly I heard his voice within. "I am here, Granddaughter. It will be over soon. Breathe." They laid me down in the center of the circle. Crystal spoke from outside the circle, asking me what I had learned in the ceremony, what vows I wanted to take about changes I needed to make in my life. I lay still, staring at the garage ceiling, trying to think. What had I learned? That I would never again do this ceremony? That I was right not to trust these people? Maybe. I searched my mind for some positive lesson. Well, once again, I had seen my own capacity to withstand what felt like abuse. I had felt the words bounce off me like raindrops on an umbrella. I also knew this capacity to shield myself was not easily dismantled. It offered me some sort of protection, but it also stopped me from taking in the light, love and caring offered by those in my life. I did not know what to say but knew I must speak if I wanted this to end. Finally I spoke. "I want to stop using my capacity to defend against the dark to block my receptivity to the light."

"Good," Crystal replied.

Denise closed the pipe and I rose and distributed my medicine gifts to everyone who had participated. We were all tired. We had been there for almost five hours. Some people began to clean up the broken glass from the door window, while others took up a collection to pay for its replacement. Everyone laughed nervously as they spoke about telling Raven. It felt strange, like kids hiding out after one of them has put a baseball through the neighbor's window.

I left feeling confused. The ceremony had added to the uneasiness I'd felt during my reading with Raven. Had my own resistance defeated the ceremony's potential for transformation? Was it me? Them? The ceremony? I didn't know. Something was off. I wanted to go home.

7

I jump in my chair as the telephone rings. Jarring, it pulls me out of the memories the journals have opened for me. It rings again and I decide to let the answering machine take a message. I have been reading for more than four hours. I rise and stretch. I have not eaten yet today, and going down to the kitchen, I absentmindedly get an apple and return to my desk, mulling over the Walk-Talk ceremony. Sitting down, I continue to read, following the dreams of the past.

The dream was of darkness. I could hear the voice of a Grandmother, but I could not see her. It was like looking at a darkened movie screen. Suddenly her face floated onto the screen. I recognized her as the Grandmother who sat in the north of the circle. She was tiny, with gray curly hair falling in tangles to her shoulders and her eyes were bright, with a mischievous glint. Again her voice was in a language I did not understand but, in my head, I heard the words in English.

"Oriah. See the image of this man." As she spoke, the face of a man appeared on the screen. It was a strong face, somehow familiar. He was blue-eyed and blond, his skin a deep tanned brown. Then I realized where I had seen him before. He was the man who had materialized across from me in my first vision quest, when I'd asked to see my inner warrior. The Grandmother spoke again. "This man is to be your husband. His name is Many Shields."

I was confused. Many Shields was the medicine name of Raven's Navaho teacher. I looked at the man's face again. "But Many Shields was an elderly Native man and he's dead. This man appears to be in his mid-thirties and he doesn't even look Native," I said.

"Do not be fooled by appearances. He is indeed Native. He is Grandfather's grandson, and he is to be your husband."

"Grandfather" was the name Raven called his teacher Many Shields. I had assumed this was who she meant. I looked closely at the man's image again. He reminded me of a friend of mine. "Is this Sam?"

"No. This man is Many Shields. He will be your husband," she repeated.

I woke up. What was this all about? The man in the dream looked like the one who had appeared on my first vision quest. That, combined with the knowledge that Many Shields was dead, led me to conclude that the meaning was symbolic. Since my return from Arizona four weeks earlier, Morgan and I had ended our relationship of two years. Doing so was difficult and painful for us both. Being single, I was spending time considering what it might mean to be more in touch with my own inner male, to develop the sacred marriage within. I wasn't having much luck in my life with external relationships. Perhaps it was time to look within. I guessed that the Grandmothers were trying to give me guidance, directing me to the image of my own inner warrior, which had appeared two years earlier on the quest.

I wrote the dream in my journal, and over the next two days shared it with just three people—Bea, Morgan, who I was still in contact with, even though we were separated, and another friend. I described the image of the man to each of them, explaining how he looked a little like my friend Sam, although he seemed about ten years younger and had a slightly broader face.

The day after I told him, Morgan called. His voice was agitated. He spoke rapidly and seemed short of breath. "Oriah, something's happened. Oh, my God, I don't believe this . . . I just don't believe it!"

"Morgan, are you all right?"

"Yeah, yeah, I'm O.K. It's just . . . I don't believe it. It pisses me off! Part of me doesn't even want to tell you . . . but I have no choice."

By this time I was really beginning to feel alarmed. "Morgan, please, just tell me what happened."

"O.K. I got a call from a man wanting to talk to me about my work. His name is Ray Green. We had lunch together. All of a sudden, in the middle of lunch, he asked me if I'd heard of a medicine man who is in the area doing some teaching. I told him I hadn't and asked him the man's name. He said his name is Many Shields. I almost fell off my chair!"

I felt my stomach turn as Morgan continued. "So, I asked him what Many Shields looked like and he said, 'Well, it's funny. He's Native but he doesn't look it. He has blue eyes and blond hair.'"

My legs felt shaky and I sat down, holding the telephone. "So, to check this out further, I asked him if he knew Sam," Morgan continued, "because you mentioned the man in the dream looked like him. Turned

out he did, at least by sight, and so I asked him if this man looked anything like Sam. He said, 'Yeah, sort of, except he's about ten years
younger and his face is a bit broader.' Those were the words he used."

My head was spinning, my voice hesitant. "Is this man still around?
Does Ray Green know how to get in touch with him?"

Morgan sounded weary. "Yes, I knew you would want to get in touch
with him. He's staying with people I know in the city and I have their
telephone number. I can't believe I'm doing this. Our relationship has
ended and now I'm going to be the one to line you up with your next husband. I feel like I'm being used and I don't like it!" I could hear his pain.

The whole thing was bizarre. For some time I had been teaching
weekly classes. Students often told me about other teachers in the area,
and yet no one had mentioned this man. That Morgan would be the one
to bring me this information felt like a sadistic joke. Why? But the
synchronicity between this information and the dream was too overwhelming to ignore. There was no way I could have made it up. It all
fitted together. Morgan gave me the telephone number and I thanked him
for calling me. Only after I hung up did I realize the additional irony of
Morgan's meeting with Ray Green. The English name of Raven's
teacher, Many Shields, was Roy Green! Was someone having fun at our
expense?

After I calmed down I called the number Morgan had given me and
asked about Many Shields. The woman who answered told me he would
be in Toronto for another week and was doing some classes and personal
readings using medicine teachings. I decided to book a reading for the
next day.

That night I went over it a million times. Many strange and wonderful
things had happened in my life since I had started to walk the medicine
path. But a part of me always looked at these things with a healthy skepticism and searched for other logical explanations—suggestion, chance,
imagination. None of these worked in this situation. Too many pieces
were verifiable. I had written the dream down and shared it, word for
word, with three people I trusted. The name was the same. The description was the same. And the Grandmother said he would be my husband!
I called Raven's office in Arizona and asked if they had ever heard of a
medicine man called Many Shields, who was presently alive and teaching. They had not.

I arrived at the address the woman on the phone had given me fifteen
minutes early and very nervous. I sat in the car and sent out my prayer to

Grandfather. "Grandfather, I ask that you be with me today. Help me to understand what meaning this has in my life."

I could immediately feel his presence. "I am here" was all he said.

Feeling a little calmer, I got out of the car and went to the door. A man answered my knock and led me inside, telling me Many Shields was waiting for me. We walked down a long hallway and into a split-level room, overlooking a huge kitchen and dining area. Standing in the kitchen watching me with a wide grin on his face was the man I had seen on my first vision quest. The lights in the room seemed to flicker, and my knees wobbled as I descended the stairs. He moved toward me and reached out an arm to steady me, his hand touching my arm. A tingling, like an electric shock shot up my arm, down my body and out the soles of my feet. I struggled to keep my composure, frantically calling for Grandfather within. I heard his voice, calm and reassuring, with just a hint of amusement.

"Easy, granddaughter. Relax. One step at a time. Breathe." Suddenly I realized I had been holding my breath since entering the room. I let it out and managed a weak-sounding introduction. "Hi, I'm Oriah."

"Welcome, Oriah. We were just making coffee. Would you like some?" Many Shields replied. I shook my head, not trusting myself with any more words. "We'll be meeting in here," he said, leading the way to a tiny room off the kitchen. I sat in a wooden straight-backed chair next to the door. I thought it would be wise to stay close to the door, in case a speedy exit became necessary. The room was only about eight feet by seven feet, crowded with a bed, a desk, two chairs and numerous boxes. Many Shields closed the door and squeezed past me to the other chair, brushing against my leg. A surge of energy swept through me. I thought I might pass out.

Frantically I tried to think straight. What was happening? This was crazy! I have always prided myself on my self-possession around men, even attractive ones. I am not one of those women who swoon in proximity to any man. I commanded my disoriented self to get a grip!

Many Shields sat silently watching me, a smile tugging at the corners of his mouth. "So what brings you to me?" My mind raced. I did not want to tell him everything in the dream. What could I say? I'm here because a Grandmother in the dream told me you'd be my husband? Great opener. I cleared my throat nervously.

"Well, to be truthful," I said, preparing to be otherwise, "I had a dream about you. I saw a Grandmother who showed me a picture of you and told me your name. I didn't even know you existed, but I told the dream

to a friend of mine, and he heard about you the next day. I was curious
. . . so here I am."

Many Shields leaned forward in his chair. The smile was gone. His
deep blue eyes were serious. "In what direction on the circle did the
Grandmother sit?"

I had not told him there was a circle. "The north," I answered.

He nodded. "Did she speak English?"

"No, actually she didn't. I don't know what language she spoke. It had
short clipped sounds, but I heard her words in my head in English."
Again he nodded, looking thoughtful. What was going on here?

"Was she Native?"

"I think so. That was the impression I got, yes. Her skin was brown—"

He interrupted. "Her hair—like mine? Kinky, curly, only gray?"

"Yes," I responded in amazement. Her hair had been like his. "She
was—"

"—tiny." We both spoke the word together. Who was this Grandmother? Why did he know who she was?

"This woman is my grandmother," he said slowly. She raised me and
taught me much about the medicine. I am named after my grandfather."
Well, the dream had said his name was linked to Grandfather; it just
didn't say which one. He looked at me steadily. "What else did she tell
you about me, or why we would meet?"

I hesitated. My resolve not to tell him the whole dream was dwindling
with the mounting evidence that it had some meaning for both of us on
the tonal. Inwardly I called to Grandfather. "Grandfather, can I tell him
the whole dream?"

I heard his voice, "Yes, little one."

Instantly Many Shields leaned forward. "Who are you talking to?"

I was startled. I knew I had shown no outward sign of calling on
Grandfather. I often asked for his guidance in the presence of others
without anyone realizing it. I do not become glassy-eyed or tranced-out.
The fact that Many Shields could sense this impressed and unnerved me.
There seemed little point in subterfuge if he could tell what I was doing.
I made up my mind. "She told me you would be my husband."

Many Shields blushed to the roots of his curly blond hair. "Aha, I
thought so." He looked up toward the ceiling. "Always looking out for
me, huh, Grandma? O.K." He shifted his weight in his chair, scraping it
noisily on the floor. Somehow his embarrassment and nervousness were
comforting. I felt a little calmer. He seemed at a loss to know how to
proceed.

"Well, how about we do the reading you came for?"

I nodded, relieved to have something else on which to focus. He moved his chair over to the desk, much closer to where I sat. He pulled out a few sheets of paper with circles drawn on them and motioned for me to move my chair so we could both look at the sheets spread on the desk. We sat inches from each other, and I was acutely aware of his proximity.

"When is your birthday?" I jumped and looked blankly at him. He smiled and spoke more softly. "Your birthday—when is it, Oriah?" I told him and he wrote it at the top of one sheet. He paused for a moment and shook his head.

"What is it?" I asked.

"Oh, I don't want to say right now. It's not real important. I will show you after we have finished the reading." He began to work with the wheels in front of him, drawing colored lines and explaining to me the nature and direction of my Earth Walk, my time in this life. I tried to appear as though I was listening, nodding and looking at the sheets. Very little of what he said filtered through to me. I was hardly aware of his words. I was aware of his leg pressing against mine under the desk, of his hand brushing mine as he pointed to the wheels. I berated myself for acting like I was thirteen, but I seemed incapable of doing anything else. Many Shield completed the reading and turned in his chair. We sat facing each other, our knees touching. He gazed at me for a moment.

"Now I will show you what I was thinking of when you told me your birthday." He pulled out a binder from one of the boxes on the floor and flipped through the sheets. He showed me a wheel covered with colored lines in a similar pattern to the ones he had just created for my reading. "This is my wheel. My birthday is exactly one quarter turn on the wheel from yours. The elders say that many people can walk this life together, but there is only one combination on the wheel that ensures a lifetime together. This is the combination." He held the sheet with my wheel up next to his. The two were different and yet fitted together. He explained, "Because of our birth places we each cover different aspects of the wheel. Together, we cover all aspects."

I nodded to show I understood. He put the book away and leaned closer. "What do you want to say to me?" he asked. Say to him? Was I supposed to say something? Words were how I worked. They usually slipped off my tongue easily and rapidly. Not now. Now I felt tongue-tied, incapable of even thinking straight, let alone saying anything. He waited and then finally spoke. "I want to do something that will help you. May I?"

I had no idea what he had in mind. I nodded. He moved his chair next to me so that he was facing my left side. He put one hand on my solar plexus, the other on my back. His hands were large, muscular and warm. I tried to breathe. I was afraid. Touching me, he would be able to feel how much I was shaking inside. I struggled to maintain some shred of dignity. He leaned forward, smiling, and spoke softly. I did not turn my head but gazed straight ahead. "Breathe, Oriah. Send your breath down into your body where I have my hands." I tried to relax. "You are shaking. Are my hands cold? Are they giving you a chill?" I shook my head. "Perhaps not a chill. Perhaps a thrill, eh?" He laughed.

I did not think it was funny. Again I tried to relax, closing my eyes. I felt a glowing warmth in the center of my body where he touched me, like the fire of an inner sun. The light grew larger and larger and spread through my body, warming and relaxing me. I stopped shaking. Many Shields removed his hands and sat back. He pulled his chair around to face me again and unwrapped an eagle feather from a piece of newspaper.

"Now, we will speak," he said. He held the eagle feather. "I will be your husband emotionally, spiritually and sexually." He handed the feather to me. "Speak through the feather. It will give you courage to speak your truth."

I held the feather. I felt strange, as if I were watching the scene from the outside. I saw myself holding the feather. I could hear the low droning sound, but even that felt distant, separate from me. I heard myself speak. "I will be your wife and you will be my husband emotionally, spiritually and sexually." Another part of me sat up in alarm. What? This was crazy! I'd just met this man. I didn't know him. Wasn't this rushing things? Numbly I handed the feather back to Many Shields.

He spoke again. "I must return to my home in North Dakota next week. Will you come and see me before I leave?"

"Yes," I replied. "And then?"

"We must leave that in the hands of the Grandparents," he replied, smiling. He stood up. I didn't want to leave, but there seemed to be little choice. I stood and he moved toward me, pulling me into his arms and hugging me close. He was not a tall man, about five foot ten, but his body was bearlike, large-chested and muscular. I felt I disappeared in his arms. "Until next time," he said.

He escorted me through the kitchen, down the hallway and out to the front door. Dazed, I moved toward my car, walking faster and faster, feeling as if I were fleeing the house. No thoughts came to me. My mind did not seem to be working. Driving down the road, cars began honking at me. I looked around surprised, and discovered I was only moving about twenty miles an hour.

That night I couldn't sleep. I could barely take in all that had happened. I was excited and frightened. It felt like something in a movie, or at least a new age novel: a woman is directed to her soul mate in a dream. Another piece of me tried to be calm and rational. Stories of women being seduced and used sexually by magicians, sorcerers and self-appointed medicine men were plentiful. I did not want to become another story. On the other hand I was not, I reminded myself, a complete novice on this path. I had been studying intensely for more than three years. I'd handled myself well up until now.

The inner debate was a facade, a futile attempt to appear in control. My will was sleeping. I had no choice but to return.

I called Many Shields the next day and we set up a time the following week to see each other. The week dragged by and night after night I dreamed of him. On one night I met the Grandmother who had originally shown me Many Shields' face. We moved out above my house into the starry sky.

"We are going to get Many Shields," she said. I saw the house he was staying in and moved inside to his room. The Grandmother and I stood next to his bed. He lay on one side, snoring loudly. We looked at each other and laughed quietly. "Now," she said, "I want you to pull him into the dream with you." I didn't know if I could do it. Past attempts to do this with Mitch or others had been only partially successful. I looked to the Grandmother for guidance. "Go to the place you can see on his left side," she said. I moved to his side and tried to "see" a spot. I felt disoriented and couldn't figure out which side was his left—I felt unbelievably stupid.

The Grandmother waited as I turned my head parallel to his and oriented myself to the way he was sleeping. He was lying on his right side, with his left side up. As I gazed at him I could see a change in color, a slight oval darkness about six inches long just beneath his rib cage. I extended my arm, and my hand moved into his side. Gently I pulled on a feeling of substance and withdrew my hand. As I did so, Many Shields appeared, light and smiling, standing next to me by the bed. His sleeping body continued snoring.

"Good," the Grandmother said. "Now, take his left hand and we will show him the stars." I took his left hand in my right and the three of us moved effortlessly out of the house into the star-studded sky. Flying up into the stars, the Grandmother finally paused and pointed ahead. "Look," she instructed, and as I looked into the darkness, a scene appeared. I saw myself seated with several others, including Many Shields, in front of a large group of people. We were on the shore of a small lake, in a clearing surrounded by rocks and a pine forest. Different people were speaking. At times I saw my own lips move, but I could not hear the words. It was obviously a gathering for teaching and ceremony. The crowd was mixed: predominantly Native and white, with a few people of African and Oriental heritage.

The Grandmother spoke. "This is the beginning of the Gathering Together Circle. You are both Rainbow People and your task is clear: the Sacred Hoop of the human family must be repaired if the People are to survive. This will happen."

The scene vanished. I turned to Many Shields, but he was gone. I wondered if he had seen the image in the stars. The Grandmother spoke again. "He will not remember it in the same detail. Come, it is time to return." I woke up in my bed at home.

The day before I was to again visit Many Shields, Morgan called. He, too, had been for a reading with Many Shields. Cautiously we exchanged impressions. He asked if I would be seeing Many Shields again before he left. I told him I would.

"I was talking to a woman in the house after the reading," Morgan said, "and apparently he'll be back. He's trying to find a way to move up here, but has to make living arrangements for his wife and six children."

Wife and six children! I forced my voice to be calm, neutral. "Yes. Well, we'll see what happens. I have to go now. Thanks for calling, Morgan. I'll speak to you soon." I hung up the phone.

How could this happen? It had never occurred to me to ask him if he was married. Why would the Grandmother go to so much trouble to set all this up—the dream, Morgan finding him, his being here—if he was married? Why hadn't he told me? What was he doing pledging to be my husband? I tried to picture what I would do if a man came for a reading and told me he'd had a dream and been told I was to be his wife. I felt fairly certain that I'd tell him right away if I was married. I felt sick and tried to calm myself. Perhaps the woman Morgan had spoken to was wrong. Perhaps the marriage was over. I had never been involved with a married man. In fact, I was proud of my inner radar that could pick out and avoid any man who was married or alcoholic like the plague, no matter how attractive or interesting he seemed. Had my radar failed me? It was conceivable that this previously infallible but subtle sixth sense may have been overridden by my out-of-control libido. Clearly my brain had stopped serving me fully.

Full of nervous anticipation, I arrived the next day at the house where Many Shields was staying. He suggested we go for a walk. The house sat at the edge of a large field. We walked for a while with little conversation and then sat down in the tall grass, now dry and brown. We were both nervous, and started to talk about what had happened the week before.

"The ways of the Grandparents are not always easy to understand," he said. "And now they have sent a beautiful woman to me to be my wife." He looked at me and smiled. "Did we not dream together this week? Were you aware of this?"

I was excited. He knew I had come to him in the dream. "Yes," I replied. "Your Grandmother brought me to you. Do you remember the scene she showed us?"

He nodded. "In part. But why don't you tell me what you saw."

I thought perhaps he was testing me. After all, how did he know if I could dream at all? I told him the dream I had had. He nodded again. "This is what I sensed. Well, we shall see what the Grandparents have in mind. I do not know what will happen, but I will follow their wishes."

I felt both envy and irritation with how easily he could surrender any desire to know or control what was happening. We told each other about our lives: where we grew up, how we had learned the medicine teachings, our work, loves, health, hopes and dreams. He told me he lived in North Dakota, in a tiny cabin in the mountains, a seven-mile hike from the nearest road. I held my breath and asked, "Do you live there alone?"

"Yes," he said.

"And do you have any children?"

"Yes, I have six."

"Six! Where do they live?"

"They are in Georgia with their mother." Georgia? Clearly he and his wife were separated. He lived in North Dakota, she in Georgia with the kids. He was not with anyone after all! I felt relief and . . . something else. Was it just my judgment about any man being so far away from the children he had fathered? Part of me wanted to pursue it. Part of me wanted to leave it alone, be happy with what I had found out, not stir things up.

"You must really miss them," I finally said.

"Don't we all," he replied, suddenly looking sad. What did that mean, "we"? I didn't miss my kids; they were with me. "But we must do the tasks we are given." There was a suggestion of tragedy here. Had his children been taken from him? He did not elaborate, and I felt our connection too tenuous for more questions.

Suddenly we heard a car horn from the direction of the house. He looked up. "That's probably for me." he said but didn't move. I didn't want our time together to be over yet. Then we heard a dog bark. "That's George, the dog. They're sending him to find me." I did not want to be found. Without thinking, I pulled my energy body into a center point in my solar plexus, something Grandfather had taught me to do in the dream. It was a way of becoming invisible, reducing your presence to one tiny point of light only discernible by someone skilled in "seeing." By consciously moving the tiny point of light around at random, it was possible to sit next to someone and be, for all practical purposes, invisible. My response was automatic, an expression of my desire to extend our time together.

It seemed unlikely that it would help, since the dog knew Many Shields and was looking for him. But as I turned toward him I was amazed to see and feel that Many Shields had also pulled his energy in. We both sat very still as the dog came bounding through the bushes behind us. Barking and jumping around, he ran right past us three or four times, sniffing and searching. Whining and looking confused for a moment, poor George gave up and ran back to the house. We both laughed and breathed a sigh of relief. The brief incident seemed to solidify our connection. Although I knew of other people who said they could make themselves less visible, I had never done it with anyone.

Suddenly I felt my loneliness. I was grateful for the gifts I had been given. I never took for granted the guidance from the Grandmothers or Grandfather, or the knowledge Raven offered me. But I realized my longing for someone with whom to share these experiences, someone on the physical plane who understood the loneliness of often being the only one in a group who knew the ecstacy, terror and toll of stepping into the crack between the worlds. I didn't feel in need of comforting. I just wanted to be with someone who really knew what it was like, like sharing remembrances of a favorite place with someone else who's been there, even if they went at a different time. I had not allowed myself to hope that there would be a man who could be my lover, partner and friend with whom I could experience these adventures.

I sat silently, overwhelmed with my own thoughts and feelings. Many Shields watched me for a few moments and then stood up and extended his hand to me. I took it and he pulled me to a standing position. I was disappointed that we were leaving. But instead of walking toward the house, he stood facing me and moved his hands up my arms to my shoulders. Waves of heat rippled through me. I wondered if my legs would support me. Gently, slowly, he moved closer and kissed me. Surges of energy, like electrical shocks, flashed through my body. We stood like that for a long time. Finally he sat back down on the grass, pulling me down with him.

For a moment, my head cleared. I pulled back breathlessly. "Wait . . . this is . . . it's too fast, too much. I need to slow this down a little." He pressed toward me. I moved back, straightening my skirt, brushing the grass off. "I think we need to wait and see what happens when you return."

He nodded and rose abruptly, a smile on his face. I stood facing him. "You are the woman. I honor this. You will set the pace," he said. "We will see what happens when I return."

We began to walk back up the hill toward the house. I felt like a confused teenager. Did he think I was playing games, leading him on? I wasn't, I was just confused. So much was happening so fast. I didn't trust myself and . . . there was something else. Something was not quite right. I didn't know what. We said goodbye in the driveway. He gave me a hug and said he would call me when he returned—in two or three months. I got into my car and drove home.

8

I groan as I read the journal entries I made after my first meeting with Many Shields. There is no one to hear me except Tasha, my cat, who sits on the pages of the opened notebooks strewn about me. I flip through page after page of handwritten notes chronicling my feelings of longing, confusion and hope. I am a different woman than the one who wrote these words. I feel like an interloper prying into the private journals of another.

But the Grandmothers are relentless. "Feel the story."

When Many Shields left, the time passed quickly. I was busy teaching classes and doing workshops. While I looked forward to seeing how my relationship with him would unfold, I could not entirely shake my sense of discomfort. The events were unique, but something about them seemed familiar. They seemed to echo a pattern in my relationships. I dreamed of Many Shields occasionally. More often I dreamed of the Grandmothers, of the wheel they had given me and new wheels that expanded on the teachings of each of the directions on the original wheel— wheels of self-love and forgiveness, of the many births in our lives, of the healing power of women's spiritual-sexuality.

A month after Many Shields left I dreamed of him, Raven, my two ex-husbands and several ex-lovers. All were sitting in a circle discussing their experiences with me. I awoke with anxiety heavy in my chest. As I wrote in my journal, words and tears flowed from me as if torn from my heart.

I am Oriah
and I have betrayed the Goddess.

Each time I have given away my power
    reshaping myself to please another

damaged boundaries

215

taking care not to speak the unspeakable
    not to move too fast
        too wildly
        too wisely
        too strongly
I have betrayed the Goddess.

Each time I have sacrificed myself to please the Father
each time I have opened my body to another as my heart
    remained closed to myself
each time I have been quiet when I wanted to scream *NO!*
    to the violation
each time I have been quiet when I wanted to scream *YES!*
    to the moon and life
I have betrayed the Goddess.

I have been raped
and I have been beaten.

And, each time, I have gotten up, like all the women before me
    moving slower than before
    to take a bath and wash from my body
    what could not be removed from my heart and soul
    to bandage my own head and heart where they are torn
    to soak my muscles as bruises rise
    an ache to the bone.

I have betrayed the Goddess each time I thought
    It doesn't matter
    It doesn't matter what you do to me.

I have betrayed the Goddess in my forgetfulness of her name.
And now I turn to walk to her
    unsure of the journey
    unsure of my welcome.
Can you forgive me?
Can I learn to forgive myself?
I walk
and am encouraged by the faces
    however scared

however unsure and nervous
of the sisters also on the road home.
I know the journey will be hard
and it will be a healing
not just for me and the sisters
but for my sons and the other children
and for this tiny green planet.

But I also know—for the first time—that I cannot walk this road
    home
to heal or touch others with Beauty
to save this Earth
or even for my children
as much as I love each of these.

I must learn to walk the path home to the Great Mother
first, for myself
for Oriah Mountain Dreamer
for Debra Anne House

Grandmothers
Help me!
I need your song to keep me from slipping into forgetfulness
I begin
again.

The words moved and shocked me. I laid my pen down, and feeling drained and emptied, I slept.

It was one day before I was to teach a weekend workshop for twenty-five women. The words I had written, following the dream, felt like a gift, a guidepost for myself. I decided to share them, and my dream of the wheels from the Grandmothers. I was worried about my ability to articulate the teachings in a way that would fully honor them. Who was I to be teaching things from the dream? How did I know I was getting it right? How did I know it would have any meaning for anyone but myself?

But at the workshop, as I taught the wheel of how the Sisterhood holds the Dream for Grandmother Earth, the excitement in the room was palpable. The women were moved. The discussion flowed immediately into how this knowledge could be used in our lives to help us live from the feminine. I was overwhelmed—it was clear the wheels were not just for me.

A month later I traveled to Boston, where Raven was teaching a weekend workshop. Many Shields had called me once to tell me how much he was looking forward to returning and spending time together. In Boston I wanted to tell Raven about Many Shields and seek his advice and also share the wheels I had received from the Grandmothers and hear his comments.

About one hundred people gathered in Boston to hear Raven teach and dance chief healing ceremonies. He had taught there many times and had developed a group of regular students. Bea and I ~~had~~ drove down together, arriving about an hour after the workshop began. Raven was in full swing.

Few people can work a room the way he can. His ability to tell stories, direct his energy toward people and articulate complex, cognitive knowledge weaves a web of magic in any room. Invariably, at some point in a workshop, almost every one of the people in the room feel Raven is speaking directly and exclusively to them. His ability to read people individually and collectively is uncanny. Occasionally, in the middle of a long and complex teaching, he will direct a comment at one particular person, naming them. I later found out this is a trance induction technique, described by Milton Erickson and others, whereby the suggestions embedded in the flow of words affect the unconscious of the listener. Whether by natural inclination or studied practice, Raven is an expert.

I had been on the receiving end of this technique several times. On an earlier trip to Boston Raven was teaching to about a hundred people, talking about the balancing of male and female energies. I was busy in the front row, taking my usual voluminous notes at top speed. Out of the blue, in describing the joining of male and female energies, he said, "So, for instance, if Oriah should happen to get pregnant from our relationship and I denied the baby was mine, it would be a sort of incomplete abortion for me. Wherever we have the masculine and feminine energies coming together . . ." and seamlessly kept going. My head snapped up. Everyone in the room glanced at me curiously, and Susan looked at me with raised eyebrows. It was not so much what Raven said but how. Without preamble, my name had been incongruously woven into the steady, smooth patter of teaching, and in a manner that hinted at a level of intimacy that did not exist. As quickly as it had happened the moment was past, and I wondered if I had heard correctly.

This had occurred to me often enough when Raven was teaching to make me wary of such comments. Sometime later the Grandmothers showed me how to resist trance induction and such embedded suggestions even from the most skilled. They showed me, in the dream, how to keep shifting my visual and auditory perception by focusing on different points of light ánd background sounds to break any steady stream of words or actions that might mesmerize.

As Bea and I took our places in the room, I felt a change within. Something was different. I did not automatically take out my notebook and begin to fill it with verbatim recordings of Raven's words. I did not sit in the front row. I wanted to listen from the place of observer, and watch the other people in the room.

Hours passed and Raven continued to teach. People occasionally asked questions. As usual the teachings were dense, filled with information and insight on the human quest for healing. Suddenly Raven shifted gears. "I want now to tell you about some new teachings," he said. "The Grandmothers of the Council of Elders have told me that they will release twelve new wheels intended for the Sisterhood."

My heart started to beat rapidly. This was exactly what I had told him the Grandmothers had said to me. Was he going to ask me to share some of those wheels here? I was not prepared. I heard the droning sound again and I strained to hear Raven above its noise. "I have asked the Grandmothers to give these wheels to Susan." He nodded toward his wife beside him. "If they are to be for the Sisterhood it makes sense for them to come through a woman. These wheels would have to come through either Susan or myself—no one else. At the moment, despite my preference for Susan to get them, they are being given to me." He shrugged with a sense of resignation. "So, for now I will do it. No one else can receive these wheels directly" he repeated.

The buzzing, like a thousand bees, grew louder and louder. I could not sit still, and had to get up and walk to the back of the room as a wave of nausea swept through me. What was he doing? I tried to calm down. Perhaps it was just coincidental that he was announcing the releasing of twelve new wheels from the Grandmothers for the Sisterhood two months after I had told him of my dream. One did not necessarily have anything to do with the other. Or perhaps my dream was a small piece of the beginning of the process, a kind of verification for the wheels he was receiving in the dream and, with his years of experience and training, would no doubt understand and teach with greater clarity. Did I want to get "credit" for the wheels? But what was important were the wheels themselves, not who got them. Besides, if the wheels he was about to teach were from the council, and only he or Susan could get them, they must be different from those in my dreams. I stood at the side of the room, leaning against the wall.

Raven continued. "So I will begin with the first wheel. It is the wheel of the different births from the feminine." My heartbeat quickened. The droning had receded but not stopped. Perhaps these wheels were the same as those I had received. But as Raven continued to teach, my level of physical distress increased. My heart continued to beat even more rapidly and I felt short of breath. The droning in my ears grew louder. I felt hot and dizzy. The wheel he taught was complex and filled with the formal language of his medicine teachings: the child of adaptability and flexibility; the necessity in birth for death, change and movement; allowing the power of pure introspection and intuition; birthing the story to weave the web, maze, matrix and crystal matrix . . . . It went on and on. There were no examples, and while the birthing of physical children was mentioned once, it was given little or no emphasis. I wanted to scream. Words, words, words! What does it mean? This is birth we are talking about—bloody, painful, joyous birth. What would it look like, feel like, taste like in my everyday life to give birth to the "Great Mother Child" or the "Death Child"? It was not that I didn't understand the words, but some part of me recoiled from the masculine treatment of a teaching from the feminine wisdom of birth.

I did not trust myself to speak. A part of me kept up the inner harangue. *Who do you think you are? This wheel comes from someone who is an experienced teacher. Listen and learn.*

Raven talked about every woman's power to birth the god, the masculine, in the world. "So," he said, "the first god that each woman births must be the man she is in love with, even if she never gives birth to a physical child. If a woman refuses to do this the man she loves will feel he has been aborted."

Something in me snapped. I spoke without thinking. "Wait a minute, Raven. Isn't the first god any woman gives birth to her own inner male?"

He looked up, startled at the interruption. "Oh, of course. But I meant after that," he said, and continued with the teaching. Speaking had broken my paralysis. Feeling calmer, I moved again to the back of the room. These wheels were nothing like the ones I had received and must be an entirely different set of teachings. I was relieved. I decided to treat the fact that Raven had come up with them two months after I had told him of my dream as coincidence and dismissed my reaction as paranoid and self-important.

After the day of teaching and a dinner break, there was a healing ceremony. When Raven visited an area people with a variety of ailments came for healing. While experienced people held places on the circle and worked directly with the patient, workshop participants were invited to stay, watch and lend their support by singing the healing songs. It was a way of teaching people directly about the alchemy and effectiveness of ✓ ceremony.

On the first night of this particular workshop I was asked to hold Karma Pipe, a role I had held before, although never with Raven. The person holding Karma Pipe for a patient sits in the northwest of the circle and works with his or her medicine pipe. As the patient's body is painted with special symbols and balanced with crystal work, the Karma Pipe, as the person is referred to, smokes her pipe, leaves her body and moves into the fifth dimension. Once there she asks the Chulamadahey, the ancestor spirits who keep the Books of Life, for images from lives past, present or future that will help the patient receive the healing they seek.

I had seen several people hold Karma Pipe. Most often, when Raven was dance chiefing, Susan would hold this position. Ideally, the Dance Chief should be able to see and confirm all of the images the Karma Pipe offers. It is the Dance Chief's job to work with the patient, helping him or her understand what meaning the images have. The first time I had held Karma Pipe was in Toronto. One of Raven's senior apprentices had come to teach a workshop and dance chief a healing, but there was no one to hold Karma Pipe. After getting Raven's approval, she had asked me and given me all of the instructions on how to do this. I had been nervous. She was not a dreamer and had never held Karma Pipe. I had felt very much on my own.

Actually, this was not true. Grandfather was with me. At no other time had I felt his presence so constant, his words so reassuring, and clear directions so crucial. He taught me to relax my body and, after smoking the pipe, to send my energy up and out the top of my head. He showed me how to split my attention to remain aware of my breath, always moving it through my womb to stabilize and maintain my physical and emotional balance. He warned me about the flood of sudden images, disjointed and distracting, which often come as I leave my body, and urged me to ignore them and continue on, praying to the Chulamadahey for guidance and direction. I later learned from Raven that this flood of images comes in the fourth dimension, the crack between the worlds of matter and spirit, and often confuses the Karma Pipe. Grandfather had been there when the images were frightening or too similar to my own inner demons for me to easily maintain my detachment.

I was looking forward to holding Karma Pipe with Raven dance chiefing. Often, in healings at home, I found myself keeping one ear on what was going on in the healing circle in order to support or help Bea or Morgan in their dance chiefing if they were in need. While both were fine Dance Chiefs with different skills, we were all very new at this. With Raven I knew I had no responsibility, chance or opportunity to influence how the images were used with the patient. I could just relax and do my bit. Over time I had also learned that while I could improve my ability to hold Karma Pipe, by being calm and centered, I could not control the process. Either there would be images or there would not—I had little or nothing to do with it.

The healing circle on this night was for two patients. I was holding Karma Pipe for Louise, a woman with a degenerative eye disease that if left untreated would result in blindness. Another woman held Karma Pipe for the other patient. A young woman wanting to learn how to hold Karma Pipe sat on my left. She was to "piggyback" with me—I had piggybacked with Susan at an earlier healing—and follow me out of her body and into the dream and find out if she could see the same images. She would not have to do or say anything during the healing. Sitting next to Susan I had picked up my pipe and crystal skull. Glancing at me, she asked curiously, "Why are you holding your pipe and skull like that? Who taught you this?" Startled, and frightened that I had, in my ignorance broken some important rule, I blurted out my reply. "Grandfather did. When I first started holding Karma Pipe he told me to hold them like this." I did not even think to offer an explanation of who "Grandfather" was.

"Oh," she replied, looking bewildered. "Well, he got it right." She picked up her pipe and crystal skull and held them in the same way.

Susan was not holding Karma Pipe for this healing, but would monitor myself and the other woman. As we began, the man sitting in the northeast of the circle filled his pipe with prayers for the two patients, calling on all the ancestors who loved them to be with them. Raven had instructed him to keep the prayers short and to the point. As the pipes were smoked, the body painters started to work with the two patients in the center. For each kind of healing there is a different set of sand and body paintings. The sand painting, done in advance, represents the patient in a healed state, and sits on a framed mirror on the floor at the patient's head. The body paintings of different symbols are to help open the patient's energy centers. The crystal work done is to balance and boost each patient's energy to help him or her take full advantage of the healing. This is further aided by the constant drumming and chanting that take place from the time the pipe prayers are completed to the end of the ceremony, often many hours later.

I watched Louise, the woman for whom I was holding Karma Pipe, lying in the center of the circle. She was about thirty years old. As the body painters worked I raised my pipe and smoked over her. Settling into my low lawn chair, I closed my eyes and relaxed. I have held Karma Pipe without a chair, but it helps when I am leaving my body to have its support. At one healing, when I did not have a chair, I felt someone come up and sit behind me. It was Bea, concerned by my ever-increasing list to the left, afraid that I was going to fall over.

As I closed my eyes I called for Grandfather. "Grandfather are you there?"

"I am here, little one. I will be with you. Remember your breath." I relaxed my body and focused my breath on a point near my womb, breathing slowly in and out of this point, allowing the weight of my body to sink to the ground. I repeated my prayers for cutting my karmic tie with the patient and asking for guidance.

"Sacred Ones, Great Mystery, see this little one, Blue Lightning Snake. I call on you now to hear my prayer. At this time I cut my karmic connection with this little one, Louise, and give away any attachment I have, consciously or unconsciously, to the outcome of this healing and my role in it. I release her into her circle with love, and I into mine. And I ask for your guidance in my task of holding Karma Pipe. Sacred Chulamadahey, I ask at this time to move through space and time and see clearly, accurately, psychically, and prophetically any images in the Book of Life of this little one, Louise, that will aid her in her healing. Grandfather be with me." I kept repeating the prayer, keeping one part of my attention on my breath and moving another part of me to focus on the top of my head. Effortlessly I felt myself slip from my body, pause momentarily above my head and the healing circle, and then, with the speed of light, I moved out of the room and into the night sky.

I found myself again in the place I love. Without the physical body there is a sensation of mixing the senses—of seeing the coolness in the blue-black sky; of hearing the heat and fire of a million stars. As I spiraled upward, aware of Grandfather at my side, I sent out my prayer again. "Sacred Chulamadahey, I ask to find the road into the Book of Life for this little one, Louise. I seek the Guardians of her gateway." In the past Grandfather had me look for a kind of road in the stars as I said this prayer—a silver ribbon of light that appears suddenly and weaves its way across the sky. When it appears I follow it, knowing I am on the path to the Book of Life I seek. Each person has some kind of gateway and Guardians at the entrance to their Book of Life. Often they are two animals, and their identity can be important symbolic information for the patient and the Dance Chief.

The silver road appeared and I moved effortlessly, following it. I was only minimally aware of the noises in the room I had left. The drumming and chanting sounded very far away. Suddenly I saw a gateway, with a stone pillar on either side of the silver road. Standing in front of each pillar was a huge turtle. Both had their shells painted in swirls of patterns and bright colors. I addressed them. "Sacred Guardians, I ask your permission to pass here and enter the Book of Life of this little one, Louise, that she may find her healing." I moved forward slowly. The turtles nodded and I passed through the gate. I am often reminded, during these journeys, of *Alice in Wonderland* and wonder if I shall ever see the Dormouse or the Mad Hatter as Guardians.

Raven called to me. "Karma Pipe, have you met the Guardians for Louise yet?"

I slowly moved my lips to form a reply. Answering questions with the physical body, while maintaining the out-of-body viewing point is sometimes difficult, and always a bit tiring. "Yes," I replied.

"What are they?" he asked.

"Two large painted turtles." As soon as I said this I heard someone begin to cry. I wasn't sure where it came from. Simultaneously maintaining attentions in both the third and fifth dimensions sometimes makes it is difficult to tell where things are happening.

"Will the Guardians let you pass?" Raven continued. Occasionally I have met Guardians which are hostile, aggressive or simply blocking the way. If this occurs the Dance Chief must work with the patient's conscious or unconscious ambivalence toward the healing.

"Yes," I replied. "They have allowed me to pass." Karma Pipe must offer only the information asked for, and only when it is asked for. The Dance Chief is in charge.

I moved through the gateway with Grandfather. The moment I stepped between the pillars the night sky disappeared. I was on a road moving into a black void. The silence overwhelmed me and it felt like a huge black sponge, soaking up any sound. It weighed oppressively upon my ears, a kind of pressure that grabbed at and consumed the tiny sounds of my feet on the paved road. Nervously I walked forward with Grandfather and sent out my prayer. As the words left my lips they were snatched away by the silence around us. "Sacred Chulamadahey, this sister, Louise, seeks a healing at this time. I ask to see images of lives past, present or future that hold meaning for her now and may help her heal herself. Sacred Chulamadahey, I ask for your guidance and help." Raven always taught that the person holding Karma Pipe must "command" the Chulamadahey. Perhaps it was my own lack of knowledge and experience, but I felt more comfortable asking for their assistance.

During any healing many images come to the Karma Pipe. As I advanced, scenes and symbols appeared, I tried to feel for the presence of the woman at my side who was piggybacking. I could not sense her with me. Suddenly Raven called to me again. "Karma Pipe, what images do you see at this time?"

A moment before he spoke, a new scene had appeared. I could see the patient standing at the top of a hill. She was dressed in a simple rust-colored dress that fell to her ankles, and a white apron. Her feet and head were bare, her hair windblown. Her hands were tied together in front of her. Around her stood several men in long black robes who appeared to be priests. One was reading from a scroll. I could only catch an occasional word. The woman had been a midwife, herbalist and healer and was accused of being in league with the devil. As they stood at the top of the grassy hill, she listened to the litany of accusations, her face impassive. One of the men moved aside, revealing a large barrel. Two of the other men grabbed her roughly and forced her inside, nailing a lid on the barrel. She did not fight or make any sound. The barrel had rows of long spikes driven into it. The priest who had read the scroll nodded to the others. They tipped the barrel over and pushed it down the hill. As it rolled the woman inside was ripped and impaled by the rows of spikes. She died slowly and painfully as the barrel came to rest at the bottom of the steep incline.

As I described what I saw, I heard a scream in the room. Louise began crying and calling for them to stop, the image evoking her memory of this horrible time. I continued to see the scene over and over, through the eyes and with the feelings of the different participants: the priest in charge—deeply convinced of his moral duty and equally terrified of the woman; the woman—resigned to her fate, unable to fight anymore, writhing in pain, praying for death; the priests, each with his own feelings—sadistic cruelty, doubt, fear for his immortal soul.

Whenever I have held Karma Pipe this has been my experience. Initially I see the scene as if watching a movie, and then I experience through each of the participants. Since the patterns that create illness are never joyful, a part of me always dreads the experience. As I felt the emotions of the characters in the scene, I felt my own emotions stir and threaten to bring me back into my body. "Easy," Grandfather cautioned. "Maintain your breath and move back from the scene. This is not you. It is your sister." I slowed my breath and stepped out of the image.

I could hear Raven speaking to Louise above the sound of the drum. "Louise, this is one method they used to kill women accused of being witches. Do you feel the memory of this time?"

"Yes," she sobbed.

"Understand," he continued, "you lost your life in this time because you were a seer. This fear stays with you today. You are afraid to see."

I continued to move from scene to scene, praying to the Chulamadahey. Several times Raven asked for images and worked with Louise. I had no idea how long the healing had been going. I knew it had been hours. Raven called to me again. "Karma Pipe, how is the Book of Life laying?" I asked to see the Book of Life and immediately a large book appeared in front of me. It was open. I described what I saw.

"The book is open. The left side is a mirror. The right side is also a mirror, but a huge gold shield lies across the surface."

Immediately I heard Gunner speak, his tone impatient. "Raven, she hasn't done her giveaways yet!" He was referring to Louise. Apparently she had not yet completed a part of the ceremony entailing a naming of those things, including the illness, she wished to give away to live a happier, healthier life.

Raven answered, laughing, "I know, I know. I was just testing the Karma Pipe." Everyone in the room laughed. Generally the Dance Chief asks how the book is laying near the end of the healing, after the giveaways are done. A clear mirror on the left side indicates the patient has seen and understood the symptom of his or her illness. A clear mirror on the right side indicates he or she has also connected with the underlying cause and knows what must be done for complete healing. Sometimes when a healing has gone on for many hours there is unspoken pressure from the many tired people in the room for Karma Pipe to report two clear mirrors and indicate the healing ceremony is complete.

After what seemed a short time Raven again asked me how the book was laying and I reported the two clear mirrors which appeared. The drumming and chanting stopped. I said my prayers of thanks to the Chulamadahey and Grandfather and, turning my full attention to my breath, returned to my body. I was stiff and tired. The healing had lasted about three and a half hours, during which time I had sat absolutely still except for the movement of my lips to speak. The pipes were closed and everyone began to talk about the healing.

The young woman who had been piggybacking leaned over and said quietly, "Boy, I'm glad it was you talking when he asked about the book. I thought I heard her do the giveaways and thought we were pretty well finished. I would have said the book was mirrored on both sides."

I smiled. "That's why I try to never pay any attention to what's happening in the room."

"Good Karma Pipe." Raven spoke from the front of the room. He continued to talk about how clear the images were, and how I had passed his "test." I was uncomfortable with this unusually effusive praise, but sat silently, listening. Raven did not usually hand out praise and I was aware that whenever he did, it usually fanned the fires of envy and competition between apprentices. As everyone started to clean up the room, I walked over to where he sat. As I approached he extended his hand. "Good work, Oriah."

"Thanks, Raven, but I feel awkward accepting the praise. It's not actually something I do. I mean, I can't make it happen, either it happens or it doesn't. I'm not sure it has much to do with me. It's just a gift for the healing." I was not being falsely modest, it was a gift.

"Good attitude," he replied casually.

I gave up; my wish, to not be praised for something that was not of my doing, went unheard. Then I described the soundless void I had encountered when first passing through the gateway.

"It was very eerie. It was an oppressive silence that just seemed to devour any sound," I said. "What was it?"

Raven nodded as he listened. "You were hearing her blindness," he said.

Of course! If blindness could be heard that would certainly be the quality of its sound.

As I rose to leave, Louise approached me with a medicine gift. "Thank you so much," she said. "I really didn't know if I would trust any of this when I arrived. But when you got the two turtles as my Guardians, I knew you were seeing something that was really connected to me. When

I was a little girl I had two painted turtles, named Jake and Esther. I loved them and I used to imagine they were very large, large enough for me to ride. I would spend hours dreaming of going on trips riding on and being protected by Jake and Esther. When you said my Guardians were two huge turtles with painted shells, I knew they were the spirits of Jake and Esther." She hugged me goodbye and I went back to my motel room for a few hours of sleep.

The second day of teachings was again very full. Following the dinner break another healing was to take place. I returned from dinner and sat down on a couch at the front of the room while the ceremonial preparations were being made. I had no role in this particular healing and was looking forward to just relaxing and watching. I began to feel sleepy. The room was cool and I was glad to be wearing a light wool dress. A deep red, it had long sleeves, a fitted top and a very full, calf-length skirt. Wrapping the skirt under my legs, I dozed on the couch at the front of the room, waiting for the healing to begin. I drifted into a light sleep, vaguely aware of the glare of the fluorescent lights and the sound of voices.

I roused from my slumber as the healing began. The circle was assembled, the two patients lying in the center, and the pipe ceremony was about to begin. I felt warm and comfortable on the couch and, sitting up, stayed where I was, at the front of the room. It was only much later that I remembered that those not on the healing circle itself were always asked to sit at the back of the room during a healing. I don't understand why no one asked me to move, or why my usually meticulous Virgo mind took no note. Raven sat on the couch to my right with the two workshop sponsors. Everyone else was on the other side of the circle, at the back of the room. The ceremony began.

One of the patients, Clare, was in her mid-thirties, pale and tired-looking and diagnosed as having a schizo-affective disorder. She talked a little at the beginning of the healing about her desire to be more emotionally and mentally present in her relationships with her husband and four children. Although obviously frightened about the healing she was desperate to overcome her mental and emotional dissociation and confusion.

The drumming and singing began; the crystal work and body painting proceeded. Occasionally Raven asked for images from Karma Pipe. I watched Clare, her eyes wide as she listened intently to the words Susan and another apprentice were saying to her. At Raven's direction they urged her to give away her illness and take hold of new life. Her eyes widened, but she did not respond. They raised their voices, yelling on either side of her. She looked frightened, lost, like a child who wants to do well but doesn't know what is expected of her. As I watched her closely I could see a point of light in her eyes receding, moving farther and farther away from contact with the world around her. I wanted to call out, to ask them to stop. It wasn't working; they were losing her.

Suddenly I heard Raven's voice from the couch next to me. "Oriah." I looked up and he motioned me over. Surprised, I walked over to where he sat. "I want you to go into the circle and speak to Clare. Tell her what she must do—that she must take her power as a woman. Her husband has forbidden the use of birth control. She does not want another child, so they've stopped having sex. You must speak in one ear, Susan in the other. Tell her she must stop playing at being the little girl. Tell her she is not her mother's little girl anymore; she does not need her mother's approval! She is a woman and must take her power as one! Tell her to take control of her body, go get some birth control and start having sex again with her husband. Be forceful and strong. I want you and Susan to do this because you are both strong sexual women who know their power, who speak with authority from the feminine. Do you understand?" I nodded. "Explain to Susan what I just said and then both of you speak to her at the same time."

I moved into the circle. I spoke to Susan, relaying to her what Raven had told me, then knelt at Clare's right side, Susan on her left. Clare looked at me, her eyes wide. I thought of a frightened animal caught in a trap. I leaned toward her so she could hear my words above the sound of the drumming and chanting. I felt confused. My impulse was to touch her face, to gently stroke her hair and speak to her softly in order to connect with her, to reassure her. I hesitated. I had never seen anyone touch a patient gently, to give comfort, during Raven's healings and he had been very clear in his instructions. He wanted me to use a strong, forceful tone. Raven was Dance Chief. He had much more experience than I and he was responsible for the choreography of this healing. As I hesitated, I heard Raven's voice behind me. "Speak to her in both ears about taking her own power!"

Clare watched me lean toward her, the light in her wide eyes moving farther and farther away. I put my mouth close to her ear and spoke. I could not make my tone forceful. The words came out slowly. "Clare, you are no longer a child. You are a woman. You can feel the power of being a woman. This is your body, your life. It is not your mother's or your husband's. It is your own." Susan leaned over her on the other side and spoke into her left ear. I could not hear what she said. Clare looked frantically from one to the other. When I finished speaking I sat back. Clare looked at me stonily, the light in her eyes had disappeared from view. I glanced back toward Raven. He nodded approval and indicated I could leave the circle. Feeling sick to my stomach, I resumed my seat outside the circle.

Susan and the other apprentice continued to work with Clare, but there was little or no response. Sobs rose in my throat and I pushed them down. As the work with the other patient was completed, the Karma Pipes for both patients reported two mirrors in their Books of Life. I wondered how this was possible. Raven brought the healing circle to a close and once again we headed back to our motels.

The last day of the workshop concluded early and I went over to the house where Raven was staying. I still wanted to tell him about Many Shields and ask his advice. I found Raven alone in the bedroom, sitting on the bed, cigarette in hand. With a smile, he motioned for me to come in.

I sat on a low chair next to the bed and told him about my dream and subsequent meeting with Many Shields. "I don't know what will happen. I'm nervous. Any words of wisdom?" I asked.

"Be careful," Raven replied. He looked at me for a moment. "I don't want to lose you. Your dreaming is important to the whole group. Can you come to Arizona in January for the advanced apprentice gatherings?"

I was surprised and touched by Raven's uncharacteristic expression of my significance to him, however small. "Raven, I've thought about it. I know you are having five gatherings and asking people to commit to all of them. With airfare, kids and work, I just don't think I can do it."

He nodded. "Well, if you want to come you're welcome to do so without making the commitment. Come to one, and then let me know what you think you can do. Think about it, anyway."

I nodded, appreciative of his efforts to make it more possible for me to attend. Thanking him for his time and teachings, I rose and left. It was only after I left the house that I realized I had not even thought to ask him about the twelve wheels from the Grandmothers or what had happened in Clare's healing.

It was a long drive home. Bea and I took turns driving and discussed what had happened on the weekend. Like the gradual wearing away of anesthetic after a visit to the dentist, I felt myself shift and began to feel sick about the healing for Clare. Why hadn't I done what I knew was needed—touched her, stroked her head, spoken gently and told the terrified child in her eyes that I would not hurt her, that she did not need to perform on cue? Would it have brought her back into the process? Would Raven have stopped me? Had the pushing and pulling actually made things worse for her, done real damage? It was true I had not done exactly as Raven had instructed. I had not told her to get birth control and start having sex with this man who was telling her what to do with her body. I did not tell her she didn't need her mother. I couldn't. But neither had I said what my heart felt would have been most healing. I had fully followed neither my own instincts nor Raven's instructions. Was that why the healing hadn't worked? I felt I had failed and I prayed to the Grandmothers to help Clare.

By the time I got home I was completely exhausted and collapsed into bed. I awoke in the morning coughing and sneezing, with a slight temperature. Two days later my doctor told me I had pneumonia. My body felt as though it had crash-landed. I knew I could not go to the apprentice gatherings in Arizona. Something was not working. My body was trying to tell me something.

9

I had never waited for a man to call. Ever. Now, for the first time, I was
waiting—for Many Shields. Not just calmly waiting, while going
about the business of living. I was sitting by the phone like some
lovesick teenager. I was disgusted with myself. I did not know when he
was returning, or if in fact he still was. I have loved and been in love
with a number of men in my life, but this was different and I didn't like
it. I was not myself. Instead, this obsessed woman controlled me. Using
my finger to dial the telephone number of the house where Many Shields
stayed during his visits to Toronto, she cleverly disguised my voice with
an English accent and pretended to request a reading with Many Shields
during his next visit to the area. It was to no avail. The people in the
house did not know when he was returning either.

Finally I got "The Call." Many Shields said he had been back in
Toronto for several days visiting friends and was very anxious to get
together. Been back for several days? I made an emotional note of it to
myself and tried to get my feelings under control. He asked if we could
see each other soon and I invited him to come to my home the following
day. He was staying with some friends about an hour from the city and
had no transportation. I agreed to drive out and bring him into the city.

I picked him up about ten o'clock the next morning, with butterflies,
birds and a small herd of buffalo running in around my stomach. As we
drove we talked about his trip. He had gone to North Dakota and spent a
few weeks there. "Then," he said," I headed down to Georgia for the
holidays." Georgia? My antennae swiveled. Home of the hopefully ex-
wife. Of course, it was Christmas. He would want to be near his children.
As we started into the city the car engine began making small coughing
sounds. I had never had any trouble with the car before and now it was
going to fail me! The engine stalled, but started—and stalled again. By
the time we got close to home it was clear something was wrong. I drove
directly to the service station and left the car there. They said it would be
ready in the morning. We walked back to the house in the cold and rain.

Home at last, we sat in front of a fire in the living room drinking tea. I had never felt so nervous with a man. Talking about everything except what I was feeling, I finally fell silent for a moment. Looking at him I spoke slowly. "Many Shields, are you married?"

"Yes," he answered, and my heart sank. "My wife and I are still together, although we both have very different paths to walk. When we married I told her I would be away a lot. She accepted this. She is learning to stand on her own, to be independent and move out into the world separate from me."

A niggling little voice whispered in the back of my head. *How much "moving out into the world" can a woman, raising six children by herself, do?*

He moved closer on the couch and touched my face. The heat ran down my body again. He kissed me gently and took my hand. "This has nothing to do with her. She and I have made our agreements." He kissed me again. "My heart sings your name," he said. I never stood a chance.

We made love all afternoon and into the evening, finally rising to eat and talk. More relaxed now he told me stories of his childhood, his days in the U.S. Army, his first marriage and his current marriage to a young woman of twenty-two. The biographical parallels between he and Raven were uncanny: both had been married twice, had six children, had trained and competed as martial artists, served in the U.S. military in Southeast Asia, had been trained by their grandmothers in the medicine and taught for a living. Intrigued with the similarities, I asked Many Shields how he felt about acupuncture and needles generally. Raven, for all his macho image and attitudes, was notorious for his morbid dread of needles. Many Shields responded strongly and immediately, "I can't stand them! I don't let anyone stick needles in me!" He shuddered as he spoke.

As we talked, I tried not to think about what was to come next. We had had this time together and right now it felt like enough. I wanted to see if there were medicine ways and teachings he would be willing to share with me and he suggested we talk about it another time. He suddenly seemed very jumpy. "I will have to call the folks at the house I'm staying at and let them know I'm not coming back tonight." He laughed nervously. "Gee, I feel like a teenager telling Mom and Dad the car broke down. Wonder if they'll believe that?" Had he really expected to go back tonight, to spend the day making love and then have me make a two-hour drive? Was he really worried about what they thought? Why? We were not children. To whom did he owe an explanation?

He picked up the telephone and dialed. I sat listening, my stomach in turmoil. "Hi. Yeah, it's me. You'll never guess what." He laughed uneasily. "Oriah's car broke down on the way into town. It's at the garage now, so we won't be able to come back out until tomorrow." Again the strained laughter. "Yeah, I know, hard to believe, eh? That's what I was just sayin'—sure hope Mom and Dad believe this one." I cringed. "Yeah, well, I didn't want you to worry. We'll see you tomorrow morning. 'Bye."

I did not sleep much that night. True to my experience in the dream Many Shields snored loudly. I tossed and turned, unable to feel comfortable next to him. I watched him sleeping next to me. Who was this man? Why was I here with him? His hands, large, strong and calloused, lay on the pillow between us. Looking at them, I felt the body memory of his touching me earlier. His hands had been gentle, loving. I knew from his story that these same hands had killed people in different parts of the world. I stared at the ceiling and pondered this. To my knowledge, I had never lain beside a man who had killed someone. Should I be frightened? I was not.

In the morning Many Shields jumped out of bed and went down to the kitchen. Clearly he was anxious to get on the road. We walked to the garage, got the car and headed out to the highway. He was very quiet, distant and preoccupied. This was another first for me. I had never made love with anyone and felt them move away so quickly afterward. Finally I spoke. "So, what's going on?"

He looked baffled. "Nothing. I'm fine. What do you mean?"

"Well, you're not talking much."

"I'm not a big talker." Really? And who was that guy telling stories for hours last night? I allowed my disbelief to show on my face. He spoke again, his tone defensive. "This is just who I am. Accept me as I am."

I gave up. I did not regret the night. In fact, I felt a little less like a lovesick teenager than I had in several months. We drove the rest of the way in silence. He directed me to the shopping mall where he was to meet someone later in the day. I pulled into a parking place. With one hand on the door handle, he spoke quickly. "Well, I'll see you around. 'Bye." He opened the door and bolted. I had a vivid flash of a rabbit, a frightened rabbit, running for its life. Dazed, I watched as he disappeared, and turning the car around, I headed back toward the city.

I waited for the devastation to hit me. But nothing happened. It was all too bizarre. Here was this man, a self-professed medicine man, running away from me because of . . . of what? A wonderful day of sex? I was mystified but not in pain. I wondered if I should be. Should I feel used, cast off, misled? All I could feel was a certainty that whatever was going on with Many Shields had little or nothing to do with me.

My calm sense of inner freedom did not last. By the next day the tortured teen had reappeared. My head hurt from trying to figure it out. Why had he run? Why had the Grandmother lined us up together if he was married? And what about his wife? Twenty-two and caring for six children? What did I want? What should I do?

Later in the week I called him and he asked me to come out to the house where he was staying and I agreed. Driving out, I tried to clear my thoughts. I had asked the Grandmothers to lead me to new teachers, ones who were more accessible on the tonal and in touch with the Native traditions closer to where I lived. I decided to focus on this aspect of our relationship and I had brought a blanket and tobacco with me, intending to use them as a formal gift in asking him to teach me what he knew of the medicine ways. When I arrived there were several people in the driveway. I did not want to attract unwanted questions, so I left the blanket and tobacco in the trunk of the car.

We met in an upstairs bedroom in the large house. Many Shields apologized for his behavior in the car. "I want you to know it had nothing to do with you," he said, looking worried.

"Oh, I know that," I responded lightly. All was forgiven, and yet I felt a new cautiousness.

We talked for a while about the different medicine teachers who had been in our lives. Many Shields' descriptions were vague, nonspecific, and hinted at mysterious circumstances. He had learned "here and there" from "many teachers and in many ways." As he spoke I heard the familiar droning sound, distant, faint but distinct. Over it I heard Grandfather's voice. "Oriah, pay attention! Listen to what is said behind the words. Can you hear the truth?"

It was only then that I realized that I always heard the droning when someone else was speaking. It had been there when Raven had talked about the Scarlet Woman, when Marsha had told her story of making a "hit" in Tula, when Raven had told me it was my destiny to be a Firewoman, when Many Shields had declared he would be my husband, when Raven had taught the wheels for the Sisterhood. What was this sound? Where did it come from? It seemed to call my attention to what was being said, to trust my feeling that something was being hidden, half-spoken. The first time I had heard the sound had been in the terrifying dream of the bees when the woman's voice had told me that "all things were rent." It felt like a message: either a call to be especially alert to what was being said, or a warning that I was slipping into unconsciousness.

Many Shields had finished speaking and sat looking at me, waiting. I felt confused. Pausing a moment, I took a breath. "Will you teach me what you know of the medicine?"

Many Shields suddenly became very serious. He looked at me thoughtfully. "In two days you can come back and ask me in the proper manner." He frowned. "You know how these things are done. Why didn't you ask me properly?"

I smiled, realizing why I had unconsciously forgotten to get the blanket and tobacco from the car before I asked him. "I do know the proper way. I wanted to see if you did."

He shook his head, obviously surprised. "You were testing me?"

"In a way, yes. You are Native and you say you have studied the medicine, but I have not seen you teach or lead ceremony. I really do not know what you know." He laughed and pulled me to him, kissing me and stroking my back. Fire raced through me again, but this time my mind was not so incapacitated.

I spoke quickly. "No. This is not the time or the place. I am not interested in brief, hurried sexual encounters with you."

"I understand," he said. But he continued to caress and kiss me. Gently I pushed him away. He pushed me back against the cushions, and rolled on top of me. A part of me did not want to stop, but something about this was not right.

"No, please," I said again. I began to feel as if we were adolescents wrestling in the back of the family Chevy. My mind flashed to the others in the house. Would they hear me if I raised my voice? With a final push and a louder voice I rolled out from beneath him. "Don't!"

He pulled back and looked at me. I was obviously upset. "Of course not. This is not the time or place. I would not dishonor my friend's house. We are not animals. We are humans. I am sorry, but we must restrain ourselves." What was he talking about? Suddenly he was giving lectures on self-restraint? Confused, I rose to leave, promising to return in two days to discuss the teachings.

The emotional roller coaster continued. I was disgusted with myself. I could not believe my longing to see him. I did not trust my judgment around him and I felt as though I was losing my mind. Late that night, in desperation, I called Raven in Arizona, at his office. I knew it was a long

shot. Raven has a reputation for hating telephones and will rarely speak
to anyone who calls. To my amazement he answered the line himself
after two rings. I felt so relieved to hear his voice I could have cried.

"Raven, it's Oriah."

"Oriah! What's up?" Never much for small talk, Raven went right for
the point.

"I feel like I'm way over my head here. Do you remember the man I
told you about, Many Shields? He's back and we . . . well, we're involved. And I've been thinking about offering him a blanket and tobacco
and asking him to teach me the medicine he knows, but something about
it scares me."

"Listen, hon, you can offer a blanket to anyone you want to learn
from, you know that. But if you do it with this guy, do it as an equal.
Offer to exchange knowledge."

"But Raven, I'm sure he knows more than I do."

"Why? Because he has more Native blood? Don't sell yourself short.
You have gained a lot of knowledge."

"Well . . ."

"Only as an equal, you got it?"

"Yeah, I got it." I responded halfheartedly.

"Listen, why don't you join us for the next apprentice gathering?"

I was surprised at the suggestion. I had already missed the first of the
five gatherings, having decided I could not afford the time or money.

Raven continued before I could speak. "I know you missed the first
one, but it sounds like you could use some contact with the family. Why
don't you come to the one at the end of February and then let me know
if you can attend any others?"

"Raven, that sounds great, thanks. Sometimes I do feel like I'm a long
way out here on my own. I'll see if I can arrange it and let you know."

"Good. And remember—you go to this guy as an equal, nothing less!"

"Thanks, Raven. I'll do the best I can." I hung up feeling a little better.

Traveling out to meet Many Shields, I was determined to follow
Raven's advice. Many Shields was waiting for me. As I sat opposite him
with my blanket and tobacco, I felt very calm. "Many Shields, I offer
you this blanket and tobacco as one who has studied the medicine way,
and as a dreamer. I ask you to exchange with me knowledge of the
shamanic path of ceremonial medicine. I will share with you what I have
learned and I ask you to do the same with me."

Many Shields sat silently, obviously surprised. My tone and manner
had changed a great deal from our previous meeting. He took the blanket

and tobacco. "I will smoke this tobacco and sleep with this blanket. I must go home in several days. I will call you before that time and let you know what my dreams and guides have advised in this." I thanked him. We talked more casually for a moment, but when he reached out to touch me, I stood to leave. Kissing him lightly, I turned and went to my car.

Four days later Many Shields called to say he was willing to share medicine teachings. He was leaving for home the next day and would not return for three and a half months. He suggested we set some time during his next visit to talk about the medicine teachings. I agreed and, with some sense of both longing and relief, said goodbye. My emotion-ridden adolescent needed a break.

10

T he cave was dimly lit, a soft yellow glow cast shadows on the walls of pale-orange sandstone. The Grandmothers sat quietly in a circle, watching me. I sat on the circle, in the south. This night was different, as I had slipped into sleep I'd felt a pull, someone calling my name and summoning me to this place in the dream. I waited.

The Grandmother in the west, tall and angular, her face in the shadows, spoke. "It is time to tell you the meaning of your name."

My heartbeat quickened, and I held my breath. Oriah was not my birth name. It was a name I had been given by a woman in a dream five years earlier. It was mine, but the meaning was elusive, like mist, an image almost seen but still hidden. I waited.

The Grandmother looked at me with eyes that were of the black void from which all things are birthed. I felt a roll of fear in the pit of my stomach. "Oriah." She said the name slowly and it ricocheted in whispered echoes around the cave. "She who belongs to no man."

My breath caught in my throat; my heart ached. "What does that mean?" I whispered. But I knew. They watched me keenly, seeing the silent struggle raging within. *No!* The voice of the little girl inside me screamed, frightened, longing and lonely. I did not want to be alone. This was the Land of the Father. If I did not belong to some man—a brother, father, lover, husband—I did not belong. I saw myself as the girl child cast out, set upon a rock with a piece of meat in her mouth, exposed to the elements, naked and unprotected, left to die and refusing to do so. I did not want this: to be a woman alone in the Land of the Father, a woman who is not her Father's Daughter.

The Grandmother continued to watch me. Finally she spoke. "One who is not her Father's Daughter is a woman in danger, because she is a dangerous woman." My eyes filled with tears. Would there be no rest then? No place to be with another? No place of protection, but always alone on the road? The image of the Grandmother blurred through my tears. "Oriah." She called me gently but firmly out of my self-pity. I looked into the shining black eyes and heard her voice in my head.

"Think of what you know of the Virgin, the one complete unto herself, the one belonging to no man, the one who is full of life and love within who may choose to share herself briefly, or with a life-partner on the road she follows. She does not belong to any save herself. There is struggle here, it is true. To be one who belongs to herself alone provokes fear, anger, disappointment, longing and the desire to possess. But think. Do you have a choice? Is this not the name you have been living for many moons now? Have you been protected by the father, brother or husband to whom you tried to belong? Did belonging bring safety, or did it bring license for rape, beatings, abuse? Did trying to belong not drain the life force from your blood, until you became ill and more lonely than you have ever been. This name is not a life sentence. It is a description of who you are."

I heard the truth in her words and sat up straighter. I was still afraid. I knew I kept the illusion of a back door out of my own power, open, just in case. I had been trained well and the belief that all else was a preliminary exercise before the Right Man came along sat like old clothes in the back of a closet—hidden, rarely used, but never really forgotten or given away. "Why do you tell me this now?" I asked.

She smiled. It was a good question. "Because this illusion must be cast aside if you are to grow, little one. It is time to name it and let it go. It holds you in old patterns of searching outside yourself, of giving away your power, dishonoring your gifts, taking responsibility for men who cannot see you as you are, being afraid of the anger of those who do see you as you are. Because the illusion has put your life in danger by draining your spirit and diluting your dream, by hiding the rage of others from you so that you leave yourself unprotected. Make no mistake. You still live in the Land of the Father, and even momentary attempts to belong to yourself and not the Father are punishable by death. You know this. You see it every day in the stories of women beaten and raped, or more subtly, and therefore more dangerously, slowly worn down by poverty and ceaseless work with no room for beauty and creativity."

"How do I protect myself?"

"Know the face of the enemy, little one. Know that it too is within and not without. The enemy is not the man who rages because he cannot possess and own you in the name of love. It is the Father's Daughter within who would give herself away to meet his need because she fears his anger, his pain, his longing. It reminds her of her own. It is the Father's Daughter within who fears she is nothing and no one unless she is reflected in her Father's eyes. It is easy to protect against the enemy without. This you have already done. You can provide for yourself and your children—there is no threat to you there. You can protect yourself and your home from physical attack. You have been trained and tested."

"And how do I protect myself from the enemy within, Grandmother— from the piece of me that wants to belong to another?"

She smiled. "With love, little one. There is no other way. This Father's Daughter is a part of you, your wounded child. She has been birthed from the fear of patriarchy. Her terror is her power. Bring her to this circle, to the Goddess, to Grandmother Earth. Do not try to cast her out. It will only increase her terror and her skill in seeking the shadows, the hidden places where she can grow and move unanticipated. Bring her into the light. Love her. This will diminish her fear. But be patient. It will take time. Her fear springs from the aeons of time in the Land of the Father and is linked to the fear of all her Sisters."

I sat and gazed down into my lap, at my hands. I understood. The name was about my life, my dreams and my struggles. Something felt settled. It helped to know.

I awoke feeling refreshed and strengthened. It was one week before I was to teach a workshop for women. The theme of the workshop was initiation, and we were going to use the myth of Inanna's journey into the underworld to examine our own journey into the depths of the feminine. I knew that this new understanding of my name would manifest itself during the ceremonial weekend.

The women at the workshop moved through the weekend together, each touching the joy and pain of descent into the darkness. On Saturday night we prepared for an initiation ceremony, a time to celebrate and dedicate ourselves to the Goddess within and without. The women prepared in small groups, painting their faces and bodies, donning ceremonial costumes. Each sat in ceremonial silence, considering the vow she wished to take, writing out the words for herself and the sisters who would take the roles of Challenger and Sponsor for her initiation. The room was lit with dozens of candles and the flickering light from the fireplace. Flowers, crystals, bowls of earth and water sat on the altar. The smoke of incense and smudge filled the air. The drumbeat filled our bodies and our voices sent out our prayers in chanting and singing. I stood in the center of the circle with Bea and Martha, two friends who were to be Challenger and Sponsor for my initiation. I held my medicine pipe in my hands.

Martha, as Challenger, spoke first. "Who comes here?"

"My name is Oriah, she who belongs to no man."

"Why do you come?"

"I come to seek initiation into the way of the Grandmothers, and to make my vow to them." I paused. "I vow to listen for, to hear and to heed their voices and guidance, for now and the rest of my life. I vow to serve them, the Goddess and the Sisterhood."

Martha responded. "Are you willing to suffer to learn?"

"Yes," I answered. This I knew I could do.

"Are you willing to receive pleasure to learn?"

Again I answered. "Yes." Of this I was less sure.

Martha continued. "Know as you have made this vow that you sacrifice the illusion of control. Know the interdependence of all life."

"I do."

She turned toward Bea. "Who speaks for this woman?"

Bea replied, "I do. I have known this woman for many years. We have shared the same path. I know her heart to be true, her courage strong and her intent without guile. I speak for her."

Martha turned to the circle. "So be it."

One after another each woman, in her own words, made a vow to serve that which was closest to her heart. In dreaming of my name and taking this vow, I knew something had changed for me. My priorities had shifted. In part my pledge was to see and honor my own beauty, and I knew the Grandmothers were my teachers in this. I felt some nervousness. I sensed a future point when my commitment to the Grandmothers would conflict with other commitments I had made. Would I have the courage to keep my vow?

I decided to take Raven up on his offer to attend the next apprentice gathering in Arizona. Our contact during my frantic telephone call about Many Shields had prevented me from moving into an unequal partnership with him. I felt the need to be more connected with both Raven, as my teacher, and the other apprentices, as a family of support, though recent experience had made me wonder if the latter was possible.

Two months earlier, Jo and Lynn had called from Arizona to say they would be visiting Toronto. They both had friends and family in the area, and wanted me to arrange a workshop for them to teach, which would pay for their trip. With only two weeks' notice I didn't feel I could, or wanted to, do so. When Lynn suggested they might teach the new wheels for the Sisterhood that Raven was receiving, my regret was genuine. I had an ongoing interest in hearing more of these wheels and seeing if they were anything like the wheels from the Grandmothers I was learning. I had shared this with Lynn, but had told her I was unable to arrange the workshop. We'd met for a short time when the two of them had come to town and their anger with me, for not setting up the workshop, was apparent. When they'd questioned me about the teachings I was receiving in the dream, something made me hesitate. Jo pressed for information "in the spirit of sharing within the Sisterhood," and I had told them briefly about the nature of the wheels. I'd sensed the risk of dishonoring the teachings, and the Grandmothers who had given them to me, by offering them where they were not going to be valued.

As I journeyed now to Arizona I wondered what account of our interaction had been relayed to Raven. I did not have to wait long to find out.

The group, about forty apprentices in all, gathered on Friday evening in the large windowless room next to Raven's office. We were in the middle of the city, in a room built of concrete blocks, beneath fluorescent lights. This was to be our home for receiving medicine teachings for the next two days and nights. The small building backed onto a large paved parking lot. A few trees, boxed in by concrete, were the only sign of green life in the area.

I'd flown in during the afternoon. Raven began teaching at nine that evening and as I waited for him to begin I wondered, with the time change and jet lag, how I would stay awake and attentive. But his first sentence dispelled my drowsiness and my attention was riveted on his words.

"I want to talk about apprentices who think they are receiving teachings in the dream." he said. "I want to be clear. You may receive lessons in the dream for your own individual life, but that's it! No one," he added with emphasis, "except myself can receive teachings from the Council of Elders! If one of the elders steps into someone's dream, to give them advice, and this is very rare, it is guidance for that person and only that person. I am the only one receiving wheels that are to be taught to others. Anyone who thinks they are receiving teachings from the elders and is offering them to others is caught in self-importance."

I wrote down every word he said, my mind reeling. Surely these words were not addressed to me and my dreams of the Grandmothers. I had told him about them and about my plan to share the teachings six months earlier and he had said nothing. What was going on? I continued to write.

"This is just the way it is. You cannot receive wheels directly from the elders until you are through the twelfth gateway, and I am the only one here who has progressed that far. I do not want the proper sequence and alchemy of the wheels I am teaching being confused or contaminated with the fantasies of an apprentice who thinks he or she can receive new teachings directly from the elders in the dream. This is self-important bullshit!"

A thousand questions ran through my mind, but I remained silent. The mood did not invite discussion. What if he was right? What if I was making the whole thing up and didn't even know it? Who was I to be receiving teachings in the dream? I knew by "elders" Raven was referring to a very specific council of intertribal elders with whom he said he worked in the dream. I had never claimed the Grandmothers I saw were part of this council. It had not even been a question that had occurred to me. Did this mean I should stop sharing the teachings I was receiving? I balked. I might very well be self-important about the wheels, and a thousand other things in my life. Could I be human and not do this occasionally? But that didn't change the content of the wheels themselves. That didn't change the responses of the women with whom I had shared them. If the wheels were just a figment of my imagination or a child of my desire for self-enhancement and approval, would the women have found them so useful, so inspiring, so rooted in the feeling of the feminine?

I was amazed at the strength of Raven's response. What had instigated this? Why now? And what if he was right? He had done shamanic training and work for years. He had been raised on a reservation. He was my teacher. Would I have even dreamed of the Grandmothers if I had not had the teachings and healings with Raven? What would he do if I continued? I could feel his anger and my own fear.

Raven moved on to other teachings in sorcery, showing us how to build a mesa. A mesa is a special altar, or table of power, with representations of intent and power in each of the eight directions. Used with an understanding of alchemy and the sacred pipe, it provides a gateway into spirit and access to power. We were going to build a collective mesa, which Raven would link to the Council of Elders with whom he worked. Then each apprentice could, if he or she chose, build their own mesa and have it linked to the circle's collective mesa.

Raven continued teaching until four-thirty in the morning. Taking a break, he told everyone to get a couple of hours' rest. We all moved to different places in the room and to the adjoining offices, rolling up in blankets on the floor to get some sleep. I was exhausted; it was seven-thirty—time for breakfast, not sleeping—to my inner clock. I finally dozed off for a while, rising around nine to get something to eat. The lecture of the night before and my inner debate continued to rattle around in my head. I ate alone at a local diner in the mall across the street and headed back to the meeting room. I felt off-center, confused, unable to muster the energy to call on Grandfather or the Grandmothers for guidance.

Raven resumed teaching around noon, continuing to explain the structure and use of the collective mesa. He had provided eight figures of the Goddess, from different cultures around the world, for the mesa we were to build. He explained that we would do a ceremony that night that would "load and fire" the mesa and link each of us with it through our pipes and crystal skulls. We took a short dinner break and returned in the evening to do the ceremony.

The tension in the room mounted as Raven talked about the ceremony. He spoke with a sense of drama and emotion. "This is why we are all here. As a circle of dreamers, as the senior apprentices on this path, I have asked you to come together to increase your abilities to work directly with power, to move in the dream together and defeat the dark side. We have a chance here to do something that has not been done for hundreds of years. Each of you has a critical part in this." No one moved or made a sound. Raven looked around the room slowly. "I want each of you to understand fully what it is you are about to participate in. This ceremony has not been done for fifteen hundred years. To do it now is to open the gateway, to make a bid for real power. You must understand the possible consequences and only step into it if you are ready." The room was silent. People looked at the floor.

A man at the back of the room spoke up. "Wait a minute, Raven. Now you're scaring me. What consequences? Maybe you need to explain this a little more."

Raven smiled slightly, enjoying himself. "When you work with sorcery there are always possible repercussions. You have to be ready. You have to be willing to go for it, to do it now." He looked around the room, relishing the anticipation he was building. He had not answered the question with any specifics. "So, are we ready? Do you want to go for it?" No one answered. A few heads nodded.

The mesa had been set up at the front of the room. One woman sat behind each of the figures with her medicine pipe. Everyone else in the room sat scattered about, each with a pipe, absolutely still. Raven nodded to Susan to begin the pipe ceremony. Suddenly, before she even moved, there was a sound by the mesa and a gasp from the women who sat closest to it. The tiny stone figure of the Goddess, sitting in the north of the mesa, had fallen over. No one had touched it. No one near it had even moved. As it fell, a cup on her head had broken off. The woman seated behind it look fearfully at Raven.

"Did you bump it?" he asked calmly.

"No," she said, obviously upset. "I didn't even move." The tension in the room was unbearable. After Raven's anxiety-provoking speech about the repercussions of practicing sorcery and the importance of the ceremony, this inexplicable occurrence did not feel like a good sign. Raven looked at three of the people sitting closest to him, all senior apprentices.

"Have you three dealt with your differences?" The three looked embarrassed. I had no idea what he was referring to—obviously a personal matter, known only to the four of them.

One woman spoke. "We have had one short conversation, but no, there's been no time or opportunity for us to sit and talk it out."

Raven shook his head. "You have to deal with and clean up these things or they interfere with ceremony." He looked around the room. "How about the rest of you? Anyone else in this room got unfinished business or feelings that are interfering with the energy of this circle?"

Chris raised her hand and spoke. "Well, something doesn't feel quite right. I mean, here we are, doing this important ceremony, and we haven't really come together as a circle. We're not even sitting in a circle, and the room is full of junk. I don't feel very clear about the ceremony, and now this happens. I want to stop and hear from people."

Many people nodded in agreement. It was true we were not in a circle. People were scattered around the room, their ceremonial items side by side with clothes, shoes, food, empty drink bottles and wrappers.

Raven looked frustrated with the delay. "Look, you have a choice. You either take this as a medicine sign that means we have to stop and examine what's going on, or you see it as just a figure falling over and get on with it. I can't tell you what to do. It's up to you. How many other people feel they don't want to go ahead right away?" A number of hesitant hands rose. Raven heaved a sigh of resignation, clearly wanting to proceed without delay.

Daphne spoke softly. "I have a suggestion. What if we went into the other room and passed the Talking Stick? Anyone who needs to say something to the group, or to another individual, can say it and clear it, as quickly and directly as possible. Then we can return and resume the ceremony." Many more heads nodded.

Raven shook his. "O.K. Go do it, but make it fast. Say what you need to and then get back in here, ready to work!" Obviously angry, he rose and went to his office. Everyone else left and gathered in a smaller room next door. The movement broke the tension and seemed to lighten the mood. Daphne began passing the Talking Stick, asking each person to say one sentence about where they were at the moment.

Some felt confused by the ceremony and nervous about the Goddess figure falling. While we were all warned not to read too much into the small occurrences and synchronicities of daily life, things that happened in the ceremonial context were seen as having more significance. The trick was figuring out what they meant. Other people wanted to get on with the ceremony. Almost everyone said they felt better for the chance to speak. Although most people spoke very briefly, with forty people in the room it took more than two hours to complete the circle.

When the stick was passed to me I sat with it silently for a moment. An overpowering feeling of fatigue washed over me. I saw my life before me, an endless stream of work—cooking, cleaning, caring for my family, teaching, counseling, leading ceremony, choreographing healings, studying, doing my gateway work . . . it all felt like too much. And now, here I was, using what scant resources I had to come to Arizona. It did not feel rejuvenating or enlightening; it felt like one more task. Finally I spoke. "I feel bone tired. I am willing to do the ceremony. What I need is a rest, a place where I can feel relaxed and supported—held." My eyes filled with tears. "This is not it." I passed the Talking Stick to the man next to me.

When everyone had spoken we all returned to the meeting room, gathered up the scattered belongings, cleaned out the garbage and rearranged ourselves in a circle. Raven reappeared. By this time it was nearly two o'clock in the morning. He was plainly unhappy with how long the Talking Stick session had taken. He looked around the room. "Well, are you all happy now? You've all done your processing?" No one spoke. "Well, because of the time that took we can't do all of the ceremony now. We've missed the opportunity, minimal chance. You have to learn this. When the abyss opens, you jump! You don't process! If you need to process, you do it on the way down. Processing is just another way of going over the same old shit one more time. If you jump, the fright will scare it right out of you. When the tiger's about to get you, don't stop and process about how hard it'll bite. You have to learn to move fast, do the processing in moments within yourself and then jump!" Everyone sat silently, waiting. "Well . . . let's see what we can do with the time we have left."

Susan began the pipe ceremony and started to follow Raven's instructions on how to "load and fire" the mesa, moving around the figures with her pipe and crystal skull. After we had all filled our pipes, we were each to approach the mesa and using our fan and pipe, add and link our energy to the table of power we had created. With more than forty people present, the process took hours. Apprentices from out of town were near the end of the line.

As I awaited my turn, leaning against the wall, Jo approached me. "Raven wants to see you in his office." Starting, I looked up. Her tone was abrupt and cold.

"When?" I asked.

"Right now. As soon as you've finished doing your ceremony."

I nodded. "O.K." She turned and left the room. I wondered what this was about. I assumed it had to do with the wheels from the Grandmothers, given Raven's opening remarks the night before. I did not feel ready for a difficult discussion. In the past sixty hours I'd had two hours' sleep, flown three thousand miles and sat in a windowless room under fluorescent lights taking pages of notes. It was just before five in the morning when my turn came to approach the mesa with my pipe and crystal skull. Using a fan to bless and open my chakras, I smoked over the items on the mesa, linking my energy and crystal skull to the energy matrix that the mesa created. Too tired to see straight and preoccupied with the imminent meeting in Raven's office, I felt myself merely going through the motions. Setting my pipe down, I went to Raven's office and knocked. A woman's voice told me to come in.

Raven's cramped office was a blue haze of cigarette smoke. He sat behind his desk and in the small space in front were Susan, Lynn and Jo. I felt on guard. Jo had said Raven wanted to see me, but evidently this was to be a group discussion.

Susan motioned for me to sit and began speaking. "Oriah, we want to talk with you about some concerns we have. First, I want to tell you how much we appreciate the work you do in Toronto. You have done an amazing job building a community, and we all know how hard it is to do this, especially when you are so far away. Your newsletter is always one of the best and you are obviously well organized. But Jo and Lynn have told us about their meeting with you in Toronto, and there are some things we want to ask you about."

Raven intervened. "You need to understand that these two women," he said, nodding to Lynn and Jo, "are like my ears and eyes on the road. Everything they hear, see or sense, they report back to me. That's their job." I felt like a child caught doing something wrong. What had been "reported?" Raven looked at Jo. "Why don't you start?"

Jo sat across from me, looking solemnly at the floor. She raised her eyes to meet mine. "Well, what you need to know about me is that when I sense something is wrong I want to get right in there and find out what's going on. Lynn and I felt you were not at all welcoming when we came to Toronto. You were not interested in having us teach, and we could not get any support for the healing we had planned. When I think something is wrong, I just say it. That's the way I am. I always want to lay it out on the table." She spoke with force and determination, a woman with a mission.

I sighed. She had voiced the same feelings to me during our brief meeting in Toronto and I had responded to her then. I spoke now, repeating what I had previously told her. "Jo, I am sorry if you felt unwelcome. As I explained when you were in Toronto, I had committed myself to lead a ceremony on the night you had decided to do your healing. It's a regular monthly ceremony for women, set months in advance. You called and asked for assistance a day before the ceremony and I could not change my plans. As for your teaching in Toronto, Lynn called two weeks before your visit. It just wasn't possible for me to organize anything with that kind of notice—I'm teaching classes, leading ceremonies, organizing events, doing healings, caring for a family and continuing my own studies and gateway work." Did I sound as though I was whining? Again I felt myself burdened with a load too heavy to carry. Tears burned behind my eyes. I couldn't do more. I felt anger form like a hard ball in the pit of my stomach. Why was I asked to do so much? Who was asking me to carry so much? Why couldn't I just put some of it down? My resentment rose, a bitter taste in my mouth. No one else in the room had children, lived on their own or worked without a supportive infrastructure. And they wanted me to do more! I continued, my tone matter-of-fact. "I simply could not do more on such short notice. Since Lynn found a friend willing to do the organizing for the workshop, I offered what I could—circulation of the poster to participants in my classes. I'm sorry it didn't feel like enough, but it really was all I could do."

The anger turned sour in my stomach. All that I said was true—but it was not the truth. The truth was that I did not want to support Lynn's and Jo's desire to teach in Toronto. When Lynn first called, my anxiety had risen—I wanted to protect my territory. I was living close to the poverty line with my sons, dependent on my classes and workshops for a living. It had taken time and hard work to build a viable practice so I could do medicine work full-time. They wanted, and assumed they were entitled to, benefit from this. But that wasn't all of it. Although I had not seen either of them teach, from what I did know of them, I didn't trust them. Both had been cold, hard and humorless in their dealings with myself and others. I did not want to hand my class over to two women I did not trust or like.

I prided myself on my willingness to speak honestly and openly in confrontational meetings. Here, at five o'clock in the morning, I sat without speaking. Thoughts and feelings flooded me, but the words I spoke were aimed at surviving and getting out of there as soon as possible. My feelings were inconsistent with who I wanted to be: reasonable, generous and unthreatened. I struggled to keep the mask intact, the shadow hidden.

Raven spoke. "Oriah, I am constantly receiving and handing out new teachings. When the people who are here with me go on the road and visit your community, it offers an incredible resource to you. As the leader of the community, you need to provide opportunities for people to get these new teachings. It will only strengthen what you do."

"I understand that, Raven, but I can only do so much, and in this case I could not organize one more thing in such a short time." I tried to keep my tone even, but I could hear how strained my voice was. I was sure they couldn't miss the hollowness of my words. The anger smoldered inside me.

Raven spoke again. "Is there some fear of having your finances threatened by others teaching in Toronto? Is your lack of physical security influencing your decision?" I swallowed my immediate response. *No shit, Sherlock!* Why would I be worried about money? With a family to support and these apprentice gatherings costing more than eight hundred dollars per weekend to come to, what did I have to worry about? How would they feel about an exchange? For every apprentice who came to Toronto to teach and benefit from what I had built, they could organize a workshop for me to teach in Arizona. The dark underside of my effort to trust the universe was my terror of ending up in the poor house. And I was unsuccessfully trying to rise above it.

But that was not all. Lynn had been my student. She had met Raven after I had, and subsequently studied in classes and workshops I taught. Excited by the Raven's teachings, she had left Toronto and moved to

Arizona, where she dedicated all her time to learning with and working for him. She quickly become office manager and Raven's personal secretary, influencing the flow of information to and from him. She had been willing and able to make the one-hundred-percent commitment that Raven had pressed me for in Palenque, a commitment I probably would have made had I not had children. All my work and effort felt unseen and unimportant in comparison. I did not want to greet her with open arms when she flew into Toronto as the teacher-with-the-latest-teachings. I wanted to tell her to go to hell. I suspected she wanted to do the same to me. In Toronto she had remarked bitterly to me that "Raven always makes extra time for you whenever you are around." The sibling rivalry was mean and nasty. At the moment, my half of it was completely out of control. I did not want to be reasonable. I did not want to clear the air, kiss and make up. I just wanted to get out alive.

I nodded as I spoke. "Yes, Raven, I will admit, at times I become concerned about my financial security. It takes time to build up classes, and at the moment I'm just able to meet a minimum budget. But things have gone well, and this wasn't a major part of my response to Lynn and Jo's request." Again, all of it was true, but the truth remained unspoken.

Raven sat mute behind his desk, smoking a cigarette. My vision blurred and I felt dizzy. The droning sound swam around and through me. I tried hard to swallow the tears that rose in my throat. Raven spoke again. "We also need to talk about the wheels you say you are getting in the dream. When Lynn called and told you she and Jo could teach the wheels for the Sisterhood I was teaching here, you said you had already received them."

Had I said that? Given my juvenile response to Lynn, it was possible, but wild horses couldn't drag this suicidal admission out of me here. Raven had made his views on anyone receiving wheels from the elders very clear on the opening night of the weekend. I honestly had no indication that the Grandmothers I knew were part of the Council of Elders to whom he referred. It was possible I had not made this fine distinction on the phone with Lynn. "I do remember telling Lynn I would be interested in hearing the wheels she had received from you to see if they were the same as the ones I had received. I remember expressing my disappointment that I would not have this opportunity when they were in town." This much was true.

"Then how is it that Lynn heard you claiming to have received the same wheels?" Raven asked.

"I have no idea." I looking piercingly at Lynn, daring her to speak the truth I could not, to reveal the feelings behind the pushing and shoving. No one spoke. I wanted to scream. I had told Raven about receiving the wheels—two months before he announced he was receiving them. And I was the one being accused of "claiming" something that was untrue? The anger in my stomach felt cold and inaccessible.

"We are concerned about anyone integrating their own ideas into wheels only Raven can receive. Have you been teaching these wheels you feel you've received?" Susan asked.

"Yes, I have been sharing them with the women in the Moon Lodge ceremonies and they have found them very useful. I have been very careful to clearly indicate that they are not part of the teachings from Raven, so as not to confuse the two."

Raven spoke again. "Can you give us an idea of what these wheels you feel you're getting encompass?" I paused. Now? At five-thirty in the morning, after being up for two nights? He leaned forward. "Just a sentence or two."

"The wheels," I said, "are to help the Sisterhood hold the Dream of Grandmother Earth." He nodded and leaned back. He seemed uninterested in pursuing it further.

Raven spoke again. "We need to know whether or not you want to be part of the family."

The family? What family? Movie images of the Mafia flashed into mind, then I realized he was talking about the group of apprentices who worked with him. I felt the same insurmountable hopelessness as in Palenque. What did he want from me? Could I not be part of the "family" if I followed my own dreams and taught what they offered me? I struggled with my feelings of abandonment. Something in this was familiar, linked to my own birth family. The support, the love, was conditional. The conditions were unclear, but in some way my behavior, my attitude, called my worthiness into question. I could feel my inner child scream in terror. She was willing to do anything to keep the love, support and approval. She just wanted to be told what was required and she would do it—work faster, try harder, be quieter, prettier, smarter—anything. But some other part of me rebelled. Not this time!

"So, we just want to know if you want to remain a part of things."

I could not reply to Raven's question without releasing the tears I had held back. "I can't do this. If you feel I'm doing something wrong and want me out, then say so. I am too tired for this. I have been honest with you from the beginning about the wheels from the Grandmothers. I have never said they came from the same elders you work with, Raven. Nor have I confused them with the teachings that I've learned here." I tried to stop my tears. "I'm working as hard and as fast as I can. If you want more . . . I'm sorry, I have no more to give. If you are dissatisfied with my work and want me out, then just tell me." I looked up at Jo and Lynn, my anger hard on the heels of the tears. "But I will not be watched!"

Susan leaned forward and spoke gently. "Oriah, you have done good work up in Canada. We hear that your resources are limited." Lynn and Jo sat stony-faced, watching me, their eyes expressionless.

Raven looked away as I glanced at him. "Well, we just wanted to have a chance to talk with you. We were concerned," he said. "We want to make sure the channels of communication are open. Now let's get back out there and see how the ceremony is going."

I rose and stumbled out into the glare of the blue-white lights. I felt numb. I wanted to go home.

As I flew home that night I slipped into sleep on the plane. I dreamed of the underground kiva and the circle of Grandmothers. There was no fire, but torches set in the walls made the chamber flicker with orange light. The Grandmother in the southeast, a round, gray-haired woman with soft creamy skin, led me to the center of the circle. She motioned for me to lie down in the middle, my head in the south. As I lay on the warm stone, my tears began to flow. My body ached with fatigue, my throat raw with held-back tears. My heart felt as if it would break. I became aware of the Grandmothers sitting around me. Each held a drumstick raised over my body. I stiffened, waiting for the blows, and heard the voice of the Grandmother in the west speak. "It will pass, little one. Breathe. Allow the tears to flow. Feel the healing of the drum." As she spoke the drumsticks came down upon my body. Instead of pain, I felt and heard the beating of a great drum beneath, around and within me. As the drumsticks rose and fell on my body, I felt a vibration roll through me, shaking me gently, loosening the held emotions. My tears flowed, it was as if they were drumming the pain out of my heart and my body.

At last they stopped. My crying had subsided. I spoke, still feeling the vibrations in my body. "Grandmothers, I am grateful for all you have taught me. But I wonder if I am understanding correctly. Am I really supposed to be teaching these wheels?" I raised myself up a little to look into their faces. They sat watching me, their eyes full of compassion. "I need some confirmation. I am worried that it is all just my self-importance, as Raven says. I am flesh and blood. I need to speak to someone on the tonal, a grandmother who is alive today to give me guidance in this." I looked nervously from one face to another, afraid I was asking too much. "Can you help me?"

The Grandmother in the north spoke. "You must seek out Dorothy and Isabel, Grandmothers who are still with you. Each is an elder of a different tribe. There will be others, but these two will give you what you need now. Go and see each one as soon as you can."

I had heard of an Ojibway elder named Dorothy in Toronto and I knew one of Many Shields' teachers had been a Seneca elder named Isabel. I felt overwhelmed with gratitude for the Grandmother's help.

"Thank you," I said, the tears beginning to flow again. "And Grandmothers . . ." I hesitated.

"We know, Oriah. But the answer stays the same—you cannot save Raven. Let it go."

I awoke on the plane, my face wet with tears. My body felt sore and bruised all over, but the tension I had been holding in my muscles all weekend was gone.

11

I walk around my workroom. Reading my notes has awakened my body memory of this time. My muscles ache; I do some stretching exercises and sit down again. My hand moves unconsciously to my throat and chest, reaching for the Goddess figure that usually hangs there. The movement reminds me of her disappearance the previous night. Her absence worries me and I feel an increasing vulnerability without her, uneasy about what her disappearance might mean. Distracted by the vague feelings of worry, I return to my journals.

I arrived home from Arizona determined to find, as soon as possible, the women elders the Grandmothers had named. Nancy, a woman who had attended some of my classes, had told me about Dorothy, the Ojibway elder. She met her after doing a Purification Lodge with Bea, Morgan and I. Dorothy, apparently, had been furious when she'd heard that non-Natives were holding Purification Lodge ceremonies. I wondered about the wisdom of going to see her. Nancy gave me her phone number, and with much trepidation, I called her. I told her I was a friend of Nancy's and asked if I could see her for an hour to discuss some personal difficulties. Neither friendly nor hostile on the phone, she invited me to her home the next day.

Nervously I prepared for the visit. On the way to Dorothy's home I stopped to buy some cigarettes—Nancy had told me her preferred brand. I arrived at the townhouses where she lived and sat in my car, trying to calm myself. After my ordeal in Arizona I was feeling particularly fragile. What if she told me to stay away from the medicine? Would she think I was outrageously pompous to come to her with teaching wheels from the dream? Cautiously I got out of the car and walked to the door. A small wooden wheelchair ramp ran up to it. I knocked softly. Maybe no one was home. Perhaps she'd forgotten. A voice called out, "Come in."

I opened the door and found myself in a large living room. Lying on the couch across from the door was a small ancient being. Worn and frail, the woman on the couch smiled broadly and beckoned me to come in as she raised herself to a sitting position. She was dressed in a pale-orange dressing gown and wore a multicolored sash over one shoulder and across her body. Her thin brown arms stuck out from beneath the orange sleeves. Glasses half an inch thick magnified her eyes and the broad smile revealed several missing teeth. "Come in, come in, dear," she said.

I pulled off my boots, set them by the door and moved to a chair next to the couch. "I'm Oriah. You must be Dorothy. Thank you for seeing me." Dorothy's smile widened as she used her hands to swing her leg down onto the floor. I glanced down and realized the leg was artificial. She noticed my glance and, smiling, rapped her knuckles on the hard plastic shin.

"Silly thing. Don't like to keep it on for long." She looked at me steadily through the glass tunnel of her thick lenses. "So, what can I do for you, Oriah?"

I took the cigarettes out of my pocket and held them in my hands. I was afraid that if I tried to speak, I would begin to cry. I waited a moment, breathing deeply. Dorothy leaned forward and touched my arm. Her fingers were gnarled, wrinkled and warm. "Don't worry, dear. Anything you need to say, you can say here. It will go no further. Take it from your heart and put it to your lips and leave it right here."

I smiled at her. "Well, I'm here because I need some guidance. I have been working with a medicine man, a shaman, for four years now. Recently some things have happened that make me wonder if I should continue to work with him. He has taught me many things and I am grateful. But I'm confused about how to proceed. I have had dreams of different teachings and I need to know how to use them."

Dorothy held out her hand for the cigarettes and I gave them to her. Holding them and bowing her head, she spoke in Ojibway, obviously praying. I waited. I had heard of another woman who had come to Dorothy offering tobacco. Dorothy had refused the tobacco and told her to go away and stay away from all Native teachings, that they were not for her. Dorothy finished praying and opened one of the packages of cigarettes. Lighting one, she offered it to the four directions and continued to pray, first in Ojibway and then in English. "Creator, I ask for your guidance that I might help this little one. Be with me." She sat quietly, her eyes closed. Suddenly she opened her eyes, looked at me and spoke. "You have fallen in love with your teacher."

I sat back, shocked. In love with Raven? No, she had misunderstood. I opened my mouth to clarify why I was there, but she raised a hand to silence me. "Have you slept with him?"

"No."

"Good. It would be much more difficult if you had. Tell me about your dreams." Briefly I told her about meeting the Grandmothers in the dream and receiving the wheels. I paused, unsure of how much detail she wanted to hear or I wanted to tell her. "So, tell me the wheels," she said, sensing my hesitancy. I continued, going through the first wheel of the different aspects of the Dream of Grandmother Earth and the tasks the Sisterhood must do to hold this Dream. Dorothy listened intently, her head down. As I finished she looked up and smiled slightly. "This must have pissed Raven off," she chuckled.

I hesitated, feeling it would be disloyal to describe Raven's response to hearing of the wheels. "Well," I said minimally, "he wasn't too pleased."

"I bet," she responded. "Well, the Grandmothers have chosen to give you these wheels. They are good wheels, ones the Sisterhood needs. Most have lost their sense of what it means to be a woman, the importance of that role. You must teach these wheels. They have been given to you and they are important for the Sisterhood. If Raven has a problem with that, that is not your concern. If you have a problem with his anger, it is because you are still in love with him. You must remove yourself."

"But I feel I owe him so much. I have learned from him. When I went to him I was ill. The teachings and ceremonies were a large part of my healing. I feel I owe him."

"What? Do you owe him your life? No! You owe him what you give—acknowledgment and gratitude for what you have learned. You are a teacher. Do your students owe you because you teach them? Of course not. That is your job as a teacher, as a healer." Her straightforwardness gave me courage. I told her about some of the ceremonies I had done, alone in the woods and on the desert. She looked at me keenly through her glasses. "I knew when you came in you had Native blood," she stated emphatically. I was taken aback by her sudden change of topic.

"Well, there is a old family story, but I've never investigated it. But look at me—I am blond and blue-eyed."

She dismissed my statement with a wave of her hand. "I have grandchildren who are blond. It is not in the eye or hair color—it is in here that I can tell." She raised her hand to her heart. "I can see it in the spirit that shines from the eyes. Find out about the family story and you will find out I am right. How far back is your Native blood?"

"Well, the story is that my great-grandfather had one parent who was Native, probably Cree, since he was out near Winnipeg."

She nodded again. "That is why you are drawn to these teachings, why you have been given the task of teaching. The mixed blood flows in your veins."

I wondered again about the likelihood of this. "When I tried to investigate, my mother denied ever having told me the story in the first place. Without her help I'm not sure I will ever know for certain."

Dorothy shook her head. "Shame and racism are horrible things for our people. But you can know inside who you are."

I asked Dorothy about some of Raven's teachings on sorcery: the ceremonies for magic and power, the stories of incredible acts—jumping off cliffs, shapeshifting, dematerializing, doubling. She listened to my questions and then leaned closer, speaking in a low, conspiratorial tone. "I hear the men talking, talking all the time about these things. And do you know what I call it?" she asked with a glint in her eye, and waited for my reply.

"What?"

"Bullshit!" she said triumphantly. "I say, what does it have to do with feeding the babies? That is the knowledge we need, knowledge that will feed the children. That is what women are concerned with. Not with power and hocus-pocus!" I smiled at her enthusiasm; something about it struck a chord in me.

We talked for a while longer and then I rose to leave, thanking her for her guidance. She asked me to come back again and talk and I promised I would. I left feeling wonderful, thanking the Grandmothers for guiding me to Dorothy. I felt her presence evoke a hunger in me for something more, something beyond the huge body of cognitive teachings I had learned from Raven. I had soaked up her sense of humor, directness and quiet dignity. Her willingness to hear the wheels from the Grandmothers and her emphatic support of my teaching them filled me with wonder and amazement.

Grandmother Isabel was an elder with whom Many Shields had worked. I tracked down her telephone number, called her home and set up an appointment to visit her. I wanted to ask her about the wheels from the Grandmothers. I also wanted to ask her about Many Shields.

Three weeks after meeting Dorothy I drove south to Isabel's home in the U.S. She lived in a large rambling country house in the middle of a reservation. When I arrived everyone was just about to have lunch. Grandmother Isabel, as everyone called her, was a petite, gray-haired woman. She greeted me at the door with a warm hug and told me to take off my things and join everyone in the kitchen. Five people stood there in a circle, four women and a man. Isabel and I joined them. We stood silently for a moment and then each person offered one word, his or her prayer for the moment, which reflected how they were feeling.

"Happy."

"Sunny."

"Confused."

"Tired."

"Peace."

"Grateful."

As the last person spoke all of us raised our hands over our heads and waved them in the air, sending out our prayers into the world. We sat around the table for lunch, everyone talking, laughing and introducing themselves. There was the warmth and chaos of a family, and Isabel was very definitely the center of activity. Lunch continued for well over two hours as she entertained us with stories of the early years of her life. It was clearly her way of teaching, and both she and those gathered enjoyed it. She was dressed in a light-pink sweatsuit and running shoes, her thin gray hair struggling to escape the pins that held it back, and her eyes were bright and smiling. Though well over seventy years old, she didn't miss a trick. Just watching her made me look forward to getting older.

Most of the others gathered were also visitors. Alison, a woman in her late fifties, had been there to help out and learn from Isabel for a few days and was packed and ready to leave after lunch. Mary, in her mid-twenties, had been visiting for three days, trying to sort out her career plans. She would be leaving the next morning. Sarah, in her late teens, was there with Alex, an older man I assumed was her father. They had come, with their house trailer, to visit and help Isabel with her computer. Maria, a beautiful woman with olive skin and dark eyes, lived in the house, helping Isabel with her work and trying to coordinate the busy comings and goings of visitors and students.

I felt at home in the general hubbub of the house, although nervous about speaking to Isabel about Many Shields and Raven. After settling me in a guest room upstairs, Isabel asked Maria to sit with me and show me my medicine wheels, a system Isabel uses of understanding why you are here and what you need to do in this life. As Maria began, I realized it was the same set of teachings Many Shields had used to do my reading. I hoped I would take some of it in this time.

The group had dinner together and then retired to the living room to watch a movie on TV. I was tired and welcomed the time alone. Quietly I approached Isabel and asked if she would mind if I did a private pipe ceremony in my room. Different traditions have different rules about these things and I did not want to contravene any of hers while staying in her home. Looking a little surprised, she gave her assent and asked who I had studied with. I told her a little about my work with Raven. She didn't comment, but nodded thoughtfully. I went to my room and filled my pipe with prayers. I had to leave the following afternoon and hoped there would be an opportunity to speak with Isabel alone before I left.

In the morning we all sat down for a pancake breakfast. Afterward Mary said goodbye and Alex and Sarah went back to their work on the computer. Isabel, Maria and I stayed at the table and spread out the sheets Maria had prepared the day before with my wheels on them.

Isabel sat and talked about my wheels and what guidance they had to offer me. Maria listened as part of her training in understanding and interpreting this knowledge for others. I listened carefully and taped the session.

Isabel's system of teachings uses colors as a guide for knowledge and she explained that my entering color, given by my date of birth, was gray. "This," she said, "tells me something about where it is you lose energy in your life." I leaned forward expectantly. Losing energy, and subsequently becoming ill, had been a lifelong problem. "You lose energy when you allow others to dishonor you. For you, honoring what is sacred is critical. If you offer something that is sacred and close to your heart to someone and they dishonor the gift in some way, you must speak to them immediately. Tell them your feelings clearly and without blame. Give them another opportunity. But if they again dishonor what you offer, walk away. Do you understand this? This is where you drain all of your energy. You go back again and again to people who have dishonored you, or what you offer from your heart, and your life energy flows out. Does this make sense to you?"

I nodded thinking of all the times I had strained to be "reasonable," to reduce my expectations of people, hide my hurt, give them another chance. Why? Because I was afraid that if I drew this line so clearly I would be alone.

Isabel continued. "For you the centering color is blue. When you know you are under stress, need to be protected, centered—the color blue holds the vibration that will provide this for you. Blue is the color of intuition." Blue was a color I loved. I smiled.

She looked at me keenly, her eyes bright. "So, tell me. Do you know of any Native blood in your family?" I was surprised and told her of the story about my great-grandfather. She grinned with satisfaction and turned to Maria—"I knew it!"

I spoke with hesitation. "Isabel, I would like to speak to you of some dreams I have had." She nodded encouragement. I told her of my dreams of the Grandmothers.

She smiled. "And what did Raven have to say about this?"

"I told him about the dreams when they happened and he was interested. But since then . . . well, I'm not really sure . . . ."

"He doesn't like it."

"Well, he has some pretty serious questions about my getting the wheels. Good questions, questions I've asked myself."

She leaned forward and touched my arm. "Will you show me one of the wheels?" she asked. I nodded and began to talk about the first wheel, of the Dream of Grandmother Earth. I drew it on a sheet of paper as I spoke, and Isabel pulled her chair over next to mine to watch. I felt nervous and spoke rapidly, not wanting to take up a lot of her time. When I finished I sat silently, waiting for her response.

She looked at me intently, her dark eyes glittering. "Don't give these wheels to Raven. Write them up and copyright them. They are good wheels and the people need them." Her tone was emphatic.

I was amazed at her response. "Copyright them? I don't want to control how people use the wheels."

She nodded. "I'm not talking about controlling the wheels. But you must honor the old ones who have given you this gift, and the gift they offer, by acknowledging it. In the society in which you live, copyrighting is the way in which you acknowledge that this is something you have been given. Then you let people use it in the way they see fit, in the way it will most add to their learning."

I felt my chest tighten; my breathing became labored. "But how do you know I didn't make up the wheels?"

Isabel leaned back in her chair and shook her head. "Because of the wheel, Oriah! Because of the content of the wheel. That is why I tell you to acknowledge, honor and teach them." I fought back the tears that threatened.

Isabel leaned forward. "What are you afraid of?" she asked softly.

"Raven will be furious," I answered, my voice barely a whisper.

"Yes," she said calmly. "He probably will be. But that is his problem, not yours." She paused. "Let me tell you something. These Grandmothers you see, they are your band members, ancient teachers who have blessed you with their presence and their teachings in this life. If you do not honor what they offer to you, and to the people through you, they will stop working with you. Do you understand this?"

I nodded, the tears very close. "But I have learned so much from Raven. It's changed my life. I know he is . . . off about some things, but I owe him. I feel like I owe him my life." Tears spilled down my face.

Maria and Isabel watched me in silence. Isabel leaned forward and again laid her hand upon my arm. "Oriah, you cannot save Raven."

I jumped. These were the same words I'd heard from the Grandmothers! "What do you mean? Why do you say that?" I asked through my tears.

"Because Raven is responsible for himself. He is a man with much talent and a lust for power. He makes his own choices and must suffer the consequences of his choices, and no one, not you or anyone else, can change this." She paused. "Not even your love can change this." There was a flatness in her tone. There was no harshness, no judgment. It was a statement of what she knew to be the truth. She looked at me penetratingly. "Have you slept with him?" I shook my head. "Good. That's more to your credit than it is to his."

"Raven has never pressed me to be sexual with him," I protested on his behalf.

She smiled wryly. "I know Raven," she said, "and believe me, if this is true it, too, is to your credit, not his. Perhaps there was something in you, or in the way you have been with him, that brought out his honorable side. He, like many medicine men, has often misused his power." As she spoke Alex and Sarah joined us at the kitchen table. "In part," she said with a mischievous grin, "it is just the way men are. They get confused. They think power has something to do with that thing between their legs." Everyone, including Alex, laughed. The laughter pulled me out of my tears. I couldn't help thinking how wonderful it would be to be seventy and get away with saying anything you damn well pleased.

We all gathered for lunch and sat around the table, chatting and listening to Isabel's stories while we cleaned up and did the dishes. I began to feel anxious about finding a moment to speak privately with Isabel. I did not want to ask her about Many Shields while everyone was around. Many Shields had lived and worked here for some time and was known by the people in this community. But my time was running out and there never seemed to be a moment when there were not at least two other people in the kitchen. I wondered if I should ask Isabel to speak with me alone, but I hesitated. I did not want to reveal the strength of my feelings for Many Shields and the importance of the discussion by for me by requesting privacy. I decided to wait and see if an opportunity presented itself. If it did not, I decided, I would assume this wasn't an appropriate time or place to discuss the matter, and try to let it go.

As the thought went through my mind, Alex and Sarah rose to say they were leaving to drive into town. Simultaneously Maria looked out the kitchen window and announced she was going outside to meet the repair man who had just arrived. They all disappeared, leaving Isabel and I alone. She looked at me without saying anything, smiling, her eyes wide and expectant. I wondered if she had somehow arranged the whole thing.

"Isabel, there is something else I would like to speak to you about." She said nothing and I took a breath and plunged on. " A while ago I met a man you know, Many Shields." I carried on, telling her about my dream and my first meeting with Many Shields. When I had finished, she shook her head.

"Well, I'll say this much. He always goes for the pick of the litter, the best and the brightest." I did not feel flattered. "And it's always the blondes." She looked at me, a touch of sadness in her voice. "Oriah, this is not a man to get involved with. Oh, don't get me wrong. I know him and I love him. He is charming, funny, a good teacher and he knows the medicine. But . . . well he's not the kind of man . . ."

She hesitated and I finished the sentence. ". . . you'd want your daughter to get involved with."

"Right." She nodded. "He's not a man you could build a life with. Did he tell you he was married?"

"Not exactly," I hedged. "Someone else told me."

"He has the prettiest wife, who loves him and looks after those children on her own. She is the best little mother I've ever seen and she has her hands full with the six of them—two of their kids under two, two from her first marriage and the two from Many Shields' first marriage. She's done wonders for his kids. They were pretty lost without a mom." This was not what I wanted to hear. It was what I needed to hear. "He has a real gift for tuning in to other people's dreams and shaping himself to meet them. Be careful, Oriah."

"What about teaching together?" I said, grasping at straws. Many Shields had suggested that we might teach some medicine classes together.

She shook her head. "A man and a woman should only teach the medicine together if they are married. Otherwise there is too much room for confusion, problems, things that will interfere with the medicine. If they have developed a good, loving committed marriage, the medicine will be enhanced by this." She smiled at me slightly. "Besides, if you are going to teach with Many Shields you'd have to be careful. In anything he does, he's the boss—the only boss. You already have a group of students. He is looking for someone to set him up in a teaching position. If you teach together, he would insist on being totally in charge."

I nodded. I had already sensed this and it had made me hesitate when Many Shields had suggested we teach together.

Maria came back into the house and walked into the kitchen. I rose to go and pack my things. The conversation felt complete. I offered some tobacco to Isabel with my thanks for her time and wisdom. She kissed me gently on the cheek, walked me to the door and hugged me. "Give me a call anytime you feel you need to talk," she said. "Go and do what you know is right."

I left feeling very much as I had when I'd left Dorothy's home. I had been welcomed, seen, heard and guided in a way that left me feeling fully responsible for my own life and completely capable of doing what needed to be done. Both women, in their gentle embrace had made me feel my own worthiness. I wanted to take care of myself and my dreams in a new way, to honor what the Grandmothers offered me, to be worthy of their gift. For the first time I began to feel what speaking and acting from the feminine looked like: a gentle and unconditional encouragement and cherishing of the best in myself and others; a courage that quietly but clearly named, without moral judgment, anything that did not honor Sacred Law. As I drove home, I sang my thanks to the grandmothers I had met for their guidance and love.

I had several more brief visits with Dorothy. She was often in physical pain, unable to eat and too weak to move around, but her spirit was always strong. I told her about my visit to Isabel's and mentioned her query about my heritage. "Dorothy," I said, "why would both you and Isabel think I had Native blood? I certainly don't look like I do, and this family story is something I have only known about for a couple of years. What even made the two of you ask?"

Dorothy smiled. "How long have you been learning and working with the medicine?"

"About five years," I said.

"Well," she said, "Isabel and I have been doing it for over thirty years, maybe longer. We should have learned something you haven't yet in all that time, eh?" She laughed. I had a sense of how young I really was.

As I continued my visits, I began to feel the need to tell Dorothy about the classes I was teaching and ceremonies I was leading. I had heard stories about her anger towards non-Natives using the teachings and ceremonies. I was in a dilemma. I didn't want to incur her wrath and risk our time together, nor did I want her hearing about my medicine work from someone else and feeling I had been less than honest with her. Although I had mentioned the classes and ceremonies when we'd first met our conversations since then had focused on more personal matters.

I arrived one afternoon determined to tell her exactly what I did during my classes and the ceremonies, willing to hear her opinions and feelings on the subject. She lay in her usual place on the couch, and smiled in greeting as I came in. As we talked about her grandson, the weather, her home on a lake north of the city, I tried several times to turn the subject to a ceremony I had led the night before. Each time I made an attempt to talk about it, she changed the subject. Feeling exasperated, I finally blurted out, "I was at a pipe ceremony last night."

She sighed. "Who was leading the ceremony?" she asked with some reluctance.

"I was," I answered with trepidation.

"Well, I hope you did it right!" She spoke with some vehemence.

"Well, I did it the way I was taught—"

"Who taught you?" she interrupted.

"Raven." She nodded absentmindedly, as if she had forgotten him. I was not deterred. I wanted to get it all out in the open. "Dorothy, I know there are things I have been taught that are different from the way you do things—"

She raised her hand to stop me. I was all set for a full confessional, telling of all the procedures I thought might be contrary, or even offensive, to her way of working. She spoke softly but with an air of finality. "Oriah, listen to me. It does not matter. There are many different ways to do these things. As long as you honor the tradition you have been taught, and always honor all of the medicine you have inside you, the differences do not matter." She leaned back on the couch, looking tired. "We're all going home to the same place anyway. Do what you know is right." I nodded to her gratefully. She leaned over and put her hand on my arm. "This can be a very lonely path. You see things, know things that no one else does. The connection to the Great Spirit is a wonderful gift, but it can be very lonely, being the one chosen to do the medicine. People need so much. They are lost, and you have to help if you have the knowledge they need." Her eyes filled with tears. "Sometimes I wish there was someone, a grandmother, for me to talk to." Then she smiled at me. "But then they send me a girlfriend like you to talk to."

I could not speak for a long time. We sat quietly together in the late afternoon sun, listening to the clock ticking on the bookshelf. As I gathered my belongings to go home I leaned over and kissed her brown, weathered cheek lightly. I spoke the only words that described how I felt. "My heart is very full."

12

My own grandmother, my mother's mother, lay in an old-age home several hours from Toronto. I had not seen her in more than two years. Although she remained physically healthy, she had not recognized me on my last two visits and my mother had discouraged me from returning, assuring me that it made little or no difference, since Nana, as I called her, did not know I was there. My cowardly side, which hated seeing her tiny, wizened body tied in a chair and couldn't stand hearing her mutter to herself or call out to unseen visitors, took solace in my mother's assurances. It was easy, with my schedule of work, children and studying, for the months to slip by.

After one visit with Dorothy I dreamed of Nana. She smiled at me and I burst into tears. "Nana," I said, "I am so sorry I have not been to see you in so long."

She smiled. "That's all right, dear. You've been busy with the babies. But come and see me now. I have something to tell you." Her tone was gentle and I woke with the image of her reaching out to touch my face.

Nana had not been an easygoing woman. She held strong opinions and let them be known. A perfectionist in all she did, she expected everyone, especially my mother, to live by the same standards. She had a sharp mind, and a tongue to match, both honed to a fine edge by her inarguable Scottish Presbyterian code of conduct. As a child, when my grandparents came for week-long visits, my mother felt terrorized, her knuckle joints became stiff and swollen from anxiety and her headaches became excruciating.

I was touched by very little of this. To me, my grandmother was the one person in the world who believed I was beautiful. I vividly remember her touching my face and speaking in loving, reverent tones about my beautiful smooth skin, my silky blond hair and my pretty mouth. Whether any of this description was accurate or not was irrelevant. I knew in the eyes of this beholder I was beautiful and I loved her with all my heart for it. As I grew older, nothing seemed to change in our contact. While my grandfather and I engaged in verbal battle over short skirts, long hair and the rise of Communism in the free world, my contact with Nana was primarily confined to assisting in the kitchen; carrying steaming bowls of mashed potatoes, whipped squash and platters of baked ham to the dining-room table. It was as if she chose to ignore the things she disapproved of.

Much to everyone's surprise, Nana deteriorated rapidly after my grandfather died. The woman who had always appeared to be in charge, impeccably organized and impenetrably strong began to crumble around the edges. The previously spotless house showed signs of neglect. Her clothes were often unwashed, her hair uncombed. The shades were drawn all day, the house dark. She wandered around within, lost, forgetful and fearful. When my mother decided to put her in a home for seniors and sell the house, I wanted to put a stop to it. I talked to my husband about having her come and live with us, but I knew it was impossible. I was ill most of the time, we were living on very little money and I had a six-month-old baby. On the one weekend she spent with us I was up all night, every night, with her and the baby. She had become increasingly disoriented and frightened. I could not take care of her.

Perhaps it was my guilt that had kept me from visiting. The dream I had strengthened my resolve and I decided to visit her. On the way there I stopped in to visit Dorothy, and told her where I was going. When I told her I had not seen Nana in two years, she looked up from the cigarette package she was opening. "Shame on you," she said. I looked away, feeling miserable. She leaned forward and, softly caressing my arm, spoke more gently. "We are all human, Oriah. Go and see her now. Don't worry about whether she recognizes you or not. Just talk to her. Tell her about yourself, your sons and the life you have. Don't worry if she doesn't seem to hear or understand. Her mind may not know you are there, but her spirit will. Her spirit will know and her spirit will tell you why she has called you to her. Trust this."

Feeling encouraged, I left Dorothy's and drove out of the city. I arrived at the old-age home just past noon. A nurse directed me to the wing where Nana stayed and there a group of nurses directed me to her room. One called out to me as I walked down the hall, "Come to visit your grannie, have you? That's great." My anger flared. What did this woman know of my Nana, how she had been, who she had been to me and those around her? As quickly as my anger rose, it dissolved. True, these women had not known Merle Hildreth when she could give anyone a tongue-lashing that left them shaking in their boots, when she had touched and made a little girl feel beautiful. But they did know more of who she was now than I, her own granddaughter, did. They bathed her, fed her, took her to the window and cared for her everyday. She was someone else to them, and they were with her now.

I found Nana's room and walked in quietly. She sat in a large chair facing the window, propped up with pillows and held in by a wide cloth strap. I hardly recognized her. Always a tiny woman, who insisted she was five feet tall but was curiously absent whenever a tape measure was available, she was even smaller now. Bowed and thin, she was no larger than a child. Her silvery hair had been cut short, removing the natural curls that had been her pride and joy. She glanced unseeing around the room and out of the window, her blue eyes unfocused. She had always worn glasses and had felt frightened without them as her poor eyesight intensified her claustrophobia. My mother had told me the nurses couldn't keep her glasses on, and she had broken several pairs. They had given up and left her without them.

As I entered the room, she moved her head and seemed to be aware of my presence. Moving to where she sat, I leaned over and kissed her forehead lightly. "Nana, it's Debbie," I said, using my birth name.

She looked up and spoke loudly, as if calling to someone in the hall. "Hello, dear. Have you brought my lunch?"

"No, Nana. It's not lunchtime." I pulled a chair next to her and sat down.

She gazed distractedly around the room. "You tell Buster to get out of there!" she yelled. Buster had been her brother. Her head dropped and her eyes flickered shut as she drifted into a light sleep. Periodically she raised her head and mumbled, speaking to shadows, unaware of my presence. Occasionally she would become agitated and strain against the strap that held her in the chair.

Remembering Dorothy's advice, I began talking slowly and quietly. I told her about my life, describing my work, the kids, my home. I told her how much I loved her and missed her, stroking her hair gently when she became agitated. I wondered if she could hear me at all. I told stories of my childhood memories. She stared blankly out of the window, occasionally yelling phrases that made little sense. I continued to talk, my heart aching for the grandmother I had known and I loved. It was as if she was trapped in a fog. I wondered if she wanted to leave but just couldn't find her way out. I knew she was on medication and wondered how much it affected her lucidity and her ability to choose the time to leave this life. Stroking her hair, I spoke softly. "Nana, if you want to leave, it's O.K. I know you might be frightened, and I don't really know what happens when we die, but I have a pretty good sense that it will be all right, that you don't need to be scared. I miss you, Nana, but if you want to leave, if you choose the time, I want you to know it's all right. You've worked so hard all of your life. Maybe you can have a rest now. Look for the light and move toward it when you choose. It's up to you."

Suddenly she turned toward me, and spoke in a different tone—slow, soft and musical. "Your words are just heavenly," she said. She sighed loudly and leaned back in the chair; her eyes vacant again. Some part of her knew I was there and heard my words. Her mind might not have understood, but her spirit had heard. I continued to talk, telling her stories about the births of my two sons. Occasionally she would interrupt with loud outbursts. "Let's look over there!" "Shirley will be here by then!" "Walk on this sidewalk!" She was seeing and hearing a world I couldn't touch.

Then I realized I would have to leave soon to be home in time for an evening class I was teaching. As the thought of leaving crossed my mind, Nana squeezed my hand. She had held it steadily for more than an hour. Again she spoke in the same slow, musical voice. "You talk so sweetly. It makes people feel good. You are a sweet girl. I love you."

I rose and kissed her on the cheek. Her skin was soft and wrinkled. "I love you, too, Nana."

She let go of my hand and stared blankly out of the window. As I walked down the hall I heard her yell incongruous phrases and wondered if she knew or remembered that anyone had been there. Getting in my car, I felt I had again been blessed by the Grandmothers who had sent me. Words and stories have always been important to me. They are the way that I teach and learn, share myself and create magic for others. Nana, in her moments of dreamlike lucidity, had shown me the effect of those words.

Out of the blue, as I sat in the car, I remembered a long-forgotten dream. At the first workshop in Northern Ontario, Raven had sent us out with Gunner to do a pipe ceremony at a spot sacred to the local Native people. It was a remote, massive rock of creamy quartz, that had, for thousands of years, been used for questing and dreaming. With permission from the local band office, we had hiked to the top of the rock and gathered in a circle as Gunner filled his pipe with prayers. As he raised his pipe to the sky, sending the smoke spiraling upward, seven hawks appeared and began to circle around, high above our heads. We watched as they stayed with us, wings extended, gliding gracefully on the wind currents.

We went off individually to explore the area. I had moved down the rock just a short way, when an irresistible tiredness came over me. Sitting down where I was, I leaned on a rock and fell asleep within moments. I had no choice—my body just dropped into the dream. And for the first time, in a sleep dream, I saw Grandfather. We sat at the edge of the stream and he told me my medicine was to be a storyteller, to weave healing that would touch the hearts of others with words. The trouble was that the only stories I was telling at the time were bedtime nursery rhymes for my sons. Surprised, I asked him, "And where will these stories come from, Grandfather?"

He gazed at me for a moment and then spoke. "From the knowledge of the sacred wheel and its power. From the history of the People. From the myths, legends and fairy tales. From the dreams of warriors past, present and future. From the Earth and her children. From the stars. From the Sacred Dream of Mountain Dreamer."

I looked at him, filled with certainty. "I am Mountain Dreamer," I stated, using my medicine name, which I had just received from Raven, for the first time.

My grandmother's words felt like confirmation of this dream. This was my medicine.

I left the old-age home and started back to Toronto, and as I drove sent out a prayer of gratitude. Then a sudden change came over me. One moment I was silently sending thanks to the Great Mystery, Grandfather and the Grandmothers; the next moment I was acutely aware of the presence of the Grandmothers. Part of me continued to drive at ninety kilometers an hour, while another part of me was in the kiva. I wondered if I should get off the highway, but there was something in the activity of driving, in the necessity for split attentions, that seemed to bring greater clarity to the experience. So, while I watched the road and drove, I also heard and saw the Grandmothers.

The Grandmother in the west spoke. "Remember the Birthing Wheel," she said. In my first dreaming with the Grandmothers they had told me the west was the place where women knew the power of the feminine as Life-Giver and Death-Bringer. Later I had a dream of a wheel of "children" we could birth in this life: relationships and personal mythology, work and dreams, health and physical children, reasons for being, ideas, choices and decisions, creativity and self-concepts. Now, as I remembered each of the eight different kinds of births, I could see eight circles of different colors spinning in the air above her.

She went on, "Look and see the Serpent's Path on each wheel of birth. Here is the pattern of the Great Mother's movement in creating life. For each kind of birth there is a different movement, a separate dance." As she spoke I could still see the holographic images of the wheels above her head. Within each, as they spun in the air in vibrant blues, greens, pinks and purples, were infinity loops. Each figure eight was in different position on each wheel. The Grandmother continued. "The wheel is the womb and contains the Serpent's Path. Along this path, where the figure eight touches the wheel, are each of the stages in this movement of creating life—lovemaking, conception, pregnancy, labor, birth and nursing. On either side of the path, in the two directions not touched by the figure eight, are the tasks of preparing the child and releasing it to stand in the world."

I could see it vividly. From working with Raven I was familiar with using the infinity movement within a medicine wheel and numbering each of the places on this movement. Driving with one hand, counting on the fingers of the other and muttering, I tried to sort out the insights and understandings that cascaded over me. "The Grandmother said there were eight, yes, eight stages in creating life. So then there are six where the Serpent's Path touches the wheel . . . and the other two are where it doesn't touch the wheel. Hmm, so this means that if each birth has a different Serpent's Path . . . then each of the eight powers on the medicine wheel hold a different role for each of the eight births. Right!"

Suddenly I was afraid I would lose it, that my words couldn't possibly hold all this. I looked around for something to write on. With one hand on the steering wheel I rummaged around in my purse for a pen, and found a black felt-tipped marker. There was no paper, but the napkins from my fast-food lunch were still on the passenger seat. I propped the napkins on my purse and, with one eye on the road, began to draw the circles for each of the different births, with figure eights inside them, numbering the places around the Serpent's Path from one to six, and the two other directions, seven and eight.

The Grandmother had said that birth was the fifth stage in creating life—this made sense. Five, as I had learned from Raven, was the number of heart-to-heart communication, of being fully human. Five was the expression of the process of birth—the child—and our full humanness came in giving birth in each of the eight directions. When I moved the infinity movement around the wheel, changing the position of each of the numbers, the Serpent's Path told a different story for each birth.

I continued mumbling. "So if I put the five place on the Serpent's Path in the south, then, because it's the south, the child that's born is a relationship. So where's the first place? Ah, the lovemaking's in the west. So if I want to birth a relationship then I have to make love in the west. Because the west is the place of the body, holding with intimacy, intuition and death and change, then the beginning and coming together in a relationship has to happen through intuition and the physical body."

I thought of the stories of the Star Nations, those ancestors who live on sister planets other than Grandmother Earth, but are not in physical form. The stories told that the Star Nation People had much knowledge and wisdom but felt incomplete—they could not touch each other—and yearned to come to a place where they could be touched and feel whole. Grandmother Earth called to them to walk upon her robe and offered each of them an earth-lodge made from her own body. The reason the Star Nation People came here and why we chose to be on this planet, the teachings say, is that being in physical form offers the gift of touching one another.

Whether the relationship being birthed is one of being lovers or not, the "lovemaking," the intimate bringing together of the masculine energy of deciding to "touch" someone and the feminine willingness to be "touched," begins with what first teaches us of our humanness: our physical body, and the intuitive knowing it holds. This decision begins the process that is aligned with death and change. Whether conception takes place and the pregnancy comes to term or not, we are always changed in some small way—death to our old way of being—by even beginning the process of touching and being touched by another.

I continued to follow the story of this birth around the Serpent's Path. This child of relationship was conceived at the second place in the movement, in the east, the place of spirit. This, too, was consistent with what I had been taught. The east is the place of illumination and enlightenment, of fire and passion, of fantasy and illusion. All relationships are mirrors, agreements we have made in spirit, whether consciously or not, to teach each other. Here, in the place of spirit, the conception of the child called relationship takes place. I thought ruefully of the number of times I had conceived a relationship from fantasy and illusion, caught in what could be or should be, not what was.

The pregnancy, the third place in the movement for this birth, happened in the northeast—the place of how we make decisions and choose to use our life-energy. The child is formed by the choices and decisions we make. I thought of all the decisions made in any relationship that shape the growing relationship: living together or separately, how much time to spend together, how the time is actually spent together, who will make certain kinds of decisions, which parts of life are shared, which parts are separate.

The fourth place in the movement, the "labor," fell in the north, the place of ideas, beliefs, philosophies and ways of viewing the world. I could see how much of the "labor," the work in birthing any relationship, involved dealing with my belief systems about love, money, home, children, men, women, sex . . . . The list was endless.

Any relationship with another is born in the south, place of the heart, emotions, of giving with tenderness. The "nursing" of this child, caring for it when it is still vulnerable and dependent, happens in the southwest, place of the dream. I could feel how in any relationship, the coming together of two creates a third, this child called relationship, which has it's own dream, its own medicine, gifts and power connected to, but separate from, the individuals involved. This dream is how it sustains itself and its life is nurtured.

The seventh place on this wheel fell in the northwest, place of karma and dharma, the lessons we have chosen for this life, and the Children's Fire. It is across this fire, our essence or soul, that our Hokkshideh or higher self, makes agreements with another to learn together in different lives. This the place of preparing the child, teaching it all it needs to know to survive and find joy. This preparation involves tending my own Children's Fire, my sacred essence, my soul, and not allowing it to be violated, as well as not violating the Children's Fires of those I am in relationship with. Without this the child would be unprepared for what life might have in store.

The Grandmother had named the eighth and final place as the place of letting the child go. What would this look like for a relationship? Would it mean the relationship would end or just that it could stand in the world on its own? In the movement for the south birth, the eighth place rested in the southeast, place of my ability to conceive of myself as lovable, as a granddaughter of the ancestors. If I was full of self-judgment, comparisons and expectations, my relationships with others would have difficulty surviving and meeting the challenges of everyday life.

In fast thought, my mind rolled around the wheels. The possibilities for learning seemed endless. Each time I drew the infinity movement on a napkin, putting the five place in a different direction on the wheel, a new story emerged, offering me guidance on how each "child" came into the world and what it needed at each stage of its growth. I knew I was only understanding a minute fraction of the ways in which these wheels offered a way of living. I wanted to sit down and overlay them with all that I knew about the powers of the directions, the songs of the numbers and the other teachings of the many wheels I had learned from Raven and others. I continued to drive and to draw the wheels. The Grandmothers had faded. I no longer had a sense of simultaneously seeing and hearing them while I drove, but I could feel their presence nearby.

I parked in front of my house and looked, dumbfounded, at the napkins, covered with circles and figure eights, that littered my car seat. I felt overwhelmed. It was so much—the meeting with Dorothy and Nana, the gift of a body of knowledge that I knew went well beyond my present understanding. I felt touched, as if I had received an incredible blessing—and I wanted to be worthy of it. I had been handed a cup filled with precious liquid to carry. I wanted to take great care in walking with it.

I got out of the car and walked to my backyard. Offering tobacco to the four directions, the earth and sky, I thanked the Grandmothers once again for their guidance. Standing silently on my diminutive rectangle of green grass, I listened to the constant roar and rumble of the huge city around me. "I will do my best not to spill a drop," I whispered.

Two weeks after visiting Nana, I received an invitation to the opening of a Native craft show. Many Shields was returning to sell some handmade items in the show. He telephoned shortly after the invitation arrived and asked if I would attend. Spending time with Dorothy, Isabel and Nana had changed something for me. I responded to that aspect of myself I saw mirrored in their eyes: a granddaughter who was forthright, honest and worthy of respect. The desire they awakened, to live from this best part of myself, and the conversation with Isabel about Many Shields, had strengthened my resolve not to regress to a swooning adolescent around this man. I also wondered if I could maintain this position. I told him I would be there, then called Dorothy to see if she would like to go with me. She had met Many Shields before and I knew having her there would support my resolve to keep some distance from him.

On the day of the opening I drove to Dorothy's house to pick her up. With her failing health, she rarely got out. She was excited and ready to go, giving me directions on fitting her wheelchair into the trunk of my car. We arrived early at the gallery. Many Shields, dressed in a white shirt, blue jeans and a fringed buckskin vest, looked wonderful. He hugged me for a long time. Aware of the others around us, I drew back self-consciously. Slowly the small gallery filled with friends and students who knew Many Shields and the other artists. I stayed close to Dorothy, helping her up and down the stairs, to the washroom and serving her food. As she chatted with other guests I stood by silently, observing the group. Many Shields had disappeared for a few moments. Then he returned, and leaning close to me so no one else could hear, he said "I was just standing there thinking how wonderful it is to have my wife here for this opening." Resisting the urge to look around the room and ask where she was, I smiled and said nothing.

Dorothy tired quickly, and we left after a short while. I arranged to meet Many Shields the following day, at the house where he was staying.

When I arrived the next day I suggested to Many Shields that we talk outside. With my medicine bag slung over my shoulder we walked to the field behind the house, and taking my medicine blanket out, I spread it on the grass and we sat down. I took care not to sit too close to him and risk another outbreak of runaway adolescent hormones. Many Shields looked at me expectantly. "I would like to speak to you across my pipe," I said. He nodded. I brought out my pipe and, putting it together, filled it with prayers for the ability to speak clearly from my heart. I asked the Grandmothers and Grandfather to be with me. Lighting the pipe, I offered it to Many Shields, he smoked and handed it back.

Holding it in my hands, I spoke. "I have something I wish to speak to you about. First, though, I have a question. Why did you not tell me you were married when we first met?"

Many Shields blushed and looked at the ground. "I thought you knew."

I was disappointed that he still could not be truthful. I continued. "I would still like to exchange medicine teachings, as we agreed on our last visit. However, our sexual relationship is something else." I looked at him for a moment and spoke more softly. "Many Shields, you have a very young wife and six children. They need you. I do not and I never will, not in that way. With the knowledge I now have I cannot step into the circle of a sister. If we were to continue to have any sexual contact it would have to be within the context of the medicine, and it would have to be clear to me that it was absolutely necessary. I am not willing to continue to be lovers."

Many Shields sat listening. His face looked strained. "Of course, that is how it should be. I am married and we must honor this and the medicine of our meeting."

Once again, he had agreed after the fact. This time I felt no anger. It didn't matter. This was my decision.

13

T he Arizona sky changed to deeper shades of blue as the sun neared the horizon. I sat on the concrete curb facing the parking lot behind Raven's offices, waiting for the evening session to begin. It had been over three months since I had attended the last apprentice gathering. A shiver ran through me at the memory of the early morning meeting with Raven, Susan, Lynn and Jo. I did not like the part of me I had seen in this meeting, nor did I want to put myself in this vulnerable position again. But a lot had changed during the three months. Morgan and I had resumed our relationship and he had traveled to this gathering with me. I was not alone. My meetings with Isabel and Dorothy had renewed my sense of commitment to the wheels the Grandmothers had given me. They had also helped me find a new strength in speaking from the feminine. While I did not like the threatened, frightened, nasty part of me that had been touched in that early-morning meeting, Isabel and Dorothy's support had somehow made it easier for me to accept all the aspects of who I was in any moment. The Grandmothers had told me repeatedly, "You do not have to be better than who you are. This is neither light nor dark. It just is who you are in this moment. See it, know it, but do not put out of your heart any part of yourself. This is how it gains power and rules from the shadows."

As I sat waiting for the meeting to begin, I sent out my prayer to Grandfather and the circle of Grandmothers. "Sacred ones, I ask you to be with me this weekend. Help me to remain conscious of what is happening within myself and around me." I could feel their presence. I wished the workshop were located in a more natural setting and not in the midst of city and concrete. It is always easier for me to stay balanced where there are trees, grass, a closeness to Grandmother Earth. The sense of connectedness to the earth helps me stay open and aware, touching my shadow sister with a softness that does not drive it into the hidden corners. As I felt the longing for a place with more green and less concrete, I heard the voice of one of the Grandmothers.

"Oriah, look around you. Remember what Grandmother Isabel told you. Blue is your centering color. Look at what Grandfather Sky offers to you here, an endless expanse of changing blues. Drink it in." I gazed at the magnificent sky now deepening in color, indigo in the east and a paler blue in the west where the sun had disappeared. It was true. Even here in the city what I needed was at my fingertips. I breathed in the color of the sky, letting my weight drop into the earth. I heard someone call for everybody to come into the meeting room and felt myself tense. I wondered if I could carry the color of the sky into the concrete-block room. As I reluctantly got up form the curb to go inside I heard the Grandmother again. "What you need is always provided."

As I slipped off my boots and stepped into the room I suddenly realized the entire space was covered in deep blue-mats—they had always been there, but I had not really noticed them before. I smiled to myself. The color that helped me to stay centered within had always been there above me and beneath me—I just needed to use it.

Morgan and I went to a back corner of the room, sitting diagonally across from Raven. He began by talking about a conflict within the local group of apprentices. I knew nothing about this. For the next two hours the group discussed the past month's events: who had offended whom, what agreements had been made and violated, what should have happened and should not have happened. Morgan, who had been ill for a week with a respiratory infection, fell asleep. I sat listening, my frustration growing. I tried to relax. If I was here and this was happening, perhaps there was something of value in it for me, something I needed to hear and learn. Much of the conflict centered around Lynn and Jo. Other apprentices felt the two had violated their trust by reporting back to Raven the contents of a confidential meeting. My little inner shadow sister poked her head up, anxious to take some pleasure from the attacks on both women. Inwardly I shook my head. I would not deny her existence, but neither would I give her bitterness free rein.

Finally Raven ended the discussion and I waited for him to begin the teachings scheduled for the weekend. Instead he started talking about Jamie, the senior apprentice who had left Raven shortly before the trip to Tula two years earlier. Jamie had apparently been teaching and living with Lorne Fire Dog. Lorne said he was a shaman and medicine man. Raven said he was a fraud. Lorne and Jamie had been sending letters to individuals in Europe who had sponsored Raven's workshops in the past, warning them about the "dark sorcery" he was using and telling them to stop sponsoring workshops. Raven read one of the letters—obviously written by a disturbed individual—to the gathering. It contained charges that Raven forced apprentices to drink urine and allowed "faggot dykes" to run things. I couldn't see how anyone would take it seriously.

Raven, however, was incensed. He vowed to "take the guy out," pledging not to kill him, but to just hurt him badly. Responses in the room were varied. Jack, the large man whose violent side I had seen during the paint-ball games at the desert retreat, enthusiastically volunteered to give Raven a hand. Several of the women shook their heads and looked discouraged. I raised my hand and Raven nodded for me to speak.

"One of the things I have learned and valued from your teachings, Raven, is the necessity of always examining the inner meaning of outer events. If I am feeling plagued by someone externally, feeling as if someone is making my life miserable and threatening me in some way, I understand that I have to examine what mirror that person holds up for me. I have to ask myself what I am refusing to acknowledge and deal with in myself that is being projected outward and manifesting in this person's actions. Perhaps we need to do this here, collectively. What is the shadow aspect of this group, this family as you call it, that we are not dealing with, that is being mirrored by this man, Lorne, and his behavior?"

Raven shook his head. "I don't buy that. This guy has to be dealt with directly. He has offended the Texan in me. That's what you hear now— not Raven the spiritual leader but Raven the Texan. And that's where I want to deal with him from."

"But Raven, I don't understand the threat. It's clear that the letter is written by someone who is unwell. Who would take it seriously?" I couldn't understand the degree of anxiety that this man created in Raven.

"Well, it has affected some of the people we deal with and I want it stopped. Jamie is completely taken in by this man!" His tone was angry and I wondered which part of the Texan had been offended. A kind of John Wayne, nobody-takes-my-woman tone had crept into the discussion. Other people offered their opinions and several, including Lynn, tried to bring the discussion back to my suggestion that we needed to look inwardly to see why this was happening. Raven refused. The tension in the room grew.

Eventually the discussion petered out and we all sat quietly. At last Raven spoke. "This is all about loyalty. I don't trust any two-legged, including Grandfather," he said emphatically, referring to the man who had been his teacher. "But you have to give absolute loyalty in order to gain knowledge. A warrior must give this loyalty to his or her president, partner and teacher."

Being Canadian, I assumed I was off the hook for the first one. I've never heard Canadians refer to "my prime minister" the way Americans say "my president," a cultural difference with which I am quite comfortable. I wondered where the discussion was leading. What exactly did loyalty mean? Scenes of my previous visit flashed before me. Could I be loyal to Raven and follow my own dream?

Raven went on. "Loyalty to someone means you do not speak against them, you never judge them as a two-legged and you accept them completely for who they are. These three things must be the intent behind any agreement in a relationship."

I mulled this over. Did I do this with Raven? Certainly I had spoken to others about my struggles with some of what he did. Was this speaking against him? I did not judge him as anything more or less than human. Somehow I doubted this was enough; he was pulling for something more. What was it?

Raven carried on speaking. "I want to ask you all something right now." He put his head down and seemed to struggle with the words. "I don't really want to ask it, but it has been given to me as a warrior task assignment by my teachers, the elders." He paused again. "What is it about me that makes it difficult for you to be loyal to me?"

There was silence in the room. I heard in the question an echo of my own terrified little girl within who begs to know what it is about her that makes her unlovable, easy to abandon or hurt. The silence in the room lengthened. I spoke softly. "What makes you think we're not loyal, Raven?"

He jumped slightly as if jabbed in the side and spoke quickly, looking around the room. "I know you're not. I know there are times when you speak against me, or do not defend me when others speak against me. What I want to know, what I have been told to find out, is why. What is it about me that makes it difficult for you to make this commitment of loyalty?"

Several people raised their hands and Raven nodded for them to speak. One at a time apprentices spoke of their loyalty to Raven as their teacher, assuring him that they had not been disloyal. Several differentiated their loyalty to Raven as a teacher and spiritual leader from their ambivalence about Raven the man and some of his personal views. They referred particularly to his desire to go after Lorne Fire Dog and their discomfort with this. Raven responded. "That's fine. You don't have to agree with everything I do as a man. What I want to hear about is your loyalty to me as the leader of this community. What makes this loyalty difficult?"

The droning sound had begun in my head as soon as Raven asked the question. I had immediately relaxed my body, focused by breath on my womb and dropped my weight into the ground in an effort to stay clearheaded. I raised my hand to speak and kept it raised, but Raven ignored me. Many others spoke and my frustration and impatience grew. Morgan had wakened from his nap to watch the process unfolding in the room. I looked at him and wrote on my notebook, "He will not let me answer the question he asked!" Not surprised, he smiled and nodded. Perhaps I would not get a chance to speak and I wondered if I should just stand up and begin talking. Immediately I heard one of the Grandmothers.

"No, Oriah. If you do not want to give your power away you must speak from the feminine. Hold your place and he will have to acknowledge you. Speak from your heart. Allow all of your feelings to flow into your words. Wait. Your turn will come."

Another fifteen minutes of discussion passed and most of the group had spoken. I remained with my hand in the air, following the flow of my breath in and out of my body. At last, with no one else asking to speak, Raven nodded to me. "Oriah?"

I lowered my hand and took a breath, trying to relax my body. I reminded myself to speak slowly and from the heart. "Raven, you have asked a very serious question. I want to honor you as my teacher by answering it as honestly as I am able. Like my brothers and sisters who have spoken, I am grateful for all I have learned from you. It has changed my life. I, too, do not always agree with some of what Raven the man chooses to say or do. This does not diminish my loyalty to you as teacher or my acceptance of your humanness." I paused. Everyone in the room was silent, expectant. "Where I find it difficult to be loyal, where I have remained silent as others have spoken against you, is when I feel the medicine being dishonored." The tension in the room rose sharply.

"Can you give some examples?" Raven asked tersely.

I raised my hand, palm forward, to indicate I had not finished. "Yes, I can offer some examples here. When I see people slipping off during the Sun Dance to take a shower, I feel the medicine is not honored. When I hear people entering life-changing ceremonies in order to respond to your push to get them ticked off the list, I feel the medicine is not honored."

Raven interrupted defensively. "Now, I don't know if I can be responsible for how everyone behaves. In the one instance—"

Again I raised my hand. "Raven, I do not offer this for debate or argument. You have asked a serious question. Out of my love and loyalty for you as my teacher, I am offering you my answer. You may do with it as you will. I offer these as examples as illustration, but I do not wish to debate each point." I paused. "I have been fortunate recently to meet some women who are elders in the Native community. When a seventy-year-old woman tells me of the years it took her to earn the right to hold the sacred pipe, learning to grow tobacco, finding and picking sweet-grass, carving a bowl, choosing a tree for her stem . . ." I paused again. "I do not want to do everything as it was once done. These are different times. But when I hear her story—and I know that within this group there are many who have been passed as Sacred Pipe Carriers, who claim this title that the Native community holds in such high regard, after holding a pipe for only a short time, rarely using it, never having held Karma Pipe, not meeting even the minimal conditions laid out by you for this honor—I am ashamed." Tears rose within me and I didn't fight them. I let them roll down my face as I spoke. "When I sit with this woman and know that something that is so sacred to her and her people is treated in this way, when this honor is claimed by those who have not met even your minimal requirements, I feel ashamed of this family, my family."

Raven responded immediately and with a touch of anger. "And what does this woman feel when she is on the reservation and sees her people desecrate Grandmother Earth with garbage?"

"She, too, feels shame for her family and their dishonoring of the medicine."

"And where does that get us, all this shame?" His tone was derisive and I responded immediately, matching the rapidity and forcefulness of his voice.

"It gets us right here with me honestly answering your question, naming the dishonoring that happens!"

Raven sat without speaking, his head down. No one moved or spoke. "Ah, well . . . maybe I do push for too much speed." Everyone waited. "Perhaps that is my fault." He looked up. "But I cannot be held responsible for how each of you works with the medicine." His tone became lighter as he warmed to his own defense. I was silent—I did not want to engage in any discussion. I had said all I had to say. I leaned back in my chair. Raven continued, "After all, you know what the medicine requires—"

"Raven, what Oriah talks of has happened right here." Roger, an apprentice and gifted artist from Texas, sitting next to me on my left, broke in. He, and some others, had spent six hours before the gathering creating a beautiful sand painting on a framed mirror. The painting now sat in the center of the room. "You asked me to do this sand painting," he said, pointing to it. "I do not ask for acknowledgment for myself, but I know this painting is a powerful medicine tool. You haven't seen to it that the painting, or the people walking around it, are smudged. It hasn't even been mentioned, so people will know to walk around it in the proper manner. This does not honor its medicine."

Raven looked startled. "Well, yes, people should walk around it sunwise and not just cut across the room." By this time others in the room had recovered enough to raise their hands in a bid to speak. Raven acknowledged several, and each pledged their loyalty to Raven. With these assurances the discussion abated and Raven called for a break before beginning the teachings for the weekend.

As I walked out into the parking lot, I raised my face to the sky. It was a deep indigo, lit with a million stars. Silently I thanked the Grandmothers. For the first time I felt I had spoken in a way that was true to my own heart. I did not know if Raven had heard me or if my words would have any impact, but it didn't matter. I had not sat in silence. I had not betrayed myself. I had spoken from a place of strength that felt different from what I had known. It was not an act of disloyalty to Raven. It was an act of loyalty to my truth. Was there any greater tribute to a teacher? As I stood there, Chris came up behind me. She touched my arm and spoke softly, her voice barely a whisper. "I think we should take up a collection and pay to have you attend these things." I smiled, grateful for the support. I was sure some were feeling otherwise.

Raven continued to teach well into the night. I took copious notes. After the usual early-morning nap we continued through Saturday and late into Sunday morning. By Sunday Raven began to share teachings about different medicine bundles, giving us each a long list of items to create our own Soul Bundle. Each person's bundle was to contain items representing his or her quest for self-healing. As he taught I felt my excitement rise. The idea of creating a bundle appealed to me, even though it would take me months to accumulate all the necessary items.

Two of the women in the group who had previously received these teachings had completed their bundles. Raven explained that he would bless and awaken their bundles, and link them with his own, using his pipe and the sand painting as we ended our time together that weekend.

At noon he moved into the ceremony, laying out his medicine pipe and asking the two women with completed bundles to sit close to the sand painting. The rest of us sat in a circle around them.

Raven rarely did a group pipe ceremony. Whenever he did, the Native half of his heritage came to the fore in its fullness and his prayers reflected the home his heart had found in the tradition of his Native ancestors. Now he filled the pipe with tobacco, saying his prayers and calling in all the powers of the universe for the ceremony. The pipe passed around the circle and we each smoked. Holding his pipe again, Raven began the ceremony to bless and awaken the bundles of two women who sat on either side of him. He sat in silence for a moment and then spoke to them. "Do you pledge at this time to make my enemies your enemies?"

My heart sank. I knew then and there that I would never have any Soul Bundle of mine awakened and linked with Raven's. I could not answer this question with an unqualified yes. I would have to ask what it meant and why it was being asked. What was an enemy, and what would be required of me in making Raven's enemies mine? What did this question have to do with the stated intent of a Soul Bundle? Was this truly a part of the ceremony or had it been instigated by the earlier discussions about loyalty and Lorne Fire Dog? I watched the two women. Both were in their late fifties. I wondered how they felt about the question. Had they known it was coming? I doubted it. To my surprise, neither hesitated but responded with a clear "Yes." The bundles were blessed and awakened, the ceremony was brought to a close and we began cleaning up.

Morgan and I were not going straight home. We had arranged to participate in an advanced spiritual-sexuality workshop on the following weekend and were going to spend the intervening week exploring a little of the Arizona desert and enjoying the sun. Before we left I stopped by Raven's office. He was by himself, sitting behind his desk, and motioned for me take the chair opposite him. He looked at me intently.

"So what's happening with you and Morgan? You're back together?"

I was surprised. Raven never showed any interest in the ever-changing personal relationships between apprentices. "Yes, we have been for about three months."

"Well, it seems to be a good thing for him." I smiled, unwilling to comment on the unspoken implication—that it was a bad thing for me. I had not asked for, nor did I want, Raven's commentary on my personal life. He looked around the room distractedly. "So have you decided if you're with us?"

"Raven, I never decided I wasn't," I answered quietly.

"Well, I know, but there seems to be some ambivalence."

I stood to leave, turning toward him at the door. "Morgan and I will be at the spiritual-sexuality workshop. I'll see you next weekend."

"Good."

14

Deep in the memory of what it was like to truly speak from the center of who I am, tears run down my face. It feels so elusive, this place of power within. I whisper my prayer to the empty room, the years before me in handwritten scrawl and typed notes. "Grandmothers, I want to live in this place. Can you show me how?"

The answering voice is patient and gentle. "Read the story, Oriah. It's all in the story."

My love for the desert had grown with my work on the medicine path. Although the land of my heart was still the rocks, lakes and evergreens of the Canadian Shield, I had grown to appreciate the incredible variety of life and the subtle colors of the desert. Morgan was still feeling ill and spent most of the week resting in our hotel room or lying by the pool, soaking up the sun. Both seemed to help and by the end of the week he was feeling better. I spent my time similarly resting and sunning and hiking out into the desert to sit with my pipe. Any apprehension I had felt about the upcoming spiritual-sexuality workshop with Raven had diminished to a tiny, almost-forgotten flicker. My experience at the apprentice gathering bathed me in new confidence about my ability to be true to my own heart.

Both Morgan and I had attended Raven's basic spiritual-sexuality workshops before, although never together. This was to be an advanced workshop, held in the home of Robert and Marsha who were coleading with Raven and Susan. We had been given the addresses of several motels in the area and the day before the workshop Morgan and I drove back into the city and found a place to stay. We arrived the next morning at Robert and Marsha's, a little after the time we had been told the workshop would begin. We were the first to arrive. I inwardly shook my head at my own inability to ever be late, despite the overwhelming evidence that nothing in this group ever happened at the appointed time.

Slowly the other workshop participants wandered in, and Raven and Susan arrived. Two hours later the workshop began. Marsha and Robert did a pipe ceremony and called in all the spirits to be with us for the weekend. Raven began the teaching by warning each of us that we were responsible for our own circle during this time. Each participant was then required to take a vow. As Raven told us the prerequisite vow, I heard the familiar droning sound, faint and distant, in my ears. It lasted only a moment and then faded completely. One by one each man and woman in the room took their vow. As my turn came I felt my lips move and heard my own voice speak. I felt a numbness settling over me and I could not think straight. The words were Raven's.

"My name is Oriah. I vow this weekend not to step into my needy, wounded, abandoned child or my vengeful, angry, manipulative adult. If I do so it is my responsibility to handle this and step out of it. I vow to assume authority, take responsibility and step into my power." The numbness spread down from my head over my shoulders and across my chest.

Raven began with teachings on relationships, teachings on how we must gather together to find happiness, share with each other to achieve health, teach one another in order to have hope and care for one another to find harmony. The wheels described the agreements we make with each other in relationships. Morgan and I, along with six or seven others in the room, had heard all of these teachings the previous weekend.

"Some of the people here have already heard these teachings at the advanced apprentice gathering last weekend," Raven said. "I hope you will be able to take your understanding of these teachings to a new level this weekend." While it was true that hearing teachings more than once was a good way to deepen understanding, part of me resented the huge investment of time and money Morgan and I had made to attend two weekends that had been billed as completely different, only to find out the teaching content was to be identical. I let my resentment go and focused on what Raven was saying. "They are part of a group of apprentices who have been working with the teachings the longest, the crème de la crème on this path." I suppressed a groan and sunk into my chair. We were the "crème de la crème" of apprentices learning to dream together, to battle the dark side in the fifth dimension? I hoped not, or we were all in a lot of trouble.

"We had an interesting weekend," Raven went on. "One of the things that happened was a kind of test. I posed a question to the group about loyalty in order to see who had advanced to the point of being able to trust themselves. I asked the question and waited to see who would answer with some kind of complaint. Those who did had not advanced to a place of trusting themselves. It was very interesting."

What? I sat up straight. It had all been a test? A way of revealing the infidels? What was this business of "trusting yourself"? I had no idea. The buzzing in my head returned. He made it sound as if it had all been a trick. I wanted to respond and looked around the room at Morgan and the others who had been at the apprentice gathering. No one seemed disturbed by Raven's reworking of reality. I remained silent, the buzzing sound receded and Raven continued teaching.

We took a break and were told to return after dinner wearing our west costume. In the first-level spiritual-sexuality workshops Raven teaches a wheel about the different faces or masks we wear in our sexual relationships. Each direction holds an archetypal energy—playful, adventurous, lusty, dominant, submissive, contractual, priest/priestess and healer—that can be brought to life in a costume. Putting together these costumes and experimenting with the different aspects of myself had been, for me, one of the most pleasurable and freeing parts of these workshops. A friend of mine in Toronto had helped me make several for this weekend. The only limitation stipulated is that all masks must be worn and acted out for the mutual pleasure and knowledge of participants, without any physical pain. The west mask is that of the wanton, lusty lover, one that Raven often asks people to step into.

We returned after dinner and, donning our costumes, gathered in the living room. As I walked into the room I noticed the arrival of a new participant, a lesbian woman and apprentice. One of the men in the group came up behind her. "Hey, Marilyn, what are you doing here?"

Marilyn looked up grimly, the tension in her face plain to see. "Oh, y'know, I got my warrior task assignment from Raven. Have to fuck a bunch of the brothers to open my closed symbols." She was obviously not looking forward to it. I paused and turned toward her. I looked at her a moment, wanting to ask her not to do this. Her face was cold, hard and steeled to any emotion she felt. I turned away.

As I moved to my place, I crossed in front of Raven, who looked up and eyed my costume: black lace garter belt and stockings, high-heeled shoes, a minute flared leather skirt and a black waiter's-vest halter top. "You look good," he said slowly, drawing out each syllable. I nodded my thanks and sat. The numbness spread down through my belly and back.

For the next two days we put on costumes, listened to Raven and acted out "exercises" that were assigned. The words Raven used were ones that touched a longing in my heart: "intimacy through trust, giving pleasure and knowledge, honoring the Sisterhood, knowing our partner as a mirror, making a soul connection, sensuously healing each other . . . ."

Some of the people were there with a partner, husband or wife. Others were there alone, choosing other single participants with whom to do the exercises. While the exercises assigned at the first-level workshops did not involve intimate sexual contact, I had known that the goal of this third-level workshop was to go much further. This was one reason I had not attended one before, waiting until I had a partner with whom I felt comfortable. Raven urged us to open up our "closed symbols" and push the edge by moving beyond what we had previously experienced.

I could not make the jump. To move from hearing about touching heart to heart to lying intimately on the floor with Morgan, beside two other couples, one of whom had met ten minutes earlier, required something I did not have. The numbness spread through my womb, my vagina and down through my legs. I saw myself moving through the activities from a distance. Dimly I heard and saw others around us: arms, legs, sighs, movement. I ignored my view of the others and my awareness of their viewing me.

On the afternoon of the second day I sat waiting for Morgan as an exercise began. One of the couples caught my attention. Teresa and John were having difficulties in their marriage—they had hoped that coming to the workshop would help. Teresa was obviously upset and angry with John. She got up and marched outside into the small backyard. I knew what she was doing. She, like all of us, had taken the vow at the beginning not to step into her hurt or anger. As it surfaced she kept her vow to deal with it alone and not express it within the context of the exercise. After doing her giveaway prayers at a tree in the backyard, she marched back in and flopped down next to John. "O.K.," she said with determination, "let's do this." They resumed the "lovemaking" exercise. I wanted to tell them to stop, talk to each other, go for a walk, anything, but don't continue. For a moment I thought I would throw up, but pushed the feeling down. The numbness moved into my hands and feet.

Morgan came in and sat in front of me. He knew something was wrong and asked me what it was. I could not speak. Each time I tried, my throat closed. I loved him and I knew he loved me and I knew he wanted to continue with the workshop. When Raven had suggested at the beginning of this exercise that people consider playing together in threesomes, I was surprised when Morgan suggested approaching one of the other women. I struggled with my feelings. I had no moral problem with people, in any numbers, loving each other physically, sexually and spiritually. But I did not know, or care about this woman, nor did Morgan. Anything we did together would be prescribed by Raven's exercise and not by any heart connection between us. I knew I could not do it and had told Morgan. I could see his disappointment, although he did not press me. Part of me was angry. How could he ask me to do this? We had been back together only three months and I felt the fragility of our new relationship. Why did he want to do this? How would we feel after the titillation was over? What would we see in each other's eyes?

The war within me escalated. I, too, had taken a vow to stay out of my hurt and anger. I knew that Raven or any of the staff present would tell me I was locked into my own beliefs about possessiveness, and my feelings of fear and jealousy. They would urge me to let these go and gain a new freedom in the pleasure being offered. I had been trained well. The arguments revolved in my head like an endless cassette. But my heart said no. Something was off, missing, twisted. There was no sense of ceremonial honoring of the joining of heart and spirit. I loved the lusty celebration of sexuality found in the meeting of bodies, but to really feel this, to bring it to its fullness, I needed to feel my link with spirit at the same time. The words of Raven's teachings affirmed this, but their practice widened the split between my spirituality and my sexuality. As I continued, trying to go through the motions of what was required of me, my spirit retreated and the numbness took over.

I knew that if I told Morgan my feelings he would be only momentarily disappointed and would insist that we not participate where I was not comfortable. I knew to say one word was to begin an inevitable chain of events: stepping out of the exercise, leaving the workshop, leaving Raven as my teacher and being seen as the woman who could not overcome her own fear and moralistic views to really push her own edge sexually and spiritually. I could not say the word. The numbness claimed my throat and advanced down the center of my body.

After the exercises we took a break. Morgan and I went into the adjoining garage, where we had stored our clothes and medicine items. As I entered the room I noticed there were five or six people lying together on the floor. Carefully stepping over them, I reached for my bag and pulled out a shirt. As I raised my arms to put it on I suddenly realized that the people in the room were involved in a group sexual "exercise." I had walked all the way across the room and not realized it—there was no erotic energy in the room at all, no sense of stepping into a private moment, only indifferent, perfunctory movements. It struck me as inappropriate to just walk through their midst as if nothing more than a game of Parcheesi was taking place. I walked out quietly and met Morgan. He had walked into the garage, picked up his clothes and quickly stepped out, feeling ill. We both returned to the main house.

As we entered Raven was calling for everyone to gather. His tone was serious. We walked into the living room. Marsha sat holding the medicine pipe she had filled at the beginning of the weekend. It had been sitting on the altar at one end of the room. She explained that a group of four people acting out a sexual fantasy in the living room had picked up the pipe to use in their scenario. Looking very worried, she warned everyone that the pipe should not be touched or used in this manner. I was stunned. Someone had touched the pipe? None of these people were new to the medicine. All had been at pipe ceremonies. How could they have not known that touching someone else's pipe, let alone using it in a sexual fantasy exercise, was not appropriate and was breaking Sacred Law? I felt sick. I looked at the individuals involved and knew it was not entirely their fault. They had taken their cue from the tone of the weekend, from the attitude toward the medicine they had seen from those leading.

We all sat down. Raven asked for feedback on the exercise and everyone responded enthusiastically about their experiences. I was silent. As I listened I heard the droning sound again and the voice of the Grandmothers speaking to me. "Oriah, get up and get out! You're life is in danger. Your soul is at risk. Get up now and leave!"

I could not move. Raven asked for a couple to volunteer to demonstrate one of the other lovers' masks. Morgan looked at me expectantly. I knew he wanted to do it. I knew I could not. The numbness was by now a coldness that had spread through my inner organs. I felt my heart, a lump of ice in my chest. I looked at him silently, beseeching, praying he would read the desperation in my eyes. *Please don't ask me to do this here, now, in front of Raven.* Another couple volunteered.

During the dinner break Morgan and I went to a local restaurant. We sat at the table without talking. My mind was blank. Halfway through the meal I felt a sudden wave of exhaustion roll through my body. I slumped in my seat as if someone had injected me with anesthetic. I could hardly keep my head off the table. My body felt watery, heavy. Concerned, Morgan leaned over and asked what he could do. My mouth felt full of cotton batting. Struggling, focusing all my attention on each movement, I managed to get to the washroom and splash cold water on my face. Looking up into the mirror, I saw my eyes, dazed and confused. Using every ounce of will I could muster, I walked back to the table and Morgan and I drove back to the house.

The final day of the workshop dawned and we continued with more teachings and exercises. I watched myself move through it from a distance. I became more and more exhausted; a migraine headache exploded behind my eyes. As the workshop came to a close we packed up. I could hardly put one foot in front of the other. Before we left I went to the room where Raven was staying. I stood at the door, unwilling to enter. Raven, looking discouraged, sat at a desk. I stood in quietness for a moment. "Goodbye, Raven." My voice was flat and expressionless. I could not think of anything else to say.

He looked up and spoke, his voice also devoid of feeling. "Goodbye, Oriah." It was the last time we would speak on the tonal as teacher and apprentice.

I sat, outwardly silent, in the car as we drove to the airport. Inwardly the voice of reason declaimed, harangued and argued. What was the problem? Everyone at the workshop had been an adult, free to choose their level of participation. Did I have a moral judgment about people's various sexual preferences or practices as long as they did not inflict pain? No. So what was the problem? No one had forced me to be there. No one had stopped me from leaving. This was probably just the rigid Christian mores of my childhood stopping me from really stepping into sexual pleasure and the spiritual enlightenment it offered.

But it wasn't. And I knew it wasn't. Suddenly I burst into tears, crying uncontrollably, as we sped along the highway. Alarmed, Morgan spoke. "Oriah, what is it? What's the matter?"

I could hardly speak past the tears, and the terror that gripped my throat. "Oh, my God, Morgan, what have I done? I promised . . . I made a pledge to them . . . . They have always been there for me and already I've broken my vow." Sobs broke from me with a violence that shook my body. "I took a vow . . . . I promised the Grandmothers I would ask for and heed their guidance. They . . . they told me to leave—to get up and get out—and I didn't, I couldn't . . . and I'm afraid—I'm so afraid they'll leave me." My voice rose in a crescendo of terror. What would I do if they left me, refused to teach or guide me anymore? And why shouldn't they? Look at what I had done. I had asked for their guidance and then I had sat there dishonoring myself, ignoring the violation of my Children's Fire even when they had told me to get out. The droning sound, the warning that came to me when I was slipping into an unconscious acceptance of what I was being told, had been there right at the beginning. I had ignored it and it had faded. They had spoken to me directly, and I had still been unable to move.

At that moment I realized what the source of the droning sound was—and had always been. The Grandmothers. Even before I had been conscious of their presence in my dreams and life they had come to me and given me a way of knowing when I was ignoring my own truth. The memory of the first time I heard the droning sound came flooding back—they had touched me in the dream with their presence. I had been terrified; it was indeed a time when, as the woman's voice had said, "all things are rent"—when old ways died, when the fibers of my life were torn apart. They had touched me and changed my life forever—and I had disregarded them. I was overwhelmed with my feeling of unworthiness.

As I spoke my worst fears, my crying subsided. The numbness was receding. My head and body ached as if I had been beaten. All the arguments in the world were worthless. It was not a question of being moralistic about sexual behavior. It was a question of heart, and there had been little or none in most of the weekend. All the words in the world about the beauty of spiritual-sexuality could not compensate for this lack. I had known this from the first hour, and I had not been able to leave for fear of incurring Raven's disapproval. My sense of self-confidence from the previous weekend was shattered.

We arrived home early the next morning. I sat alone in my house and wept. I felt ill; my head and body ached. The following morning it was worse. The migraine was so severe that if I moved, I threw up. I crawled to the phone and called Bea. Barely able to speak, I told her I was ill. "Can you come?" I asked weakly.

In moments she was at my door. Bea was a professional bodyworker, the best I knew. She laid me out flat on the floor where she had found me and started to work. As she touched me gently she drew back her hands, a shocked look on her face. "My god, Oriah, what happened? I've never felt anything so terrible. It's as if your electrical system has been wired backwards. It's hard to know where to start."

I knew she was right. I knew I was not sick with a virus or infection. It was as if the energy in my body had been entirely scrambled, a physical manifestation of the violation to spirit I had allowed. Slowly Bea was able to reduce the pain enough to get me back into bed. As she sat by my side, the tears slid down my cheeks. Speaking increased the pain that roared in my head. My voice was weak and strained.

"Promise me, Bea. Promise me that if I ever buy a ticket to go see Raven again you'll remind me—just remind me—of how I'm feeling right now, O.K.?"

She nodded.

I opened my eyes to see branches and dense foliage above me. Beyond, it was dark. As I tried to raise my head, waves of pain washed over me. I looked down at my body. My legs were covered with blood. Nausea swept through me and vomit rose in my throat. I was too weak to do more than turn my head to the side. The smell of sweat, vomit, feces and blood mingled with a hint of wood smoke. The light was dim, flickering. Every muscle in my body throbbed. I closed my eyes, exhausted.

I felt movement beside me and heard the splashing of water. I opened my eyes with effort and struggled to focus on the figure next to me. The Grandmother who sat in the southeast of the circle knelt by my side, wringing out a cloth in a basin of steaming water. She smiled as I opened my eyes and gently began wiping my face and neck, cleaning away the vomit and sweat. I labored to speak, my throat hoarse. "Grandmother . . . where am I? What—"

"Sshh, little one. Do not talk now. It will be all right. You have had a difficult birth, but everything is fine now." A birth? That would explain my condition. The Grandmother disappeared for a moment and returned with fresh water. She continued to bathe my body. I was filled with a sudden shame. This was one of the Grandmothers of the dreaming, my teacher and guide. I did not want her to see me this way, to have to clean my soiled body. I turned my face away, my eyes brimming with tears. The Grandmother spoke as she worked, her tone low, her voice soothing.

"No, no, little one. There is no need for shame. The birth was difficult and dangerous. We thought we might lose you. You were alone, unable to call for assistance. But you are here now. You are alive. This—this cleaning up—is nothing. Rest now, let me take care of you." She smiled. "It gives an old woman pleasure to feel useful."

Her words brought me back to my exhaustion and I sank into unconsciousness. I was roused to semi-consciousness by many hands rubbing my body from head to toe. The anonymous hands lifted me up and placed me gently on a clean, dry, sweet-smelling blanket. Another blanket covered me and I sank further into the darkness. When I awoke the Grandmother was still there, sewing something made of leather, sitting by my side. As I opened my eyes she smiled. "Ah, you are awake. Good. Here, I have something for you to drink." Putting aside her sewing, she gently raised my head with one hand and set a metal cup to my lips. The liquid was warm and pungent and I drank for a few moments. My head felt clearer, although my body still ached. I surveyed our surroundings—we were in a small domed structure, about twelve feet in diameter and six feet high. A fire burned in the center sending smoke out of a hole in the roof. The floor was covered with multicolored medicine blankets and I was lying on a bed of blankets and cedar boughs. As I took this in, the words of the Grandmother came back to me: "The birth was difficult and dangerous." I was stunned. When had I been pregnant? "Grandmother, the baby? Is the baby all right?"

She beamed. "The baby is just fine, a little girl. She was tiny and struggled for her life also, but she is fine now." Memories of my sons' births came to me, and panic rose in my chest as I remembered the sleepless nights and endless nursing. I did not have the strength. I couldn't do it again. The memories brought tears to my eyes and the Grandmother clicked her tongue softly, soothing me as she tucked the blankets around my body.

"Grandmother, I can't nurse her. I'm too weak, too tired. I have nothing left to give to her. Will she be alright?" The tears spilled over.

"Yes, granddaughter. She'll be fine." She moved to the opposite side of the structure and raised a blanket that covered an opening in the wall. A large black woman entered carrying a small bundle. She smiled at me, her teeth white in her glowing ebony face. She spoke gently and leaned toward me to show me the baby in her arms. The baby was tiny and red-faced, sleeping with one fist curled under her chin.

"Don't worry. I have plenty of milk for her. She will grow and be strong. You rest now." As she spoke both she and the baby seemed to vanish. They didn't walk out of the door; they simply disappeared. Dazed, I looked at the Grandmother.

"You have given birth to the heart of the woman whose name is Longing." As she spoke I felt my breath catch, deep in my chest my heart ached.

"I was so afraid, Grandmother, so afraid that all of you would leave me."

"We will never leave you, little one. Now rest. There is still some risk to you. We will do all we can to help you, to guide you. We will never leave you." I felt my body drop into the earth.

I woke up in my bedroom. Gingerly I moved my body—my headache was gone, I was sore and bruised, but the pain had subsided. Painstakingly I rose, washed my face and went out to my backyard with some tobacco. A light mist filled the air. I raised my face to the sky, offered some tobacco at the base of the maple tree and spoke. "Grandmothers, thank you for staying with me. I will try to be worthy of your guidance." I sat quietly for a moment, part of me still in the morning's dream. I heard the Grandmother who had taken care of me speak again.

"Oriah, you do not need to be better than you are. Be who you are, that is all we ask."

15

T he tapping at the door was persistent and annoying. It pulled me out of my sleep and then stopped. As I drifted off again the tapping resumed. Irritated, I raised myself up on my elbow and looked around. I was at my trailer with Brendan and Nathan. It had now been a week since the spiritual-sexuality workshop. After the dream with the Grandmother I had recuperated rapidly. I was feeling a new sense of physical energy and well-being.

I looked out of the trailer window and across the lake. Nathan popped his head out of his sleeping bag and looked at me. "Mum, what does he want?"

I raised a finger to my lips, warning him not to wake his brother, and groped for my watch in the dim light. "Who, Nathan?"

"The bird. What does he want?" As if on cue, the tapping started up again, and raising my head further, I could see a huge black crow walking on the ground in front of the trailer, tapping on the wall.

"I don't know, Nath, but it's not time to wake up yet. It's only five o'clock. Go back to sleep," I whispered. He nodded and obediently snuggled down next to his brother. Peeved, I lay back down, I probably wouldn't be able to get back to sleep. I sent out a silent prayer. "Winged-one, I ask for more rest. Please, go away," and started to drift back to sleep.

Tap, tap, tap, tap, tap, tap, tap, tap, tap. The noise bored its way into my half-doze—nine taps on the skylight above my bed. He was determined.

"Damn," I muttered out loud. What did he want? We had never had a bird behave this way before. What had I been taught about crows? Crows were the Keepers of natural law, the Teachers of civil and social law, and they danced with magical law. The laws were about the cycles in our lives, honoring ourselves, learning the lessons for which we've taken birth. So why wasn't this crow going to let me sleep?

Again it came, nine taps. "O.K., O.K. You've got my attention. What? What!" By now I was fully awake. I lay listening to the wind in the trees, watching the light grow. I felt my body relax as if going to sleep, but my mind was alert, awake. Suddenly I could hear the Grandmothers singing. I tried to sit up to see if the sound was coming from outside the trailer, but I couldn't move my body. So I relaxed, closed my eyes and listened to their voices. The singing continued and I heard a woman's voice rise above the soft chant.

"Oriah, you have reached the end of the last cycle of nine in this life. A change will soon come." I did not know what she meant. Then I saw a circle with figures written on it. In the south was written "0-9," in the west "9-18," in the north "18-27" and in the east "27-36." The woman continued to speak. "This is the cycle of your life, a picture of your working place." I thought about this. My birth place on the medicine wheel was in the southwest, so my working place was opposite, in the northeast. My working place was the direction in which I would have the greatest struggles and the hardest lessons in this life. For me, this was in determining how to design and choreograph my energy, in the choices and decisions of where to live, what work to do, how to be in relationship. The numbers associated with the powers of the northeast are nine and nineteen.

The Grandmother continued. "You were born on the ninth day in the ninth month of a year totaling nineteen." Quickly I did some addition—it was true. "Every nine years, as your age becomes a nine ($18 = 1 + 8 = 9$; $27 = 2 + 7 = 9$; $36 = 3 + 6 = 9$) that year totals to nineteen." This was also true. "Think about what has happened during these years."

I reviewed my life. When I turned nine my family moved from Southern to Northern Ontario. My whole identity as a "Northerner" was born. In the year I turned eighteen I left home, returning to Southern Ontario as a young single woman. In the year I turned twenty-seven, my first son was born—and my identity as a mother. Now I was about to turn thirty-six. I wondered what new identity or sense of self was about to be revealed.

I began to feel anxious. I thought about the different directions on the medicine wheel where each of the nine years was placed. I had moved through the south, place of the child, emotions, family, trust and innocence; the west, place of change, intuition, introspection and the body; the north, place of the mind, philosophies and beliefs, harmony and balance; the east, place of spirit, illumination, enlightenment, fantasy and illusion. I could certainly see how the past few years had involved a spiritual search with alternating flashes of illumination and long journeys into fantasy and illusion. What was next? The only place left for me to go on the wheel was into the center. Raven said the center of the medicine wheel held the catalyst energy, sexuality. I recoiled at the thought of what chaos this might lead to.

Immediately the voice of the Grandmother spoke. "No, Oriah, the catalyst energy, the energy that creates great change, is not sexuality alone."

"But that's what I have been taught. What will it look like in my life?" I asked.

"First you must examine the catalyst energy. There is a center wheel of the different aspects of the catalyst energy that moves the whole wheel, the energy that brings about change without itself being changed. In the south is the love for children. Think—did not the birth of your sons make you aware of your capacity to love more deeply? Did this not change who you were?" Yes, it was true. Few things had changed me as quickly or profoundly.

"In the west is sexuality, the physical touching with intimacy, that is the gift of your world," the Grandmother went on to explain. "This also has the power to transform. Misused, as in rape and abuse, it brings chaos. Used in a sacred manner, it can heal and revitalize body and soul. This is the catalyst energy of which Raven has spoken." She paused and then continued. "In the north is compassion. This is the love and bonding between those who share the pains and joys of being human. It is what moves the man or woman to dash into the burning building or dive into the water to save a total stranger, risking her own life. It is what touches and transforms people when they hear each other's stories. It is the love that defeats the illusions of separation—racism, sexism, class divisions, homophobia, ethnocentricity.

"In the east is spiritual passion, what the Christian mystics of earlier times would have called man's passion for God. It is the fire that runs through you as you do ceremony and touch the unseen. It is the lovemaking that takes place with spirit—your own, another's—the spirit that lives in all things. It is the vision that gives light, life and purpose to the one who has beheld its beauty."

"And what's at the center of this circle, Grandmother?"

"In the center of this wheel, in the language of your Christian ancestors, is God's love for you. It is the love of the Great Mystery, the God or Goddess. But while you may experience this as being outside yourself, it becomes the catalyst when mirrored in self-love, the ability to love your own humanness."

I was overwhelmed with this new and unexpected teaching wheel. Like most things that are true it seemed almost too obvious. Love was the catalyst energy, and sexuality was but one of the five manifestations of this power that creates change in our lives.

I thought about the cycles of nine the Grandmother had said I was now completing. Did this mean I was now entering the center, the place of the catalyst energy, love?

"Yes." I heard the word spoken and sat up, instantly coming fully awake. The sound of the voice seemed to hang in the air. My heart beat rapidly and I swung out of my sleeping bag, sure someone outside must have spoken.

There was no one there. I reached for my journal and began to write down the dream, recording the wheels I had been shown. I tested the pattern of the nine and nineteen in my life. It was true. The pattern ended with this upcoming birthday and did not repeat as far as I could project into the future.

"Is he gone?" Nathan sat up, my movement waking him.

"Yes, hon. The bird's gone."

"Did you figure out what he wanted?"

"I think so, Nath. I think he was just trying to wake me up."

16

I lean back wearily in my chair, pondering my notes on the catalyst energy. It strikes me that I had usually been tired and ill when I returned from other teaching sessions with Raven, but had never felt as much physical pain or disruption in my body as I did after the spiritual-sexuality workshop. Why? I realize it was because that weekend had used only one aspect of the catalyst energy, sexuality. Only now, as I read the Grandmothers' wheel on love as the catalyst energy, am I aware how much damage I could have done to myself. I remained in a situation where sexuality was being used in a way that was in direct opposition to loving and honoring myself. Within my body two catalyst energies were pitted against each other. The result—an explosion. A shudder runs through me. Now I understand why the Grandmothers' warning, and their insistence that my life was at risk, had been so vehement.

I get up to take a break and wander around the room. I cannot shake this new understanding I feel in my body of the power of this catalyst energy, its capacity to create change or wreak havoc, depending on how it is used. It is truly Fire medicine. A flash of anger rises in me as I think of the medicine men I know who have misused this power for personal sexual gratification. As quickly as it rises, the anger fizzles. I and other women I have met who have felt used in this way must face the truth of our responsibility. We are not children. This is one lesson the Grandmothers made sure I learned.

I sit down and absentmindedly open my journal again, and as if to make sure I don't forget, I begin to read about my lesson.

It was Many Shields' birthday and I had been invited to a party at the house where he was staying. A lot had changed since I had last seen him. I had changed. But my experience in Arizona, of being centered and speaking my truth one weekend and giving away all of my power less than six days later, had made me wary—particularly of myself. It was a lesson in humility. Despite my inner clarity about the nature of my relationship with Many Shields, I knew the romance-ridden, libido-driven adolescent still clung to her hopes. I approached the festivities with prudence and caution.

As I entered, Many Shields greeted me with a long and enthusiastic hug. There were more than fifty people in the room, chatting, eating and watching. Before I pulled away he turned his head and whispered in my ear, "I love you. You know that, don't you?"

I stepped back, bemused—but only slightly. Where had this come from? I moved into the room as other guests arrived and Many Shields turned to greet them.

There were very few people in the room I knew. I wandered around, smiling and introducing myself. Suddenly I saw a woman I did know. Myrna had attended a number of my classes and one of the vision quests I'd led. She was a beautiful blonde who exuded a sensuality that was heightened by her often provocative, and somewhat eccentric, way of dressing. She approached me smiling and we embraced, both pleased to see an old friend among so many unknown faces. As we stood and chatted, I sensed Many Shields watching us. Myrna told me she had been spending a lot of time at the house where Many Shields was a guest, taking workshops and classes. Isabel's words rang in my memory: "It's always the blondes . . ." As we talked more people arrived, to be greeted noisily by Many Shields. We both turned and observed the commotion.

"Quite a character, isn't he?" Myrna observed.

"Many Shields?" I asked.

She nodded. "Some around here call him The Walking Hormone," she said with a grin.

"I don't doubt it," I replied.

"Actually . . ." she hesitated ". . . I would like to talk to you a bit about something that has happened between he and I. I'd like your sense of it." I nodded slightly. Myrna began to describe her contact with Many Shields: her sense of being seen by him, the feeling of his power, his approaching her during a vulnerable time, touching her with his words about the medicine and her loneliness—and their subsequent sexual contact.

My stomach did a nauseous double flip and headed in the direction of my feet. I was aware of Many Shields watching us, his tension and nervousness increasing. "When did all this happen Myrna?" I asked.

"About eight weeks ago," she said.

Yes, right after my last meeting with Many Shields, when I had told him I would no longer relate to him sexually. Inwardly I shook my head, remembering his response, his speech about honoring the medicine and his marriage. It was a crock. "Myrna, my opinion on all this is not likely to be very objective. In fairness, I feel I should tell you a little about my interaction with Many Shields. It, too, has had its element of intimacy," I said delicately.

Myrna nodded. "I thought so," she said. We moved to a couch in the corner. "Have you noticed how panicked he seems?" she asked, referring to Many Shields, who was moving in high gear around the room, laughing and talking much louder than usual.

I smiled grimly. "As well he should be," I replied. I was prepared to take full responsibility for my own willing participation in the this so-called medicine man's philandering, but I would not stop myself from taking some small pleasure in his discomfort as two women spoke openly and honestly together. It seemed like fitting justice that this was occurring at his birthday party. Now I understood his unexpected declaration of love at my arrival—insurance against the fallout from the inevitable conversation between Myrna and I.

For the next two hours we shared our stories. Not surprisingly, there were many similarities. As Myrna rose to get some food, Many Shields dashed over and took her place on the couch, sitting between us when she returned and talking agitatedly. He spoke of the medicine and all he had learned, of the many conflicts in the Native community, of the need for forgiveness and the energy that could be wasted in shame. He didn't get much response from us. We sat listening, smiling and waiting—as he got up from the couch we laughed together and resumed our conversation.

Suddenly I felt very tired. I put on my coat and said goodbye briefly to the hostess and Many Shields. When I was safe in the solitude of my moving car, the anger mushroomed. How could I have been so stupid? "My heart sings your name." "You are the woman. I honor that." "We must leave it in the hands of the grandparents." He had used these or similar phrases from the medicine teachings in his interactions with Myrna, weaving a spell of mystery, alluding to deep, meaningful spiritual contact. What a load of crap! And I'd fallen for it, hook, line and sinker! How could I have been so stupid?

I knew something had not been quite true in his words, but I had stubbornly persisted because of . . . because of . . . the dream! That was it! It was so undeniable: the Grandmother had shown me his picture in the dream and given me his name; the name was identical to Raven's teacher; the way I had found out about him; he had described the Grandmother—and I had even seen him in my first ceremony, years before. It had all been credible, conclusive and verifiable.

I was enraged. "You set me up!" I yelled to the Grandmothers as I drove along the highway. "I never would have pursued it if you hadn't given me such watertight, convincing information. You set me up!"

"Yes, we did." I heard the voice of one of the Grandmothers speak within. "But it was a pretty cheap price to pay for such an important lesson, wasn't it? No real harm done."

"Wh-what?" I spluttered, momentarily rendered speechless by her easy admission. "What lesson?"

The voice of a second Grandmother spoke. "You have always been aware of the dangers of your own fantasy and illusion creating or influencing what you receive in the dream. That is why you have learned to ask for verification and examine carefully what you receive. This is good. Now you must take this to another level. You must learn to judge the truth and value of something you are offered according to your own feelings, regardless of the evidence, inner or outer. Evidence that can be rationally verified offers useful pieces that are true. They do not necessarily give you the truth. The truth you find in your own heart."

With her words my anger collapsed. She was right. From the beginning, and certainly after Morgan had told me about Many Shields' wife and six children, I had felt uneasy about our contact. But I had wanted to believe something else. I had used the evidence, the authenticity of our meeting being set up in the dream, to override my own feelings that something was not right, clean and open between us.

The Grandmother spoke again. "You have learned this lesson before, in different ways. How often did you know that something was out of balance with Raven, but remained silent because you could not back up your feelings with irrefutable evidence? You knew that what was true for you was true regardless of the evidence from the physical world. Now you also know that what is true for you is true regardless of the evidence from the dream world. You are a dreamer, Oriah. Many gifts of teachings, prophecy and guidance are offered to you in the dream. Verifying your understanding of them is important, but equally important is your own evaluation of what you are offered. If you ignore your feeling about what is offered, you will always be at risk of betraying yourself."

"So you tricked me," I said resentfully.

She laughed. "Yes, we tricked you. But what did it cost? You are not irreparably damaged. Your pride is hurt. You again meet your guide, humility. Is that so large a price to pay for the wisdom you have gained?"

"No," I admitted. Then I remembered the reading Raven had done for me ten months earlier. My path card for the year was the Heyoka Grandmothers, those who teach by tricking. Now I knew what that meant. Mentally I saw myself once again sprawling face-first in the dirt, getting up, brushing myself off and moving forward. I resolved to keep humility close at hand.

But humility can be an elusive companion. As my strength grew with my understanding of the lessons I thought I had learned, so did my confidence. As I felt myself move farther away from Raven a part of me grieved and longed for the earlier times of unquestioning excitement. From this place of longing I decided to go to the Sundance in Arizona. I bargained away my memory of the pain of my last visit and my resolve never to return. I had heard good things about the Sundances held since I last attended people had told me Raven had made an effort to have a more traditional ceremony. I would stay out of the politics, the group interaction; it was a ceremony; Raven would do a minimal amount of teaching; I would focus on doing my Sundance. This time it would be different.

I bought a plane ticket to Arizona and made my Sundance shield. A different shield is created for each dance, marking a different aspect of self. As this would be my second dance, the shield was to represent my inner woman, the part of me that decides how to present and use my medicine, my gifts, in the world in a way that supports my personal dream—home, family, money. I had painted the shield intuitively during the year. It was of two women—one was surrounded by darkness, holding a red-and-pink basket above her head, the lower half of her body a strong tree trunk rooted firmly in the ground; the other moving in orgasticness in the deep blue night sky, seven stars above her, turquoise lightning running from her extended hands and feet into the ground on either side of the woman below her. I didn't understand it or try to analyze its meaning. It was my Woman Shield.

One day after the ticket arrived in the mail I was getting ready to take a group of twenty people on a wilderness vision quest. Rushing around packing and preparing, I ran down the stairs and yet again flew off the steps several feet from the bottom. This time, I turned my right ankle. The cracking sound was all too familiar. Once again I had torn the ligament out of the bone, fracturing it. There would be no sundancing this year.

With crutches, the quest took on a new dimension. Other people had to carry my pack, put up my tent and get my food and supplies for me. I hobbled through the bush and collapsed in a lawn chair by the fire circle. And that's where I stayed. The group looked after me, and I taught and guided the process from my place by the fire like a premature grandmother. I had no choice. I had to slow down and ask for assistance.

This was the second group of people I had taken out to do a vision quest that summer. On the first quest I had heard something in people's stories I had missed in previous years. Over and over people described sitting in the darkness, listening to the sounds of the bush around them— rain, wind, mosquitoes, squirrels that sounded like bears, and occasionally bears who were surprisingly quiet. Each person faced their fears, loneliness, longing, boredom and questions as they moved through the ceremony watching, listening and waiting. Most of the time what they did not do was pray. I was surprised. Why had they so rarely asked for help from the Great Mystery or their ancestors? The quest is a ceremonial container for constant prayer, of sending out a voice to the Great Mystery, a crying for a vision for oneself and one's people. We had talked about this often, but it only now occurred to me: most people did not know how to pray. For many, their experience with prayer had been born in churches and synagogues, wrapped in rituals that no longer held any meaning for them. They didn't know how to talk with the Great Spirit, nor did they trust that the words from their heart would be heard.

This hadn't occurred to me before. While I had spent most of my early churchgoing days editing the minister's prayers by making comments to myself like "No, count me out on that one, God" or "Could we talk about this 'wretch, like me' business?" I had always had a sense of an ongoing conversation between myself and spirit. When I met Grandfather in the dream I knew he had been a part of the "someone out there" I had been talking to since childhood. I think it was a gift I was born with. But how could I help others begin their own conversation with spirit?

On the second quest we began talking about prayer, our previous experiences and levels of comfort with the idea and reality of talking with "something or someone unseen." Naming the feelings of awkwardness, disappointment, doubt, shame and fear seemed to free us to explore together. We moved into a ceremony of praying, not in the first person but in the third. We each spoke to the circle as one of a council of Gods or Goddesses addressing his or her peers, speaking on behalf of a human.

In my fireside chair I reflected on my prayer. What did I wish to say about this human, Oriah? What did she need? What did she deserve?

Why would I want to speak for her? As I beheld this woman, hot and tired, her bandaged foot elevated on a bucket, I felt a great tenderness for her and I spoke.

"Sacred Ones, I come before you to speak on behalf of this human, Oriah Mountain Dreamer, born Debra Anne House. I ask that you see her tiredness and grant her rest. She has made mistakes. She has often chosen a path that is difficult. She sits now at a new threshold, and I ask you to guide her, to make your voice clear and loving to her so that her choices may be guided by the Goddess.

"I ask that she be allowed to go home, to the place within and without where she can lay down the burdens she has taken up along the way—the need to work hard all of the time, cooking, cleaning, listening, reading, studying, organizing, speaking, caring for her sons, packing, unpacking, journeying. I ask that you touch her and help her lay down the constant striving and hoping to somehow make a difference by what she does in this world for the people and the earth she loves.

"She can feel the winds of change that surround her and blow within her as she approaches this next and final movement of the nine in her life, and she is afraid. As her mother and grandmother near death she feels the blackness of being alone—no mother, no grandmother, no aunt or sister; the only female in all her family. She feels the weight of the burdens carried by the women in her family before her—unlived lives, constant work, unspoken words. I ask that this inheritance be removed from her.

"Sacred Ones, I speak to you on her behalf because I am moved by her courage, and by her faith and her humanness. Although she has never been able to find her home, she carries on, trusting she will find it. Even when her choices have led to pain, bruises on her body from beatings, scars on her heart from rape, discouragement from trying to please and prove her love and loyalty to those who would not receive either, she has held within her the hope of change and the trust in the Grandmothers. She seeks that change now even in the midst of fear and I ask you to grant her safe and easy passage. I ask that you show her the way home."

Two weeks later I sat outside my trailer next to the lake, crutches at my side. My leg, now in a cast, rested on an old plastic milk box. There was nothing that had to be done. There were no trips, or healings or classes to organize. Many Shields had left a message on my answering machine saying goodbye. He was returning home. I watched the wind scurry across the water and listened to it move through the trees around me.

I sat in the shade and dozed, moving in and out of the dream, writing down what the Grandmothers said. They sat again in the kiva. The place was by now familiar to me. I sat on the stone floor worn smooth by the countless feet that had visited this place. The Grandmother in the west nodded to me and smiled. The smile softened the strong angular features of her face and made her eyes shine. "Ah, now that we have you sitting still, perhaps we can do some more teaching."

I chuckled. "I'm clearly not going anywhere, Grandmother. I would like very much to learn."

She gazed into the fire for a moment. "I will teach you the wheels of the west, the wheels of birthing. Do you remember the birthing movement we showed you on these wheels?" I nodded, remembering the luminescent wheels with figure eights inside them. "These wheels are about how you give birth to yourself, and it is always yourself that you are birthing in order to know yourself. This is not to say that what you birth does not separate from you and develop a life of its own, and in turn give birth to new life. But you are not what you birth. That which you birth is but a mirror of some aspect of yourself, inner and outer, that you need to bring balance into your life. It is your Sundance, your way of touching yourself, life and others with Beauty.

"Part of the mirror is the what is actually birthed—the child. Remember the wheel of the different children each person may birth—relationships, personal mythology, dreams, medicine and work, physical children, health, home, purpose in life, ideas, choices, connection with spirit, creativity, artistic originality, a new concept of self and knowing of the ancestors. In any one life you may give birth repeatedly to all or some of these children.

"As important as the children that are born are the mirrors offered by each stage in the birth—lovemaking, conception, pregnancy, labor, birth, nursing, preparing and releasing the child. These are the places on the Serpent's Path. But they are only signposts. The real journey happens in the movement between the points. How each occurs—the ease, difficulty or energy—tells you something and shows what is needed in the moment. This birth is not an end point or prize. Even the releasing is part of the cycle as each releasing creates a space for new conception. You may simultaneously be at different points with different births—conceiving one while preparing another to go into the world, though there are human limits to this.

"These wheels are life wheels. They mirror the process of life—the innate yearning of the human heart, mind and body to create and recreate in an effort to know and be connected with the life force that creates all. To know yourself as God and Goddess, capable of connecting so fully with the life force of Grandmother Earth and Grandfather Sun as to bear new life in the now, and to see yourself in that child. All birthing is evidence of hope, faith and creativity in the human community. Even people whose future is uncertain, who are in the midst of war, feel the stirring of hope for the future in the newborn child.

"Remember I speak here of all of the children you may give birth to, not only the two-leggeds. It is the feminine that gives birth, but all pregnancies require the seeding of the egg, the marriage of the masculine and feminine. Both are contained within each child and so each child has an outer masculine and inner feminine mirror for its mother. This, like every aspect of these wheels, is most easily described and understood by looking at the birthing of physical children. This experience, personal for everyone on the planet as they were indeed birthed by a physical mother, is a guide, a gift for understanding how to live this wheel in every aspect of life. Women are the Keepers of this gift and the silencing of their stories robs the people of the knowledge for birthing new life individually and collectively. Women, whether they have had physical children or not, hold within their bodies the knowledge of the feminine—Life-Giver and Death-Bringer. It is the right and responsibility of the feminine to consciously choose the births and deaths needed for balance.

"This knowledge that is held by the feminine offers you clear insight on the human struggles involved in creating new life in any aspect of self. Many are unable to make love wholeheartedly, splitting heart and spirit from sexuality. How does this effect the fullness of the orgasmic experience? What do you know of the elements that effect this decision to make love—neediness, distrust, past pain, violence. How does the nature of the lovemaking effect conception? Remember this may be the lovemaking needed to conceive a new idea or a new concept of who you truly are.

"And what do you know of conception from your own experience? When does the desired conception fail to occur? Where do you conceive when consciously you say you do not want to? How does a woman feel when she has conceived? Afraid, joyful, used, full, elated, petrified? Why? What of the woman who remains unaware of having conceived? How often do you agree to make love and conceive and then hide the pregnancy—the development of a new relationship, state of health, belief—even from yourself? What of the woman who is conscious of the moment of conception? What of the unplanned conceptions, the ones that are a 'surprise' or a 'shock'?

"It is in the journey along the Serpent's Path from lovemaking to conception that you first cross the medicine wheel and move through the Lodge of Self-Reflection at the center. In the eyes of the lover, inner or outer, you see a mirror of some part of yourself. In the conceiving there is the death of the illusion of separation.

"And what do you know of pregnancy? Its undeniability, diversity, tiredness, vulnerability, its demand to turn inward, its taking precedence over all else. What are the abortions, the miscarriages? Why do they happen and how does the way they are carried out effect other pregnancies? Why are some births, some ideas, some creative efforts, repeatedly aborted? What of the things 'gone wrong'—disease, toxemia, water retention, the turned baby? What do the wise women, the midwives, say of their causes and cures? What do the doctors say?

"And the labor—what do you know of the timing and nature of labor? Even as it is common to all women giving birth each labor is unique and distinct, some early, some late, some fast, others slow, painful, hard work, calm, frantic, unpredictable, orgastic, endless, over in the blink of an eye. Is it not also true that labor births a healed self? This is the place of surrender, of doing the impossible, of allowing, of giving up control and trusting. This is the place where your failure to do these things brings pain and destruction to yourself and your child. This is the place where the feminine must be relied upon, where it truly knows its power in the messy, uncontrollable, painful, noisy throes of giving birth. Every attempt to make it otherwise, to make it clean, scheduled, quiet, neat, controlled from outside, tears this power from the feminine and leaves you less than you truly are.

"Make no mistake—this power is raw! And no matter what the birth, for those around you and those parts of yourself that rely on control and predictability, this power is terrifying. For it is in the process of labor that you again cross the medicine wheel and move through the Lodge of Self-Reflection. Here we see a mirror—on one side birth, on the other, death. There is no birthing without blood, a giving of that which carries the life force, and therefore it has risk. Here you pass close to the edge of other worlds and may step out of the one you know.

"Labor is work that demands sacrifice, blood and sweat and that is what makes it sacred. To avoid this is to lose the sacredness. But it need not be unbearable. Think of what you know of how to ease the way without stripping the woman of her power—the gifts of midwifery, of women with knowledge guiding, supporting, reassuring, following the lead of the body and heart of the one who gives birth, not imposing their will, help that does not seek to rob another of her power but enables her to experience it to its fullest.

"And what do you know of 'problems' in labor? Do you know what the midwives say of a woman whose labor stops repeatedly? That often there is something wrong in the relationship between the mother and father, the feminine and masculine. How is the relationship between the masculine and feminine within you, in your life, in your world? Is it any surprise that the laboring to give birth to yourself and your world seems to go on forever?

"And what do you know of the birth, for the one who has been supported, who has felt her power even in the pain and fear, and for the one who has been pushed and pulled, strapped down, cut open, kept quiet? What do you know of the feelings a mother has as she sees her child for the first time—the desire to hold, to lick clean, to stare, to speak, to look away, to have the child taken away? The fear, exhaustion, tears, disappointment, elation. The knowledge of something ended, something begun.

"And what of the child who is different than expected or hoped for— the 'wrong' gender, too drugged to nurse, bruised by forceps, stillborn, brain-damaged, misshapen? What of the grief, the fear, the exhaustion of the mother?

"You have asked, 'Do we give birth to what is dark or wrong?' Here is your answer. You give birth to all that is in your life, whether you are conscious of it or not. There are women unaware they are carrying a child in their belly, who give birth in the bathroom, and you ask, 'How could they not know?' But they did not.

"What mirror is offered if the child, the relationship, the home, the job you birth does not look like the one you had wished for? How much of this is in your control? Some. More than you are often willing to acknowledge. If you smoke and drink during pregnancy you know it will influence the child you bear. If you took drugs the child will probably be formed differently. Be careful. There is no blame here, only responsibility—the need to respond to the best of your ability. Can you in every moment control all things that effect your pregnancy—internal upsets and emotions, the air you breathe, the water you drink? No.

"The child is neither light nor dark. It is life as mirrored to you and manifest in this moment. The more you are who you are, the easier you are able to see the beauty and have it touch you as every child, every aspect of self and every change in your life, is born.

"And what do you know of nursing, the stage where mother and child are physically separate but the child is still dependent upon the mother for all sustenance? What does each gain? What bond is forged? You know nursing gives the child immunities from outside viruses and bacteria. What happens where the mother is unwilling, unable or not allowed to nurse? What happens to the mother as she nurses—sore nipples, cracked and bleeding, full breasts seeking to suckle, exquisite release, unspoken communication, intimacy? And what of weaning? Who decides—child, mother, doctor, social convention? What of ambivalence, the child's and the mother's? What does the nursing, the sustaining, of the other children on the wheel—your concept of yourself, your relationship to the ancestors, your health or home—look like?

"And now it is time to prepare and teach the child so it will survive in the world without you. How do you do this? Timing is everything. Do you really want this child, a physical two-legged or an aspect of yourself, to go out into the world at all? Are you aware of how others perceive your child? You want to be sure the child is safe, but how much of your fearfulness do you want to send with the child? Are you preparing the child based on how things are now or on how it was for you, or for your other children in the past?

"And then you must release the child to go into the world. Is this a child who will come back and visit? Can you live with what the world will say about your child, the manifestation of your creativity, your medicine, your sense of self? What part of yourself is mirrored in the releasing? What does the child birth?

"And the cycle continues. You create and recreate. Some pregnancies last nine days, some nine years. There are abortions, miscarriages, easy pregnancies and ones filled with discomfort. What happens is a mirror of self, neither bad nor good, neither light nor dark. It is what is. You can learn to give birth in pleasure, with ease, and know, on the one hand, the fullness of the gift of creating and on the other, the inability of humans to control how any of this is done."

The sun was close to the horizon and the air had cooled. I had been sitting for hours, alternately drifting into the dream and waking to write. I felt my orende, my energy, surge as I read my notes. I began to draw the Serpent's Path for different births on the medicine wheel and to ask myself the questions the Grandmother had raised for each step. There was so much more to understand and to live—and this was a way of living from the feminine in each moment.

As darkness fell I gathered my papers and went into the trailer to put on a sweater and jeans. Pulling my canvas lounge chair behind me, I limped down to the lake. The sky was a deep indigo, the lake a smooth mirror of polished obsidian, reflecting the stars. I dragged the chair out onto the rocky point that jutted out into the lake and lay down flat, looking straight up. I had a clear view of the sky, uninterrupted by trees. The Milky Way swept over me, millions of silver stars. I felt held by the sky.

Suddenly I heard a song, long and lonely, like the call of a loon over the lake. The words came from deep within me; the melody came from deep within the stars.

Sacred Grandmothers hear me
I am lost without your light.
Sacred Grandmothers guide me
through the night.

17

"T his will be the first of the teachings of the Heartflame."
I woke up with a start, the sound of the Grandmother's voice still
ringing in my ears. Heartflame teachings? What did she mean? The
Heartflame, the Heartflame . . . those were the teaching wheels of the
east, which showed how to repair the torn Marriage Basket, how to stop
the inner and outer war between the masculine and the feminine and create the Sacred Marriage that would help us hold the Dream of the Ancestors and the Dream of the People.

I could not remember the dream that had preceded the voice. I lay in
my bed, feeling inwardly for a thread that would lead me back to the
dream. As I relaxed my body, bits and pieces of the dream returned to
me: a girl, ten or eleven years old, sitting in front of an old woman. The
old woman smiled and spoke to her, touching her cheek, her hair with
love, laughing at something that was said, the girl asking questions. As I
drifted back into sleep I heard the Grandmother's voice.

"In the south of the Heartflame Wheel, place of the heart, is the meeting of Grandmother and Granddaughter. Here the young girl, about to
enter womanhood, learns of her spiritual-sexuality. She sees mirrored in
the eyes and words of the Grandmother, love for her physical body and
an honoring of the sacredness of human sexuality. All questions are per-
mitted, as the girl brings her fears, doubts and excitement to the Grandmother. This is the beginning—the foundation upon which her sense of
self as a sensual, sexual, spiritual being, capable of holding the sacred
Marriage Basket inside her, is built."

A wave of grief swept over me. How many women in my time had
been given this beginning? How many more had been taught to hate their
bodies, fear sexuality, feel ashamed of their own desires, fears, questions? The Grandmother spoke again, her voice gentle. "This is where
you must begin, Oriah. The sisters must learn to be Grandmothers to one
other, to re-member this process. This will be the first Heartflame weekend."

The first Heartflame weekend? My mind raced. Since my experience at the advanced spiritual-sexuality workshop with Raven in Arizona I had felt a sense of despair about ever being able to share the medicine teachings on spiritual-sexuality. Gunner had asked me twice to teach a spiritual-sexuality workshop with him. I had waffled, first saying yes, then no, then maybe. I wanted to give people an opportunity to learn a tradition that did not separate spirituality from sexuality, but even before the advanced workshop I had reservations about the way it was being taught. I had not felt critical—I could see the difficulty in keeping a balance between honoring the sacredness of sexuality and celebrating its physical vitality, without either ascending into the esoteric ozone or sliding down into the sleazy side of the raw sex mentality prevalent in our culture. While Gunner assured me he understood my concerns and wanted to shape a workshop to keep this balance, I had reservations about my ability to do this any better than Raven or others who had far more experience. Finally, having risked Gunner's understandable frustration with my indecisiveness, I told him I would not teach the workshop with him, and resigned myself to not working in this area of the medicine.

But the Grandmothers seemed to have other things in mind. Clearly the Heartflame Wheels were a different approach to the teachings of spiritual-sexuality. As I lay in my bed the Grandmother continued to talk about the other places on the wheel, describing the movement of learning about, and healing, our sexuality from a spiritual perspective, and vice versa.

"The west is the place of the body. Here the woman learns that her body is a living Heartflame, as she joins the fire at the center of Grandmother Earth with the fires in her heart and womb. With this energy, experienced in the sensuality, orgasticness and beauty of her own body, she can heal herself and others.

"In the north the woman moves into the mind, beyond the limitations of the conscious mind, to meet her inner lover. They unite in the Sacred Marriage, balancing, supporting, loving, exploring each other, and the woman is complete. From this wholeness she can enter into relationship, or be alone, as she chooses, with an open heart.

"In the east, this union creates the Marriage Basket, the container for the woman's own creativity, for the manifestation of spiritual-sexuality is in the living of one's own creativity. It is the fire, the passion that creates Beauty in the world from the very heart of the womb of woman."

I awoke abruptly again and reached for my journal, feeling over-whelmed. They had given me a way, a road map for teaching, that felt true to my heart. As I wrote, tears of gratitude coursed down my cheeks.

Two months later thirty women gathered to participate in the first of the Heartflame weekends. On our first night together we entered the Purification Lodge. The heat rose as the women sent out their prayers, asking for help in healing the shame, fear and woundedness that enslaved their sexuality. In the final round, as I poured twenty cups of water on the red-hot rocks, I heard again the voice of the Grandmother who had spoken to me in the dream.

"Take them down, granddaughter. Take them to the Heartflame."

Speaking slowly, I directed the women to relax their bodies as the heat in the lodge continued to build. Closing my eyes, I felt myself sink into the cool darkness of the earth beneath us. I continued to speak. "Direct your attention down, into Grandmother Earth. Feel yourself begin to sink into her cool dampness. Smell the earth around you. See the rich earthen colors—browns, reds. Feel yourself move effortlessly around rocks and roots, sinking farther and farther down. And as you go down, through the seemingly endless blackness, be aware of a faint, glowing light beneath you. As you move farther down, the earth becomes warmer—feel the tin-gling warmth as it moves through your arms and legs. Embrace it, wel-come it into your body. And as you sink deeper the glow becomes a bril-liant light—the light of the fire at the center of Grandmother Earth, her Heartflame. Feel now, within your own body a similar light, a fire that burns in your womb and your heart. It may be a tiny flicker, a glowing ember, or a strong flame. Within your mind send out your prayer to Grandmother Earth. Ask that the flame within you be joined with the flame at her center. Feel how the two are joined—the vast, pulsing fire within Grandmother Earth, and the small but steady flame within you. Feel how, as they are joined, both grow stronger. They feed each other."

Slowly I opened my eyes. The lodge was pitch-black: I could not see my hand in front of my face. As I looked through the blackness I began to see tiny flickers of light, small blue flames in the wombs of about a dozen women in the lodge. I rubbed my eyes and looked again. The im-ages remained. I sat mesmerized and awestruck. Slowly the images faded, and guiding the women's attention back into their bodies in the lodge, I finished the ceremony and we moved out into the night.

Later that night, as I lay sleepless in my bed, I saw the scene again and again in my mind. I had seen the Heartflame in the women's bodies! It had been like a tongue of fire. Something about this was familiar. I searched my memory. Of course—in the Bible! After Christ's ascension, at the Pentecost, the disciples had experienced "tongues of flame," coming down from the heavens and resting over their heads. I sat up in bed, the full import of this slowly sinking in. The men in the Bible received the flame of spirit from the heavens, into their heads. The women in the Purification Lodge received the flame of spirit from the earth, into their wombs!

The following day the women divided into two groups: Grandmothers and Granddaughters. Each group dressed in costumes and stepped into the silence to connect with the appropriate place within her: the young adolescent girl, about to seek the advice of a loving Grandmother who could teach her all she needed to know about her budding sexuality, or the wise Grandmother, wanting to affirm this little one's beauty, sacredness and sensuality. The groups joined and each Granddaughter sat with a Grandmother and re-membered what could have been. Later in the day the two switched roles, giver becoming receiver, student becoming teacher. Many tears were shed, much laughter ensued and we prepared for an evening of firebreath, music and dancing.

The firebreath is a method of moving energy through the body that I had learned from Raven. With intent and breath, the energy from the earth is pulled up into the body. On each inhale, by contracting the muscles around the first chakra at the genitals, the energy is moved up through the chakras and circulated back into the earth. If enough energy is raised to the fourth or heart chakra, it will continue up and out the top of the head, into the earth and back up through the first chakra, creating wave after wave of full-body orgasms. This orgastic wave builds one's overall energy level and helps heal physical, emotional, mental and spiritual woundings.

For some unknown reason the firebreath had come easily to me. Many people experience blocks in different parts of their body and subsequent emotions of grief, sadness, fear or anger. I had been teaching a monthly women's firebreath class for two years, and I never ceased to be amazed at the level of grief and sadness that was often released in tears, screaming and crying during these sessions.

I began this firebreath session as I always did, by explaining and then demonstrating the method. Somehow I always manage to pull into myself and move the energy in my body, temporarily blocking my awareness of the people watching me. Demonstrating it once for a friend and lover, who was not on the medicine path but had expressed a desire to learn the firebreath, I had been surprised by his response. As my breathing returned to normal and the waves of energy rippling through my body diminished, I opened my eyes.

He sat, wide-eyed, next to me on the bed. "Well," he said forcefully, "you don't need me here, do you?" He got up to get dressed, our planned lovemaking forgotten.

I was astonished. "No," I replied, "I don't need you here. That's not why you're here. You're here because I like having you here and I assume you like being here." I reached for his arm, trying to explain. "The firebreath is wonderful, but it doesn't replace the sexual and emotional intimacy of touching another person."

He was inconsolable. After this I became more cautious about requests from men to learn the firebreath.

When I had finished demonstrating the firebreath to the women I had them lie down and, while drumming, began to talk them through the breathing. Guiding them first through a relaxing meditation, I asked them to send their prayer out to Grandmother Earth asking that the Heartflame come into their bodies for healing. While Raven always had people "pull" the energy into their bodies, I had discovered that many women found it easier to "welcome" the energy by focusing on opening more and more, creating a place for and "allowing" the energy to flow into them. While still holding and moving the energy through their bodies this seemed to avoid the more masculine go-for-it attitude of constant pulling.

As I drummed I watched the women around me: thirty women lying naked next to each other, each welcoming and moving the energy of Grandmother Earth through her body. Lucy, a seventy-seven-year-old Jamaican woman, had been anxious to learn the firebreath. She had called me a month before the weekend. "Oriah, I just read a description of your weekend and I want to know if I am too old to come. I've had a good life—children, grandchildren, a nice home—but I just realized what has always been missing—passion, real passion. My mother died when I was eight and no one ever told me anything about sex. I married my husband when I was young and thought that was how it was supposed to be. It wasn't pleasant, but I didn't expect anything else. But now I want to find what I'm missing. I want to find some passion in my life. Do you think it's too late?" I had assured her I did not. I watched her and the others moving their bodies, raising their voices in sighs, moans, screams, laughter and tears. Each woman was unique, each wondrous and awesome, an embodiment of the Goddess. I felt their courage, as the pain and fear from past incest, rape, violence, abuse and terror was reawakened in their bodies. I felt their courage as they dared to feel the ecstacy, the fire that makes us whole. My throat tightened with emotion and I sent out my prayer.

"Grandmothers, they are all so beautiful. They are all trying so hard to heal themselves and the Sisterhood. Be with us, Grandmothers—teach us, guide us. I am filled with gratitude to be here, to see this, to be part of it."

As the women ended the firebreath they lay silently together, relaxing and listening to the music that I had put on the tape deck. One woman, her face glowing, raised herself on her elbows and looked around the room. Eyes wide, she looked at the room full of naked, shining women. The air was electric with the pulse of feminine power. She looked at me, a flicker of fear visible in her eyes. "This is what women were burned for once, isn't it? For knowing this power?"

I hesitated, feeling my eyes fill with tears. "Yes," I said softly. "It is." Inwardly I let the fear melt away. Not this time. Not this time!

18

My life, or at least the parts I have chosen to record, is scattered around me on the floor. Binders, notebooks, sketch pads, tapes— they hold the pieces of my journey. I have been reading for more than six hours, moving through the past, watching the story unfold.

It is January, four months since I was held by the stars and sang my prayer to the Grandmothers. Yesterday I wrote a letter to Raven, separating my life and work from him. The letter lies on my desk, and I read the last paragraph for the twentieth time:

> This is very difficult for me. My heart aches as my words speak the unspeakable. Separation is painful. What I have learned from you, Raven, has changed the course of my life and has given me a way of understanding the dreaming that has been a part of me and my loneliness since I was a child. Our connection is very precious to me, a gift of this life. I do not want to lose this. I may be wrong. A separation may be completely unnecessary, or even damaging, but it is what my spirit calls me to do at this time. I offer this to you as my truth. I have nothing more precious to give. I would offer you nothing less.

Suddenly I feel very alone. A shiver runs up my spine as I remember the dream of the night before: the dark sorcerer in the yellow streak, trapped in the vacuum cleaner, in the ruler that speared my body; the need to calmly and clearly state my intent and rid myself of his energy. How can I do this on my own? Who do I think I am? Raven is the one who brought me to the dreaming and the medicine teachings. My understanding of my own dreams is grounded in the knowledge he has shared with me. Would the Grandmothers have taught me if he had not trained me? Do I not owe him my life, my loyalty?

Engrossed, I continue to leaf through the journals. Two of the binders are filled with notes I made before I met Raven. One dream catches my eye—a dream recorded over a year before I met Raven.

"I was in a dark place, surrounded by a group of old women. I felt nervous, afraid to speak, but I had a question I needed to ask them. Gathering my courage, I whispered my question. 'I want to have a third child. Will my husband and I have another baby?'

The women's faces were blurred; their voices came from very far away. One spoke. 'There are many ways to have another child. You have given birth to two human children already. There is a wheel of birth. We will teach you of the many different kinds of children you can give birth to in this life. It is this desire, the longing to give birth to the different, unborn aspects of yourself, that makes you consider a third baby.'

I nodded to them and whispered, 'Thank you, Grandmothers.'"

How could I have forgotten this dream? I check the date and the entries before and after to verify it. I remember the time period. My husband and I had in fact been considering having a third child. But I had forgotten the dream.

It seems incredible: I met the Grandmothers more than a year before I met Raven. For the past four years I have assumed that my learning of the medicine began with and was linked to my meeting Raven. Only now, as I read this dream, am I aware that it's not true. The Grandmothers had spoken to me in the dream about the Birthing Wheels before I ever heard of a medicine wheel or Raven! And if they were with me before I met him, there's no reason to suppose they will leave me now. I have been so afraid that leaving Raven will mean the end of learning the medicine in the dream.

My heart begins to pound. I try to calm my breath and continue to scan the pages. I follow the thread, moving like a blind person wanting to see the picture, to feel the texture. I stop at the dreams of the crystal skull. The skull had said I was called by the Dreamers, long before I had any understanding of what this could mean. I find a copy of a letter written to Raven ten months after we met, telling him about my dreams of the crystal skull directing me to dream it "back to the circle of Grandmothers." None of it had made sense to me at the time. In the letter I'd asked Raven for advice and direction. "What does this mean? Who are the Grandmothers?" I had received no reply.

Agitated, I pace around the room, feeling my anxiety rising. In all my time with Raven, during all the dreaming with the Grandmothers, I had not remembered this dream, the very first time the Grandmothers came to me. And yet here it is, written in my own hand more than five years ago. It's like a giant jigsaw puzzle. Many of the pieces had been in place before I had the knowledge to use or understand any of them. Anger flashes through me—I didn't have the knowledge, but Raven did! Why had he never answered my questions about the Grandmothers and the skull? My anger leaves as quickly as it came. Perhaps he didn't know—he had always shared everything he knew. Would I have understood what the Grandmothers were trying to teach me without Raven's teachings of the medicine wheel and ceremonial alchemy? Perhaps there would have been another teacher—but that was not what happened—I had learned these things from Raven.

A wave of tenderness for Raven washes over me. He saw me in ways others did not, and in doing so enabled me to see myself in new ways. He knew what it was like—this working in the dream. Am I strong enough to be alone with this knowing? I feel an ache in my chest. Can I bear the grief of missing him?

I feel like a thread, one thread in a giant tapestry. Who is the weaver? I don't know. Perhaps there are many weavers. I do know the tapestry is larger than the small fragment I can see at this time.

Unable to sit still, I walk into the bathroom and look into the mirror. My hand pushes my hair back from my face, revealing fine streaks of gray at the temples. My face, the amount of gray in my hair, the tint of the gray, the change around my temples—all these suddenly coalesce and I am pulled back to the dream of walking into the cave, holding the crystal skull, returning it to the Grandmothers and dancing inside the circle along the Serpent's Path. My hair in the fourth and final sequence of that dream was streaked with gray at the temples. I lean closer to the mirror, my heart pounding. The gray in my hair almost matches that of the dream. I will reach the age I was in the dream within the next year. I remember Raven's rage in the dream when the Grandmother refused him entry to the cave.

I go back to my workroom and begin to pick up the scattered papers. I put the letter to Raven in an envelope and address it. I will mail it now, not because my journey out of the Land of the Father toward the Grand-mothers is affirmed by my dream journals—yes, the evidence is there and it's true and gives me comfort—but because the truth is in my heart.

The post office is just around the corner, and ten minutes later, letter dispatched, I walk through the front door to the sound of the telephone ringing. It's Bea.

"It's been a strange day, Bea." My hand moves down my throat and across my chest. I gasp.

"What is it?" Bea asks, alarmed.

"I can't believe it," I whisper, not knowing if I want to laugh or cry. There, hanging from her silver chain, is the tiny silver Goddess, holding the deep-blue lapis lazuli above her head. She vanished the night before. Except for trips to the bathroom, kitchen and post office, I have been in my workroom all day. I'd searched my bedclothes when I woke up and couldn't find her. And now here she is, hanging over my heart.

"Oriah, what is it?" Bea asks again.

"My Goddess is back," I say, and begin to laugh.

If you would like to share your insights about this story or receive information about workshops and vision quests, please write to:

Oriah Mountain Dreamer
Dream Star Lodge
Box 22546
300 Coxwell Ave.
Toronto, Ontario
Canada M4L 2A0